# MANCHESTER MEDIEVAL LITERATURE AND CULTURE

## TRANSPORTING CHAUCER

Manchester University Press

# MANCHESTER MEDIEVAL LITERATURE AND CULTURE

The Manchester Medieval Literature and Culture series publishes new research, informed by current critical methodologies, on the literary cultures of medieval Britain (including Anglo-Norman, Anglo-Latin and Celtic writings), including post-medieval engagements with and representations of the Middle Ages (medievalism). 'Literature' is viewed in a broad and inclusive sense, embracing imaginative, historical, political, scientific, dramatic and religious writings. The series offers monographs and essay collections, as well as editions and translations of texts.

**Titles Available in the Series**

# Transporting Chaucer

HELEN BARR

**Manchester University Press**

MANCHESTER AND NEW YORK

distributed in the United States exclusively by Palgrave Macmillan

Published by Manchester University Press
Altrincham Street, Manchester M1 7JA, UK
and Room 400, 175 Fifth Avenue, New York, NY 10010, USA
www.manchesteruniversitypress.co.uk

Distributed the United States exclusively by
Palgrave Macmillan, 175 Fifth Avenue, New York,
NY 10010, USA

Distributed in Canada exclusively by
UBC Press, University of British Columbia, 2029 West Mall,
Vancouver, BC, Canada V6T 1Z2

British Library Cataloguing-in-Publication Data
A catalogue record for this book is available from the British Library

Library of Congress Cataloging-in-Publication Data applied for

ISBN    978 0 7190 9149 0  hardback

First published 2014

The publisher has no responsibility for the persistence or accuracy of URLs for any external or third-party internet websites referred to in this book, and does not guarantee that any content on such websites is, or will remain, accurate or appropriate.

Typeset in 10/12 Imprint MT by
Servis Filmsetting Ltd, Stockport, Cheshire
Printed in Great Britain by
by TJ International Ltd, Padstow

# Contents

# List of plates

# Preface

Transporting Chaucer has, happily, engaged me in quite a bit of toing and froing. I thank His Grace the Duke of Northumberland for permission to consult MS Northumberland 455 at Alnwick Castle and the archivist Chris Hunwick for facilitating my work on the manuscript. The librarians at the Shakespeare Birth Place Trust Library and Archive, Stratford-upon-Avon, were unfailingly patient in enabling a novice user to make the most of their recordings and publications. I thank the Dean and Chapter of Canterbury Cathedral for permission to reproduce images of the intriguing story of Eilward of Westoning from the stained glass in Trinity Chapel and I am very grateful indeed to Antony Gormley for his generosity in allowing me to include in this book a photograph of *Transport,* which hangs in the crypt of the Cathedral, and an image of his earlier work *Bed.*

Professor Mary Robertson at the Huntington Library, San Marino, California, made my research visit in March 2012 one of the highlights of researching this book. I was thrilled to be able to examine the Ellesmere manuscript in person, and I thank Mary for expediting all the arrangements and for her insights as we looked at the images together under 3D binoculars. I would have missed so much without her expert eye. I thank the Huntington Library for permission to reproduce newly digitised images of the Squire, Prioress, Man of Law and Chaucer from MS EL 26 C 9; the Bodleian Library for permission to reproduce the lawyer from MS Douce 104, and the British Library for Chaucers from MS Royal 17.D.VI and MS Harley 4866. Wes Smith kindly took a new photograph of Fettered Cock Pewters's replica pilgrim/ vulva badge and allowed its reproduction here, and Cambridge University Press gave me permission to reprint material from 'Wrinkled Deep in Time: Emily and Arcite in *A Midsummer Night's Dream*', *Shakespeare Survey* 65 (2012).

Much of this book has grown out of conversation and exchange especially from teaching. Students at Lady Margaret Hall, Oxford, have galvanised and sharpened my thinking over many years and I thank them for indulging me in some of my more outlandish readings of Chaucer and Shakespeare and for gently rebuffing those that were even more preposterous. I also want to acknowledge the participants of the 'Chaucer: sacred and profane' group in the 2012 Summer School run by the Department of Continuing Education, Oxford. Without their discussion when the sun suddenly streamed through a window in the Morris Room, Exeter College, in an otherwise exceptionally rain-sodden and dark summer I should probably never have realised that Chaucer allows us to imagine the Virgin Mary thrusting her nethers out of an Oxford window.

Friends and colleagues have kindly read portions of this book, discussed ideas, and helped with particular aspects where they knew so much more than me: Helen Cooper; Vincent Gillespie, Isaac Harrison Louth, Amanda Holton, Anne Hudson, Maarit Kivilo, Nicholas Perkins, Roberta Staples, Annie Sutherland, Helen Swift, Cathy Swire, Julie Taylor, Laura Varnam, John Watts and the anonymous readers for Manchester University Press. I especially want to thank Emma Smith and Paul Strohm. While they cannot be held responsible for what I have gone and done, their responses to what they read of this and their intellectual generosity in developing ideas and thoughts only beginning to take shape have enabled me to take Chaucer to places that I would not have reached on my own. Ayoush Samardi Lazikani and Anouska Lester were wonderful research assistants in the latter stages and I thank them both very warmly for their help in bibliography and checking. Thank you also to Carol Harrison for introducing me to Iain McGilchrist's *The Master and His Emissary*, and for graciously forgoing the pleasure of my company at the Bearpark prize leek and onion show to give me the space to read her copy. Vincent Quinn has contributed more to this book than he can know. His friendship sustains my academic work and my sense of its purpose. The Souter family, as ever, have helped in so many ways. Frances and Anna have heard rather more about arses than I suspect they liked, and I am enormously grateful to Martin for making me think much harder about what they might mean. His expertise in scatology – and music – has been a touchstone. Felicity has assisted me greatly with visual materials. I am delighted that she agreed to design the image for the cover and has produced something that is so brilliantly responsive to what she read in preparation.

Quite a lot of this book is about the continuing importance of persons no longer 'here'. Thomas Carney Forkin was my graduate student for most of this book's making. I am sorrier than I can say that he did not live to see it come out because his hilarious erudition made it possible for me to think I could write it. Especially when it can seem that the only thing that now counts is what can be quantified; Tom's commitment to making academic work speak of things that matter is a lasting inspiration. He achieved this in ways that I can scarcely shake a stick at. All the same, *Transporting Chaucer* is for Tom.

Oxford
December 2013

# List of abbreviations

*DMF*  *Dictionnaire du Moyen Français (1330–1500)*, 2012
       edition. ATILF – CNRS & Université de Lorraine
       www.atilf.fr/dmf
EEBO   Early English Books Online http://eebo.chadwyck.com/
EETS   The Early English Text Society (1864–)
  OS   Original Series (1864–)
  ES   Extra Series (1867–1920)
  SS   Supplementary Series (1970–)
LION   Literature Online http://lion.chadwyck.co.uk/
*MED*  *Middle English Dictionary*, ed. Hans Kurath and
       S. M. Kuhn (Ann Arbor: University of Michigan Press;
       London: Oxford University Press, 1952–) http://quod.
       lib.umich.edu/m/med/
*OED*  *Oxford English Dictionary*, 2nd edn ed. John Simpson
       and Edmund Weiner, 20 vols (Oxford: Clarendon Press,
       1989) www.oed.com/
*PMLA* *Publications of the Modern Language Association of
       America*
RSC    Royal Shakespeare Company
SATF   Société des Anciens Textes Français

# Introduction: Transporting Chaucer

At the gate of Canterbury Cathedral in February 2011, a porter informed me that access to the Becket stained glass in Trinity Chapel I had come to research was off limits. There was a service happening. There was, however, a new statue of Becket in the crypt that might interest me. The statue seemed some compensation for having to wait for the glass so I dutifully trotted off to the crypt and searched with increasing puzzlement for the new artwork. Only, there was no statue. Nor, seemingly, Thomas Becket. At first.

The sculpture had been unveiled only a week before my visit. I had not seen the press release from Canterbury Cathedral, embargoed until 16.00 GMT, 30 January 2011:

> On Sunday 30th January at 16.30hrs TRANSPORT a new sculpture created by the artist Antony Gormley will be unveiled at Canterbury Cathedral. Antony Gormley is credited with a radical re-investigation of the body as a zone of memory and transformation. The two metre long work uses handmade antique nails from the Cathedral's repaired south east transept roof to construct a delicate filter-like membrane outlining the space of a floating body. The membrane is suspended above the site of Thomas Becket's first resting place in the Eastern Crypt of the Cathedral.[1]

The sculpture, it transpired, is not of Becket (see Plate 1). But it could be. Gormley writes: 'the body is less a thing than a place; a location where things happen. Thought, feeling, memory and anticipation filter through it.'[2] Suspended above the martyr's first resting place, *Transport* anticipates recall of Becket, in part because of the sculpture's location. It extends an invitation to conjure bodies that are and are not there; to enter into dialogue with the body mould suspended *above* our heads and the bodies remembered or expected *within* our heads. There is no literal referencing of any of the details of Becket's martyrdom: no representation of knights, archbishops, Thomas's famous head wound, or his healing blood. Contemplation of the nails, however, prompts an association of Becket's resting place with wounding and piercing. That the antique nails are rescued from the roof suggests Becket's spiritual transformation through martyrdom. But Becket's is not the only body that *Transport* bodies forth. To see a body of nails, hanging, calls both to mind and to feeling, an image of Christ suspended on the cross, riveted with nails, crowned with gouging thorns. As a metonym of crucifixion, the nails fuse the body of Christ in first-century Jerusalem with Becket's in twelfth-century Canterbury in twenty-first-century time. *Transport* conveys Becket's body with Christ's.

Crucifixion iconography is both courted and refigured. The membrane does not hang between the nave and the chancel. Its axis is horizontal, not vertical. In ecclesiastical space a horizontal body is an effigy on a tomb, or a corpse in a grave beneath a slab stone underfoot. The raised height of the sculpture reconfigures these associations of space, position and axis without necessarily leaving any of those associations behind. Suspended by a scarcely visible cable, the body appears to float in free space. Neither in nor affixed to stone, glass or wood, and with spaces between the nails, it remains unbound by any material attachments save those that an observer projects from within its Canterbury setting. While its constituent materials of nails and space suggest the tactility of marking and incision, because the nails make up the place and shape of the body while creating a membrane that is multiply pierced, *Transport* exceeds definitive representation of any particular human body. One of the ways that bodies are told one from another is through the way that they are marked; marked through anatomy, costume, paint or incision.[3] The nails in *Transport* however make up both an outer shape and an inner density. Even as the sharp materials of the nails deter the desire to touch, they inscribe spaces for the observer's projection: for the observer to fill those spaces and the space around with bodies remembered, anticipated, historically vibrant and/or angrily rejected.

One hostile respondent to the sculpture complains it is simply a model of the body of Gormley himself. Honest John from Wakefield in West Yorkshire writes, 'did you know he bases all his work (which is all the same – it is all figures) – on himself? He has a massive ego ... I have more talent in my right testicle.'[4]

John's testimony notwithstanding, *Transport* has no signs, genital or otherwise, that make it definitively male, or female. It has adult dimensions but no sign of age: no face, no limbs and no costume. But the Wakefield dissident has a point about all those other Gormley bodies. To an observer familiar with Gormley's oeuvre, the membrane can't help but prompt recall of those Gormley bodies elsewhere, even though this particular sculpture is not cast from the sculptor's own body mould. Anticipated from memory, Gormley's body co-exists with those that are prompted from what he has made. Gormley's 'own' body re-fuses distinction between sculptor and sculpted. And yet this is not Gormley's body any more than it is Becket's or Christ's. The body mould is what it is made to become. My first response when I saw it was to wonder why someone had strung up a giant hedgehog in a cathedral.

There is no one stable 'source' for *Transport*. An observer can walk all around the body, looking up, and around. But not down. There is no superior vantage point, no place assigned from which to look. *Transport* yields no directed itinerary, nor point of origin. Or destination. That is one of the reasons why I choose *Transport* as a figure for the work of this book, and hence its title. *Transport* suggests movement between place(s) and/or person(s), and also to be beside oneself; a state of being elsewhere.[5] Crucially, 'transport' is both a noun and a verb. Something that is substantive is indistinguishable and inseparable from something that is in process. The *Transport* body in the crypt of Canterbury cathedral creates a movement in time and place that takes observers beyond themselves in their encounter with multiple bodies in durable time.

Why turn to this twenty-first-century sculpture to explore the movement of Chaucer through time? Are there not 'bokes ynowe' as Ymaginatif reminds the narrator of *Piers Plowman* without 'medlying with makynges' to explain such matters?[6] Yes and no. There are wonderfully supple studies of Chaucer's works in relationship to what comes after him. Sources and allusions have been richly mined. Movement between manuscript and print studied meticulously. Chaucer has been imaginatively explored as a congenial soul in future textual company and as a corpse who persists in turning up amongst the living. A huge range of Chaucer's works have been placed in fruitful conversations with those that come later, whether or not they explicitly refer back to the medieval poet.[7] My exploration in this book of encounters between

Chaucer's oeuvre, Chaucerian apocrypha, and early modern texts has been informed and enriched by this scholarship. *Transporting Chaucer* does not dispense entirely with source and analogue study, or depart wholly from the tracing of allusions, and ideas of literary followings. But, rather than reading through chronological and genealogical succession – Chaucer and Sons inc., script and print, or its flipped incarnation of ghostly presence and anxious hauntings – my analysis inhabits a temporality that is neither successive nor bounded. There is no argument between 'medieval' and 'after'; no struggle between canon and apocrypha. In a sense, this is a book about reading between the lines; the lines that have been drawn up to make sense of literary corpora to discipline them into manageable time and place.

This book explores a question. What is going on when we encounter Chaucer's characters, including 'himself', in works he did not make? I argue that when we pay attention to what happens when Chaucerian bodies – their physical appearance; their costume; their names and their sounds – travel between textual corpora (whether or not Chaucer wrote all of them), then authorised versions of literary time and place cease to hold. Meeting Chaucer where he isn't supposed to be rearranges normative understandings of before and after, time and place. *Transporting Chaucer* explores the imaginative possibilities that such encounters open up. Recognition of Chaucerian bodies between texts written at different historical junctures upsets linear chronology. The movement of Chaucerian characters back and forth plays out in movements of time experienced as continuous rather than a sequence of temporal units that has been fabricated to tell the time in segments. Freed from unitary measurement and free to play, Chaucerian bodies cross the material borders of physical books and the drawn-up borders of literary history. This book ravels strange meetings with Chaucerian bodies between works that Chaucer wrote, works deemed apocryphal, and early modern plays. Between all of these works, Chaucerian bodies are in transport whether or not Chaucer can be proved to have had a hand in them. These bodies are figures of resistance to teleological versions of literary history. They are bodies that don't keep time, and they make free with place. The bodies I explore in this book travel in and between works from around 1340 to 1700. Only, they are not held up by boundaries of periodisation. At least, not in the regular ways that these have come to be told.

I use Gormley's *Transport* to form the title of this book not because I am on some grand mission to explain the process of reading through sculpture, but because – quite simply and honestly – encountering this sculpture gave back to me, viscerally and intellectually, a recognition of how bodies are thought and felt to travel across time that I had already started to write about. *Transport* bodied forth the experience of reading between Chaucer's works and those that come after him in a way that kept getting lost when I tried to account for it in verbal language; not in the writing about the traffic between the texts themselves but in trying to give an account of what I was doing at a metacritical level. With its play with matter and space, and its room, both literally and figuratively, for the movement of an observer, *Transport* showed me a realisation of what it was that I had been trying to articulate verbally. Words, however, are supposed to be put into normative syntax and grammar. Such institutionally policed arrangements are an impediment to temporal congruity and co-existence between bodies and persons. Tense grammar and disciplined relationships between parts of speech tell out versions of experience that necessarily privilege linearity, teleology, emphasis and subordination. For reasons of clarity, written language distinguishes between sentences, and between subject and object in sentences; between who is doing what to whom and when. On a micro-level, editorial conventions about language usage predetermine the versions of bodiliness that readerly experience may or may not recognise. That certainty of unambiguously separated persons in clearly articulated relationships may not always be desirable because, as I discuss in Chapter 2 of this book, it may give only a version of some of the facts. In stumbling across *Transport*, unexpectedly (accidentally), I encountered a work of art that bypassed such regulation in its invitation to meet bodies past and present on different terms. Had the trains been on time, I should probably never have seen the sculpture; I should have gone straight to the stained glass that was the purpose of my research trip. Had I not seen the accompanying plaque which prompted reflection on the kinds of bodies I could meet there, I should probably have persisted in thinking about delusional hedgehogs or grumbling about being sent on a wild goose chase for a seemingly non-existent statue. That serendipity is important to the work of this book. On one level, this work ducks prevalent academic requirements to set out the journey in advance and meet its destination within required timelines and trajectories: to give advance notification of its outcomings and its inputtings.[8] Put less contentiously, coming across *Transport* enabled me to articulate what happens when bodies meet up between medieval

times and after that in ways that felt consistent with my experience
of those unsought encounters.

It matters that my understanding of *Transport*'s coincidental
bodiliness was informed both by physical artefact and by accompanying text.[9] The relationship between verbal and non-verbal
forms of art informs a great deal of the work in this book. Its
narrative travels in and between written texts and material artefacts: stained glass, pilgrim badges, musical instruments, mouldy
bread, manuscript illustration and medieval architecture. It is
also important that *Transport* hangs in a medieval cathedral, one
located in Canterbury. As I explore in Chapters 1, 2, 5, and 6,
Canterbury is a destination that is, and is not, reached, both in
Chaucer's own works and in those that take up the narrative
of what Chaucer's works are become. Chaucer's works shuttle
backwards and forwards between ecclesiastical milestones that
are insufficient to contain them in fixed place and time. Set in the
history of a medieval cathedral for present, past and future times,
the work of *Transport* re-presents a bodily confection that is so
characteristic of medieval cultural practices. Within its religious
setting the twenty-first-century sculpture produces bodies that are
coterminously historical, contemporary, human and divine in a
mould whose synthesis would have been recognisable to a medieval
mind, even as it takes an unfamiliar shape.

As is very well known, cycles of mystery plays stage redemption history in local time and place. Within the duration of Corpus
Christi Day, townsfolk would watch their fellows become biblical characters performing Old and New Testament stories with
the materials of local guilds. With the Crucifixion staged by the
Pinners, the nails of Christ's body are the tools of the soldiers'
trade. With the Death of Christ staged by the butchers at the
Shambles in York, Calvary is the site of the civic slaughterhouse.[10]
Cycle plays would have been performed in the streets; outside the
bounds of ecclesiastical buildings. But the merging of the contemporary and the scriptural with townsfolk becoming persons
from the Bible has its counterpart within the walls of the church.
Donors of medieval stained glass take their place alongside figures
from biblical history in the windows of churches. Even as they may
not take centre-stage, their persons form part of vitrine drama in
which divisions of time and place are glazed over. The *Pricke of
Conscience* Window in All Saints, North Street, York, combines
a paraphrase of the text of the Middle English poem from which
it now takes its name with depictions of the end of the world.

The tenth glass panel shows the destruction of buildings by an earthquake. To bring home the horror of the event to the present congregation, the newly built spire of All Saints is depicted falling. At the top of the window two panels in the quatrefoil tracery lights show St Peter admitting redeemed souls into heaven and demons ferrying the dammed to hell. At the base of the window contemporary figures look with consternation at the events going on in the panels above. Whether or not they represent members of the Henryson and Hessle families who paid for this window, or figure the parish congregation of All Saints, the kneeling figures take part in an apocalyptic history which shows the destruction of their own parish church as a sign of the end of the world. The congregation of All Saints are invited to contemplate a version of themselves facing the end of time even as they stand within the very building whose future demise the window records.[11]

The overall scheme of the window suggests that it is designed as a prompt for repentance. Such penitential mingling of the contemporary and the eschatological in stained glass was not without its critics. The narrator of *Piers Plowman* exposes the potential for financial corruption in lay sponsor of ecclesiastical glass when he recounts a mutually incriminatory conversation between Meed and the friar in Passus 3.[12] Yet the folding of contemporary persons into biblical and salvation history is a staple characteristic of the narrative of the poem. At the start of Passus 18 the events and persons of liturgical holy week unfold in scriptural history and in recognisable fourteenth-century place: in Jerusalem, at the gates of a medieval city, in a church and in the lists of a tournament. Christ's entry into Jerusalem on an ass is dramatised through the liturgy for Psalm Sunday. Will the narrator wakes from his dream to the sound of glory and praise and 'osanna' sung to the sound of the organ (19.7–8). Latin quotations score the narrative with snatches of liturgy woven into the drama of the fourteenth-century alliterative line to recreate in verse how liturgical performance in a church already made present and dramatic to the assembled congregation the scriptural events of the day that the service commemorates. The singing church also welcomes a nobleman, barefoot on a donkey coming to be dubbed a knight. Abraham as Faith, first introduced in Passus 16, is present in the episode as a herald. Standing in a window from an overhanging street like a character from a mystery play, or a figure in stained glass, he announces the name of the anonymous jouster with words from Matthew 21:9: 'cryde "*A fili David!*"' (18.15). Abraham/Faith/Evangelist/Tournament Herald/

Figure in Glass speaks in scriptural, historical, and contemporary
times and places all at once:

> This Jesus of his gentries wol juste in Piers armes,
> In his helm and his haubergeon – *humana natura*.
> That Crist be noght biknowe here for *consummatus Deus*,
> In Piers paltok the Plowman this prikiere shal ride
> For no dynt shal hym dere as in *deitate Patris*.
>
> (18.22–6)

Christ is costumed, socially marked, both as a knight in armour
and as a ploughman in a worker's jacket. He is both God and man;
triumphant and scarred. His body is divine and human; his name
Jesus, Christ, *Deus*, and Piers. To scrape out any one of the inscriptions of time, place, body and name from this episode is to gouge its
theological and poetic immediacy for all of time.

The figure of Piers Plowman however, for all of his timely fullness of personhood, is not available to be confused with its maker
William Langland in the way that the *Transport* body can be seen
to incorporate that of its sculptor Antony Gormley. Even those
later works that take up the project of rewriting *Piers Plowman* for
their own times and interests do not appear to have confused the
ploughman figure with the poem's author.[13] In the case of *The Book
of Margery Kempe*, however, the voice and actions of its historical
author become inseparable from the scribes who wrote her. She
becomes conscripted into ecclesiastical space resonant with figures
from contemporary devotional writing and salvation history. As the
scribe recounts in chapter 62, Kempe's behaviour becomes devo-
tionally legible to him, intellectually and emotionally, as he recalls
the *Life of Mary D'Oignes*.[14] A lay woman with no established place
in ecclesiastical structure becomes recognisably religious as she is
reassembled alongside existing models of devotional practice: those
of recent vintage and those in the Bible. How far this recognition
is Margery's and to what extent the scribes' is a boundary that is
probably impossible to determine.[15] One example must suffice
for illustration. When Kempe is examined in Leicester before the
abbot of St Mary's monastery, and the Dean of Leicester in the
church of All Saints, the abbot and his assessors (with great spatial
appropriateness) sit at the altar as she details an orthodox account
of the sacrament of the Eucharist (p. 234). Quoting from the Bible
in English, Margery publically challenges the Mayor's moral standing, while in retaliation the Mayor scoffs at the sanctity of her white
clothes and accuses her of coming to lead away the townswomen

(pp. 235–6). All this while, the townsfolk stand on stools to gape at a parish drama which bears more than a passing resemblance to Christ's interrogation before the high priests in a mystery play. When she is sent to the abbey for further interrogation, the canons come out to give her shelter. To Margery, they appear as the 'Lord comyng wyth his apostelys'. She is so ravished into devotional contemplation that she is unable to stand up, 'but lenyd hir to a peler in the chirche' (p. 238). In Leicester's pre-eminent ecclesiastical space, and with consummate theatrical blocking, Margery is supported in her mystical vision of Christ's second coming by one of the pillars of St Mary's Abbey. Margery takes her fifteenth-century place in scriptural time and salvation history by using a fixture of the church as a prop for her body. The daughter of the mayor of King's Lynn, erstwhile brewer and mother of fourteen children, a woman without place within contemporary religious structures and categories, is conveyed dramatically into theological and social orthodoxy. She takes up a place in and through narratives that otherwise would exclude her on account of having no room to recognise her devotional irregularity.[16]

Chaucer's writing occupies a recognisable place in this blurring of boundaries between historical materiality, scriptural history and contemporary fictions. As in *The Book of Margery Kempe*, it is hard to separate confections of the author and 'somebody else', and it is difficult to tell text from voice. But those confusions are differently inflected from those encountered in *Kempe*. In Chaucer's writings, it is Chaucer as author who reads between the lines. Chaucer transports textual versions of his own body in and amongst those other fictional bodies he brings into being. Between diverse fragments of *The Canterbury Tales* and beyond, a body that is available to be recognised as Chaucer's, whether through voice or through narrative appearance, becomes transitive amongst bodies that are multiply told, heard and seen. Shuttled back and forth in and amongst *The Canterbury Tales* and between other Chaucerian works, bodies are confected in ways recognisable from religious texts and material cultural practices. Versions of personhood play out in vernacular poetry that confound distinctions between discrete textual productions, between maker and made, and between sacred and profane. In the process – and this is what is distinctively Chaucerian – that traffic of human bodies transports literary corpora. Literary works written in the past keep present company with those in the process of being made. The movement of Chaucerian bodies makes texts float free through the boundaries that have come to be seen to hold

them up in proper place.[17] Chaucer arrives before later writers and
critics at a future he has already fashioned. *Bodily transport between
Chaucer's own works anticipates the transport that is yet to be made of
them in works that he did not compose.*

I discuss the movement of Chaucerian bodies (including
Chaucer's own) between fragments of *The Canterbury Tales*
'authentic' and 'apocryphal' in Chapters 1 and 2. Chapter 3 shows
how a specific body part, Chaucer's hand, moves between a brico-
lage of other hands that he wrote, and hands that later illustrators
made of them. Chaucer's hand gets caught up in the telling not only
of Chaucerian literary history but of critical stories of its reception further afield. These corporeal movements are anticipated by
Chaucer's writing even before the writing of *The Canterbury Tales*
and their aftermath. The fashioning of the narrator in *The Book of
the Duchess* projects a version of physical and literary bodiliness that
sets in motion a translation of persons – and corpora – that anticipates the work of *The Miller's Tale*. Between a dream vision written
for the most powerful nobleman in the land, and a fabliau voiced by
a churl, Chaucerian bodies and Chaucerian corpora are trafficked in
and through some rather startling incarnations of the Virgin Mary.

When the scene of Gabriel's Annunciation is figured in stained
glass windows, the Virgin Mary is seated with a book in her lap.
There is a window behind her. A beam of light, often issuing forth
from a dove, streams through the glass. In its passage through
the glass without fracturing it the light represents the Holy Spirit
penetrating Mary's human body whilst leaving it intact. The word
of God is made flesh within the body of a mortal woman without
breaking Mary's virgin seal. Thus is the unfathomable mystery of
the Virgin Birth blazoned. Placed in front of a window, in a window,
Mary becomes bathed in the artificial light of the glazier's craft,
the light of the Holy Spirit, and the natural daylight of the world
beyond the church's stone walls.[18] In *The Book of the Duchess* these
iconographical figurations come to tell a story of literary production
in which the body of the dreaming narrator becomes the body of
the Virgin Mary. The Dreamer falls asleep 'ryght upon' the book
he has taken to bed (274–5). The Virgin's book that symbolises the
Word of God she is to bear is become an anonymous tome that the
narrator is unable to keep open before his eyes. There is a 'gret hep'
of birds outside (295) whose singing fills the whole chamber with
a heavenly harmony that the narrator has not hitherto experienced
(307–20). His chamber is full of windows glazed with stories of
Troy and its walls are painted with the *Romance of the Rose*:

And sooth to seyn, my chambre was
Ful wel depeynted, and with glas
Were al the wyndowes wel yglased
Ful clere, and *nat an hole ycrased*,
That to biholde hyt was gret joye.
For hooly al the story of Troye
Was in the glasynge ywroght thus,
Of Ector and kyng Priamus ...
And alle the walles with colours fyne
Were peynted, bothe text and glose,
Of al the Romaunce of the Rose.
My wyndowes were shette echon,
And thrugh the glas the sonne shon
Upon my bed with bryghte bemes,
With many glade gilde stremes.[19]

Line 324 explicitly draws attention to how the glass is not cracked; there is no *hole* in it. Light shines through the 'shette' windows and bathes the narrator's bed with bright beams. As he announces the onset of his dream just before this description, the narrator has told us, in a seemingly comically irrelevant detail, that he lies in his bed 'al naked' (293). When we aggregate all the details of book, birds, window, uncracked glass, texts, and vulnerable body, we see that this is not just a dream vision; this is an Annunciation scene retold. The light that travels in through the sealed window quickens the narrator's naked body with new word from previous literary works. God's Word becoming flesh becomes the light of literary precedent that in-forms a new body of text. A new literary corpus, a naked text that is the narrator's body, becomes glossed with the spirit of Classical and Continental literary heritage. Transported to an English poem, the foundational moment of human salvation history becomes an originary scene of English vernacular writing that will fuse what has already been written with a new body of work produced by this Chaucerian narrator.

The narrator's body is simultaneously the body of the Virgin Mary and a textual corpus produced in the fullness of time. Humble, ordinary, the narrator is picked out to produce new work that will transform what has already been written in the present moment of the poem. The feminised narrator becomes pregnant with pre-existent word that forges a new testament of literary history that is already prefigured by the old and which it is in the process of fulfilling. In his textual incarnation as Mary, the narrator is intermediary between word and body, male and female, past

and future, sacred and secular. As Mary, the male narrator embodies writing as reception that plays between temporal boundaries.
Material borders (the glass windows) are sealed but the images
they contain are uncontained. In a literary chamber that refigures
the Virgin's womb, textual containment and dissemination cannot
be told apart. The dreamer is not literally Chaucer, of course; not
in the historical sense. But if we follow the invitation to figure
that is cued both by the reprise of iconographical signs and by
the collocation of 'peynte' with 'bothe text and glose', then the
windowed body is Chaucer's just as much as the *Transport* body in
Canterbury Cathedral is Gormley's. The dreamer of *Duchess* narrates into being the present and future work of the poet Geoffrey
Chaucer. With this audacious arrogation of incarnational theology,
the Mother of God is the Father of English poetry.[20]

Even more audacious perhaps is what this annunciatory scene
becomes in *The Miller's Tale*. Old Testament Noah's Flood is
restaged by fourteenth-century New Testament fictional characters. In a 'legende and a lyf / Bothe of a carpenter and his wyf'
(I.3141–2), John the carpenter becomes Joseph. Alison, his wife, is
the Virgin Mary. She receives a somewhat secularised version of
Gabriel's salutation to Mary, as Nicholas, the singer of 'Angelus ad
virginem' (I.3216), grabs her by the 'queynte' (I.3274). The foundational moment of salvation history is become a student's sexual
assault on his landlady. At the end of the tale, the Annunciation
glass of *The Book of the Duchess* becomes the open bow shot
(hinged) window in an Oxford side street. The Oseney window is
not sealed and uncracked, but hinged. It can be thrown open, and
'clapte to' (I.3740). It reaches (significantly) down to the waist.
Memorably, of course, it is a window out of which body parts
protrude, fart and are met with kisses, and/or red hot pokers. And
it is out of this window that the Virgin Mary as Alison thrusts out
a body part that goes unmentioned in the Bible:

> Derk was the nyght as pich, or as the cole,
> And at the wyndow out she putte hir hole.

> (I.3731–2)

Partly because the scene is set in pitch black night (no gilded dove-
like beams shine through *this* window), quite which 'hole' Alison
presents is left unspecified (I.3732).[21] That remains a matter of a
woman's 'pryvetee' (I.3164). The inscrutability of Alison's 'hole'
is a secular retelling of the theological mystery of the Virgin Birth.
Neither the window nor Alison's body is unsealed in *The Miller's*

*Tale*; but the guarded silence about the nature of her aperture still cloaks the permeability of a woman's body in mystery. Absolon's disgust about encountering what he thinks is a beard gets us no closer to understanding exactly what hole of Alison's body he has encountered. Neither does Nicholas's gleeful riposte, '[a] berd! A berd! ... by Goddes corpus' (I.3742–3). In its yoking of unclassifiable pubic hair to God's body the oath simply serves to intensify the confusion.[22] Between *The Book of the Duchess* and *The Miller's Tale*, the body of Our Immaculate Lady and the body of 'Chaucer' are become an Oxford 'prymerole' (I.3268). The translucent purity of an Annunciation window, and an originary writing scene of English vernacular poetry, is become a woman scandalously thrusting her nethers through an open window in a fourteenth-century public street. While John Joseph the carpenter tries to keep Alison/Mary 'narwe in cage' (I.3224), she escapes the spatial and temporal boundaries that would narrowly confine her. Eternal time, salvation history, fourteenth-century carnality and transport between earlier and later Chaucerian texts all come together as she (or should that be Chaucer?) plays her part faultlessly in the story of the rear window.

*The Miller's Tale* restages the incarnational poetics of *Duchess* in theologically resonant fleshliness. The *Duchess* scene explicitly raises questions of how you read a text/body; the end of *The Miller's Tale* revisits these questions through the unreadability of Alison's *hole* as a figure for the inscrutability of God's body. Chaucer's dreaming corpus travels through time and through text to become incorporate with the bodies of the Virgin Mary and the coltish wife of an Oxford carpenter. Theologically quizzical fabliau keeps place with aristocratic dream vision in-formed by Classical and Continental reading. Written by Chaucer the poet and told by a miller who usurps the speaking place of a monk, Alison's body in the window incorporates past and present Chaucerian corpora with dark theology in contemporary vernacular voice.

It is fitting, perhaps, that the body who in her earliest incarnation is a Chaucerian narrator should turn out to be one of Chaucer's most well-travelled fictional creations. Alison's is a body that is transitive not just in the work that calls her by name but also in other fragments of *The Canterbury Tales* and beyond. It is a critical commonplace that Alison has already appeared in *The Canterbury Tales* by the time she gets told by the Miller. She is, of course, Emelye from *The Knight's Tale*, still clinging to vestiges of her Marian identity from *Duchess* as she is introduced

as fairer than the lily flower (I.1035–6).[23] Set in a rather different garden from *The Knight's Tale*, the Merchant's narration of
the encounter between Damien and May up the pear tree turns
Mary/Alison/Emelye into Eve. Helen Cooper's classic study of
the girl with two lovers is also a story of bodies in transport
between *The Canterbury Tales* and beyond.[24] Alison's body floats
through Chaucerian corpora beyond those works that Geoffrey
Chaucer wrote. I explore some of her avatars in Shakespeare's
plays in Chapters 4 and 5. In Chapter 2 I show how Alison meets
Chaucerian incarnations of herself in the unique fragment of
*The Canterbury Tales* now known either as *The Prologue to the
Tale of Beryn* or as *The Canterbury Interlude*. This 'apocryphal'
Canterbury narrative upsets chronological linearity and confounds
normative co-ordinates of time and place. Although *The Interlude*
comes two-thirds of the way through MS Northumberland 455, its
story is placed in Canterbury. Not only does the pilgrim assembly
arrive at a destination that is never reached by other narratives of
*The Canterbury Tales* but they set off for the return to London
even as the remainder of the Northumberland sequence tells the
tales of the pilgrims as they are still striving – and failing – to
reach their journey's end. Alison is one of the many persons in
*The Canterbury Interlude* who has already been met several times
on a reader's journey through the Northumberland codex. As
I show in Chapter 2, Kit the tapster, the woman who plays such
a central role in *The Canterbury Interlude*, plays out a part that is
conscripted with the words and actions of Alison. In turn, Alison/
Kit reprises the voice of a Chaucerian heroine from another work
entirely: Criseyde joins the all-star cast of the *Interlude* bringing
Troilus as the Pardoner along with her.

Like Alison, the Pardoner also does the rounds between
Chaucerian works. But in contrast to Alison, the Pardoner's name
does travel with him as he commutes between the canonical fragments of *The Canterbury Tales* and *The Canterbury Interlude*. So
too, do recognised fragments of his body. I argue in Chapter 1
that the Pardoner's body in the *Interlude* anticipates the memorial
newness of Gormley's *Transport* body in Canterbury Cathedral.
Dramatised in the spaces between the inn and the cathedral, suspended somewhere between London and Canterbury, the Pardoner
is become a portable Becketian relic whose ontology is as inscrutable as his sexual anatomy. Signed with signs of Becket's murder
and his healing ampullae of blood and water, the Pardoner's stig-
matised sexuality conflates the desire for the revelation of hidden

human anatomy with the parading of pilgrimage trophy. With his apparently tortured phallus, and his wounds to head, back and arms, the Pardoner is a concealed display of an abjected Becket and a tormented Christ as he rides away from Canterbury in the midst of his pilgrim group.

The first two chapters of *Transporting Chaucer* attempt to keep track of some hectic intra-travel between constituent parts of a continuously evolving Chaucerian oeuvre. I show in Chapter 2 how the work of editors has swollen the volume of traffic. Through punctuation, capitalisation and emendation, persons are brought into an already populous pilgrim band from the memory of Chaucerian works beyond the *Canterbury Tales*, and beyond the oeuvre of Chaucer's canonical texts. In one instance, Furnivall's supplying of a line to *The Canterbury Interlude* is prompted by his memory of the Great Chaucer window unveiled in Westminster Abbey in 1868. Trailed into the poem are not only versions of Chaucer but an assembly of ladies from a blend of apocryphal Chaucerian texts. *The Canterbury Interlude* has become part of a recognisable landscape of Chaucerian literary criticism. Not so the text that follows it in MS Northumberland 455. Partly because it is a long redaction of an even longer fourteenth-century Anglo-Norman romance, *The Tale of Beryn* has been seen as a no-through-road back to Chaucer. Chapter 2 argues for a different version of events. The plots of *Beryn* and *Bérinus* depend on the instability of the signs of personhood. As a consequence, characters are made up back and forth between the French version of the story and its English redaction. In their Canterbury setting, narrated by a Merchant pilgrim, preceded by a Chaucerian Prologue and in the midst of a codex of *The Canterbury Tales*, the foreign bodies of *Bérinus* become persons rather familiar from the works of Chaucer. The most striking re-semblance is between the mysterious shape-shifting person of Gioffrey/Geffrey and the inconsistent cameo appearances of Chaucer's body in different parts of his oeuvre.

The re-citation of personal names plays a significant role in the border crossings I analyse in Chapters 1 and 2. While Proper Names create the appearance of separation and distinctions between bodies, that illusion is shattered when individual names turn out to be rather more common. Names shared between texts, even when written more than a century apart, trail the memory of bodies into narratives where they ought not (strictly speaking) to appear. Names play a vital part in *A Midsummer Night's Dream*. It is often remarked that in this play Shakespeare took the name

of Philostrate and Egeus from Chaucer's *Knight's Tale*. I argue in
Chapter 4 that the dramatic reality is far more complex. Nothing
in *A Midsummer Night's Dream* is just a name. When Shakespeare
includes Philostrate and Egeus in *A Midsummer Night's Dream*,
he recalls and foretells a complex interweaving of past, present
and future bodies in which *The Knight's Tale* gets caught up in an
unravelling of the borders of literary history. Chapter 4 shows how
the anticipated memory of characters who ought to feature as part
of a story but do not appear to be on stage folds three tellings of
Chaucer's *Knight's Tale* into co-temporality. When Theseus lets
slip in Act 5 that he has already returned a conqueror from Thebes
before he has actually razed the city to the ground he unfolds a
wrinkle in time that discloses the memorial presence of Emily and
Arcite from *The Knight's Tale and Two Noble Kinsmen*. Emily
and Arcite cannot be properly admitted to *A Midsummer Night's
Dream* because they would wreck the couplings of the play on
which Theseus's dynastic desires depend. As *Two Noble Kinsmen*
shows, the intratemporal presence of Emily and Arcite frustrates
diachronic arithmetic and plays havoc with normative couplings.
When Emily and Arcite become available to the temporal imagination of these three works, chronology and heteronormativity will
not work.

The chapter shows how Emily and her avatars course through
the language and imagery of *A Midsummer Night's Dream*, shaping
up and back like the temporally incontinent moon that dominates
the play. Once noticed, neither Emily nor those other unruly
women she brings in train (Alison included) can be dismissed.
Philostrate is Arcite in disguise at Theseus's court, stalking the
boards all along, weaving in and out of the stage directions and
textual cruces between Folio and quartos. For all that the Knight
and Theseus try to manage time in a fashion that suits their dynastic plans, temporality is not theirs to determine. Like guardians of
normative disciplines of literary history, their attempts to control
temporal succession are defeated by the unruliness of bodies that
refuse subjection to superimpositions of time and place. The con-
temporaneous bodies that spill the borders of *A Midsummer Night's
Dream* pose a challenge to the placing of literary texts in genealogical succession. Although I do not present it first (my own subjection to a semblance of chronology in the ordering of the chapters in
this book), Chapter 4 was written before the other chapters. I had
not gone looking for Emily and Arcite in *A Midsummer Night's
Dream* on purpose. Discovering them to have been lurking there

all along prompted the question I explore throughout the work that appears in this book: what is going on when we encounter Chaucer's characters in works he did not make?

Chapter 5 continues to address that question in relation to the personnel that flit in and out of *The Knight's Tale*. *Two Noble Kinsmen*, William Davenant's wholly neglected seventeenth-century play *The Rivals*, Lydgate's *The Siege of Thebes* and Dryden's *Palamon and Arcite* inhabit a complex intratemporality in which poetic and royal lines of succession lack distinction. While *Two Noble Kinsmen* jestingly replays the genteel apologia for vulgarity that has become so familiar from *The Canterbury Tales*, Davenant attempts to strip sexual licence from his 1664 version of Shakespeare and Fletcher's play as part of his theatrical restoration of Charles II to the English stage. But the play cannot be rid of unruliness so easily; in part because of Davenant's meddling with names. One reason why *The Rivals* has so low a critical profile is that the names of its characters are not those of *The Knight's Tale* or *Two Noble Kinsmen*. Some names are invented, but others are the names of Lydgate's characters in his telling of the 'prequel' to *The Knight's Tale* in the *Siege of Thebes*. Davenant can be seen to swerve in and out of Fletcher and Shakespeare and Lydgate and Chaucer to tell the story of legitimate royal succession. His choice of names, however, cues the memory of noble annihilation and revolution yet to come. Only by diverting the course of Theban history and the end of *The Knight's Tale* can Davenant stave off complete disaster. But he is unable to control how his revisions spark new contention; this time, between royal mistresses. Lineage and literary succession are doubly upset, on stage and off. Davenant's contributions to the Restoration stage celebrated the joining of the laurel with the Crown, but his successor in the Poet Laureateship, John Dryden, presents a rather different tale of noble collaboration. In the Preface he writes to his version of *Palamon and Arcite*, Dryden ignores his erstwhile friend and collaborator William Davenant (and William Shakespeare, and William III) by going right back to *The Canterbury Tales* and to the Tabard when he stakes his claim to poetic lineage and Chaucer's supposed bays.

Dryden's attempts to 'restore' the Canterbury pilgrims to their rightful place and time is bound up, as is well known, with his desire to be buried in Chaucer's tomb in Westminster Abbey. We find ourselves again on a road well-travelled. Chaucerian bodies and those that would tell their time and place get shunted back and forth in time between ecclesiastical powerhouses. But as Chapter 6

argues, these churchly monuments are not as solid or as perma-
nent destinations as they are made out to be. Chapter 6 picks up
on where the Canterbury journey finished in Chapter 1; with the
prescient disclosure in Chaucer's *House of Fame*, that Canterbury
Cathedral, for all its wealth of stories told in stained glass, is a
feeble foundation on which to base enduring narrative. Chapter 6
shows that Shakespeare's 'man of gret auctoritee' in *Troilus and
Cressida* is not the Chaucer who tells *Troilus and Criseyde* but the
figure who does not want his name told in *The House of Fame*. The
action of the poem and play is told not in London but in the unruly
suburb of Southwark. The poem and the play share a distinctive
soundscape that collapses the distance that normative literary
history would put between them. As Chapter 2 has already discussed, voices and their sounds reverberate over time in ways that
override temporal segmentation and division. Trojan laud becomes
the tittle-tattle of Southbank stews. The levelling of value and
reputation is accompanied in both works by an acute sonic emphasis that eliminates difference between voice, sound, noise and air.
In both works, the trumpet plays a key role. Resulting from its
brazen lack of valves, the trumpet blows literary repute and stinky
fart with insouciant caprice. The final part of the chapter considers
the crucial role of silence and name in each work. The Chaucerian
narrator refuses to anchor the free-floating tidings of Troy with the
authority of a Proper Name. The figure of Antenor in *Troilus* is his
opposite: a name without a voice. On stage, but mute, Antenor is
a silent physical reminder of the fall of Troy that the audience will
already have known even through it remains explicitly unspoken
during the course of the play. And yet, directorial choices in the
play's performance history have yielded a scenario in which this
speechless body becomes spokesperson for all the characters in
Troy. Antenor and the narrator of *The House of Fame* are mirror
images of each other.

A mirror image of a Chaucerian narrator will already have been
encountered in *Transporting Chaucer*; only in Chapter 3 it is a
mirror image of 'Chaucer himself'. This chapter explores how
hands are intermediated between visual and verbal *Canterbury
Tales*. Medieval thinking about hands was conflicted. In scientific
writings the hand is the supremely articulated part of the body:
what distinguishes a human from a beast; the maker of civilisation, indeed the instrument of the soul. In Christian penitential
writings, hands are always potentially agents of sin; especially
of wrath, avarice and lechery. Meanwhile, in courtesy literature,

hands are exquisite agents of delicacy and taste. Hands in *The Canterbury Tales* reproduce this confusion. Chaucer writes about the pastoral hand that is simultaneously the agent of sodomitical congress; the groping hand of knowledge that is simultaneously the agent of the devil's work of alchemy, and hands costumed with signs of aristocratic taste as the markers of death and erotic transgression. The hands in illustrated copies of *The Canterbury Tales* continue to confound distinction. The visual pilgrims of Ellesmere and Cambridge MS CUL Gg.4.27 are placed by the start of the tales that they narrate. But their place as ordinators is unsettled by the work of their hands. 'Ordinatio' is compromised by details that make available to the eye information that has yet to be read. Or information that does not textually 'belong' to earlier textual incarnations of a pilgrim. Or information that is derived from a place other than that of *The Canterbury Tales*. Readers who come to illustrated copies of *The Canterbury Tales* are brought face to face with bodies that may tell anticipated memories of textual hands they have encountered elsewhere. Their recall and their expectation replay text and image back and forth across the visual and verbal texts of the *Canterbury Tales* and other places besides.

The temporal movement of Chaucer's 'own' hands is especially complex. His left hand in the Ellesmere Manuscript is inseparable from the memory of his right hand in the image of Chaucer from the Harley Manuscript that contains Hoccleve's *De Regimine Principum*. Chaucer's left hand is a little text hand: a manicule. Manicules have lives of their own. They provide orderly navigation through a text for readers even as they re-present its contents with unruly disregard. Chaucer's left hand dramatises the full range of textual movement that manicules can orchestrate. Remembered and anticipated between Ellesmere and Harley, the work of this left manicule conflates the roles of poet, narrator, pilgrim storyteller, writer, reader; both living and dead. Without doubt, the most famous image of Chaucer, the one that is most frequently reproduced, is his Ellesmere self, pointing with his left hand. When translated to other contexts – whether, academic books, leather bookmarks or biscuit boxes – his left index finger, as in Ellesmere, points into an empty space. For all its authoritative iconicity, however, the work of the left hand in Ellesmere can no more fix Chaucer than his shape-shifting namesake in *The Tale of Beryn* can be formally identified. After all, the narrator of *The House of Fame* wishes no one to have his name 'in honde' (1877).

A twenty-first-century readership is probably aware of how handedness has become part of a developing scientific discourse unavailable to Chaucer, but of whose significance his left hand seems pointedly prescient. Iain McGilchrist's *The Master and His Emissary: The Divided Brain and the Making of the Western World* explores the different characteristics of the right and left hemispheres of the brain. The right hemisphere is associated with the left hand and vice versa. This is how McGilchrist accounts for the left-handed work of the right hemisphere. Time is experienced as duration rather than a series of individual, chronological, measured and marked-up segments. The right hemisphere processes the relational aspects of experience; knowledge in the form not of facts but encounters that are rooted in experiential encounters between one thing and something else: one person and another, or others. The right hemisphere, the part of the brain in relationship with the left hand, yields a world that is changing, evolving, interconnected, implicit, incarnate, but never fully graspable, always imperfectly known. It's the right hemisphere that allows us to understand metaphor, or to get a joke. The left hemisphere, the part of the brain in association with the right hand, produces knowledge in the form of division: clarity, fixity, and separation. Its work produces things that are known, fixed, static, isolated, explicit, disembodied: lifeless. As McGilchrist argues, we need the right and left hemispheres to work together to allow us to get around; to navigate our experiences.[25] Both hemispheres are obviously crucial to the work of scholarship. But which is the master and which the emissary? It's a coincidence (but to me, one of wonder and delight) that iconic Chaucer points with his left hand. It's a coincidence – not least, as I argue in Chapter 3 – because his left-handedness is simply a consequence of the space that was left for him to fill on a verso page. Although I have written this book with my right hand, I have tried to make it work through the guidance of Chaucer's left.

## Notes

1  http://canterbury-cathedral.org/assets/files/docs/pdf/home-news/Gormley_Sculpture.pdf [accessed 6 February 2011].
2  Text cited from the explanatory notice accompanying the sculpture in the crypt.
3  As Gary Taylor remarks, 'once humans learnt to sign bodies, they could artificially mark differences between one set of bodies and

another', *Castration: An Abbreviated History of Western Manhood* (London and New York: Routledge, 2000), p. 162.

4  www.dailymail.co.uk/.../Antony-Gormley-unveils-new-artwork-Transport-Canterbury-Cathedral.html, posted 2 February 2011 [accessed 7 February 2011].

5  *OED* 'transport' (n) and (v).

6  William Langland, *The Vision of Piers Plowman: A Complete Edition of the B-text*, ed. A. V. C. Schmidt (London: Everyman, 1991), 12.16–17.

7  Caroline F. E. Spurgeon, *Five Hundred Years of Chaucer Criticism and Allusion, 1357–1900* (New York: Russell & Russell, 1960), 2 vols; D. S. Brewer (ed.), *Chaucer and Chaucerians: Critical Studies in Middle English Literature* (London: Nelson, 1970); Alice S. Miskimin, *The Renaissance Chaucer* (New Haven: Yale University Press, 1975); Ann Thompson, *Shakespeare's Chaucer: A Study in Literary Origins* (Liverpool: Liverpool University Press, 1978); E. Talbot Donaldson, *The Swan at the Well: Shakespeare Reading Chaucer* (New Haven and London: Yale University Press, 1985); Seth Lerer, *Chaucer and His Readers: Imagining the Author in Late-Medieval England* (Princeton: Princeton University Press, 1993); Theresa M. Krier (ed.), *Refiguring Chaucer in the Renaissance* (Gainesville: University Press of Florida, 1998); Daniel J. Pinti (ed.), *Writing after Chaucer: Essential Readings in Chaucer and the Fifteenth Century* (New York and London: Garland, 1998); Thomas A. Prendergast and Barbara Kline (eds), *Rewriting Chaucer: Culture, Authority, and the Idea of the Authentic Text, 1400–1602* (Columbus: Ohio State University Press, 1999); Kathleen Forni, *The Chaucerian Apocrypha: A Counterfeit Canon* (Gainesville: University Press of Florida, 2001); Stephanie Trigg, *Congenial Souls: Reading Chaucer from Medieval to Postmodern* (Minneapolis: University of Minnesota Press, 2002); Thomas A. Prendergast, *Chaucer's Dead Body: From Corpse to Corpus* (London and New York: Routledge, 2004); Gordon McMullan and David Matthews (eds), *Reading the Medieval in Early Modern England* (Cambridge: Cambridge University Press, 2007); Helen Cooper, *Shakespeare and the Medieval World* (London: Methuen, 2010); Andrew Higl, *Playing the Canterbury Tales: The Continuations and Additions* (Farnham: Ashgate, 2012).

8  'Shew them the form of the house, and of the fashion thereof, the goings out and the comings in, and the whole plan thereof, and all its ordinances, and all its order, and all its laws, and thou shalt write it in their sight: that they may keep the whole form thereof, and its ordinances, and do them' (Ezekiel, 43.11).

9  And also, a very long-standing personal interest in Gormley's work. While I had no idea that the sculpture had been unveiled just before my visit; I should certainly have wanted to visit it when I had caught up with the news. I first encountered Gormley's works in an exhibition

at the Tate Modern in St Ives in 2001. One of those exhibits, *Bed*, informs my discussion of Chaucer's hands in Chapter 3.

10  Richard Beadle and Pamela King (eds), *York Mystery Plays* (Oxford: Clarendon Press, 1984), pp. 211–36.

11  The window can be viewed at http://allsaints-northstreet.org.uk/stainedglass.html.

12  The friar offers to absolve Meed of her sins if she will help with the glazing of a new window in their cloister, and promises her that she will have her name engraved therein also (*Piers* 3.47–50). The narrator provides an unambiguous gloss on the conversation, '[a]c God to alle good folk swich gravynge defendeth – / To written in wyndowes of hir wel dedes – / An aventure pride be peynted there, and pomp of the world' (*Piers* 3.64–6).

13  In *Pierce the Ploughman's Crede*, for instance, while the figure of Pierce commands the highest voice of authority in the poem even as he stands in a muddy field in abject poverty, he is not invested with the multiple roles of Langland's figure, and nor is he conflated with the author of the poem. While the voice of Pierce at the end of the poem merges with that of the narrator, the poem does not merge character with creator.

14  *The Book of Margery Kempe*, ed. Barry Windeatt (Harlow: Longman, 2000), pp. 291–7.

15  The issue of authority in the book, and the extent to which it can be seen to be Margery's, is explored by Lynn Staley, *Margery Kempe's Dissenting Fictions* (University Park, PA: University of Pennsylvania Press, 1994), pp. 1–38; Roger Ellis, 'Margery Kempe's Scribes and the Miraculous Books', in H. Phillips (ed.), *Langland, the Mystics and the Medieval Religious Tradition* (Cambridge: Brewer, 1990), pp. 161–75, and Jacqueline Jenkins, 'Reading and the Book of Margery Kempe', in John H. Arnold and Katherine J. Lewis (eds), *A Companion to The Book of Margery Kempe* (Woodbridge: D. S. Brewer, 2004), pp. 113–28.

16  Prior to 1934, however, Margery Kempe was known exclusively as a religious woman as a result of Wynkyn de Worde's printing of a seven-page quarto pamphlet that contained extracts from the more devotional parts of *The Book*. When Henry Pepwell reprinted them in an anthology of mystical pieces in 1521, he described the author as a 'devoute ancres', Allyson Foster, 'A Shorte Treatyse of Contemplacyon: The Book of Margery Kempe in Its Early Print Contexts', in *A Companion to the Book of Margery Kempe*, pp. 95–112. Foster notes the virtual absence of Kempe's own voice in these extracts, p. 97.

17  While I shall not be pursuing the concept of erotohistoriography, the arguments of Elizabeth Freeman, *Time Binds: Queer Temporalities, Queer Histories* (Durham, NC, and London: Duke University Press, 2010), have helped to shape my own; not least that bodies are a relentlessly plural sign of being in time rather than escaping from it.

Memory and anticipation detach bodies from the contexts that may be seen to have produced them. I return explicitly to this work in Chapter 3 in my discussion of 'temporal drag'.

18 An example of a fifteenth-century Annunciation window which follows this schema exactly can be found in the Church of St Peter and St Paul, East Harling, Norfolk. Discussion of the glass can be found at *Corpus Vitrearum Medii Aevi: Norfolk: East Harling*, www.cvma.ac.uk/publi cations/digital/norfolk/sites/eastharling/history.html. A photograph of the glass is available at www.flickr.com/photos/stiffleaf/8244695806/.

19 Geoffrey Chaucer, *The Book of the Duchess*, 321–37, in *The Riverside Chaucer*, ed. Larry D. Benson et al. (Oxford: Oxford University Press, 2008), 3rd revd edn. All further references to Chaucer's works are to this edition unless otherwise stated.

20 Dryden dubs Chaucer so in his *Preface to Fables, Ancient and Modern* (1700), 'In the first place, as he is the father of English poetry, so I hold him in the same degree of veneration as the Grecians held Homer or the Romans Virgil'. *The Works of John Dryden: Volume VII, Poems 1697–1700*, ed. Vinton A. Dearing (Berkeley: University of California Press, 2000), p. 33/342. I return to this text in Chapter 5.

21 The indeterminacy of whether the hole is vaginal or anal is discussed by Elaine Tuttle Hansen, *Chaucer and the Fictions of Gender* (Berkeley and Los Angeles: University of California Press, 1992), pp. 224–6. She argues that the indeterminacy makes possible the substitution of male for female bodies.

22 Laura Kendrick discusses the play with the signs of genitalia and the Word of God in this Tale, *Chaucerian Play: Comedy and Control in the Canterbury Tales* (Berkeley: University of California Press, 1988), pp. 20–33. Though chiefly concerned with male genitalia, she does also note that the Miller's advice that men should not be too inquisitive about 'Goddes pryvetee', nor that of his wife, invites the desire to be curious both about female sexuality and God's inscrutable power. Her argument does not extend to the discussion of the sexual theology of Alison's 'hole'.

23 In Annunciation iconography a potted lily flower is placed in the scene to symbolise the Virginity of Mary. The East Harling window places the lily in front of Mary. A mischievous version of this iconographical symbolism reappears in *The Nun's Priest's Tale*, when the claws of the vigorously sexual cockerel Chanticleer are described as being whiter than the lily flower (VII.2863).

24 Helen Cooper, *The Structure of the Canterbury Tales* (London: Duckworth, 1983), pp. 227–30.

25 Iain McGilchrist, *The Master and His Emissary: The Divided Brain and the Making of the Western World* (New Haven, CT, and London: Yale University Press, 2012), pp. 67–70; 76–9; 95–6; 113–18; 137; 174–5.

# The figure in the Canterbury stained glass: Chaucerian Beckets

Canterbury is the destination that Chaucer's pilgrims never reach. While 'folk' from every 'shires ende' go to seek the cathedral shrine of the holy, blessed martyr Thomas Becket, the saint who helped them when they were sick, neither the assembly that gathers in Southwark nor those other persons who emerge en route come to their journey's end.[1] The narrative's topographical momentum falters about two miles away from Christ's Church at the end of an unknown village somewhere not far from Blean Forest.[2] With this unspecified shortcoming, the desire for Thomas Becket remains intact; remains *as desire*.

Two early responses to *The Canterbury Tales* rescue the pilgrims from their enmirement in the Kentish countryside: Lydgate's *Siege of Thebes* and the early fifteenth-century Canterbury fragment now known either as *The Prologue of the Tale of Beryn* or as *The Canterbury Interlude*.[3] But the rejuvenation promised by the reputation of Becket's miraculous healing remains elusive. The dismal annihilation of *The Siege of Thebes* is discussed in Chapter 5. This chapter explores Chaucerian pilgrimage practice in *The Canterbury Interlude*.[4] The sole surviving material copy of *The Canterbury Interlude* and *The Tale of Beryn* is in the unique copy of *The Canterbury Tales* in MS Northumberland 455, now in the possession of the Duke of Northumberland in Alnwick Castle. Occupying fols 180a–235a, *Beryn* is embedded between *The Canon's Yeoman's Tale* and the end of *The Summoner's Tale* (III.2159–294). Although the work is situated in the middle of *The Canterbury Tales*, this is a poem that gets the pilgrim to their avowed destination: the shrine of Thomas Becket. *The Interlude* traverses an established devotional pathway through the cathedral: its stained glass is perused, prayers and offerings are made at Becket's shrine, and the pilgrims buy their souvenir badges. The poem showcases pilgrim activity with such abundance and attention to detail that

it has often been mined as a document of literal social practice.[5]
Such approaches fail to notice however, that *The Interlude* toys
with the extensive play with figuration that shored up Becketian
devotion. Signs are so prolific, multivalent, and performative that
substance becomes impossible to determine. Far from leaving
Canterbury in a state of unequivocal spiritual refreshment, the
pilgrims of *The Interlude* are touched by a notional Becketian
'healing' that both courts and questions the transparency of belief
in pilgrimage practices as agents of spiritual cleansing. Faith in
the outward, temporal, signs of spiritual tourism is exposed as a
double-edged sword, both literally and metaphorically.

Crucial to this project is the reappearance of the figure of the
'Pardoner' in *The Canterbury Tales*. This chapter argues that
the *Beryn*-poet recognises that Chaucer's Pardoner is fashioned
from the signs of Becketian relics. Further, the poet reproduces
the interplay between body and relics to question the ontology of
both anatomy and devotional practice. The Chaucerian Pardoners
in *The Canterbury Tales* and *The Canterbury Interlude* are figures
for the work of figuration. On the road to Canterbury and within
its walls, the Pardoners' bodies reproduce the desire for the traffic
in relics so closely bound up with the body of Thomas Becket in
Canterbury Cathedral and beyond. They reproduce the devotional
work of the cathedral industry that is enshrined literally and metaphorically in the architecture of Christ's Church. In particular,
they reproduce the Becketian healing miracles associated with one
Eilward of Westoning in Bedfordshire. Eilward's story is told,
and not told, in a variety of Canterbury media. Its most graphic
inscrutability is to be seen in one of the stained glass windows in
Trinity Chapel.

With no tangible proof available either for sexual clarification
or for spiritual teleology, Eilward's window, *The Canterbury Tales*
and *The Interlude* offer up versions of Thomas Becket which
remain suspended between the sexual and devotional discourses
in which Chaucer's *General Prologue* initially placed him. The
*Canterbury Interlude* delivers what *The General Prologue* promises:
travel to Canterbury inspired by 'moisture' that is both sexual and
devotional (I.1–3). Only, those highly prized relics of Becket, the
glass phials that contained his blood and water – liquid proof of
his sainted martyrdom – turn out to be pilgrim 'a-trophy'. The
souvenir that the *Interlude* Pardoner carries away from Canterbury
makes no difference between Becketian healing and brutal damnation. Apparently, it makes no difference at all.

## Healing Canterbury bodies: Becket and Eilward

When late medieval pilgrims stepped inside Canterbury Cathedral
they became part of its theatrical performance of Becket's sanctity.[6] Between 1172 and 1174 two monks of Canterbury named
William and Benedict compiled the biographical materials which
helped to secure the murdered churchman's canonisation, and
to lay the foundations for its recreation in architectural form.[7]
Four sites within Christ Church were focal points of reverement:
the crypt where his body was first buried; the site near the altar
where he was murdered; his elaborate shrine; and Trinity Chapel
with its mimetic architecture and stained glass miracles.[8] Pilgrims
followed a devotional route which traversed all these sites rather
as a mini-pilgrimage.[9] Signs of Becket's miraculous body were,
and still are, manifold.[10] Dispersed in material witness throughout the fabric of Canterbury and beyond, the overinscription of
Thomas's physicality is proportionate to its unrecoverable spiritu-
ality. A vessel for healing and reincorporation, Becket is as emptily
full and as lastingly unfathomable as those Chaucerian Pardoners
he comes to re-present. Suspended between literal and allegorical,
devout imagination produces Becket's physical saintly body to
satisfy the pressing need for spiritual transformation and physical
wholeness.[11] Physical fragments of the saint, together with testimony of their healing powers, were dispersed through Canterbury
Cathedral and even further abroad.[12] Pilgrims paid elaborate
devotion to the splendid shrine, inserting their own bodies into
its holes to get close enough to be able to kiss the remains of
the saint.[13] Only it remains doubtful whether Becket's material
remains were ever buried there. If his body were still interred
in the crypt, then the suppliants abased themselves at an empty
mausoleum.[14] Material witness of Becket's miraculous powers,
however, sustained belief in their efficacy.[15] The stained glass in
the ambulatory windows of Trinity Chapel illustrates many of the
healing miracles that Thomas and his bodily relics performed. One
window has a detailed depiction of the original medieval shrine,
and shows Becket emerging from it to succour a man supine with
sickness who has prayed to the saint for help. The repetition of the
image of the shrine in the window and the depiction of Becket's
bodily emergence from its confines reinforces the spiritual profit of
visiting the murdered archbishop's tomb.[16]

Visitors to Canterbury were guided round the ambulatory glass.
The windows reinforced the healing message of the Becketian

cathedral script. An early biographer records that cathedral monks treated pilgrims to a pre-tour lecture on the miracles depicted.[17] One story in particular has a powerful resonance with the body of Becket and the bodies of the Chaucerian Pardoners. Eilward of Westoning in Bedfordshire was wrongfully accused of stealing, and punished by having his eyes and genitals mutilated. Neither monk is very precise in telling us exactly what genitalia was cut off in the first place, but both agree that whatever was excised was buried in the earth.[18] When Eilward prays to Thomas Becket for help, the saint miraculously restores all body parts. Benedict records a letter of testimony from the town of Bedford which affirms the authenticity of Eilward's restoration. It refers straightforwardly to his 'oculos', but more guardedly to his 'pendentia'.[19] William is much more forthright; the Bedford townsfolk offer incontrovertible proof of Becket's miraculous powers in healing the poor man's eyes and testicles.[20] When Eilward presented himself to them in his cured state, he allowed anyone who wished to do so to touch his genitals. Restored, the said testicles were smaller in size than those of a cockerel. Eilward's healing is palpable.[21] His testicular completeness is not simply seen and heard; it is proved by the good folk of Westoning who can hold his testicles in their hand and compare them with a bird that was known for its sexual potency.[22]

Unsurprisingly, the vitrine version of the story in Trinity Chapel lacks such explicit detail. The depiction of the punishment obscures the genital butchery by showing a man with menacing knife leaning over a naked torso (see Plate 2).[23] When Eilward appears to the townfolk after his cure, he points only to his eyes.[24] And the roundel that shows Becket actually healing Eilward takes refuge in sign language. The illustration does, and does not, follow William and Benedict's narrative that the saint imprinted the sign of the cross with his pastoral staff on Eilward's forehead and restored both eyes and privy members.[25] In the window, Eilward lies in bed, coverings keeping the lower part of his abdomen under decent wraps. Becket appears above him, pointing at his head. Only on close examination, however, is it clear that the saint has not one (as in the Latin narrative) pastoral staff; but two. One staff must heal his eyes, the other stands in for the healing of his unshown testicles.[26] More penile than testicular, the second pastoral staff is a metonymy for a testimonial proof that cannot be shown.[27] The window that offers confirmation of the saint's power to restore a castrated man to sexual potency cannot depict it (see Plate 3). The story that bolsters Becket's reputation as a miraculous healer requires Eilward's restored testicles to be taken on trust. To have faith in the miracle you need to know how to read the glass signs. Unlike the good folk of Bedfordshire, you can't reach out and touch the thing itself: the palpable, living proof.

These images of bodily assault, disfiguration, and restoration are part of a widespread cluster of signs that mark the bodies of the Chaucerian Pardoners. Eilward's healing was recorded in church liturgy and not just for use in monastic offices in Canterbury. The liturgy that Benedict composed for the first celebration of Becket's feast day in December 1173 tells how Thomas blazes forth with new miracles: he gives male parts to the castrated, vision to those deprived of sight.[28] It was a text given wider currency in the Sarum Breviary: Becket endowed the castrated with male genitalia, and extended the touch of his power to unusual and unheard of signs.[29] Whether preserved in Latin narrative, engraved in glass, or sung in liturgy, material witness of the healing powers of Canterbury's famous saint credit him not only with the miraculous restoration of incomplete or damaged genitalia but with an extraordinary feat accomplished through arcane signs.[30] It is precisely within this nexus of terms – genital excision, unfathomable signs, and Becketian healing – that the figures of the Pardoners are characterised. Both Pardoners present a puzzle as to whether they are genitally intact and/or functional: an enigma that is significant not primarily because it calls into question their sexual categorisation but because the cut that may or may not leave a mark that can be displayed questions the 'very category of category itself'.[31] Toggled back and forth between the two Pardoners, markers of sexual indeterminacy that are inseparable from the signs of Becketian healing question the cultural desire for signs of religious miracles.

## The Pardoners

It is unsurprising that this role is allotted to the Chaucerian Pardoners. Their professional existence rests on a practice in which the exchange of a piece of paper wipes temporal sin off the salvational slate. Pardoners claimed the power to remove the smirch of transgression. The virulent body of anti-Pardoner satire witnesses not only the abuse of the transaction – its financial corruption or its misunderstanding – but also the questionable value of the document itself.[32] If it came from the Pope, did that validate its authenticity or render it useless? The answer depended not on the material paper but on religious conviction. Was St Peter's

successor the rock of the institutional church, or the embodiment
of Antichrist? Even if one were not a reformist, only God could
provide ultimate proof that the document was not a fake. It is not
only in the pilgrim context of *The Canterbury Tales* that Chaucer
raises these questions. In *The House of Fame*, having demonstrated
that there is no ontological difference between a truth and a lie,
the narrator spies a motley group pressing their suit for eternal
reputation in the wicker House of Rumour. Among the Pardoners
with 'boystes' crammed full of lies are palmers with their 'scrippes'
'bret-ful of lesinges' (2121–30). The observation is not a straightforward denunciation. In its poetic context, the lies could be true
given the poem has just dramatised the impossibility of telling
one from another. The *General Prologue* Pardoner's wallet, the
bag which carries his documents, is a pilgrim sign whose contents
cannot be verified. The efficacy of what Pardoners carried in their
wallets was open to question.

   In the *General Prologue*, the Pardoner's wallet lies before him
in his lap. Figuratively, it is his scrotum; the contents of which
are indeterminable. If he is a 'geldyng' or a 'mare' (I.691), have
his testicles been cut off, or are they present but defective? One
might ascertain the first by ocular proof, but the second would
take a completely different kind of demonstration, one that would
be conclusive not by whether the Pardoner were capable of sexual
performance but by the issue of any fruit from the act. The 'or'
of line 691 harbours a whole series of 'ors' with no stable base
within its terms. And when we reach the conclusion of Fragment
VI, the Pardoner's pilgrimage genitalia becomes even more frac-
tious. When the Host wishes he had the Pardoner's 'coillons' in
his hands, and wishes them to be cut off, with what status does the
modality of his utterance invest the object of his cutting intent? To
suggest that the Host's retort 'proves' that the *General Prologue*
Pardoner must have testicles that can be removed misses the point
that the utterance proves nothing of the sort. Critical anxiety has
desired to repair what appears to be a severance in resemblance
between the Prologue 'geldyng' or 'mare' and the Pardoner at
the end of Fragment D; for the Host's willingness to touch
the Pardoner's testicles to offer proof of his anatomical details,
rather like the palpable testimony that monk William supplies for
Eilward.[33] The Host's diction confounds such enquiry. The word
'coillions' (testicles) is recorded only here in Chaucer's whole
corpus. It collocates three times with 'relikes'. The Pardoner's
genital puzzle becomes entangled not just with the vexed question

of the authenticity of the pardons he traffics but with the relics he offers also.[34] This is a conundrum that has been dramatised prior to the heated exchange on the road to Canterbury; it has been rehearsed already in *Le Romaunt de la Rose*.

The French text confounds the difference between testicles and relics. When the Lover protests the indecency of using the word 'coillons', Reason's defence rests on the argument that God made both things and their names, and therefore the name 'coillons' cannot be thought coarse; 'if when I put names to things that you dare to criticise thus and blame, I had called testicles relics and declared relics to be testicles, then you, who here criticise me, and goad me on account of them, would say that "relics" was an ugly base word. "Testicles" is a good name, and I like it, and so in faith, are "testes" and "penis"' (7091–3).[35] Apparently a vindication of the divine sanction of names, Reason's argument is inadequate because of her choice of evidence. To cite testicles interchangeably with relics demonstrates not only the arbitrariness of the relationship between names and what they denote but also the inscrutability of ontological substance. For a human being to give an object the name 'relic' is not to confirm its saintly powers. The potency of relics and testicles can be proved not by naming them but only if they produce demonstrable evidence of their power to bring forth new life. How else can you prove the sanctity of a relic? And even then, proof is dependent on testimony. Forensic proof is endlessly circular. A relic is a true relic if there are witnesses to a healing transformation which state that it is true. Faith in relics depends on belief in the substance of signs. In the case of the Pardoner, the signs of his relics/testicles lack stability. It cannot be proved whether the Pardoner is a eunuch, a castrated heterosexual, a sodomite, or sexually inadequate because the words used to describe his body will not add up to a conclusive sum of their parts. That does not put an end to the desire to know for sure, however.[36] Like the desire for relics. Desire that in both instances stems from the wish for (or of) a body part that is not, under ordinary circumstances, exposed to revelation. Unlike Eilward's neighbours, Harry Bailey can only wish to have the Pardoner's testicles in his hands.

In *The Canterbury Interlude* the Pardoner's sexual anatomy poses very similar issues, though with a mischievous substitution of its relevant parts.[37] The *Canterbury Tales* Pardoner does not carry a literal pilgrim staff, except in figure: the 'stif burdoun' that he bears to the Summoner in *The General Prologue* an example

of the widely attested pun on staff and penis. The wordplay is
expressly reprised in *The Canterbury Interlude* when the Pardoner
asks the Summoner to join him in singing to '[d]oubil me this
bourdon' (413). Throughout the poem, the significance of the
Pardoner's 'phallus' is contested both sexually and religiously.
The Pardoner's first action, surrendering his pilgrim staff to Kit
the tapster, has been variously interpreted. Whether the gesture
is a sign of an emasculated heterosexual or of a sodomite the text
never makes clear. Overtly, the Pardoner is in heterosexual pursuit
of a woman who dupes him. His sexual prowess is never proved
because he never regains possession of his phallic staff. Despite his
pleas for its return, Kit gives it to her lover, a man named only in
the text as Paramour.

> And sodenly [Kit] kissed hir paramour and seyd, 'We shul sclope
> Togider hul by hul as we have many a nyghte,
> And yf he com and make noyse, I prey yew dub hym knight.'
> 'Yis, dame,' quod hir paramour, 'be thow nat agast.
> This is his own staff, thow seyest; thereof he shal atast.'

> (454–8)

Kit's instruction to her sexually active paramour to use the
Pardoner's severed phallus to give him a beating turns the apparently heterosexual phallus into a sodomitical weapon. One man
wields the phallus of another and threatens him with its 'taste'.
Physical violence figures auto-sodomitical fellatio: the pilgrim staff
an instrument not of piety but perversity. Already overdetermined
in its sexual sense, the pilgrim's staff also figures a knight's sword.
The diction 'dub hym knight' invests a pub brawl drubbing with
the ceremony in which the tap of a sword on the base of the neck
each side of the shoulders performed a symbolic act which changed
the status of the man who received the blows.[38] The touch of the
sword transformed a man into a knight. As the poem moves towards
its denouement the manifold signification of the Pardoner's staff
as pilgrim stave, perverse phallus and knightly sword intensifies.
Instead of serving the Pardoner in his heterosexual quest of Kit,
his staff is the central weapon in a fight between three men. Jak the
hosteller of the inn gets caught up in the rumpus as the Pardoner
and the paramour prowl around a kitchen in the dark in a mock
knightly tournament. Amongst all these men, the phallic staffs,
or their substitutes (the Pardoner has a kitchen ladle to match his
saucepan helmet), are trafficked throughout the spaces of a public
inn with violent force. When the Pardoner demands that the

Paramour return his staff, he gets it back in a way that he did not foresee:

> He axed his staff spitouslich with wordes sharp and rowe.
> 'Go to bed' quod he within, 'No more noyse thow make.
> Thy staff shal be redy tomorow, I undertake.'
> 'In soth', 'quod he, 'I woll nat fro the dorr wend
> Tyll I have my staff, thow bribour!' – 'Then have the toder end!'
> Quod he that was within, and leyd it on his bak,
> Right in the same plase as chapmen bereth hir pak.
> And so he did too mo, as he coude arede,
> Graspyng after with the staff in length and eke in brede,
> And fond hym otherwhile redlich inowghe
> With the staffes ende highe oppon his browe.
>
> (520–30)

The night fast and vigil that preceded a knight's investiture are comically mined for religious import. The Pardoner's supper with Kit has been withheld from him: it has been eaten by the tapster and the Paramour. And the investiture is brought forward as the Paramour beats the Pardoner on his shoulders (where chapmen bear their pack), and then gropes his way along the whole length of the Pardoner's phallus to wound him high upon his brow with the end of the staff.

This knightly sword blow in a public house invests the Pardoner with sacrilegious Canterbury significance. It replays Becket's murder in Canterbury Cathedral.[39] After the fire in the cathedral in 1174, a substantial renovation programme culminated in the building not only of the magnificent shrine but also of the spectacular new east end of the cathedral which recreated details of the archbishop's murder in stone. Descriptions of Thomas's assassination, both textual and pictorial, give the cause of his death as a blow to the head. In its most graphic form – and hence the one most widely disseminated – one of the knightly assassins sliced off the top of Becket's head with his sword. It remains unclear whether Becket was decapitated, part of his skull sliced off, his head cut open, or whether he was simply wounded with a blow that proved to be fatal. Some illustrations show a sword blow at the top of Becket's head (either to front or back),[40] some a cut below the neck. Even more pertinently perhaps, was there a literal sword at all? The proliferation of accounts is more than matched by the multiplication of monumental sites of devotion to Becket's head. Becket's severed crown became a relic of the saint in its own right. Called the 'head' of Becket, it was enclosed in a reliquary in Trinity Chapel.[41]

So placed, one Becket head nests inside another. Inspiration for the shape of Trinity Chapel itself is drawn from severed top of Becket's skull. Known to this day as the Corona, the sign of the sliced head built into the scallops, columns and flying buttresses informs the very stones of the easternmost part of the cathedral church.[42] In *The Canterbury Interlude*, the staffless pilgrim receives a knightly d(r)ubbing that is a performative recitation of the ignoble assassination of the Archbishop of the Realm; a sign of saintly transformation that the architectural theatre of Christ's Church commemorates and repeatedly performs through its manifold images.

As I have already discussed, the ambulatory glass windows of Canterbury's Corona are an extensive witness to Becket's sanctity and to his continued power to work miraculous healing. At an earlier point in the poem, the Pardoner is one of a number of pilgrims who attempt to work out the iconography of a window in the Cathedral before they reach Becket's shrine. One object in particular proves impossible to decipher:

> The Pardoner and the Miller and other lewde sotes
> Sought hemselff in the chirch, right as lewd gotes,
> Pyred fast and poured highe oppon the glase,
> Counterfeting gentilmen, the armes for to blase,
> Diskyveryng fast the peyntour, and for the story mourned
> And ared also – right as rammes horned!
> 'He bereth a balstaff,' quod the toon, 'and els a rakes ende.'
> 'Thow faillest,' quod the Miller, 'thowe hast nat wel thy mynde.
> It is a spere, yf thowe canst se, with a prik tofore
> To bussh adown his enmy and thurh the sholder bore'.
> 'Pese!' quod the Hoost of Southwork. 'Let stond the wyndow glased.
> Goth up and do yeur offerynge. Ye semeth half amased.'

(147–58)

The identity of the stick-like object over which the pilgrims squabble is never revealed. Nor is it possible conclusively to identify the window in question.[43] There are numerous windows in Trinity Chapel which feature such an implement: either as weapon, pilgrim staff or St Thomas's pastoral staff. With no localisation of the window, what the pilgrims see has the potential to figure an implement that has a range of significances from healing to injury across the whole social spectrum. The possibilities offered in the poem range from a farm implement, a 'balstaff' most usually associated with affrays and brawls, and a knightly spear. Faced with a devotional stained glass window in the space sacred to the murder of an archbishop, these pilgrims see the record of an unruly brawl or an aristocratically delivered shoulder wound. What the Pardoner fails to see above his head is a proleptic image of his own punishment as he impersonates Thomas Becket in the Cheker of the Hope. Struck by a staff that is also a sword, the Pardoner becomes a victim in a *buffa* replication of Becket's martyrdom.

He also becomes a figure of the wounded Christ taking on the sins of the world to redeem humankind from eternal punishment in hell. While it is the wound to his head that receives dominant textual focus, it is not the Pardoner's only injury; he dissuades himself from retaliation against his assailants by considering the blows he has already received:

> And thought that he had strokes ryghte inowghe,
> Witnes on his armes, his bak, and his browe
>
> (597–8)

Wounded not only on his brow by the knightly dubbing, he also receives strokes on his arms and back which are witness to his torment. The diction of these lines invests the Pardoner with the topos of the Complaint of Christ. Especially in devotional writing, Christ is figured, hanging from the cross calling on humankind to examine the marks of his bodily suffering; wounds that bear witness of his torment for the sake of human souls: his back that has been scourged, his arms that have been bound, and the brow scored with the crown of thorns.

> ... thi lithe armes wel streit itent ...
>
> And on his body so mony swappys ...
>
> Myne [armes] for the on rode
> With the Jewes wode
> With grete ropis todraw ...
>
> Under mi gore
> Ben wndes selcowthe sore.[44]
>
> Youre gyltes on my bak I bare ...
>
> Suffre pyne for the, me nedid nought
> In hed, in hand, in foot ne ton.
>
> (11/101–2)[45]
>
> Of sharpe thorne I have worne a crowne on my hed,
> So rubbid, so bobbid, so rufulle, so red.[46]

The Pardoner's witness of his own wounds turns his body into a perverse spectacle of Christ's tortured redemption. Humiliated in a kitchen brawl in Canterbury, this victim of sodomitical affray is a figure of Becket, overlaid with the marks of Christ. Although the *Beryn*-poet switches the signs of genitalian inscription, there is palpable awareness of Chaucer's sexual religious play with those concealed parts of the Pardoner in the epilogue to his *Tale*.

The lines in which the Pardoner offers his relics to the pilgrim assembly as guarantors of spiritual healing are rich in complex wordplay:

> I have relikes and pardoun in my male,
> As faire as any man in Engelond,
> Whiche were me yeven by the popes hond.
> If any of yow wole, of devocion,
> Offren and han myn absolucion,
> Com forth anon, and kneleth heere adoun,
> And mekely receyveth my pardoun.

> (VI.920–6)

What the Pardoner offers to the pilgrims are both relics and remission from a pilgrim's wallet *and* his genitalia, as fair as any man's in England. Though these items, release is figured that is both sexual and spiritual. The Pardoner boasts of his devotional regalia with insouciant sodomitical bravura. It is not sufficient that the pilgrims simply take the pardon into their hands, they have to kneel down in meekness to receive it. As the Pardoner's subsequent command to Harry Bailey makes clear, they have to unbuckle their own purses and kiss the Pardoner's own. Absolution from sin is figured as communal fellatio in a public place at the side of the pilgrimage route to Canterbury. Pilgrims are invited to bestow their devotions on 'relics' whose vintage is guaranteed by no less an authority than the hand of the Pope. The staff that passes from male hand to hand in *The Interlude* is prefigured here by the hand to mouth simulation of Papal succession as the Pardoner's testicles are passed down from the Pope, to the pilgrim congregation and, in desire at any rate, to the hands of Harry Bailey – the Host.

Sodomy is inscribed within salvation history. The Pardoner invites the pilgrims to regard his body as a document of Pardon.[47] In its material form, a pardon is a document with a dangling seal that authenticates its terms. The Pardoner's offer to reveal his 'pendentia' to his fellows plays on the visual likeness between a document and the shape of male genitalia.[48] As an instrument of absolution it also plays on the well-attested image of Christ's body as a Charter.[49] The image of Christ's flayed skin as the scored parchment of a document blotted with blood, and sealed with the promise of Atonement, is transformed at the end of Fragment VI of *The Canterbury Tales* into an allurement of sexual congress that would ensure certain damnation. The Pardoner's devotional offering conflates salvation theology, ecclesiastical history, and sexual transgression considered so pernicious that confessional handbooks skip over it in silence.[50] The multivalency of the signs unsettles any stable level of representation and plunges pilgrim practice, and the hope for spiritual healing, into scandalous sexual congress.

The Host's response renders the Pardoner's outrageous invitation topical in every sense:

> Com forth, sire Hoost, and offre first anon,
> And thou shalt kisse the relikes everychon,
> Ye, for a grote! Unbokele anon thy purs.'
> 'Nay, nay,' quod he, 'thanne have I Cristes curs!
> 'Lat be,' quod he, 'it shal nat be, so theech!
> Thou woldest make me kisse thyn olde breech
> And swere it were a relyk of a seint,
> Though it were with thy fundement depeint!
> But, by the croys which that Seint Eleyne fond,
> I wolde I hadde thy coillons in myn hond
> In stide of relikes or of seintuarie.
> Lat kutte hem of, I wol thee helpe hem carie;
> They shul be shryned in an hogges toord!'
>
> (VI.943–55)

Harry's awareness that to accede to the request would incur damnation registers its sodomitical import. Hence the extreme measure of desiring the Pardoner's castration to protect the ultimate fate of his own soul. Even so, the elected governor of the pilgrim assembly recognises that the sexual abomination threatened by the Pardoner's body is also a version of the martyred saint who is the goal of the Canterbury pilgrims.[51] By likening devotion to the Pardoner's relics to kissing an old breech that masquerades as the relic of a saint, the Host brings into this heated exchange the material sign that was greeted as the first indication of Becket's transformation from worldly cleric to holy martyr. When his dead body was unclothed, Becket was found to be wearing a hair shirt and breeches crawling with lice.[52] The revelation of penitential undergarments beneath elaborate vestments of clerical office was received as a sign of the spiritual regeneration of the once worldly archbishop. Thomas's filthy, coarse breeches reformed him, and in turn were a hopeful sign for the regeneration of all Christian souls.

Becket's underwear was blazoned in the liturgy that honoured him. The second antiphon 'summo sacerdocio Thomas sublimatus' in the office for the Translation of St Thomas Becket honours how the prelate raised to the highest priestly office was suddenly changed into another man. Secretly hair-shirted, the monk under the clothing of a cleric is stronger than flesh in his conquest of fleshly desires. Lectio III records that his hair garments covered the length of his thighs right down to his knees.[53]

Harry's retort conflates the sexual pollution of the Pardoner's body with the material sign of the archbishop's underclothing that precipitated moves for his canonisation and was the foundation (or fundament perhaps) for England's most sought-after site of pilgrim healing. The shrine full of pigshit in which the Host wishes to house the Pardoner's testicular relics is the elaborate reliquary of Becket's tomb, into whose holes pilgrims inserted their bodies in order to get as close as possible to the saint's material remains, believing them (rightly or wrongly) to be lodged inside. The body parts of Thomas Becket that brought such lucrative pilgrim trade to Canterbury Cathedral are displaced on to a sexual outcast. The promise of saintly absolution, invested in material signs whose substance is recursively transacted through competing, and apparently oppositional, codes of reference is subjected to scandalous scrutiny. Inscripted with the signs of Christ's redemptive pardon, papal succession and Becketian transformation, the Pardoner's unspeakable body is an obstacle to the recovery of any primary substance, sinful or saintly. Rather as the 'lewd sottes' cannot deliver up an agreed figure in the Canterbury stained glass, neither the *Canterbury Tales* pilgrims nor their future readers can get through the maze of signs to the body 'itself'. Remaining beyond ratification, the signs of the Pardoner's body pose a scandalous challenge to the efficacy of the signs of Becket's body that the pilgrims go to seek, and the powers of healing with which it is believed to be invested.

It is a scandal that the journey never resolves because its end is never met. The violence of the quarrel between Harry Bailey and the Pardoner is resolved by the intervention of the Knight. As Harry follows the Knight's bidding in bestowing a kiss on a wayward Becketian body, placing his lips on a sodomitical simulacrum of the martyr's relics, he prefigures the *Interlude* pilgrims kissing Becket's shrine in Canterbury. As the highest figure of secular authority on the *Canterbury Tales* pilgrimage, it is appropriate that it should fall to the Knight to restore peace and amity. But amidst the Becketian signplay his governance enacts a rewriting of ecclesiastical biography. To write about, or to illustrate, a knight attacking the crown of the Archbishop's head with a sword is to create a potent allegory of sacrilege. For a knight to take up arms against a priest in his own church is violation enough; but capped when the point of the sword delivers a fatal blow to the sacramental tonsure of the archprelate of the realm.[54] Becket's body was mutilated by a knight; the mortal sword blow that apparently severed his skull is lastingly petrified in the fabric of Canterbury Cathedral. Chaucer's pilgrim Knight prevents the threat of severance to Becketian body parts, which for all the Pardoner's zeal to have them palpably presented, resist verifiable demonstration. In stepping in to prevent a replay of the archbishop's mutilation, the Knight preserves the mystery of the Pardoner's Becket body intact.

The *Beryn*-poet's play with these body figures tells a slightly different story, but one that is sourced from the same stock of materials. Although the Pardoner receives a version of Becket's sword blow on his brow, no part of the skull is sliced through. Instead, the Pardoner is terminally separated from his own phallus. To the outside world, at any rate, he bears no public sign of his ordeal. After they have beaten him up, Jak the hosteller and the Paramour lay a plot to trap the Pardoner by preventing his escape:

> ... make the gates fast; he may nat then astert.
> And eke of his own staff he bereth a redy mark
> Whereby thow maist hym know among al the route.

(611–13)

The ready mark of the Pardoner's own staff is his head wound: the sign of Becket so prominently displayed by the East End of the Cathedral across the road.[55] Except that the Pardoner takes careful steps to ensure that his own martyrdom remains under wraps:

> Yet or he cam in company, he wissh awey the blood,
> And bond the sores to his hede with the typet of his hood,
> And made lightsom chere for men shuld nat spy
> Nothing of his turment ne of his luxury.

(661–4)

He disguises the evidence of his torment through administering to himself a perverse version of the aftermath of Becket's head wound in Canterbury Cathedral. With his skull gaping open, Becket's brains were hoiked out and scattered on the pavement. The mash of red blood and white brains on the cathedral stones was likened

by early biographers Edward Grim and William Fitzstephen to
the rose and the lily; symbolism that was marmorealised in the
pink and white of the Purbeck columns of Trinity Chapel.[56] When
the archbishop's gore was washed from the stones, the water
and blood were collected and bottled. Of all the available relics,
these phials were most particularly associated with regeneration.
Pilgrims to Canterbury took away ampullae of Becket's blood
and water in the hope that it would heal them;[57] pilgrim badges
featured miniature replicas of the salvific phials.[58] The privileged
role of the phials in healing was reiterated in the stained glass of
Trinity Chapel. Two pilgrims wearing oversized ampullae are
depicted suspended from cords, and a wounded man drinks from
a phial in his quest for healing.[59] Possession of the ampullae that
commemorated the action conferred prestige on those pilgrims
who left Canterbury with either a phial itself or its sign on a pilgrim
badge.[60] For the *Interlude* Pardoner, Canterbury blood and water
bring about no healing, nor any pilgrim bounty. The staff that
marked him out as a devotional figure has scored him with wounds
of humiliation that he uses Becketian devotionalia to conceal.

His choice of laundry cloth is also significant: he wipes his
wounds with his headgear. In the sanctity of the Cathedral,
the Pardoner is amongst those pilgrims who proceed straight
from kissing the holy relics of St Thomas's shrine to acquiring
pilgrimage badges to commemorate their visit:

> They preyd to Seynt Thomas, in such wise as they couth.
> And sith the holy relikes, ech man with his mowth
> Kissed, as a goodly monke the names told and taught ...
> Then, as manere and custom is, signes there they boughte,
> For men of contre shuld know whom they had soughte.
>
> (165–9)

The desire to display their journey's goal to their own 'contre'
prompts some fraudulent practice. Sharing out their spoils between
them, a trio of pilgrims secrete in their pouches signs for which
they have not paid:

> And in the meenwhile, the Miller had i-piked
> His bosom ful of signes of Caunterbury broches:
> Huch the Pardoner and he pryvely in hir pouches
> They put hem afterward, that noon of hem it wiste,
> Save the Sompnour seid somewhat, and seyde to hem 'List!
> Halff part!', quod he, pryuvely, rownyng on hir ere ...
>
> (174–9)

These contraband signs become part of public display: 'they set hir signes oppon hir hedes, and som oppon hir capp' (191).[61] For the Pardoner, however, the process gets reversed. His final head covering, a payment he did not anticipate, becomes the means to efface the signs of his beating. In one sense, the Pardoner's self-healing through his concealment of Becketian signs is efficacious. He escapes detection. With his 'sores' bound by his 'typet' and the blood from his wound washed away, Jak the hosteller is unable to identify him amongst the pilgrims when the assembly embarks on its return journey:

> And the hosteler of the house, for nothing he coude pry,
> He coude nat knowe the Pardoner among the company
> Amorowe when they shuld wend, for aught that he coude pour.
>
> (665–7)

Despite his attempts to pry and to 'pour' (the word that is used of the attempt to decipher the body in the stained glass window), Jak's search for the Becketian head wound is in vain. Nursing an injury of his own, having cut open his shin on a pan in the kitchen (585–90), Jak is unable to see beyond the Pardoner's fabrication of Becket's healing wounds. The headgear that ought to be a triumphant display of achieved pilgrimage shrouds the Pardoner's head in a displacement of signs that preserve his tortured skull from detection. In *The Interlude* the pilgrims ride away from Canterbury without noticing that a humiliated Becket lurks in their midst in wounded anonymity.

> And evermore he held hym amydward the route
> And was ever synging to make al thing good,
> But yit his notes were somwhat lowe, for akyng of his hede.
> So at that tyme he had no more grame,
> But held hym to his harmes to scape shame.
>
> (670–4)

While the signs of Becket's healing powers were sung out in liturgy, the Pardoner sings low to escape detection; his unhealed harms are kept to himself. He alone knows that his head still hurts. For his fellow pilgrims, the telltale signs are overlaid too thickly.

The Pardoner is become a returning version of the pilgrim badge sported by his avatar in *The Canterbury Tales*. Of all the pilgrims assembled, only the Pardoner parades a pilgrim sign. He wears it in his cap; a vernicle: the sign of the image of the veil of St Veronica. Translated into a pilgrim brooch, St Veronica's veil, thought to have been imprinted with the image of Christ's face when used to wipe his wounds, is a sign of a sign of a sign.[62] Neither Christ's blood nor his body is physically available; they are endlessly displaced; unrecoverable. As we have seen, the version of Christ's salvific body that the Pardoner offers is a sodomitical performance of communal redemption; one that is countersigned with Becket's breeches and an abject version of his reliquaried shrine. The body of the *Interlude* Pardoner is not identical to that of his fellow Canterbury pilgrim; a genitalian jest perhaps at the expense of belief in dispersed body fragments as relics of a once whole saint. But his body is wrapped in veiled signatures from a common exemplar. A perverse version of Becket lurking undetected in the return pilgrimage journey, marked with Canterbury torment, his phallus left in the keeping of two men in a hostelry, this wounded knight cannot be paraded as a pilgrim spoil. Like that of the *Canterbury Tales* Pardoner, his unrestored body, with its devotional tattoos, remains unrecoverable beyond the signs of his bodily inscription. Both Chaucerian Pardoners are bodies in parts; an assembly of signs dispersed between fragments.[63] The body of the *Canterbury Tales* Pardoner circulates chiefly between the first and sixth fragments of the canonised Chaucer corpus. That of the *Interlude* Pardoner is secreted into the apocryphal end of a pilgrimage in the middle of a defective Canterbury sequence. MS Northumberland 455 is not a sound (nor a whole) witness to Chaucer's Canterbury project – or so it might seem.

In their splintered signings and their textual transportations, the Pardoners replicate the fragmentation and dispersal of sacred body parts that were so highly desired as media for spiritual healing. In its early history, the church prohibited the dismemberment of sacred bodies. They were to be kept whole: sacrosanct. Precisely to encourage and then to meet the demand for saintly devotion however, holy bodies were cut up, dismembered and disseminated.[64] Once dispersed, the body fragments performed healing miracles on their own. The more body parts put into circulation, the more demand exceeded supply. With the currency of relics and miracles swollen beyond a single locatable source, the grip of the institutionalised church over their significance was loosened. Efficacious body parts became obtainable not just from holy sites but from the trading centres with which they became associated, like the shops outside the gates of Canterbury Cathedral.[65] With the proliferation of the material signs of divine healing, their valency becomes subject to change. Passed out from an institutional normative hierarchy into more popular currency, they become part of an economy of desire that is resistant to the control of the ecclesiastical body that created the demand. Signs of God's miraculous workings that were once stamped with institutional authority become objects of desire in their own right. Official church practice turns orectic. Circulated to meet demand, divided and replicated to supply it, the signs of holy bodies are let loose as objects in a financial economy whose appetite turns ludic; they become part of organised play.[66]

The process of this spiritual economy reaches its apogee in the manufacture of obscene badges. In a replication of the replications that matches those of the Pardoner's bodies, profane brooches fuse the desire for devotional objects with the desire for sexual exhibitionism. These erotic devotional objects parade a variety of saintly re-presentations. A religious procession, for instance, in which a saint is carried on a bier, is fashioned from three phalluses bearing up a crowned vulva. An oval-shaped brooch which looks like a pilgrim turns out, on closer inspection, to be a vagina (see Plate 4). Genitalia and pilgrims cannot be separated. The purpose of these objects has been much debated.[67] Clearly, however, they represent something rather more complex than simply conflating the sexual with the spiritual, the sacred with the profane. They make elaborate play with the whole process of signing, and of signing off, a devout pilgrim and the object of their journey. One surviving badge has a vulva dressed up as a devout pilgrim complete with hat, staff and rosary. Both male and female, this profanely sacred object has pinned meta-badges of devotion into its pilgrim garments: giant phalluses/pilgrim staffs. There is no telling where the signs begin and end. The whole object is one convoluted conundrum of religious/sexual desire. These material witnesses of the dissemination of pilgrim trophies into ludic entertainment provide an analogue to the devotional play with the Chaucerian Pardoners' insignia. Like the material objects they traffic and replicate, when unfixed from ecclesiastical jurisdiction because transported into vernacular poetry, these mobile devotional signs carry the potential to turn the demand for spiritual wholeness into fragmented, individualised desire that threatens the very mainstay of the institutionalised church.

The author of *The Canterbury Interlude*, whoever he may have been, was very well read in Chaucer's *Canterbury Tales*. From an echo of it in *The Interlude*, he may well have read *The House of Fame*.[68] Preserved there is an early indication of Chaucer's play with Becketian reputation. Because of its radiance, the Temple of

Fame in Book 3 appears to be made of glass (1124–5). But when the narrator inspects its 'congeled matere' (1126) more closely, he discovers that it is made of ice.[69] The names of the famous folk engraved thereon are scarcely decipherable because the material has thawed, and letters in every name have melted away. This is the dissolving story of the house of Fame, the record of the glorious fabrication of Canterbury Cathedral, perhaps even its brilliant stained glass in Trinity Chapel where written inscriptions, like that for Eilward's story, are worn away:

> Thoughte I, 'By Seynt Thomas of Kent,
> This were a feble fundament[70]
> To bilden on a place hye.
> He ought him lytel glorifye
> That hereon bilt, God me so save!'

(1131–5)

In *The House of Fame*, the cathedral of England's most famous saint, object of desire from the limits of every shire, is an edifice whose substance is so precarious that the person who built it ought to be ashamed. The commemorative inscriptions that hold up the reputation of Canterbury Cathedral and its lauded martyr are engraved on materials that are disappearing into their own brittleness. Glorification is built on an unsound base. But, as the end of the poem makes clear, that does not stop hoards of petitioners scrambling brutally for admittance, imploring that they be granted lasting reputation and enduring glory. Amongst the scrum, as mentioned above, are the Pardoners with their wallets. And pilgrims, called 'palmers', after their sign. The end of *The House of Fame* showcases a motley throng of folk frantic for a memorialised part in a theatre of pilgrim dreams that the poem has already melted into thin air. The final chapter of this book argues that the concluding vignette of *The House of Fame* is located in Southwark. Yearning for material endorsements of glorification, the pilgrims have not even left first base.

For all the desire to seek Thomas Becket, martyr, saint and healer, he remains a figure stained in glass.

## Notes

1  Geoffrey Chaucer, *General Prologue* to *The Canterbury Tales* I.15–18.
2  For the topographical references see *The Prologue to the Manciple's Tale* IX.2–3, and *The Prologue to the Parson's Tale* X.12.

3 The intervention in the journeys and the contesting of the pilgrimage itinerary are discussed by John M. Bowers, 'The Tale of Beryn and The Siege of Thebes: Alternative Ideas of The Canterbury Tales', Studies in the Age of Chaucer 7 (1985), 23–50.

4 The scribe has been identified as a copyist in seven other manuscripts, including five that contain the prose Brut chronicle, see Linne R. Mooney and Lister M. Matheson, 'The Beryn Scribe and His Texts: Evidence for Multiple-Copy Production of Manuscripts in Fifteenth-Century England', Library 4 (2003), 347–70. Simon Horobin argues that the Beryn scribe was also responsible for the copy of The Canterbury Tales in the Helmingham Manuscript, now Princeton Firestone Library MS 100, 'The Scribe of the Helmingham and Northumberland Manuscripts of the Canterbury Tales', Neophilologus 84 (2000), 457–65. The textual history of the poem is discussed by Peter Brown, 'Journey's End: The Prologue to The Tale of Beryn', in Julia Boffey and Janet Cowen (eds), Chaucer and Fifteenth Century Poetry (Kings College London: Exeter University Press, 1991), pp. 143–74. Although not included in early printed versions of Chaucer's works, The Interlude and Beryn were printed in John Urry's posthumous The Works of Geoffrey Chaucer, Compared with the Former Editions, and Many Valuable MSS. Out of which, Three Tales are Added which were Never Before Printed (London, 1721). Thomas Wright included a version of Urry's text in his The Canterbury Tales of Geoffrey Chaucer: A New Text with Illustrative Notes in Early English Poetry, Ballads and Popular Literature of the Middle Ages (London: Percy Society, 1847 and 1857, vols 24, 26). But Skeat excluded Beryn from his Chaucer canon, The Chaucer Canon, with a Discussion of the Works Associated with the Name of Geoffrey Chaucer (Oxford: Clarendon Press, 1900), p. 143. The poem was edited for the Early English Text Society under the title The Tale of Beryn with a Prologue of the merry Adventure of the Pardoner with a Tapster at Canterbury by F. J. Furnivall and W. G. Stone (EETS OS, 1901). For ease of reference I quote from the more recent edition by John Bowers, ed. The Canterbury Tales: Fifteenth-Century Continuations and Additions (Kalamazoo, MI: Medieval Institute Publications, 1992). Bowers calls the Prologue The Canterbury Interlude, a practice that I follow here, partly to disambiguate discussion when I turn to examine The Tale of Beryn in the next chapter.

5 E.g. Brown, 'Journey's End', pp. 149–50; Howard Loxton, Pilgrimage to Canterbury (Newton Abbot: Readers Union, 1978), pp. 171–9, and Benjamin John Nilson, Cathedral Shrines of Medieval England (Woodbridge: Boydell, 1998), p. 96.

6 Anne Harris, 'Pilgrimage Performance and Stained Glass at Canterbury Cathedral', in Sarah Blick and Rita Tekippe (eds), The Art and

*Architecture of the Late Medieval Pilgrimage in Northern Europe and the British Isles* (Leiden: Brill, 2005), pp. 243–81 (p. 245).

7  These are collected in J. C. Robertson and J. B. Shepherd (eds), *Materials for the History of Thomas Becket, Archbishop of Canterbury* (London, Rolls Series, 1875–85), 7 vols. William of Canterbury, I.137–546; Benedict of Peterborough, II.21–281.

8  Paul Binski, *Becket's Crown: Art and Imagination in Gothic England 1170–1300* (New Haven and London: Yale University Press, 2004), p. 18.

9  As discussed by Harris, 'Pilgrimage Performance', p. 243, and Nilson, *Cathedral Shrines*, p. 98.

10  Diana Webb, *Pilgrimage in Medieval England* (London and New York: Hambledon, 2000), pp. 51–2.

11  Harris, 'Pilgrimage Performance', p. 279; Loxton, *Pilgrimage to Canterbury*, p. 100.

12  See Loxton, *Pilgrimage to Canterbury*, pp. 85–100.

13  John Butler, *The Quest for Becket's Bones: The Mystery of the Relics of St Thomas Becket of Canterbury* (New Haven and London: Yale University Press, 1995), p. 17.

14  His actual remains, reportedly entombed in a feretum for safekeeping by the monks after his murder, are shrouded in mystery. It remains unclear where in the crypt Becket was actually interred, and if he was ever moved to Trinity Chapel. In 1538, when Henry VIII ordered the shrine to be destroyed, appropriating its choicest ruby to make a ring for his finger, what the monks had done with Becket's body remains unknown, Butler, *The Quest*, pp. 23–7.

15  Jonathan Sumption pithily notes the tension between desire for miracles to happen, and desire to stage them: 'a miracle constituted certain proof of the authenticity of a relic and a common method of testing relics was to provoke one', *Pilgrimage* (London: Faber and Faber, 1975), p. 39.

16  As noted by Richard Gameson, 'The Early Imagery of Thomas Becket', in Colin Morris and Peter Roberts (eds), *Pilgrimage: The English Experience from Becket to Bunyan* (Cambridge: Cambridge University Press, 2002), p. 75. Harris writes extensively on the role of the stained glass as a crucial part of the ritual performance that sustained Becket's sanctity and healing powers, 'Pilgrimage Performance', pp. 243–62.

17  *Materials for the History of Becket*, III.151.

18  *Materials for the History of Becket*, II.177; and *Materials for the History of Becket*, I.157. All the relevant vocabulary is in the plural: 'genitalibus', 'membra' and 'virilibus'. But it is by no means clear whether these words are semantically equivalent, or quite what part of the male genitalia they signify. Do they denote testicles, or testicles and the penis? The sense matters. Although neither author uses the word

'castratus', Eilward's punishment is surely that of castration, a penalty which targeted injury to genitalia, but of precisely which parts was not absolutely fixed. Castration in the Middle Ages usually involved disabling or excision of the testicles, but, in a case of criminality, the penis could be removed also. Matthew S. Kuefler, 'Castration and Eunuchism in the Middle Ages', in Vern L. Bullough and James A. Brundage (eds), *A Handbook of Medieval Sexuality* (New York: Garland, 1996), pp. 279–306 (pp. 286–89). The diction used by both William and Benedict in describing the punishment does not explicitly rule out the possibility for understanding total dismemberment.

19  *Materials for the History of Becket*, II.181.

20  '[Q]uod oculis et testiculis, quand primo apud eum hospitatus fuit, omnino caruit; qui postea saepins invocans merita sancti Thomas martyris, gloriose et mirifice apparitione praedicti martyris sanitati restitutus est'. *Materials for the History of Becket*, I.157.

21  '[G]enitalia vero, quae cuilibet palpanda praebebat, infra qualitatem testium galli poterant aestimari'. *Materials for the History of Becket*, I.158. Translations of many of Thomas's miracles can be found in E. A. Abbott, *St Thomas of Canterbury: His Death and Miracles* (London: Adam and Charles Black, 1898), 2 vols. Interestingly, while Abbot preserves the Latin text at this point in his volume, he does not provide an English translation of this palpable moment, II.87. I am very grateful to Dr Maarit Kivilo for ensuring accurate sense of this crucial piece of censored Latin.

22  In *The General Prologue* Harry Bailey is the 'aller cok' of the pilgrims and 'of manhode hym lakked right naught' (I.757). The proximity of cockerel and plentiful manhood is a testicular jest; one that is reprised with the Host's merry banter about the size of the 'trede-foul'/Nun's Priest's stones in his breeches (VII.3448).

23  Becket's healing of Eilward is displayed in the third window on the north side of the ambulatory of Trinity Chapel. The four large panels which form a roundel narrate a truncated version of the narratives given us by William and Benedict. The panel on the right side of the frame shows the scene of Eilward's mutilation. Its Latin inscription reads [VDVTVR]ECTA SVNT LVMINA. MEMBRA RESECTA: ([his eyes] were put out, his members cut off). Photographs of this window, description and transcription of the inscription are in Madeleine Harrison Caviness, *The Windows of Christ Church Cathedral Canterbury* (London: Oxford University Press, 1981), pp. 190–1 and plates 127–9. The castration scene is plate 127 fig. 279.

24  The bottommost panel in the roundel has Eilward walking amongst the townsfolk pointing to his eyes and giving alms to a cripple. Plate 127 fig. 279.

25  According to Benedict, the saint appears to him dressed in white garments, painting the sign of the cross on his forehead and on his eyeless

sockets with his pastoral staff, 'baculoque pastorali signum crucis in frontes ejus et oculorum foraminibus depingens', *Materials for the History of Becket*, II.158. William has Thomas imprinting the sign of the cross with his pastoral staff between his eyebrows, 'sibi inter supercilia baculo pastorali signum crucis imprimentem', *Materials for the History of Becket*, I.157.

26  This is the D-shaped pane on the left underneath the punishment roundel, Caviness, plate 129 [284].

27  By a bizarre coincidence, the Latin text round the window has suffered damage at this point and the text that describes the missing parts has to be supplied from the record of the written accounts. The Latin inscription reads: 'REDDITA SVCCRE[FVRTVM. BES] SENSIQ' RECRESCVNT. This is how Caviness translates it: 'Supplying [*membra*] and *succre*[*scunt*], the sense is: His [members] are restored and swell up and gradually grow again'. Caviness, *The Windows of Christ Church Cathedral*, p. 190. The expert restores both the gaps in the sense of the verbal inscription caused by the ravages of time and the gaps in the original visual display. In contrast to the white garments described in Benedict's account, the window dresses Becket in red.

28  The text is from the third responsory of the third nocturn of the matins 'Novis fulget Thomas miraculis, / Membris donat castratos masculis; / Ornat visu priuatos oculis', quoted in Anne J. Duggan, 'A Becket Office at Stavelot: London British Library Additional MS 16964', in Anne J. Duggan, Joan Greatrex and Brenda Bolton (eds), *Omnia Disce: Medieval Studies in Memory of Leonard Boyle O.P.*, Aldershot: Ashgate, 2005), pp. 161–82 (p. 164).

29  The eighth response and the ninth lesson read, 'ad inusitata quoque et inaudita signa potencie sue manum extendit', Kay Brainerd Slocum, *Liturgies in Honour of Thomas Becket* (Toronto: University of Toronto Press, 2004), p. 89 and pp. 142–4. An additional prosa to the response of lesson nine of the Sarum Office for Thomas's feast day, found in just one manuscript, changes the details. In a bodily inscription which is not semantically identical to other accounts, it turns Eilward into a eunuch: 'Illuc datus est *spandoni* / sexus, ordo visio', Slocum, *Liturgies*, p. 292. The manuscript is BL Add.28598, fol. 125v.

30  As noted above, the Papal Bull which guaranteed Becket's canonisation is concerned with the signs of his body.

31  Taylor, *Castration*, pp. 155–6.

32  There is a rich tradition of satire against Pardoners for selling indulgences on false grounds, see Jill Mann, *Chaucer and Medieval Estates Satire: The Literature of Social Classes and the General Prologue to the Canterbury Tales* (Cambridge: Cambridge University Press, 1973), pp. 152–4, and Andrew Galloway, *The Penn Commentary on Piers*

*Plowman* (Philadelphia: University of Pennsylvania Press, 2006), pp. 86–92.

33 The arguments in this paragraph follow the discussion by Robert S. Sturges, *Chaucer's Pardoner and Gender Theory: Bodies of Discourse* (London: Macmillan, 2000), pp. 36–70. He provides detailed analysis of the critical debates surrounding the Pardoner's physical and meta-phorical body and interpretations of his sexuality.

34 My discussion here is indebted to Carolyn Dinshaw, *Chaucer's Sexual Poetics* (Madison: University of Wisconsin Press, 1989), pp. 157–84, though I have left Freud's fetishism to one side.

35 *Le Roman de la Rose*, ed. Daniel Poiron (Paris: Garnier-Flammarion, 1974), 'Si ne vous tienz pas a cortoise / Que ci m'aves coilles renomees / En bouche a courtoise pucele' (6928–31), and 'Et quant tu d'autre part obices / Que villain et lait sont li mot, / Je te di devant Dieu qui m'ot, / Se je, quant mis les nons as choses / Que si reprendre et blamer oses, / Coilles reliques appelasse / Et reliques coilles nomasse, / Tu qui si m'en mort et depiques, / Me redeisses de reliques / Que ce fust lais mos et vilains. / Coilles est biaus mos et si'l'ains, / Si sont par foi coillon et vit, / Je fis les mos, et sui certainne / Qu'onques ne fis chose vilainne' (7106–20). My discussion owes much to Marijane Osborn, 'Word and Image in Chaucer's Enshrined "Coillons" Passage', *Chaucer Review* 37 (2003), 365–84.

36 Or to deny strenuously that the Pardoner's body can have anything other than a heterosexual signification; see C. David Benson, 'Chaucer's Pardoner', *Mediaevalia* 8 (1982), 337–49, and, in the same journal, endorsing Benson's arguments, Richard Firth Green, 'The Sexual Normality of Chaucer's Pardoner', pp. 351–8.

37 Though the *Interlude* Pardoner has been seen as a heteronormative corrective to Chaucer's figure, Trigg argues that the *Beryn* Prologue covers over the Pardoner's homosexuality with an ostensibly hetero-sexual misadventure, *Congenial Souls*, p. 94. Other critics have been more strenuous in disavowing his sodomitical potential: B. Darjes and T. Rendall, 'A Fabliau in the *Prologue to the Tale of Beryn*', *Medieval Studies* 47 (1985), 416–31, especially pp. 429–30; Glending Olson, 'The Misreadings of the *Beryn Prologue*', *Mediaevalia* 17 (1994 for 1991), 201–19, especially p. 215. Sturges, *Chaucer's Pardoner*, pp. 153–6, is an exception, though he does not press his arguments as far as they could go; seeing the Pardoner as a marker of gender trans-gression within an impulse towards normalisation.

38 We might compare *Piers Plowman* 18.14–15, where Piers as Christ comes as a 'knyght ... to be dubbed'. In this case, the punning draws resemblance between the wounds in Christ's feet and 'gilte' spurs on slashed shoes.

39 Robert Sturges discusses the staff as a detachable phallus which is invested with sodomitical association in the mock-knightly

tournament in the kitchen in his more recent discussion of the *Interlude*, 'The Pardoner in Canterbury: Class, Gender and Urban Space in *The Prologue to the Tale of Beryn*', *College Literature* 33 (2006), 52–76, pp. 68–9. He does not note the Becketian symbolism.

40  For instance the illustration in British Library MS Harley 5312, fol. 28v shows a knight standing behind Becket, who kneels at the altar. The knight raises his sword behind Becket's shoulders. See also British Library MS Harley 5102, fol. 32 where the knight points his sword high upon the brow of Thomas Becket.

41  Binski, *Becket's Crown*, pp. 7–11; Nilson, *Cathedral Shrines*, p. 54.

42  Francis Woodman, *The Architectural History of Canterbury Cathedral* (London: Routledge, Kegan and Paul, 1981), p. 125.

43  For example Caviness, *The Windows of Christ Church*, Plate 65 fig. 156; plate 116 fig. 254; plate 121 fig. 265; plate 136 fig. 300; plate 139 fig. 307. Plate 159 fig. 364 features a group of men carrying shovels, but so far as I can see there are no rakes anywhere in the stained glass windows. Bowers, *Fifteenth-Century Continuations*, suggests that the window is that of Adam delving in the West End window, pp. 167–8.

44  Douglas Gray, ed., *A Selection of Religious Lyrics* (Oxford: Clarendon Press, 1975), p. 45/8; p. 23/29; p. 30/15–18 and p. 28/17–18.

45  *The Digby Poems: A New Edition of the Lyrics*, ed. Helen Barr (Exeter: Exeter University Press, 2009), 10/116 and 11/101–2.

46  Gray, *Religious Lyrics*, p. 26/25–6.

47  Prendergast makes the connection between reading Chaucer's body and a legible pardon, *Chaucer's Dead Body*, p. 4.

48  While I had arrived at this reading of the Pardoner's body independently, I note corroboration in my reading of its sexual puns in Eugene Vance, 'Chaucer's Pardoner: Relics, Discourse, and the Frames of Propriety', *New Literary History* 20 (1988–89), 723–49; Anne Laskaya, *Chaucer's Approach to Gender in the Canterbury Tales* (Cambridge: Cambridge University Press, 1995), p. 192, and Rory B. Egan, '*Bulles, Coillons*, and Relics in *The Pardoner's Tale*', *ANQ: A Quarterly Journal of Short Articles, Notes and Reviews* 21 (2008), 7–11. I thank Thomas Forkin for drawing this last article to my attention.

49  One of the fullest expositions of this trope is 'Christ's Testament' in the Vernon Manuscript, see F. J. Furnivall (ed.), *The Minor Poems of the Vernon Manuscript Part II* (EETS OS 117, 1901), pp. 637–57. See also Hope's patent in *Piers Plowman* B.17.5–8. Woolf discusses the tradition, *The English Religious Lyric in the Middle Ages* (Oxford: Clarendon Press, 1968), pp. 212–14, and, more recently, Emily Steiner, *Documentary Culture and the Making of Medieval English Literature* (Cambridge: Cambridge University Press, 2003), pp. 49–53 and 61–75. Charters with hanging seals are illustrated on pp. 78, 80, 81 and 82.

50  'Maner þer ys of foule kyssyng / As ys of dede and of handling, / Þat falleþ*. [falþ.] ofte yn pryuyte, / But þat shal nat be tolde

for me', *Handlyng Synne*, ed. F. J. Furnivall (EETS OS 123, 1903), ll. 8118–22.

51 Melvin Storm argues that the Pardoner stands as a meretricious substitute for what the pilgrims seek at Becket's shrine, 'The Pardoner's Invitation: Quaestor's Bag or Becket's Shrine?' *PMLA* 97 (1982), 810–18, p. 810. Noting the reference to Becket's breeches at line 947, Storm sees the Pardoner to threaten the pilgrimage because of his fraudulence and his spiritual sterility; hence the Host's intervention. See also the earlier discussion by Daniel Knapp, 'The Relyk of a Saint: A Gloss on Chaucer's Pilgrimage', *English Literary History* 39 (1972), 1–26, and Siegfried Wenzel, 'Chaucer's Pardoner and His Relics', *Studies in the Age of Chaucer* 11 (1989), 37–41.

52 Anne Duggan discusses how Becket's martyrdom and subsequent canonisation were inseparable from the recording of miracles associated with his body. Over four hundred are recounted, a process that appears to have started as early as January 1171, *Thomas Becket* (London: Arnold, 2004), pp. 225–33. See also Loxton, *Pilgrimage to Canterbury*, p. 74.

53 Slocum, *Liturgies*, p. 6. Slocum quotes the relevant texts of the liturgies: 'Thomas sublimatus / Est in virum alium / subito mutatus', 'Monachus sub cleric / clam ciliciatus / Carnis carue forcior / edomat conatus', p. 142, and 'Cilicium clam inuit, femoralibus etiam uses est [usque] ad poplites cilicinis', p. 178.

54 Gameson, 'The Early Imagery of Thomas Becket', p. 59.

55 To my knowledge, the connection with Becket's head wound has not previously been made. Sturges, *Chaucer's Pardoner*, interprets the head wound as a mark of castration, p. 155.

56 Binski, *Becket's Crown*, discusses the elaborate biblical symbolism of the colouring, pp. 7–9. Elaborate pavement tiles came to commemorate the spot where the brains were dashed and then mopped.

57 Gameson, 'The Early Imagery of Thomas Becket', p. 49.

58 Anne Duggan notes: 'the pilgrim demand for tangible tokens of their pilgrimage created a veritable industry for the manufacture of ampullae, badges and small figurines', *Thomas Becket*, p. 234. Sarah Blick discusses how badges which reproduced the ampullae were thought to ensure the wearer's safe return home, 'Reconstructing the Shrine of Thomas *Art and Architecture*, Becket in Canterbury Cathedral', in Blick and Tekippe, pp. 405–41 (p. 453).

59 Caviness, *The Windows of Christ Church*, pp. 197–8, plate 142, fig. 313, and p. 202, plate 148 fig. 331.

60 Jennifer M. Lee, 'Searching for Signs: Pilgrims' Identity and Experience Made Visible in the *Miracula Sancti Thomae Cantuarensis*', in Blick and Tekippe, *Art and Architecture*, pp. 473–91 (p. 479).

61 Duggan notes how pilgrim badges functioned as personal mementoes, sacred objects and even as passports. Pilgrims were a recognised

category of privileged persons, allowed free and secure passage in the
regions through which they passed, and the wearing of a badge was a
sign of their good faith, *Thomas Becket*, p. 235.

62 Sturges, *Chaucer's Pardoner*, discusses the Pardoner's vernicle in relation to Baudrillard's ideas of simulacra, pp. 65–70.

63 Sturges, *Chaucer's Pardoner*, discusses the dispersal of the *Canterbury
Tales* Pardoner's bodies between fragments in which he appears, and
the textual instability of Fragment VI itself, pp. 141–51.

64 Dinshaw, *Chaucer's Sexual Poetics*, p. 163.

65 Noted by Nilson, *Cathedral Shrines*, p. 113.

66 The argument of this section is indebted to the anthropological
analysis of Victor and Edith Turner, *Image and Pilgrimage in Christian
Culture: Anthropological Perspectives* (Oxford: Blackwell, 1978),
pp. 143–6; 196–9 and 247.

67 Jos Koldeweij, 'Naked and Shameful Images: Obscene Badges
as Parodies of Popular Devotion', in Blick and Tekippe, *Art and
Architecture*, pp. 493–510; Nicola McDonald (ed.), *Medieval
Obscenities* (Woodbridge: Boydell, 2006), pp. 1–16.

68 See Chapter 2, pp. 58, 72–3.

69 David K. Coley argues against a deconstructive reading of the vitreous
materials in *The House of Fame*, arguing that, while they are a sign of
the brittleness of literary materials, they are also a beacon of hope for
their endurance, '"Withyn a temple ymad of glas": Glazing, Glossing
and Patronage in Chaucer's *House of Fame*', *Chaucer Review* 45 (2010),
59–85.

70 The 'feble fundament' of Christ's Church will have become the 'fun-
dement' on St Thomas's breeches as reportedly worn by a Pardoner
who traffics in relics as though he were a portable Becketian reliquary.

## 2

# Crossing borders: Northumberland bodies unbound

Right from its opening *The Canterbury Interlude* dissolves the boundaries that mark out bodies in time and place. This is how the pilgrims from the Tabard are introduced as they come into Canterbury:

> When all this fressh feleship were com to Caunterbury,
> As ye have herd tofore, with tales glad and mery,
> Som of sotill centence, of vertu and of lore,
> And som of other myrthes for hem that hold no store
> Of wisdom, ne of holynes, ne of chivalry,
> Nether of vertuouse matere, but to foly
> Leyd wit and lustes all, to such japes
> As Hurlewaynes meyne in every hegg that capes
> Thurh unstabill mynde, ryght as the leves grene
> Stonden ageyn the weder, ryght so by hem I mene.
>
> *(The Canterbury Interlude 1–10)*

'This' (line 1), holds up the 'fressh feleship' in the here and now. But quite 'when' remains undetermined. The audience 'ye' (2) of *The Canterbury Interlude* has not already heard that the pilgrims have arrived at Canterbury. As the previous chapter has discussed, the Tabard company falls short. At this point in MS Northumberland 455 the 'feleship' is only half-way through the sequence of *The Canterbury Tales*. In their place on fol. 180a, the pilgrims both have arrived at Canterbury and are not yet at the final destination that they do not reach.[1] The syntax of the opening sentence mirrors that ateleology. For all that it purports to describe a journey's end, the grammar fails to deliver its subjects to a conclusion. A sequence of seemingly parenthetical subordinate clauses tumbles out but is never finished up with a main verb. The action promised by the opening 'when' never arrives. The 'fressh feleship' is left stranded somewhere between

two similes: '[a]s Hurlewaynes meyne in every hegg that capes'
and 'as the leves grene' (8–9).

To be a member of Hurlewaine's retinue is to be neither living
nor dead. In medieval French texts, Hurlewain, or Hellequin, is a
figure from charivari. He leads processions of cavorting tricksters
who wear disguises or masks and dress up in outlandish costumes.
Illustrations show Hellequin as a leader of the 'undead'.[2] Prior
to any formal introductions on first-name terms, the pilgrim
assembly of *The Canterbury Interlude* is become a harlequinade
of persons suspended somewhere between life and death. That
'somewhere' is in a hedge. A hedge is not a naturally occurring
feature of landscape. A hedge is an artificial living border planted
as a territorial marker or as a defence to divide one place from
another. These Hurlewaines, however, are neither on one side nor
the other. Capering in the leaves, even becoming like the leaves
themselves, the pilgrims cannot be assigned a place by the border
because they are in and of the border itself. Whether or not its
leaves are evergreen, a hedge forms a boundary that is permeable;
you can peer through it. And if you are in it, you can look out in
both directions.[3]

These transitive border bodies prefigure and recapitulate how
persons in *The Canterbury Interlude* and *The Tale of Beryn* do
not keep time or place. I argue in this chapter that they exceed the
material borders of the works that contain them. Titles and names
that ought to separate one person from another lose distinction.
'Individual' characters cannot be identified by clothing, accessories,
or voice. Primary characteristics conjure notions of singularity
only to frustrate the enterprise of telling personhood apart in
textual company. Features that seem to be individual turn out
to be nothing of the sort. This blurring of boundaries between
fictional bodies is an integral cause of the border crossings between
textual corpora. In their travel back and forth across material and
epistemological boundaries they render the borders of these texts
as capaciously accommodating as that transitional hedge populated
with Hurlewaynes cavorting through its leaves. In their 'wandrynge
by the weye' in and among fragments of *The Canterbury Tales* and
beyond, the bodies of *The Canterbury Interlude* and *The Tale of
Beryn* render literary boundaries indefensible. These are borders
that cannot be firmly policed by guardians of chronological versions of literary history. Their check points cannot manage the
volume of traffic back and forth.

## Between London and Canterbury via Northumberland

The traversal between boundaries begins even as the characters appear to be stably penned within the folios of the manuscript in which they appear. The presence of capitalised nouns that describe persons is usually seen to confer special, and distinctive, status even if, philosophically speaking, a Proper Name does not define some pre-existing ontological entity.[4] But the scribal practice of punctuation in MS 455 does not, consistently, confer distinction upon the persons it writes into being.[5] The scribe's erratic deployment of capital letters fails to discriminate between proper and common nouns, and between an individual person and a generic type.[6] Apart from one instance, to which I shall return, the Pardoner is always referenced by his occupational name, not his personal one. Because of the inconsistent use of capitals, he appears sometimes as the singular Pardoner, and at others as a generic pardoner.[7] Before she acquires the name Kit at line 65, 'Tapster' is capitalised on her first appearance but thereafter shifts back and forth between large and small 't'.[8] The Paramour, nameless throughout a text in which he plays such an important role, is sometimes capitalised, sometimes not, and, like Kit, appears both with and without his preceding definite article.[9] The innkeeper of the Checker of the Hope is sometimes 'the hosteler', sometimes 'Jak Hosteler', and sometimes 'Jak the Hosteler'. Between lines 536 and 538, the hosteler becomes simply 'Jak'.[10] Printed editions confirm no stability. Between the sole surviving manuscript witness and the editions of Furnivall and of Bowers, characters take their places irregularly between Proper, generic, singular, and ordinary. Understandably, given that he produces an edition that is concerned to make a neglected text accessible, Bowers standardises much of the punctuation according to modern conventions. So while Furnivall retains the manuscript reading at line 104, '[t]yll the Preest & the clerk [ful] boystly bad me goon', Bowers puts both persons in lower case.[11] On fol. 185b/l. 410, the scribe uses the definite article before both capitalised characters: '[b]ut þe Miller and þe Coke, drunken by the moon'. Bowers silently, and Furnivall with a superscript number, emend to 'Butte Miller'. Their interventions create an inequality of status between the two characters and present their readers with a figure who either is preceded by an adversative conjunction or has acquired a somewhat unfortunate forename. Any sense of stable, prior ontology is completely confounded: in the manuscript; in Furnivall, in Bowers and across all three of them.[12]

Quite simply, the characters become hard to call. They move
between singular, plural and type, and between script and print.
Even when personal names are used, they hover between the recognition of a specific person and a generic model. Kit's name suggests
the role of a common woman; a prostitute. The narrator says as
much at lines 443–4: 'lewd Kittes / As tapsters and other such'. Kit
has her personal name capitalised by Bowers, but Furnivall and the
manuscript pluralise her into a common woman and places her in
the company of lower-case tapsters.[13] The Pardoner is also briefly,
and once only, invested with a personal name that scripts him into
a typecast role. Prompted by his readiness to offer to confess her (as
a precursor to bedding her), Kit assumes that the Pardoner's name
is 'Jenkyn'. The Pardoner neither confirms nor denies the appellation, replying only that he was informed as such 'of hem that did
me foster' (64). Jenkyn is also the name of Kit's first dead paramour, or so she tells us (30), and readers of other Middle English
texts will recognise the name 'Jenkyn' as a byword for a seducing
cleric.[14] Even at those moments in the text when the Tapster and
the Pardoner are identified by personal names, singular distinction
is compromised by the knowledge that these are generic names of
character types that have been encountered elsewhere.

This epistemological quandary is intensified because the majority of the characters in *The Interlude* have the same name as pilgrims
and tale tellers in *The Canterbury Tales*. As Brown remarks, '[t]he
author has studded his composition with references to Chaucer's
poetry which operate at various levels of subtlety but which do not
work at all if the recipients are ignorant of what Chaucer wrote'.[15]
Most prominently, those references are to names. It has proved
difficult for critics to articulate the relationship between these
names and the characters they identify. The knowledge that they
have met these characters before and elsewhere challenges the
desire to assign to them 'a primary or transcendent unity to the
notion of individual, isolated character'.[16] Nonetheless, the dominant emphasis in the critical reception of *The Interlude* has been
to measure how consistently *The Interlude* rendered Chaucer's
'original' characters. Towards the beginning of the twentieth
century, editors and critics opined that the *Beryn*-poet had done
a decent job:[17] in the last two decades the relationships between
*The Interlude* and *The Canterbury Tales* have been discussed in
more querulous and often openly hostile terms. At their most
extreme, these critics berate the author in no uncertain terms.
For Jost, he is the 'clumsily incompetent *Beryn*-jester' who cannot

hold a candle to the Chaucer 'original' – his 'more polished and sophisticated ur-creation'. His outrage is closely matched by Olson, who argues that *The Interlude* is a TV version of *The Canterbury Tales*.[18] More recently, critics have argued that the *Beryn*-author challenges Chaucerian conceptions of character; seeing rewriting as a critique, a correction or extended play of a kind that one may find in twenty-first-century computer games.[19]

All these critical positions confront the same thorny issue: the characters in *The Interlude* that share a name with characters in *The Canterbury Tales* are beside themselves. In MS Northumberland 455 they are beside themselves materially even as the teleology of the Canterbury sequence is upset. They are also beside themselves epistemologically; they occupy more than one place simultaneously. Characters with shared names acquire a sense of personhood that is in transit between time and place. They cannot be regarded as individual, isolated characters because they exist in more than one place and time within the mind of the reader that encounters them. They travel across the boundaries between *The Canterbury Tales* and the works of the *Beryn*-poet.

From reading the description of the Knight in *The General Prologue* and his rusty stained 'habergeoun' (I.76), we might be surprised that, when he arrives in Canterbury, he pulls on a fresh shirt (231). Given that the narrator of *The General Prologue* observes that the Wife of Bath knew 'muchel of wandrynge by the weye' (I.467), we might not expect her to take the weight off her legs to have an afternoon chat in a herb garden with the Prioress (281–5). From the description of the Parson in *The General Prologue*, or his sermon, which we may or may not have yet read (materially, it has yet to be delivered; epistemologically, it has already been heard), we might not expect him to knock back the wine with the Monk and the Friar (267–80). But once names, so foundational a way of telling personhood apart, travel across the borders of texts, then horizons of expectations are expanded; indeed become unbounded. It becomes difficult to chart where one character begins and ends. Even as the 'Wife of Bath' does not appear to 'keep up' in Canterbury, she is not left behind. And even as characters *do* seem to keep up, it remains difficult accurately to pinpoint quite how much of them has made the journey. The Squire receives extensive physical description in *The General Prologue*. His characterisation as a lover is expressed through similes which turn not only his gown, embroidered as though it were a meadow, but his very person, his body, into a May morning literary convention (*General Prologue* I.89–98).

That nothing in his description in *The Interlude* contradicts the
impression of this Squire leads Sturges to remark, 'the Squire
himself is represented exactly as Chaucer represents him in the
*General Prologue*'.[20] But is he? Here he is:

> He was of al factur after fourm of Kynde,
> And for to deme his governaunce, it semed that his mynde
> Was much in his lady that he loved best,
> That made hym offt to wake when he shuld have his rest.
>
> (*Canterbury Interlude* 247–50)

This is not *exactly* as Chaucer represented him. Being composed
completely according to the form or mould of nature (247) does
not contradict the impressions of Chaucer's Squire, but nor does
it explicitly include those extensive similes and the abundant
details of the natural world. And yet Sturges has a point. While
the *Interlude* portrait excludes the precise wording of *The General
Prologue*, it is hard to banish the memory of Chaucer's words
when one encounters the *Beryn* Squire. Readers have already met
the Squire, and remember the impression he made when they
encounter his avatar once more. His appearance in *The General
Prologue* carries through to his description in *The Interlude*.
The Squire, like all those other characters who share a name,
commutes between texts. While in terms of chronological order of
composition, Chaucer's characters come first, and the *Beryn*-poet's
later, in the present moment of readerly engagement the categories
of first and second place are reforged. The boundaries between
textual bodies and, by extension, of literary corpora are traversed.

The process of con-fusing before and after, here and now,
time and place is not only confined to names. Voices also carry.
They resonate across time.[21] While voice may seem to embody
features that are 'natural', their recognition depends on remembering where that voice has been encountered before. Voices travel
between the fragments of *The Canterbury Tales* and beyond such
that is becomes impossible to determine where one person's voice
stops and someone else's begins.[22] Between them, the Pardoner and
Kit the tapster sound like a reduced company version of Chaucer's
collected works. This is the Pardoner's response to Kit's dream:
'"Now Seynt Danyel," quod the Pardoner, "yeur sweven turne
to good!"' (106). In sounding like the dreamer at the start of *The
House of Fame* (1) and Chanticleer lecturing Pertelote (VII.3128),
the genitally inscrutable Pardoner speaks 'the cokkes wordes' of a
Chaucerian narrator. And with the Pardoner sounding, at least in

part, like a chicken, Kit makes a becoming hen. In their second encounter, the voices of Kit and the Pardoner become even more multiply resonant. This is the Pardoner, anxiously trying to secure his night's assignation:

> ... 'Lord! Who shall ligg here
> This nyghte is to comying? I pray yewe tell me.'
> 'Iwis, it is grete nede to telle yew', quod she,
> 'Make it nat over queynt, thoughe ye be a clerk.
> Ye know wel inowgh iwis by loke, by word, by work'.
> 'Shall I com then, Cristian, and fese awey the cat?'
>
> (346–51)

Although neither the Pardoner nor the cat (so far as we are told) fetches up sleeping with Kit, Jenkyn's offer to sweep the feline from the bed sounds the voice of the Summoner reporting the actions of a friar (IV.1775). For her part, Kit sounds like Simkin from *The Reeve's Tale* as he swears he will outwit the 'sleights' of clerks 'the moore queynte crekes that they make' (I.4051); words that resonate with the Miller's narration of 'clerk' Nicholas's advances towards Alison's 'queynte' (I. 3276). Kit and the Pardoner also speak in the voices of Troilus and Criseyde, patched with resonances, appropriately enough, of their go-between Pandarus:

> 'Nowe sith ye be my prisoner, yeld yewe now', quod he.
>
> (*Interlude* 317)

> This Troilus in armes gan hire streyne,
> And seyde, 'O swete, as evere mot I gon,
> Now be ye kaught; now is ther but we tweyne!
> Now yeldeth yow, for other bote is non'.
>
> (*Troilus* III.1205–8)

> And fond hir liggyng lirilong, with half sclepy eye,
> Poured fellich under hir hood and saw al his comyng.
>
> (*Interlude* 310–12)

> With that she gan hire face for to wrye
> With the shete, and wax for shame al reed;
> And Pandarus gan under for to prie.
>
> (*Troilus* III.1569–71)

> ... 'how have ye fare
> Sith I was with yew last? That is my most care.
>
> (*Interlude* 333–4)

> 'I have i-fared the wers for yewe'.
>
> (*Interlude* 337)

> ... 'How stant it now
> This mury morwe? Nece, how kan ye fare?'
> Criseyde answered, 'Nevere the bet for yow'.
>
> (*Troilus* III.1562–4)

Sexual congress never takes place between Kit and the Pardoner. But by speaking through the voices of Criseyde, Troilus and Pandarus before and after the consummation scene in *Troilus and Criseyde*, it sounds not only as if sex will happen but that it already has.

Thus far, I have been arguing that bodies travel across the borders of *The Canterbury Interlude* and Chaucer's oeuvre between script and print; through names and through voice. Their encountering is conditional upon the meeting of textual memory with material place. These Chaucerian bodies exist both in the place where they were once con-scripted – and elsewhere. In the final part of this section I want to show how these border crossings have become contagious. Editors have helped them along. Through their decipherment of marks on the page, or through supplying information felt to be inexplicit or lacking, editors have introduced persons into *The Interlude* from much further afield, and persons whom, it could be argued, ought not properly to have gained admittance. Readers of Loomis and Willard's partly modernised text published in 1948 will have encountered a Pardoner named Hugh. No such person, even by *The Interlude*'s policy of open access, properly exists. The editors misread the capitalised relative pronoun at the start of line 176 'Huch the Pardoner'.[23] Trivial though the point may seem (after all, Hugh is simply an accident of grammatical misrecognition), for readers of this edition with no access to any other text, 'Hugh' will have carried substance; his sudden baptism no more bizarre perhaps than any of the other haphazard nomenclature of *The Interlude*.

While John Bowers introduces no persons into his text through pronominal accident, he adds them in via his commentary notes. When the 'fresh feleship' enters the cathedral at Canterbury, the Friar attempts to wrest the springle from one of the Canterbury canons ('a monk' – not the Monk) because he hopes that aspersing the pilgrims will allow him 'to se the Nonnes fase' (144). Bowers's note runs: 'Huberd's longing to see the Second Nun's face may be shared by many of Chaucer's readers since this faceless pilgrim is given no real portrait in the *General Prologue* (I.163–4)'.[24] To satisfy (or maybe to tickle?), readers' desire for a face to be supplied to a nameless nun, Bowers reunites the anonymous Nun of *The Interlude* with 'another nonne' of *The General Prologue* (I.163) and with the teller of *The Second Nun's Tale* who acquires that name only in the rubrication of Fragment VII. Without the running titles, she exists only as an unclassified voice. Through transporting the name of Huberd from the Friar's description in *The General Prologue* (I.269), and through deciding that the nun's face belongs to the Second Nun, Bowers creates a doorway drama in Canterbury Cathedral that is played out by characters from diverse fragments.[25] Bowers goes one stage further at line 271 when the Monk invites the Parson and the Friar to visit his 'brother in habit'. Bowers suggests that the canon 'might be another Benedictine confrere of the author, perhaps a witty reference to the author himself!'[26] The desire to connect persons with versions of themselves that may or may not be fully present and correct in their textual place extends to inviting his readers to imagine the *Beryn*-poet in the body of a nameless canon who goes out on a drinking spree with an assembly of clerics in Canterbury.[27]

Bowers's incorporation of a version of the putative author amongst *The Interlude*'s drinking companions places him in Canterbury. Furnivall adds a figure of another author. He places him in the whole company of pilgrims in his text, and takes him on much further than Canterbury: right back to London. A break in the rhyme at line 682 suggests that a line is missing in the manuscript. While Bowers supplies a line of dots to mark the absence, Furnivall inserts a line of his own:

> [When Chauceres daysyes sprynge. Herke eek the fowles syngyng]
> The thrustelis & the thrusshis, in þis glad morning,
> The ruddock & the Goldfynch; but þe Nyȝtyngale ...
> ( Furnivall, 683–5)[28]

It has not gone unnoticed that, in filling a metrical gap in the manuscript, the name of Chaucer is introduced into a poem that lacks it. Chaucer is not one of the pilgrims in the 'fressh feleship'.[29] Stephanie Trigg has argued that Furnivall's introduction of Chaucer brings into the poem notions of propriety and textual ownership that are alien to it. The introduction of Chaucer's name countersigns the authority of Furnivall's text.[30]

My concern here is less with notions of authorship and Chaucer than with the significance of the daisies. Their introduction intensifies the confusion of time and place already present in the text. The *Beryn*-poet heralds the return of the pilgrims to Southwark with a reprise of the spring Prologue opening which assembled them there.[31] Furnivall's daisies revive another spring Prologue from another of Chaucer's works: the *Prologue to the Legend of Good Women*. There, the narrator's worship of the 'daysye' prompts a recitation of a catalogue not only of Chaucer's literary oeuvre but also of a company of good women. A complex symbol of womanly virtue that the narrator honours almost like a relic, the daisy has been taken to represent a variety of goodly woman: those named explicitly in the text, and those that are merely suggested. Candidates include Alceste, the Virgin Mary and Anne of Bohemia, wife of Richard II.[32] But this is not the only place where Chaucerian daisies appear. They are also present in the fifteenth-century poem *The Floure and the Leaf,* a poem which lurks in the hinterland of Chaucerian apocrypha.[33]

> And at the last there began anon
> A Lady for to sing right womanly
> A bargaret in praising the daisie:
> For, as me thought, among her notes swete,
> She saide, Si douce est la Margarete.
>
> (p. 134)

> Then the Nightingale, that all the day
> Had in the laurer sate, and did her might
> The whole service to sing longing to May,
> All sodainly began to take her flight;
> And to the lady of the Leaf forth right
>
> (p. 136)

> The Goldfinch eke, that fro the medler tre
> Was fled for heat into the bushes cold,
> Unto the Lady of the Floure gan fle
>
> (p. 136)

When Furnivall added daisies into *The Interlude*, he introduced them into lines which already contained a goldfinch and a nightingale. I suggest that it was the presence of these birds that prompted the daisies. The passages from *The Floure and the Leaf* that I have quoted here are taken from Furnivall's transcription of the inscription in the Great Chaucer Window that was unveiled in Westminster Abbey in 1868. Daisies feature prominently in the glass; the lines from *The Floure and the Leaf* are in the roundels. In his detailed description of the window he wrote that its installation 'renews the bond between London and Canterbury that Chaucer wove'.[34] I think that Furnivall rewove that bond in composing line

683 for *The Interlude*. The goldfinch and the nightingale already
present in the text cue the memory of the daisies and the birds in
the Westminster window. Given that those daisies are freighted
with the textual memory of Margaret and all those other women
in *The Legend of Good Women*, Furnivall's returning *Interlude*
pilgrims keep company with a very densely populated assembly
of ladies. It is a 'compaignye' into which they have fallen not so
much 'by aventure' (I.25–6) as by editorial memory of text from
another place and a former time. While the returning *Interlude* pilgrims never reach London, in his editing of MS Northumberland
455 Furnivall supplies a memory of that future destination from
another borderline Chaucer work. Fresh from puzzling out stained
glass windows in Canterbury Cathedral, the *Interlude* pilgrims
become located in a spring Prologue that has been transported
from the memory of the Chaucer window in Westminster Abbey.

## Canterbury to London via the Continent

When we turn to the tale that takes the 'fressh feleship' out of
Canterbury and back to London, it looks as though England gets
left far behind. The Merchant's telling of *The Tale of Beryn* appears
to sever relations with *The Interlude* and its textual company of
*The Canterbury Tales*. Drawn out of a redaction of an Anglo-
Norman romance, the action of the story unfolds in Rome and in
an unnamed Mediterranean seaport. Its characters are probably
foreign to readers of Chaucer: in any copy of *Bérinus* I have read,
the majority of its pages were uncut. Persons within the story are
also unrecognisable to each other. Between the English and French
narratives, persons tell stories about themselves and each other
that do not tally. Bodies tell versions of themselves that belie their
outer appearance. Characters and readers are confronted with a
series of persons that are like a Russian doll that refuses reassembly.
When the outer body is opened up, the inner ones won't go back
inside. They are unfittingly self-contained. And yet, even as the
story appears to travel ever further away into a no-man's-land
where bodies and words have no sustainable relationship to each
other – themselves or anyone else – readers find themselves back in a
place and with a person that seems familiar. The endlessly dynamic,
unbounded bodies in the story of *Beryn* turn out to be intimately
related to the Chaucerian characters in Canterbury after all.

Before going any further, a synopsis of the plot of Beryn's strange
story is probably in order. Beryn is a wayward, selfish youth.

Born in Rome to pious parents named Faunus and Agea, he spends
his time robbing the poor, drinking and gambling. He refuses to
leave a game of dice even when his father sends him news that his
mother is dying. Beryn's absence from her sickbed serves to hasten
Agea's death. When Faunus remarries, his second wife alienates
him from his son. Beryn's allowance is cut off, and, when he returns
home destitute, he is refused help. Shunned by everyone, Beryn
begins to feel remorse, and when he visits his mother's tomb in a
church he is overcome by grief and repentance for his dissolute life.
Having atoned for his misdeeds, he is reunited with his father, who
offers his son new clothes, a horse and a knighthood. Beryn refuses;
his only wish is to forgo his inheritance and instead to chance his
fortunes by travelling overseas as a merchant. Faunus accedes to
his request and equips him with ships laden with goods. Beryn
and his fellow mariners set sail from Rome and after surviving a
tempest they arrive in an unfamiliar seaport. During his stay there,
Beryn is cheated out of his goods and falsely accused of crimes by
every person that he meets. First, he plays at chess with Syrophane,
a burgess of the town, and is beguiled into playing the last game
with a forfeit. Beryn loses the wager and is left wondering how he
will be able to make good his pledge to drink all the salt water of the
sea. Beryn then enters into an agreement to exchange all his cargoes
for the goods he can find in the house of Hanybald, the provost.
Only when he arrives there, he finds the house empty. Beryn's
fortunes get worse: a blind man accuses him of stealing his eyes; a
woman claims that Beryn is the father of her child and has abandoned them; and a man named Macaign accuses him of murdering
his father. All these plaintiffs take their accusations to court, and
Beryn is summoned to answer the charges against him.

It transpires that the seaport has a legal system in which substantive proof is supplied through the collective verbal evidence
of its speakers. If sufficient members of the community swear that
an account is true, then it is held to be so. The plaintiffs have a
plentiful supply of compurgators to indict Beryn on the charges
they lay before the court. He escapes from what seems certain
punishment only by the intervention of a mysterious character
who conducts an ingenious form of defence. Beryn's unlikely – and
unexpected – barrister turns the tables on the plaintiffs and indicts
them with the same criminal charges that they laid against Beryn.
Now safely delivered from the seaport's wily inhabitants, Beryn
determines to set sail back to Rome. His defence lawyer makes him
promise to give him a berth on ship since he is pining to see his

native city. Beryn agrees. The narrative concludes, however, with Beryn marrying the daughter of Isope, the overlord of the seaport. Whether anyone makes it back to Rome remains untold.

On the face of it, this tale is not unfitting to its merchant teller. With its emphasis on 'encrees of his wynnyng' (I.275) and sea trade, albeit sea much more expansive than that betwixt Middelburgh and Orewelle (I.277), the concerns of the tale chime with those of the Merchant in *The General Prologue*. Only the Merchant does not consistently sound like himself. In agreeing to tell the tale for the homeward journey, the Merchant's first words suggest an East Anglian provenance that is not out of character with the places mentioned in his indirect free speech in *The General Prologue*: '"By the Rood of Bromholm", quod the Marchaunte tho' (*Interlude* 717). An ear alert to oaths, however, will recognise the voice of Simkin's wife roused from her laborious slumbers with John the clerk in *The Reeve's Tale* (I.4286). In making his pre-narrative apology for lack of eloquence, the Merchant asks to 'be excused of [his] rudines' (*Interlude* 729). Here, he sounds like the teller at the end of Chaucer's *Merchant's Tale* who claims that he is a 'rude man' who cannot gloss (IV.2351). But when he expands on his shortcomings and says 'I cannat peynt my tale but tell as it is' (V.730), he also sounds like Chaucer's Franklin who asks to be 'excused of rude speche' because he claims to know no colours of rhetoric save those which men use to 'dye' or to 'peynte' (V.717; 725). This indeterminacy between voice, person and tale-telling that begins the end of *The Interlude* is a narrative staple of the story of Beryn.

One episode must suffice to illustrate something of the continuous bewilderment that this confusion brings about. At the point when Beryn is grieving over his many woes, a man appears to offer him spiritual comfort. Pledging himself as his 'trew frend' (2248), Macaign (for he it is, it would seem) offers to help Beryn out of his difficulties. He tells him that he owns a knife that has long been coveted by the Steward of the town. If Beryn were to take this knife to the Steward as a gift, and promise him some money as well, then he would help him in his misfortunes. Beryn agrees and hands over five marks for the knife. Macaign tells Beryn that, in order to advance his suit, he will come with him to the Steward. But, he adds, just to be on the safe side, 'sey ye be my cosyn, the better shull ye spede' (2257). Macaign accompanies his new friend to the Steward: '[b]ut Beryn bare the knyff' (2264).

Once arrived, Macaign falls straight to his knees and accuses Beryn of murder. Seven years ago, Melan, Macaign's father,

travelled to Rome and has disappeared without trace: missing
presumed dead. Beryn is carrying Melan's knife so Beryn must
have killed him to get it. Beryn is required to answer the charge
in court. Macaign repeats his story. There is no question, says
Macaign, over the identity of the knife:

'The knyff I knowe wel inowe; also the man stont here
And dwelleth in this town and is a cotelere,
That made the same knyff with his too hondes,
That wele I woot there is noon like, to sech al Cristen londes.
For thre preciouse stones been within the hafft
Perfitlych i-couched and sotillich by crafft
Endended in the hafft, and that right coriously:
A saphir and a salidone and a rich ruby'.
The coteler cam lepeing forth with a bold chere,
And seyd to the Steward, 'That Macaign told now here,
Every word is trew; so beth the stones sett.
I made the knyff myselff – who myght know it bet? –
And toke the knyff to Macaign, and he me payd wele.
So is this felon gilty. There is no more to tell'.

(3293–306)

The knife becomes an accessory that marks a murderer; not
because it is a true sign of a homicide but because the stories that
are told about it make it become one. The knife is told between
several stories: it is a knife coveted by the Steward; a knife that
belonged to Macaign's father; a knife that the cutler made; a knife
that Beryn carries, and a knife whose stories told by Macaign and
the cutler are verified as truth by the burgesses in court (3307–10).
Beryn is made into a murderer in the eyes of the court because he
carries an implement on his person that can be used to tell the story
of his past actions and his moral condition.

The interplay between an accessory, the body that carries it and
the stories told about them characterises not only this individual
episode but the process through which fictional characters and their
readers recognise the persons who play out the action. It becomes
hard to tell who someone really is because the signs of their appearance and the narratives attached to them are unverifiable. Here is
how Macaign is introduced into the story as he approaches Beryn:

... he hym wold engyne, as he had purpensed,
And had araid hym sotillich as man of contemplacioun,
In a mantell with the lyste, with fals dissimilacioune,
And a staff in his hond, as thouh he febill were.

(2214–17)

As a fictional character in the story, Beryn can see only what is on outward show, and measure Macaign's words against the body he sees in front of him. For a reader of the English narrative, the signs of dissimulation in his appearance are clear: 'engyne', 'sottilich' and 'fals' and the triple counterfeiting similes. But for a reader who is familiar with both French and English versions of the tale, the signs are not so clear. Between the French and English stories, and between Beryn's perspective and a reader's, Macaign's body becomes an intercontinental puzzle. This is Macaign as he is told in French: 'Ainsi que Berinus se dementoit et estoit en celle destresse, uns escachiers la seurvint, qui avoit nom Martains' (*Bérinus* I.51).[35] Martains/Macaign is an 'escachiers': one who is lame, and who needs support to be able to walk. The narrative focalisation in the French story, however, gives no indication of his dissimulation, and his crutches are told only implicitly. Macaign, however, holds a staff in his hand 'as thogh he febill were'. Macaign's body exists between versions of a story in two different languages and between competing narrative perspectives. And it is the presence of the staff that marks him out as if he were infirm that is the sticking point. Just as the knife in the episode orchestrated by Macaign can be made to yield up different narratives about the body that carries it, so too the staff that Macaign/Martains does and does not appear to carry. Produced from a tissue of tales, a knife can make out that an innocent man is a murderer. Transacted between narratives of the 'same' story, a lame man's staff can be taken as the sign of a man who is hale and hearty.

The differences in detail and in perspective may seem trivial: after all Macaign still turns out to be a dissembler whichever version of the story we read. But there is more to this than meets the eye. Macaign is not the only character in the English story who uses a staff that has no direct correspondence in *Bérinus*. And he is not the only character whose body becomes signed by a staff that makes misleading statements about the condition of his body. In the French version of the story, Beryn meets a blind man who accuses Beryn of having stolen his eyes. The blind man is led by a nameless guide: 'Berinus ... encontra un aveugle que l'en menoit.'[36] There is no such person ('en') in the English story: the Blind Man is guided by a staff. Alarmed by yet another mysterious person who hails him, Beryn attempts to ride off. In order to stop him, the Blind Man 'cast[s] awey his staff' (2013) so that he can seize man and horse with both hands. It turns out, of course, that there is nothing lame or blind about this assailant, whatever his testimony in court. The staff is also an accessory that is the distinguishing mark of Geffrey, the mysterious lawyer who saves Beryn from the accusations against him in court. Geffrey's first appearance in the poem is seen through Beryn's eyes. He rushes in with a stilt under his knee and a crutch under his arm. His sticks identify him as a cripple:

> A crepill he saw comyng with grete spede and hast,
> Oppon a stilt under his kne bound wonder fast,
> And a crouch under his armes, with hondes al forskramed.

(2379–81)

He bears resemblance to his French avatar: 'un homme qui sembloit contrais, qui venoit vers lui a grant exploit sur deux escames' (*Bérinus* I.56). But at this point in the story he is only pretending to be a cripple. The French 'sembloit contrais' hints as much.[37] Later, when Geffrey reveals his 'true identity' to Beryn, he explains that he has adopted the disguise of a lame man to save him from the machinations of the people in the seaport:

> 'My lymes been both hole and sound; me nedeth stilt ne crouch'.
> He cast asyde hem both and lepe oppon an huche,
> And adown ageynes, and walked too and fro,
> Up and down within the shipp, and shewed his hondes tho,
> Strecching forth his fyngers in sight over al aboute,
> Without knot or knor or eny signe of goute.

(2509–14)[38]

In his English redaction, Geffrey reveals his 'real body' by the casting away of the props of his affliction and showing, for all to see, his fingers stretched out with no sign of disease. Geffrey's 'new' appearance is displayed as a sign of his authenticity. The sticks which identified him as a cripple, now abandoned, are a sign that he is 'substancial' (2518). Only there is nothing very substantial about Geffrey between the stories of his body: at the corresponding moment in *Bérinus* there is neither crutch nor staff for him to discard.[39] He acquires them in the English story only to throw them away. Having promised to help Beryn, Geffrey then disappears for a great chunk of the narrative. During his absence the Roman crew give up any hope of Geffrey's return. But then 'therewithall cam Geffrey on his stilt lepeing / And cried wonder fast by the water-syde' (2840–1). His arrival reassures Beryn but his men still grumble about betrayal to the point where Geffrey loses patience:

And for veray anger he threw into the see
Both stilt and eke his cruch that made were of tre.

(2853–4)

In *Bérinus* Geffrey has no crutches or stilts when returns, so he
has none to throw into the sea in his dramatic gesture of exaspera-
tion.[40] The *Beryn*-poet supplies Geffrey with sticks that he did not
find in *Bérinus*. He does so again when Geffrey appears in the
courtroom '[p]leyng with a yerd, he bare in his honde' (3415).[41]
Stephen Harper has argued that the 'yerd' marks Geffrey as a wise
professional fool in order to act as a foil to Beryn's immature errors
of judgement.[42] Persuasive though this is, it does not mark the end
of the story about sticks. In the court room, Geffrey plays with the
rod of a fool not because he *is* a fool but because sticks and staves
in the works of the *Beryn*-poet are unreliable signs of personhood.
In translation from the French story, there are several English
persons who have acquired a stick that marks them out as someone
other than who they seem. None of these sticks is a reliable sign
of the character that bears it, and they are thrown off with some
regularity. For Macaign, the Blind Man, and Geffrey, sticks are no
more guarantees of authentic identity than Macaign's knife.

Sticks are introduced into the English narrative on two further
occasions. Beryn twice berates himself for having been such a fool
as to have been beaten with his own staff. This is the first:

For ther nys beting half so sore with staff nether swerd
As man to be bete with his own yerd.

(1313–14)[43]

Twentieth-and twenty-first-century readers will recognise these
staffs as material that the *Beryn*-poet has added to the story only
if they have sliced between the pages of an unread edition of an
old Anglo-Norman romance. Almost certainly, however, they
will be familiar with the *Interlude* that frames *The Tale of Beryn*
in which staffs, as I argued in the first chapter, feature prominently. The Pardoner's staff is a pilgrim accessory and his phallus.
When wielded by the paramour the staff delivers a queer-bashing
and dubs a knight who murders Thomas Becket in Canterbury
Cathedral. The proverbial staff of Beryn's self-beating proverb
contains all those different narratives: a beating with a balstaff
that is a beating with a sword; a beating that is self-inflicted; and
a rod of punishment that is also a penis ('yerd'). The multiple
staffs in Beryn's proverb reprise the pilgrims' attempt to decipher
the staff in the window in Canterbury Cathedral. The body of

that stained glass figure is never revealed. Nor is Geffrey's in
the story of Beryn. Geffrey's is the body that is most frequently
and enigmatically invested with unfathomable sticks and staves,
and it is Geffrey's body that remains most conspicuously under
cover. When Gieffroy from *Bérinus* is translated into the English
story of Beryn he becomes invested with the riddling sticks not
from the foreign source but from the Canterbury prologue to the
Merchant's tale.

By the same token, when Geffrey becomes incorporated into the
Canterbury narrative of MS Northumberland 455, he also becomes
recognisable as someone else who is very familiar: someone who is
adept at inhabiting different persons, assuming their voices and
changing his physical appearance. Before Beryn's trial, when
Geffrey exchanges his cripple's staff for a fool's 'yerd', he appears
with his head and beard shaved, and speaks in riddles. Hanybald
the Provost is completely taken in by Geffrey's new appearance:

> Hanybald loked on Geffrey as he were amased,
> And beheld his contenaunce and howe he was i-rased,
> But evermore he thought that he was a fole,
> Naturell of kynde, and had noon other tool,
> As semed by his wordes and his visage both.
>
> (2933–7)

Geffrey is so good at playing a fool that nobody in the courtroom
recognises Geffrey as 'the cripple'. Everyone is taken in, and
'knewe hym noon other but a fole of kynde' (2965). But Geffrey's
words are just as unreliable as his sticks and his shaven head. When
he speaks on behalf of Beryn in court to defend him from the
charge of murdering Macaign's father, he does not alter the details
of Macaign's accusation: there is no more 'opyn pryve' (3795). But
Geffrey's narration makes these details carry different significance.
He narrates a 'prequel'. Seven years ago, on the Tuesday of Passion
Week in Rome, Beryn's father went early to church to perform his
devotions. Beryn also went to the same church and was surprised
not to find his father there. Quaking with fear, he went home and
rushed instantly to his father's chamber where he found him lying
stone dead, naked, on the straw of his bed; the bedding all ripped
away. 'Out! Alas,' quod Beryn, 'that ever I sawe this day!' (3816).
On hearing Beryn's cry, the servants rush in, and searching the
body 'fond this same knyff, the poynt right at his hert / Of Beryns
fader' (3823–4). Geffrey authenticates his account by saying that he
witnessed Beryn's reaction to this scene with his own eyes:

Then stan-dede I sawe hym fal doun to the ground
In sighte of the most part that beth with hym nowe here.

(3826–7)

The assembled court affirms Geffrey's account 'for sothe, as
Geffrey did hem lere' (3828). Geffrey is a supreme chameleon: in
appearance and in words. Through translating a version of his past
self to Rome, and narrating the vignette of Faunus's death as seen
through his own eyes, his narration carries conviction. In assuming the voice of Beryn, he takes his part. Geffrey is the ultimate
character witness because he is always somebody else.[44]

A reader of the story of Beryn, whether in English or French,
knows that Geffrey's narration probably cannot be true. But as
they never discover Geffrey's true identity, present or past, they
cannot be sure. Hanybald the provost asks him directly who he is:

... 'What is thy name, I prey?'
'Gilhochet', quod Geffrey, 'men cleped me yisterday'.
'And where weer thow i-bore' – 'I note, I make avowe',
Seyd Geffrey to this Hanybald; 'I axe that of yewe,
For I can tell no more but here I stond nowe'.

(3045–9)

'et lui demandoit comment il avoit a nom. Et Gieffroy lui respondi:
"Sire, on m'appelle Guinehochet. – Et ou fu tu nez? – Par ma foy,
sire, je ne sçay; or gardez comment je le vous diroye ..."'

(Bérinus I.79)

Between the English and French versions, Geffrey's autobiogra-
phy shifts. In both he claims ignorance of the place of his birth and
redirects the questions back to his questioner. The most faithful
statement Geffrey utters about his identity is 'here I stonde nowe'.
The derivation of his name is even more enigmatic. He is called
Guinehochet in French, and in English, Gilhochet is a name he
acquired only yesterday. Consistent with the slipperiness of names
throughout The Interlude and Beryn, Geffrey's assumed names
do not deliver a stable and prior sense of selfhood. Even Geffrey
appears to have no idea who he really is. Nor do readers. Up
until this point the dazzling impersonator has gone by the name
of Gieffroy/Geffrey. From this point onwards both narratives
alternate between calling him Gieffroy/Geffrey or Guinehochet/
Gilhochet. Depending on narrative perspective, the story's most
accomplished fabricator is between two different versions of his
name. 'Guine' probably means a wink, or a movement of the eye as
a sign of complicity. 'Hochet' is either a toy rattle given to children

or a derivation of a verb meaning to move or to shake. As a whole,
Guinehochet might mean a 'nod and a wink'. The most likely
explanation for 'Gil' is that it is related either in English or French
to 'guile', 'cunning' or contrivance.[45] Geffrey's alternative names
suggest a tricksy, dissembling body; a plaything, a winker.

So much for the moniker. What about Geffrey's proper name?
The simplest explanation is that it is a translation of his French one.
But that is not the end of the matter. It has not gone unnoticed that
Gilhochet shares a name with Geoffrey Chaucer. Stephanie Trigg
argues that Chaucer's name appears 'with no apparent irony in the
ancient cripple named "Geoffrey"'. Given that she argues that the
Beryn-poet shows no signs of authorial competition with Chaucer,
Trigg does not pursue the point. Andrew Higl comments that 'for
readers, his name may evoke the name Geoffrey Chaucer'.[46] It is
worth exploring further what the name 'Geoffrey' may mean for
readers of Chaucer; beginning with the Beryn-poet himself. It
is clear from the wealth of Chaucerian allusion in The Interlude
that the Beryn-poet was familiar with a range of Chaucer's works,
including The House of Fame in which the narrator is named
'Geffrey'. It is also clear that names interested the Beryn-poet.
Although he redacted only a third of Bérinus, he chose to retain a
massive 'digression' to start his narration: forty lines that list all the
names of the seven sages of Rome. It is not just a catalogue: he states
his desire to 'declare yewe the cause why they hir names bere' (793).
He also plays with names by introducing them when there is no
prompt in Bérinus. At line 2450, Geffrey appears as 'Sir Clekam';
a name whose sense is even more obscure than Gilhochet.[47] How
likely is it that this astute reader of Chaucer, with his interest in
onomastics, remained oblivious to the fact that the most compel-
lingly enigmatic character in his telling of the story of Beryn shared
Chaucer's first name?

That question must remain unanswered, but there is evidence
that other readers of Beryn made connections between the names
of its characters and authors who were not really present in the text.
In the synopsis of Bérinus that is included in Furnivall's edition,
Geffrey is described as 'a kind of Æsop in body and mind'.[48]
Chaucer is nearer the mark than Aesop. Geffrey is a superb storyteller and is well able to take other characters' parts and to speak in
their voices. He is able to inhabit the past lives of characters who
may or may not have any substance. He has no stable origin within
the narrative or without it. No one, not even Geffrey himself (or
Gilhochet?) seems to know who he is. His physical appearances do

not add up; accessories that ought to mark his physical state or his moral condition are misleading. And he exists between intercontinental versions of a story told by a merchant pilgrim coming out of Canterbury.

And Geoffrey Chaucer? Son of a wine merchant, superb taleteller, ventriloquist. A persona within *The Canterbury Tales* and beyond that adopts multiple identities.[49] His body and voice is as unstable in representation as his narrative perspectives. From the eagle's quip in *The House of Fame* 'thou art noyous for to carye' (574), he would appear to be portly. It is an impression found in other works.[50] Between *The Prioress's Tale* and *Sir Thopas* the Host tells a different story. Chaucer is a 'popet' (VII.701). While it has been suggested that this means a puppet – a reading that chimes engagingly with the similarly post-eventful translation of 'Guinhochet' as a hand-puppet clown – the *MED* suggests that 'popet' is a diminutive person, perhaps a doll.[51] Certainly a figure small enough in 'an arm t'enbrace' (VII.701). This 'popet' is an 'elvyssh' (703) shrinking violet fit to tell some 'deyntee thyng' (711).[52] Through the words of the Host, the pilgrim teller version of Chaucer assumes proportions at odds with those that suggest his narrative shape elsewhere. Well might the Host, speaking on behalf of many readers, ask '[w]hat man artow?' (695). To which the most truthful reply is probably the one that the narrator gives in *The House of Fame*, 'I wot myself best how y stonde' (1878). When the *Beryn*-poet expanded those lines on Gieffroy's inscrutable origins to include the statement 'I can tell no more but here I stond nowe' (3049) were Geoffrey's words in *The House of Fame* on his mind?[53]

Helen Cooper has observed that readers of Chaucer are faced with many Chaucers, a bewildering series of multiple representations.[54] For readers of Chaucer who encounter Geffrey in the works of the *Beryn*-poet, it is hard to banish the memory of Geoffrey Chaucer's multiply elusive performances. Geffrey Gilhochet becomes made up between the French and English stories of Beryn *and* memory of the textual incarnations of Geoffrey Chaucer. He takes shape for readers between all of these because of the place where he is encountered. Although Geffrey is derived from French, he is narrated in a story by a Canterbury pilgrim told after *The Canterbury Interlude* in the middle of a manuscript of *The Canterbury Tales*. Geffrey Gilhochet is materially embedded in Chaucerian Canterbury storytelling. As such, he becomes unmoored from his Anglo-Norman origins and becomes available to be read as a likeness of the elusive Geoffrey Chaucer. The author of *Bérinus* could not have been aware that his figure of Gieffroy could be taken for a version of Geoffrey Chaucer. Set in Canterbury, however, Gieffroy Guinehochet forms a striking impression of an author he could not have resembled in his native text. Because of that setting, borders between time and place cannot hold. Gieffroy crosses continents and literary cultures. His incorporation into a Chaucerian codex as Geffrey escapes him from the clutches of linear chronology.

Translated to a borderline Chaucerian text from the uncut leaves of an edition of an Anglo-Norman romance, Gieffroy becomes free to be remembered and anticipated as Geoffrey Chaucer. He takes place between materiality and epistemological memory like those pilgrims in *The Canterbury Interlude*. As I have argued, the persons one encounters in *The Interlude* depend on the place in which that text is found. So readers of Willard and Loomis will meet up with Hugh; readers of Bowers will renew acquaintance with Huberd; and readers of Furnivall fall into company with a Chaucer and an assembly of ladies traced from the memory of a window in Westminster Abbey. The bodies of the fictional characters in MS Northumberland 455 become available for transport in ways that cannot be contained by linear versions of textual chronology and literary history. They, like the body of Gormley's 'Transport' mould hanging in the crypt of Canterbury Cathedral, invite investment with the anticipated memories of bodies that are before and after, absent and present at the same time. Found in Canterbury, all these bodies slip through borders between time and place and between the made up boundaries of literary history.

## Notes

1   Peter Brown, 'Journey's End', argues that *The Interlude* is an alternative ending to *The Canterbury Tales*, as does Andrew Taylor, 'The Curious Eye and the Alternative Endings of *The Canterbury Tales*', in Paul Vincent Budra and Betty A. Schellenberg (eds), *Part Two: Reflections on the Sequel* (Toronto: University of Toronto Press, 1998), pp. 34–52. Bowers suggests a reintroduction of a pilgrimage that can be mapped out in time and place, 'Controversy and Criticism: Lydgate's *Thebes* and the Prologue to *Beryn*', *Chaucer Yearbook* 5 (1998), 91–115. More recently Andrew Higl has argued that the Northumberland manuscript represents an alternative traversal path

which explores new territories and borders of the story canon, *Playing the Canterbury Tales*, p. 76.

2 An illustration of such a procession in *Le Roman de Fauvel* shows men dressed as monks who moon at the spectators and hurl excrement at them. At the head of this scurrilous rout is Hellequin. All the figures are wearing masks, simulating otherworldly creatures; see Michael Camille, *Image on the Edge: The Margins of Medieval Art* (Cambridge, MA: Harvard University Press; Warwick: Reaktion, 1992), p. 145. The manuscript is Bibliothèque Nationale Paris MS fr.146, fol. 36b. The entry in *MED* does not quite capture this sense, see 'Hurlewain' (n.) 'A mischievous sprite or goblin; 'hurlewaines meine' (kin) [cp. ML familia Herlechini & OF maisniee Hellequin], pranksters, rascals'. The phrase appears in *Richard the Redeless*, to warn against duplicitous counsellors who are employed in defiance of 'kynde', or nature, I.177 in *The Piers Plowman Tradition*, ed. Helen Barr (London: J. M. Dent, 1993). The commentary note, p. 259, provides inadequate lexical commentary on the phrase. Later usage associates hurlewains with the fear aroused by their uncertain shapes and their propensity to lurk in border places, *OED* 'harlequin' n.1. The obsolete verb 'to harlequin' means to conjure away (*OED* 'harlequin' (v) 1).

3 A border whose permeability – and provisionality – is so prominent a feature of its make-up that in its form as a verb it has acquired the figurative sense to leave ways open. *OED* 'hedge' (v) 9.

4 John Searle argues that a Proper Name is not a shortcut to an object; nor is a Proper Name a description of an object. Neither sense nor reference according to logical definitions, a Proper Name is not a description, but a peg on which to hang descriptions. Use of a Proper Name evokes sets of characteristics thought appropriate to it; it is a description of secondary characteristics attached to an object that allow the formation of notions of primary being, John R. Searle, 'Proper Names', *Mind* 67 (1958), 166–73 (p. 172).

5 See Chapter 1 n.4 for studies of the scribe's work on other manuscripts, including the Helmingham manuscript of *The Canterbury Tales*.

6 The discussion that follows owes much to the essay by Random Cloud, 'The Very Names of the Persons: Editing and the Invention of Dramatick Character', in David Scott Kastan and Peter Stallybrass (eds), *Staging the Renaissance: Reinterpretations of Elizabethan and Jacobean Drama* (London and New York: Routledge, 1991), pp. 88–96.

7 On fol. 180a, for instance, we have the Pardoner at lines 40 and 43, and the Pardoner at lines 19 and 47. The Pardoner is capitalised more consistently than some of the other characters but while both Furnivall and Bowers consistently capitalise the Pardoner there is variation even with this major character.

8 Kit is introduced by name at line 65. In the MS, she is 'the Tapstere'

(fol. 180a/line 22) 'the tapster' (fol. 180b/99) and 'the Tapster' (fol. 181a/122). Bowers uses lower case for line 22 and capitals for lines 99 and 122. Furnivall has capitals for line 22 and 122 and lower case for line 99. Thereafter there is no consistency of usage in the MS or either of the editions.

9   In the MS the Paramour is capitalised fol. 186a/447; fol. 186a/457 but in lower case fol. 185b/427. Bowers has lower case for 447, 457 and 427. Furnivall capitalises Paramour in all these lines. As with 'tapster', there is variation throughout the MS and between the printed editions.

10   MS fol. 187a has 'the hosteler' at line 582 and 'Jak Hosteler' at 584. Bowers reproduces the practice of the MS; Furnivall does so at 582 but gives 'Jak [the] hostler' at line 584. Erratic naming extends also to animals. A proverb at line 78 tells how a singed cat retains a fear of fire. Capitalising 'Brennyd Cat' (fol. 181a) turns a proverbial moggy into a named species. The MS uses capitals fol. 181a, as does Furnivall. Bowers relegates the feline to lower case.

11   Cf. fol. 181a/137, 'Put forth the prelates, the person and his fere' and fol. 185b/427 'The tapster and hir Paramour & the hosteler of the hous'. Bowers retains the capitalisation of fol. 183b/267 'The Monke toke the Person then and the Grey Frere' but Furnivall puts all in lower case.

12   For ease of reference, variation in practice has been recorded alongside the punctuation habits of the manuscript in the preceding notes.

13   *MED* glosses 'Kit' as a lecherous woman, Kit(te (n.(2)b). Cited in support are *Piers Plowman* C.8.304: 'Ich haue ywedded a wyf wel wantowen of maners. / Ich may nat come for a kytte, so hue clyueþ on me'. Beryn refers to his father's maid-servant as a 'lewd Kit' (line 1011). Robert J. Sturges discusses Kit's role as a prostitute in 'The Pardoner in Canterbury: Class, Gender, and Urban Space in the *Prologue to the Tale of Beryn*', *College Literature* 33 (2006), 52–76, 60–2.

14   *MED*, 'Jankin (n.) Also janekin. A man's name; – also, applied contemptuously to priests. c1275 *LSSerm*. (Clg A.9) 56: And þeos prude maidenes, þat luuieþ Ianekin. (c1390) c1450 *As I went on Yole* (Sln 2593) p. 309: Knew I joly Jankyn be his mery ton ... Jankyn began the Offys on the Yol Day.'

15   Brown, 'Journey's End', p. 154.

16   Cloud, 'The Very Names', p. 93.

17   Furnivall argued that 'most of the characters are well kept up', see F. J. Furnivall and W. G. Stone (eds), *The Tale of Beryn with a Prologue of the Merry Adventure of the Pardoner with a Tapster at Canterbury* (EETS ES 105, 1909), p. vi, and E. J. Bashe argued that the *Interlude* characters were consistent with those of Chaucer, 'The Prologue of the *Tale of Beryn*', *Philological Quarterly* 12 (1933), 1–16.

18   Jean E. Jost, 'From Southwark's Tabard Inn to Canterbury's Cheker of the Hope: The UnChaucerian *Tale of Beryn*', *Fifteenth Century*

*Studies* 21 (1994), 133–48, p. 144. Glending Olson, 'The Misreadings of the *Beryn* Prologue', *Mediaevalia* 17 (1994 for 1991), 201–19, p. 206. For further comparative evaluations, see Stephan Kohl, 'Chaucer's Pilgrims in Fifteenth-Century Literature', *Fifteenth Century Studies* 7 (1983), 221–36; Bradley Darjes and Thomas Rendall, 'A Fabliau in the *Prologue to the Tale of Beryn*', *Mediaeval Studies* 47 (1985), 416–31; Frederick B. Jonassen, 'Cathedral, Inn and Pardoner in the *Prologue to the Tale of Beryn*', *Fifteenth Century Studies* 18 (1991), 109–32. Karen A. Winstead is an exception to these pejorative readings, arguing that the *Beryn*-poet was an astute reader of Chaucer's experiments in genre, especially fabliau and romance; 'The *Beryn*-Writer as a Reader of Chaucer', *Chaucer Review* 22 (1988), 225–33. In his *Chaucer's Pardoner* (2000), Sturges discusses the *Beryn* Pardoner in relation to his Chaucerian predecessor, pp. 153–6. In his 2006 article, 'The Pardoner in Canterbury', he attempts to separate them by mapping gender and space in *The Interlude* without nagging recourse to Chaucer. Even so, the presence of 'the Pardoner' in the title of the journal article is a sign that the Chaucer 'Pardoner' will not so easily be put aside.

19 Ben Parsons, '"For My Synne and for My Yong Delite": Chaucer, *The Tale of Beryn*, and the Problem of *Adolescentia*', *Modern Language Review* 103 (2008), 940–51; Elizabeth Allen argues that the *Interlude* delivers a humiliating punishment on the Pardoner by depriving him of narrative control, and literacy, and instead, raising the Host, and the overall narrator's voice to one of regulatory control, 'The Pardoner in the Dogges Boure: Early Reception of *The Canterbury Tales*', *Chaucer Review* 36 (2001), 91–127; Higl, *Playing the Canterbury Tales*, pp. 75–90.

20 Sturges, 'The Pardoner in Canterbury', p. 57.

21 Wai Chee Dimmock argues that meaning literally resounds through time because of the travel of noise, 'A Theory of Resonance', *PMLA* 112 (1997), 1060–71. It is a theory that is applicable also to voice. I revisit this argument in Chapter 6.

22 I doubt that Joke Dame's essay 'Unveiled Voices: Sexual Difference and the Castrato' in Philip Brett, Gary Thomas and Elizabeth Wood (eds), *Queering the Pitch* (London: Routledge, 1994), pp. 139–54, was written in anticipation of being cited in a discussion of *The Canterbury Interlude*. Not just for its play with name however, but for its insights on relationships between bodies and voices, it has been extremely useful.

23 *Medieval English Verse and Prose in Modernized Versions*, ed. Roger Sherman Loomis and Rudolph Willard (New York: Appleton-Century-Crofts, 1948).

24 Bowers, *Fifteenth Century Continuations*, p. 167.

25 Readers of MS Northumberland 455 will already have encountered *The Second Nun's Tale* because of the distinctive ordering of the tales

in that codex. Higl discusses this as part of his argument that the scribe joins in with the games of the text, *Playing the Canterbury Tales*, p. 76.

26  Bowers, *Fifteenth Century Continuations*, p. 170.

27  Several candidates have been proposed for authorship of the *Beryn* works. The colophon at the end of *The Tale of Beryn* reads 'Nomen Autoris presentis Cronica Rome / Et translatoris Filius ecclesie Tome'. For Furnivall this is conclusive proof that '[a] Canterbury monk wrote this tale', p. vii.120, a confidence shared also by Manly and Rickert: 'the most natural interpretation of "Filius ecclesie Thome" makes him a monk of Canterbury, and this is confirmed … by his intimate knowledge of the town and the doings of the pilgrims' (*The Text of the Canterbury Tales*, 8 vols, ed. John M. Manly and Edith Rickert (Chicago: University of Chicago Press, 1940), VIII. 392)). Other critics have been similarly persuaded, though with more circumspection: Brown, 'Journey's End', suggests that the author was a Canterbury canon because of his detailed knowledge of practices of the Cathedral, and the poem could have been written as part of the festivities for the Jubilee in 1420, p. 153. From the knowledge of legal practice in the *Tale of Beryn*, R. Firth Green, 'Legal Satire in *The Tale of Beryn*', *Studies in the Age of Chaucer* 11 (1989), 43–62, suggests that the author may have been one Thomas Astill, rector of Winchelsea.

28  Although the line is in square brackets, readers of Furnivall's edition have become so habituated to matter supplied thus that by this stage in the poem the editor's self-confessed tic of additions appear as a normative part of the story, 'unluckily, when editing it, I was affected for a time with the itch of padding out lines by needless little words in square brackets. The reader can easily leave them out in reading when he finds them unnecessary, or gratify his resentment at such impertinence by drawing a pen through them. But he will agree that the MS is often faulty in metre, and is not a correct copy of the original poem', p. xi.

29  I explore this further in Chapter 5.

30  Trigg argues that narratorial self-fashioning in *Beryn*, especially in contrast to Lydgate's reproduction of the Prologue pilgrims in his *Siege of Thebes* is worn very lightly, *Congenial Souls*, p. 91; pp. 103–4.

31  *The General Prologue* starts in April. By the time that the pilgrims are ready to depart, it is nearly May. Appropriately enough, the *Beryn*-poet places this observation in the mouth of the ever time-conscious Host, 'how sote this seson is entring into May!' (682).

32  The allusion to the 'dayseye' of 'ye day' (*LGW* G.184) is to a text that is self-consciously concerned with the act of writing poetry and with the memorialisation of objects and persons seen and unseen. As the object of the narrator's undying love (*LGW* F.57) that he lacks sufficient English to praise (F.66), the daisy in the *Legend Prologue* takes on a resemblance to the Lover's quest for the rose in *La Romaunt de*

*la Rose*. Described as 'of all floures floure' (*LGW* F.53 and F.185), the daisy tropes the lily that is the sign of the Virgin Mary. It is also the figure of Alceste who was turned into a daisy on account of her great goodness (F.511–12).

33  Thomas Speght included the work in his 1598 edition of *Chaucer's Collected Works*. It remained in the canon until Henry Bradshaw declared that it could not have been written by Chaucer on account of its rhyming practices. Skeat included the poem in the supplement to his *Chaucerian and Other Pieces* in 1897. Derek Pearsall discusses its textual history in his *The Floure and the Leaf* (Kalamazoo, MI: for TEAMS by Medieval Institute Publications, 1990), pp. 1–2.

34  F. J. Furnivall, *A temporary preface to the six-text edition of Chaucer's Canterbury Tales. Part 1, Attempting to show the true order of the tales, and the days and stages of the Pilgrimage, etc., etc.* (London: N. Trübner & Co., 1868). Prendergast *Chaucer's Dead Body*, draws attention to the statement, p. 93, but his concern is more with the movement of Chaucer's body between Canterbury and Westminster. Furnivall's transcription is equivalent to lines 344–50, 435–4, and 441–4 in Pearsall's edition.

35  *Bérinus: Roman en prose du XIVe siècle*, ed. Robert Bossuat (Paris: SATF, 1931). Boussat glosses 'escachiers' as 'a boiteux qui marche sure des bequilles'. *DMF* does not explicitly mention crutches. One who is 'eschacier' is one who is lame and relies on the support of an arm or a leg.

36  Once more, a staff is not explicitly mentioned in the French version: 'il lui fut dit que ce estoit le marchant des nefz; ... Berinus se cuida delivrer de lui, mais, voulist ou non, l'aveugle l'emmena, par l'aide de la gent qui y seurvindrent' (I.49). The Blind man is not led in *Beryn*.

37  Higl, *Playing the Canterbury Tales*, reads Geffrey's performance of disability as part of a covert sign-based game of mimicry, pp. 100–1.

38  Read in isolation from their place in a romance tale, these lines could be taken as the affirmation of a miracle of healing. The crippled, gnarled body, supported by stilt and crutch, is made 'hole'.

39  'Et quant ilz se furent entrebaisiez, Gieffroy se leva en son estant et dist: "Beau seigneur, or me regardez, car je sui sains et haitiez ne je ne sui mehaigniez ne de piez ne de mains, ne onques ne fu, mais ainsi l'ay je contrefait pour eschever peril de mort"' (*Bérinus* I.61).

40  'Ainsi qu'il estoient sur le point de eulx mettre au retour, Berinus se prist garde et vit venir Gieffroy grant aleüre, si s'esvigora un peu' (*Bérinus* I.72). Bérinus's men have no faith from how Gieffroy appears to them that he will not send them to their death; but not because he is a cripple, but because they take him for a conniving fool, '[c]hascuns disoit qu'il ne pouoit percevoir chose en lui par quoy il ne soit un fol et un engigneux qui les vouloit mettre a mort par son engin' (p. 73).

41  The equivalent text in *Bérinus* is I.90.

42  Stephen Harper, "'Pleying with a yerd": Folly and Madness in the
    *Prologue and Tale of Beryn*', *Studies in Philology* 101 (2004), 299–314.

43  The second instance is for 'I was nevir chastised; but nowe myne own
    yerd / Beteth me to sore, the strokes been to hard' (2324–5). See also
    line 1060. Harper, '"Pleying with a yerd"', notes how the fool's sticks
    have been introduced, but not those of Macaign and the Blind Man.

44  Geffrey also assumes the voices of other characters in his defence of
    Beryn; supplying backstories to the defendant's predicament in which
    he ventriloquises all the parts. See, for instance, the exchange of direct
    speech between Beryn and the Blind Man (3707–18). Sometimes
    Geffrey claims eye-witness accounts of these dramas; sometimes he
    excludes himself: 'althoughe I were nat there' (3443); 'when we were
    at see' (3481).

45  Bowers's suggestion, *Fifteenth Century Continuations*, p. 191, is not
    wholly accurate. He is right to suggest the connection between
    'hochet' for 'toy rattle', but 'guignol' for 'hand-puppet clown' is not
    attested in early French, nor do any other of the available etymons in
    *DMF* suggest this sense. I am grateful to Dr Helen Swift for her help
    with this.

46  Trigg, *Congenial Souls*, p. 88. Of the prologue [of *Beryn*], she writes,
    direct references to the Prologue are slight, and the poet makes no ref-
    erence to Chaucer, either by name or indirectly as the original author,
    p. 91. Higl, p. 109.

47  His name may derive from 'cliken' *MED* v. 'to chatter' and/or OF
    'cliquer' to clatter.

48  These are Vipan's notes, not Furnivall's, see p. 132. The instability of
    punctuated names characteristic of *The Interlude* extends also into the
    movement between script and print of *The Tale of Beryn*. One example
    must suffice. The Blind Man is consistently capitalised in Bowers's
    edition: lines 2011; 2013 (equivalent to fol. 207a where there are no
    capitals). The same practice extends to lines 2025; 2041 (fol. 207b)
    and 2074; 2080 (fol. 208a). The seaport that is nameless in English
    is called 'Blandie' in *Bérinus*. It has the sense of 'flatter, dissimulate'.
    Furnivall's translation as 'Falsetown' (see p. 120) is too stark; it fails
    to capture the sense of deception. Furnivall's naming results from his
    reading of line 4013, 'saff the burgeyses of the town, of falshede that
    were rote'. Although he places a comma mid-line, Furnivall equates
    'falshede' with the town, rather than the burgesses who were rooted
    in falsehood. The name 'Falsetown' has been adopted by critics, e.g.
    Harper, '"Pleying with a yerd"', p. 305.

49  Criticism of Chaucer's narrative personae is legion. A recent investiga-
    tion into its history can be found in Geoffrey W. Gust, *Constructing
    Chaucer* (New York: Palgrave Macmillan, 2009). David Lawton
    argues that a distinguishing feature of Chaucer's personae and his use
    of polyvocality is its collapse of the distinction between self-projection

and self-narration, *Chaucer's Narrators* (Cambridge: Brewer, 1985), p. xiv. Foundational in the work of separating Chaucer the man from Chaucer his many personae is C. David Benson, who argues against the view that a consistent persona of Chaucer emerges from his works. Instead, the poet uses his 'flexible but disembodied voice' to produce a series of narrative perspectives that cannot add up to one distinct person, see *Chaucer's Drama of Style: Poetic Variety and Contrast in The Canterbury Tales* (Chapel Hill: University of North Carolina Press, 1986), pp. 26–7, and 'Their Telling Difference: Chaucer the Pilgrim and His Two Contrasting Tales', *Chaucer Review* 18 (1983), 61–77, p. 65.

50  He is amongst those who are 'hoor and round of shap' in *L'Envoy de Chaucer a Scogan* (27), and suggests that he is 'fat' in *Merciless Beaute* (27).

51  Ann Haskell suggests the reading 'puppet' in '*Sir Thopas*: The Puppet's Puppet', *Chaucer Review* 9 (1975), 253–9. Bowers's note, p. 191, reprises the suggestion from Mary E. Mulqueen Tamanini, *The Tale of Beryn: An Edition with Introduction, Notes and Glossary* (PhD Dissertation, New York, 1969), p. 309, that Guinehochet is formed from 'guignol' for 'hand-puppet clown' and 'hochet' for toy rattle. *DMF* does not substantiate the suggestion. 'Guignol' is unattested, though it is in use in later French.

52  Gust discusses the critical reception of this exchange, *Constructing Chaucer*, pp. 159–98. He suggests that even the most recent discussion has flinched from grasping the nettle of assigning a queer identity to this figure with confidence. The idealisation of Father Chaucer has a long and critically inhibiting legacy, pp. 192–8.

53  A few lines later, the narrator also utters the line '[t]he cause why I stoned here'. Verbal resonance of both these lines is not impossible in Geffrey's words in *Beryn*.

54  Helen Cooper, 'Chaucerian Representation' in Robert G. Benson and Susan J. Ridyard (eds), *New Readings of Chaucer's Poetry* (Cambridge: Brewer, 2003), pp. 7–29 (p. 20).

# 3
# Chaucer's hands

When the Pardoner boasts of his preaching prowess in the Prologue
to his tale, he explicitly draws attention to his hands:

> Myne handes and my tonge goon so yerne
> That it is joye to se my bisynesse.

(VI.398–9)

But who can tell what 'bisynesse' these busy hands sign: rhetorical
eloquence, inspirational moral teaching, or fraudulent extortion?
Who sees these hands, and when? Although he talks in the
present tense, at this moment, the Pardoner's hands are suspended
between his former congregations, the Canterbury pilgrims, and
future audiences. Do his present pilgrims see a show of the
Pardoner's preaching hands, or do they hear a verbal account of
their previous performances? How do future audiences form an
acquaintance with these hands? Do they hear about them, or do
they read them? Are they also able to see them in visual form? What
the Pardoner's hands mean depends on the medium in which they
are encountered, and when and where that encounter takes place.[1]

This chapter explores the transport of hands in Chaucer's
*Canterbury Tales*. The Pardoner's self-disclosure shows how
Chaucer's written hands refuse accommodation in one taxonomic
place or time. As I show in the first section of this chapter, the hand
has no settled place in medieval culture; it exceeds the disciplines
of the encyclopaedists, moralists and theologians who attempt to
contain it. The narratives of *The Canterbury Tales* capitalise on that
discursive transgression to dramatise hands that work in ostensibly
incompatible ways at one and the same time. When the verbal
hands of the Canterbury narratives are translated into visual media
their discursive waywardness is intensified. Already uncontainable
within boundaries of medieval categorisation, Chaucer's hands
become intermediated; they become composite between word

and image.[2] When the verbal pilgrims become seen, they acquire hands, whether or not their written incarnation speaks of them. As a consequence, the Canterbury pilgrims become unmoored. Their intermediated hands confect pilgrims without finite source in narrative time and place.

Told visually, these hands produce characters that are beside confounded versions of themselves. They are assembled through textual description not just in one place but from diverse fragments. They become seen through the words that they use to describe themselves and from the words that other pilgrims say about them. They also acquire attributes of other fictional characters, either those that they narrate or those in stories told by their companions. The figure that is most densely intermediated in this assembly is that of Chaucer himself. In the Ellesmere manuscript, his left hand scripts him into a performance of visual and textual roles that destabilises ontological classification. Based on a version of 'himself' that may or may not be extant, his left hand embodies ideas, memories, and practices associated with 'Chaucer' which dislodge him from his textual location while, at the same time, confirming him in his place in memorial literary history.

## Medieval hands

The most powerful hand in the Middle Ages was the Hand of God: one that 'hath measured the waters in the hollow of his hand, and weighed the heavens with his palm; who hath poised with three fingers the bulk of the earth' (Isaiah 40:12). No human hand is a match. In medieval art God's hand is a rich iconographic symbol of his actions and his voice: his power to shape and to intervene in the works of humankind. As Blanch and Wasserman have shown, the works of the *Gawain*-poet draw heavily on this tradition to contrast the might of God's handiwork with the forlornness of human endeavour.[3] This structural contrast also informs the work of Gower's *Confessio Amantis*. While the hand of Amans, the narrator, is unable to reach up to the heavens and set the world in balance and in evenness (1.1–3), the 'almighty' hand of God is capable of omniscient miracle that changes the face of the earth and shapes the lives of human beings.[4] One of the most powerful evocations of God's hand is crafted in *Piers Plowman* when the Samaritan explains the indissolubility of the three persons of the Trinity through an extended comparison of the interdependence of fingers, palm and fist (B.17.139).[5]

As we shall see, God's hand is not granted such imperious weight in *The Canterbury Tales*. Chaucer's hands are more relentlessly human. They embody the tensions and uncertainties that characterise medieval thinking about the work of the hand. Depending on the discourse that produced it, the human hand was either a supreme instrument for knowledge and civilised behaviour or a means of damnation. Writers on physiology and rhetoric profile the hand as an agent of knowledge and eloquence. Writers of penitential and pastoral texts stress that hands are agents of sin. The work of the human hand is cleft between discourses whose values are at odds. Always between dominant traditions of thought, the human hand escapes taxonomic closure. The history of the medieval hand has yet to be written. Prior to an examination of its work in *The Canterbury Tales*, I present here a short précis of how the hand takes shape in medieval thinking.

So important was the hand to the physiologist Galen that in his treatise on human body parts he placed it first. For Galen, the work of the human hand epitomises the work of civilisation:

> With these hands of his, a man weaves himself a cloak and fashions hunting nets, fish nets and traps and fine meshed bird-nets so that he is lord not only of animals upon the earth, but of those in the sea and the air also. Such is the hand of man as an instrument of defence. But being also a peaceful and social animal, man also writes laws for himself, makes altars to the gods, builds ships, makes flutes, lyres, knives, fire tongs and all the other instruments of the arts.[6]

Quoting Aristotle, Galen remarks that 'the soul is like the hand, for the hand is the instrument of instruments'.[7] The hand is excellently constructed and all its joints perfectly articulated to perform its work. Its wonders contrast with the hand of animals. An ape's hand, for instance, lacks the dexterity of a human's because the thumb is separated only slightly from the forefinger: 'a ridiculous body bestowed by nature on an animal with a ridiculous soul' (p. 108).[8]

Trevisa's translation of the *De Proprietatibus Rerum* by Bartholomaeus Anglicus made such scientific or encyclopaedic lore readily available in the 1380s. Indebted throughout to the etymologies of Isidore of Seville, Bartholomaeus begins his chapter on hands thus: 'the hond hatte *manus* in latyn, for he is þe ȝifte of al þe body, so seiþ Isider, for þe hond serueþ þe mouþe of mete ande dooþ alle werkes and disposiþ'.[9] The hand creates writing and painting and 'surete of pes is iȝeue wiþ þe riȝt hond, and he is witnes of fey, trist and sauacioun' (p. 222). The hand is a great help and ornament of the body and is the principal instrument of touching and feeling. Like Galen, Bartholomaeus quotes Aristotle on the human hand as an instrument of the soul. He celebrates the wonderful articulation of its many parts. The nails protect the fingers, and there is nothing in the body to match the way that the ends of the fingertips discern and judge so deftly between things that are 'itouchid and igropid' (p. 226).

With its dexterity of movement, the hand is supremely articulated to make significant gesture. For writers on rhetoric, hand gestures were markers of expressiveness that gave greater articulation to an orator's message. Quintilian waxes eloquently on the virtues of hands in effecting the fifth part of rhetoric, namely delivery:

> As for the hands, without which all action [i.e. Delivery] would be crippled and enfeebled, it is scarcely possible to describe the variety of their motions since they are almost as expressive as words. For other portions of the body merely help the speaker, whereas the hands may be almost said to speak. Do we not use them to demand, promise, summon, dismiss, threaten, supplicate, express aversion, or fear, question or deny? Do we not employ them to indicate joy, sorrow, hesitation, confession, penitence, measure quantity, number and time? Have they not power to excite and prohibit, to express approval, wonder or shame? Do they not take the place of adverbs and pronouns when we point at places and things? In fact, though the peoples and nations of the world speak a multitude of tongues, they share in common the universal language of the hands.[10]

For Quintilian, as for Augustine, movements of the hands are 'visible words'.[11]

Hands are also co-opted into political figuration. In the image of the body politic as articulated by St Paul, hands work in harmony with different parts of the body: '[a]nd the eye cannot say to the hand: I need not thy help; nor again the head to the feet: I have no need of you. Yea, much more those that seem to be the more feeble members of the body, are more necessary' (1 Corinthians 12:21–3). This trope is used in a range of Middle English writings. One of its fullest expositions is *Digby* Poem 15 where the concluding stanzas stress the work of the hands within a social – and spiritual – body:

And hed were fro þe body stad,
Noþer partye were set at nouȝt;
And body wiþoute armes sprad,
Were armes wiþoute handis ouȝt;
Ne handis, but þey fyngres had,

Wiþoute fingere what were wrouȝt?
Þes lymes makeþ hed ful glad –
And al þe body, and it be souȝt.

(129–36)[12]

Praiseworthy though hands be in this individual poem, the series
as a whole, penitentially inflected, warns that the work of human
hands endangers the spiritual health of the soul.[13] The last stanza of
the final poem warns that human beings will have to account before
God on Doomsday for every misdeed, no matter how small: '[e]ch
touche and mouynge with hys honde' (24/411). However laudable
the work of the hand in scientific writings, within the penitential
tradition of Christian eschatology it is marked as an agent of sin
that can condemn the soul to everlasting perdition.[14]

In accounts of the seven deadly sins, the work of the hand comes
to the fore. Throughout Gower's *Confessio Amantis*, the human
hand is often used as a metonym for action in the sense of 'deed'.
It performs atrocious examples of the seven capital sins. Hands are
agents of lechery,[15] hands commit acts of terrible violence[16] and
a person's *own* hand is responsible for monstrous acts of human
behaviour.[17] Pre-eminently, the hand is an instrument of avarice.
With its ability to grasp and to hold tight, what for Galen was a
miracle of body mechanics becomes an icon of sin.[18] Avarice never
lets gold out of his hand (5.26), and, in the story of Midas's cupidity
for gold, the king lays his hand on all that he desires to possess
(5.268) and 'in his hond al gold it is' (5.276). When he tries to wash
his hand it turns to gold (5.306). Gaius Fabricius is an antitype of
Midas: he takes some gold into his hand, but, when he tests it with
all his five senses, he abjures it (7.2792) and throws 'the gold out
of his hond anon' (7.2813).[19] Much of the force of this exemplary
action comes from Gower's reversal of familiar iconography.[20]

Christian penitential discourse attempts to reform the human
hand. To do so, it has to negotiate a fundamental conflict in valuing
its work. As a supreme agent of sense perception, the hand is
invaluable in navigating a person through the material world. But
attachment to that worldliness leads it into sin. Moralists argue
that the proper goal of sense perception is to overcome worldly
limitation and search for a deeper truth that lies beyond.[21] In
*The Book of Vices and Virtues*, the writer explains that, just as God
made humankind with a body and soul, so he has given him two
kinds of 'delitable good' to draw man's heart to him. One comes
from the five senses of the body: conduits through which the

'delitable good' of the world are experienced. But the delights that are perceived through the senses are like a dewdrop compared to the well of delight that is the soul's love of God. When a man sees a drop of dew from afar, it is as bright as a precious stone. But when he comes up to that dewdrop to take it in his hand, it falls to the ground and vanishes.[22]

Even within such reformatory discourse, however, the hand causes trouble. It upsets the neat mathematics of the schema of the five senses of the human body. At first sight, the hand appears a tailor-made metonymy for the sense of touch.[23] The other four senses, however, are each neatly governed by one organ: eye, ear, nose and mouth. The hand does not have a monopoly on the sense of touch; touch is a sensation performed by the whole body, including the skin.[24] In John Mirk's *Instructions for Parish Priests*, for instance, touch is listed as the last of the five senses, but the hand is not mentioned:

> Hast þou I-towched folyly
> Þat þy membrus were styred by,
> Wommones flesch or þyn owne?[25]

There's a further problem. In writing about the reformation of sin, hands are required to perform the work. In Robert Brunne's translation of *Handlyng Synne* not only is the hand absent as an efficient cause of wrong-doing, but the author's self-reflexive exposition on the words of his title extols the hand's constructive pastoral work, '"Manuel" ys handlyng with honde; / "Pecches" ys synne y vnderstonde' (83–4).[26] The hand as part-agent of the sense of touch may lead humankind astray, but, without hands, humankind cannot perform the work of pastoral instruction. As I shall discuss, Chaucer can be seen explicitly to draw on this conundrum in *The Summoner's Tale*, and the tale of the Canon's Yeoman.

Hands that touch may do so in ways that are laudable or damnable. The difference depends on whether hands are clean or dirty, literally and morally. The efficacy of the sacraments depends on whether the hands of the priest are spotless or soiled. Priests, says the author of *Vices and Virtues*, should bless and cleanse others, but warns, in the words of St Gregory, 'that the hand that is foul and unclean may not "do away þe vnclennesse of anoþer"' (p. 263/15–17).[27] One of the reasons why the parable of the wedding guest in *Cleanness* is so disconcerting is that the unwashed hands of a ragged labourer are equated with the unclean soul of a human being unfit to enter heaven.[28] As courtesy books make clear, clean hands are essential for serving a lord and handling food. Hands must not soil towels or leave stains on a cup; fingers must be wiped. At table, the actions of the hands are keenly policed; they must not play with the cutlery, eat bread without a knife, pick ears or nostrils, and fingers must not be put in the food dishes. Clothing and skin must not be scratched. To avoid disaster, one is advised to 'close þyn honde yn þy feste / And kepe þe welle from hadde-y-wyste'.[29]

Hands are also crucial in other public transactions; once more, for good, or for ill. The pledging of truth to another is sealed by the shaking of hands, or the placing of one hand in that of another. As the body politic trope of St Paul makes clear, hands ought to bring people together in community. Public contracts are made visible by the show of hands or by trothplight. Oaths are made visible by the placing of hand(s) on a book.[30] These outward shows of truth, however, may be deceptive. In *Confessio*, those who lay their hands upon a book to declare their fidelity have their fraudulence exposed. A lover's treachery is made plain, and the hand of God smites dead a dissembling knight.[31] As agents of touch, hands negotiate the borders between one person and another. They can do so with violation or with intimacy. When excessive pawing and holding trespass into another person's space, the hand becomes an agent of covetousness.[32] Gentle touch, however, forges tenderness between lovers and between parents and their children.[33]

It is, perhaps, because the hand is such a powerful agent, so indispensable to human action, that its value is so troublesome to calibrate. Trouble for taxonomists, however, creates opportunity for literary writers. Before turning to Chaucer's manipulation of the unruly discursiveness of the hand, in part as a prefatory contrast to that work, I want to conclude this section with some of the most hauntingly sublime moments in all Middle English literature. In each, the touch of a hand, a hand that could be capable of the most terrible carnage and chaos, produces devastatingly moving moments of transformation. In *Piers Plowman*, Christ invites the doubting Thomas to search the wound in his side to prove the truth of the resurrection:

> And toke Thomas by the hand and tauȝte hym to grope,
> And feele wiþ hise fyngres his flesshliche herte.

> (B.19.170–1)

His divine hand guides Thomas to feel his heart. The shocking alliterative tactility of human fingertips on the *flesh* of Christ's

heart is searing. Langland's poetry creates affective demonstration
of how God reaches out to humankind and directs fallen human
sense to know his mystery and his love. The motif of a hand inside
a wound courses throughout Malory's *Morte D'Arthure*. It reaches
its climax in the story of the healing of Sir Urry. From the long
list of knights who search Urry's wounds, Lancelot alone is able to
quicken them to heal: '[a]nd than laste of all he searched hys honde,
and anone hit fayre healed'. The hands of two knights, joined
neither in combat nor in pledge, closes the stubbornly open wound
that is so potent a metonym for the bleeding fracture of the whole
Round Table. Fleetingly. 'And Lancelete wepte, as he had bene a
chylde that had bene betyn.'[34]

And, in a final moment of paradox, it is the hand of Eros that
releases Amans from his desperate infatuation at the close of
*Confessio Amantis*. Touch prevails where sight is unavailable. The
hand of blind Cupid heals like that of a surgeon confessor:

> This blinde god which mai noght se,
> Hath groped til that he me fond;
> And as he pitte forth his hond
> Upon my body, wher I lay,
> Me thoghte a fyri Launcegay,
> Which whilom thurgh myn hert he caste,
> He pulleth oute, and also faste
> As this was do, Cupide nam
> His weie, I not where he becam.

> (8.2794–802)

In a work so supremely aware of how the hand is an agent of sin and
misguided sense, Cupid's groping touch achieves what Genius's
words fail to accomplish. Amans's affect is redirected to rationality:
aged lover is converted to the moral poet John Gower. The hand
of Cupid transforms the whole dream landscape and cauterises the
erotic work of the human heart. Cupid vanishes, along with the
whole company of lovers. With the fiery dart removed, the cupi-
dinous agony of desire is exchanged for a pair of penitential beads
'[p]or reposer' (8.2907).

## Verbal hands in *The Canterbury Tales*

Hands are mentioned explicitly hundreds of times in *The Canterbury
Tales*. Paradox abounds, but in a very different key from the narratives of Langland, Malory and Gower. The hand of God gets
short shrift. Outside of the Parson's sermon and the tale of *Melibee*,

it features only incidentally.[35] The most memorable hands in
*The Parson's Tale* are those of the devil: the fingers of one hand tell
the five species of gluttony, the fingers of the other five species of
lechery.[36] Attention to the moral dangers of the hand as a hazard-
ous portal for the sense of touch is fitful and sporadic across the
work as a whole.[37] Incidental references to the hand produce a
profile of its work that does not look wholly dissimilar to its deeds
in the works of Chaucer's contemporaries.[38] But when hands
feature in extended narrative an important difference emerges.
They transgress the boundaries of the normative discourses that
produce them. As a consequence, Chaucer's hands are signs of
narrative incontinence, morally and generically.

While the Monk intones some short episodes that feature
murderous hands in terms not dissimilar from those of *Confessio
Amantis*,[39] in two narratives which are told also by Gower – the
story of the crow in *The Manciple's Tale* and the story of Virginia
in *The Physician's Tale* – Chaucer's narration has a distinctive
narrative edge. The hand of vice becomes a prop in self-justifying
exercises of moral virtue. After Phoebus kills his wife in anger, he
speaks like the writer of a penitential treatise as he excoriates his
hand's cruel impetuosity '[o] rakel hand, to doon so foule amys'
(IX.278). In transferring culpability as if the hand were its own
agent, Phoebus squirms out of moral responsibility for his own
action by treating the hand as a detachable moral exemplum.
When Virginius justifies the murder of his daughter, '[m]y pitous
hand moot smyten of thyn heed' (VI.226), he not only laments the
agency of his own hand over which he has no control but turns it
into an instrument of compassion and mercy ('pitous'). A hand
that acts on virtuous principles kills a vulnerable child. Phoebus
and Virginius behave like the morally disordered Cambises in one
of the friar's preaching exempla in *The Summoner's Tale*. To prove
that wine never deprives him of his sight, nor his power of eye and
hand, the King of Persia takes a bow and shoots his own child:
'[n]ow', he asks his assembled company, do you question whether
I have a 'siker hand or noon?' (III.2069). While both Chaucer
and Gower tell of murderous hands, characters in *The Canterbury
Tales* hold up the signs of their guilt in defiant self-righteous justification. Their behaviour resembles that of the Pardoner, with
whose dissimulating show of preaching hands this chapter began.
The Pardoner's tale continues to confound moral teaching and vice
in its telling of hands. Swearing fealty and comradeship, the three
rioters claim '[l]at ech of us holde up his hand til oother / And ech

of us bicomen otheres brother' (VI.697–8). This is the Chaucerian version of Langland's hand of God. In a parody of the heresy that two members of the Trinity murdered the other, the result of the revellers' handpledge is covert mutual slaughter. Their greed for gold and individual profit overtakes any collective sense of fellowship. Having procured the means to murder his fellows, the youngest reveller 'hath in his hond yhent / This poysoun in a box, and sith he ran' (VI.868–9). The hand that signs a third of the Holy Trinity as a poisoner of his fellows is well-matched to the 'bisynesse' of the Pardoner's own. When he preaches, as he tells us himself, the Pardoner spits out his 'venym under hewe / Of hoolynesse' (VI.421–2).

Holy and heinous hands keep contiguous company in *The Canterbury Tales. The Canon's Yeoman's Tale* could well be titled 'the tale of two hands'. The Yeoman narrates the mutual greed of a canon and a priest as they grope after unholy alchemical knowledge and material reward. By laying a series of substitute materials in the fire to suggest that base metals have been transformed into finer, the canon's sleights of hand gull the greedy priest. The first decoy is a beechwood charcoal. Because the canon has drilled a hole in it, the iron can run out. He distracts the priest from his business of blowing on the flames and places the device carefully in the fire, '[a]nd in his hand he baar it pryvely' (VIII.1178). He then has another contrivance 'in his hand' (VIII.1264), a hollow stick which replays the same trick with copper. When the priest buys more of the same metal, the canon takes it into his hand to weigh it out (VIII.1297), and puts his own hand into the fire to remove the copper rod and replace it with one made of silver (VIII.1315).

Throughout the story, the priest is persuaded that serial transformations of matter are the work of his own hands. The canon takes out a crucible and tells the priest to '[t]aak in thyn hand, and put thyself therinne / Of this quyksilver an ounce, and heer bigynne, / In name of Crist, to wexe a philosofre' (VIII.1120–2). As a token of the love which the canon bears to the priest, or so he tells him, he bids that 'thyne owene handes two / Shul werche al thyng which that shal heer be do' (VIII.1154–5). After the canon has replaced the copper in the fire with a silver ingot, he announces excitedly to the priest '[l]oke what ther is; put in thyn hand and grope, / Thow fynde shalt ther silver, as I hope. / What, devel of helle, shold it elles be?' (VIII.1236–8). The priest does put in his 'hand' (VIII.1240) and, to his intense delight, expecting copper, he picks up silver. 'Grope' is the charged word here. What a

priest is meant to 'grope' is not the coals of an alchemist's fire but
the conscience of one of his parishioners. John Mirk's pastoral
manual advises the priest confessor to make sure that he has fully
examined his penitent's conscience in order to cleanse his soul,
'[a]nd when he seyþ "I con no more" / Freyne hym þus & grope
his sore' (p. 28/911–12). In *The Canon's Yeoman's Tale*, the priest
gropes in a fire associated with devils in hell. In this tale of serial
manual temptation, the canon repeats 'putte in youre hand and
looketh what is ther' (VIII.1329). Christ's invitation to Thomas
to put his hand into his side reveals the mystery of the resurrection; the canon's invitations to the priest to put his hand in the fire
implicate two clerics in a fiendish quest for gold. Greed and self-
interest drive one member of the church to outwit another. The
canon (a chantry priest who has left his parish to sing masses for
the departed dead) successfully cheats a parish priest out of £40.
The rivalry between priests who stay within their parishes to tend
their flocks and those who run away to more mobile and lucrative employments is well known from the details of the portrait
of the Parson in *The General Prologue* (I.509–10). In the *Canon's
Yeoman's Tale*, the parish priest chooses to grope around for gold
in damnable practice rather than tend the spiritual good of his
parishioners.

    *The Summoner's Tale* also dramatises the work of a clerical
hand more invested in greed than in spiritual health. The rivalry
between the Summoner and the Friar is articulated, in part, by
the duplicitous handpledges of the characters in their respective
tales. In *The Friar's Tale*, the summoner makes a pledge with
the 'yeoman', '"by my feith!" / Everych in ootheres hand his
trouthe leith' (III.1403–4). Sign of individualistic opportun-
ism and profit-making, the sworn handclasp of fealty results in
the summoner's fetching up as a possession of the devil in hell.
Thomas, in *The Summoner's Tale*, agrees to give the friar a gift
on condition that he shares it equally with all the brothers in his
convent. '"I swere it", quod this frere, "by my feith!" / And there-
withal his hand in his he leith, / "Lo heer my feith; in me shal be
no lak"' (III.2137–9). The wording of handpledge between the
two tales chimes their protagonists into verbal harmony that scores
an almost pathological desire for 'quiting'. The Summoner's friar
does keep his word, but not in the way that he foresees.

    The friar criticises those 'curatz' who are negligent and slow
'[t]o grope tendrely a conscience / In shrift' (III.1817–18), but
his own performance of 'confession' brings his comeuppance.

In extracting his gift from Thomas, the friar embarks on a pastoral manual quite unlike any other in Middle English literature:

'Now thanne, put in thyn hand doun by my bak,'
Seyde this man, 'and grope wel bihynde.
Bynethe my buttok there shaltow fynde
A thyng that I have hyd in pryvetee'.
'A!' thoghte this frere, ''That shal go with me!'
And doun his hand he launcheth to the clifte
In hope to fynde there a yifte.
And whan this sike man felt this frere
Aboute his tuwel grope there and heere,
Amydde his hand he leet the frere a fart;
Ther nys no capul, drawynge in a cart,
That myghte have lete a fart of swich a soun.

(III.2140–51)

Mentioned explicitly three times in this short passage, the friar's hand is a scatological mime of the sacrament of penance.[40] Taught by a layman, the friar gropes for what Thomas has stored in private: not some secret sin but a fart whose sound is a parody of the full confession that a priest should exact from a hoarding penitent. Expecting a gift, which in itself violates penitence and satisfaction, the friar receives rather more than he bargained for. Rummaging in the buttocks of another man, his hand brings about a release that is very different in kind and in temper from Cupid's groping of Amans, or Lancelot's searching of the wounds of Sir Urry. With scatological finesse, the spiritually cleansing hand of a 'confessor' fumbles around in another man's arse. Groping here and there, the contiguity of hand and anus conflates oral shrift with hapless sodomy. Arse-fondling and the sacrament of confession cannot be told apart. Thomas's manual instructions cause the professional confessor to commit a damnable act. The comedic one-upmanship dramatises carnal behaviour considered to be so dangerous that it was a sin passed over always in silence in pastoral handbooks.[41] Chaucer's narrative of the groping hand is more than a satirical swipe against lucrative fraternal penetrations into regular church practices. The comparison of the sound of Thomas's confessional arse to the fart of a carthorse blasts open the church's concealment of sexual practices it found too damnably attractive to spell out explicitly in pastoralia. While a confessor's groping ought to bring about spiritual cleansing through penitential speech, here, the friar's anal searching pantomimes congress of execrable carnality about which the church had opted for collusive silence.[42]

Apart from Constance receiving baptism from the hands of a priest (*Man of Law*, II.377), clerical hands in the *Tales* are consistently carnal and avaricious. The Pardoner's genitalia have received more extensive treatment than his hands, but hands are crucially implicated in what his genitalia come to represent. As I discussed in Chapter 1, the relics and pardon in the Pardoner's bag stand in for his indeterminate sexual organs. The Pardoner boasts that the items in his 'male' are '[a]s fair as any man's in Engelond', and were given him by 'the popes hond' (VI.920–2). The hand of the Pope is not only implicated in the provision of fraudulent absolution but charged with sodomy. The traffic of relics is also the touch of St Peter's successor on the attractive private parts of another man. Perilous remission of sin is authorised through papal same-sex fondling. The Pope, of course, is not the only man who wishes to touch the Pardoner's genitalia. So too does Harry Bailey. In his desire to hold the Pardoner's testicles in his hand, the Host of the Tabard stands in succession to the leader of the Church of Rome. With Harry, however, the pseudo-apostolic line comes to an unholy end. The Host's desire is for the testicles to be cut off, for the Pardoner's balls to be encased in a hog's turd. Testicular relics, handed down by the Pope, are rehoused in monumental pigshit. A filthy church shrine displays severed male genitalia as if they were the prized relict of a revered saint. It is worth recalling here two powerful strands of medieval thinking about the hand: the hand that is praised as an instrument of the soul, and the injunction for the hands of priests to be physically and spiritually clean. Through the words of the Pardoner, Chaucer gives us a papal hand that, in medieval ecclesiology at any rate, would be better attached to the body of the Antichrist than to St Peter's heir.

Persistently, in Chaucer's works, the hand is an instrument not of the soul but of transgressive bodies. In the first two fabliaux of the *Tales*, clerks are shown to use their hands in pursuit of knowledge that is not clerical but sexual. The adjective used most often of Nicholas, the clerk who uses his superior religious learning to such advantage in *The Miller's Tale*, is 'hende' (handy). At the start of the tale Nicholas's hands assault another man's wife, causing Alison to cry '[d]o wey youre handes, for youre curteisye' (I.3287), but, in the tale's climactic denouement, Nicholas finds himself on the receiving end of a handy congress that has more in common with the conjugation of body parts seen in *The Summoner's Tale* and the exchange between the male figures of the Pope, the Pardoner and the Host. When Absolon takes the coulter from Gervase's forge to scorch Nicholas's backside, the phallic property of one man in the hand of another flays the skin of a third man's arse 'an handebrede aboute' (I.3811). While handbreadth was a term used to describe the distance between knights in combat, here, rather more intimately, a blacksmith's coulter leaves the imprint of a hand on a male bum.[43] For Galen, the hand was a sign of civilised achievement, and its exquisite articulation the mark of difference between a man and an animal. For Nicholas, the hand of scalded flesh on his buttocks brands him with the mark of bestial congress.[44]

Aleyn and John in *The Reeve's Tale* are also university clerks. Hands that should seek for clerical illumination, however, grope for beds in the dark. Feeling cheated by Aleyn's sexual conquest of the miller's daughter, John goes to the infant's cradle 'and in his hand it hente / And baar it softe unto his beddes feet' (I.4212–13) so that he can 'swyve' the miller's wife by luring her to the wrong bed as she returns from emptying her bladder. The wife relies on finding the cradle to guide her back to her own bed, but as she 'groped heer and ther, but she foond noone' (I.4217). Relieved not to have found her way into the clerk's bed by mistake, she 'gropeth alwey forther with hir hond' (I.4222) and finds what she believes to be her own bed, but it is, of course, the bed where John lies in wait. Aleyn repeats the charade. After his conquest of the miller's daughter, he resolves to creep into John's bed to tell him of his exploits. As he seeks his way in the dark, he 'fond the cradel with his hand anon' (I.4251). Believing that his sense of direction has been scrambled by his night's 'swynk', he congratulates himself on the near-miss of climbing into bed with the miller and his wife only to climb into bed with Simkin and to blurt out how he has humiliated him. The series of deceptions and counter-deceptions in this tale showcase a groping hand as a creepy sign of competition between clerical and prosperous labouring estates. Clerical hands that ought to be groping after knowledge are seen to be no better than the fumblings of a middle-aged miller's wife who cannot find her way back to her own bed after pissing in the dark.

It is not wholly surprising to find sexually active hands in fabliaux, even if their work conflates the discourses of erudition and carnal adventure. More shocking, perhaps, is to encounter such hands in a tale of vaunted 'gentillesse'. As we have seen, courtesy books set out in great detail the correct behaviour of the hands in order to protect hapless individuals from social indelicacy. In *The Squire's Tale*, however, courtly hands behave with the utmost impropriety: in public and in private. The Squire narrates how the anonymous knight who turns up at Cambuyskan's court bears a mirror in one hand (V.82), and on 'his thombe he hadde of gold a ryng / And by his syde a naked swerd hangyng' (V.83–4). The knight bestows this ring on Canace to wear '[u]pon hir thombe or in hir purs it bere' (V.148). Nothing the Squire has said explicitly likens the thumb to a penis inserted into vulva, or places a vagina and a vulva in close proximity. It is hard, however, not to notice that the collocation of 'thumb', 'ring', 'naked sword' and 'purs' sets up a chain of obscene innuendo.[45] The Squire's lingering on quaint, aristocratic romance props undoes propriety. Ceremonial courtesy is thoroughly indecent.

There are many adjectives that the Squire could have used to describe Canace's gold ring. Only, he seems compelled to use the word 'queynte'. Not only does he repeat the adjective as if suffering from some unconscious libidinous tic, but he does so in collocations with unmistakable sexual resonance:

> For swich a joye she in hir herte took
> Bothe of hir queynte ryng and hire mirour,
> That twenty tyme she changed hir colour
>
> (V.368–70)

> This faire kynges doghter Canacee,
> That on hir fynger baar the queynte ring.
>
> (V.432–3)

In its anatomical sense of expandable cartilaginous tissue, 'ring', prefaced by 'queynte', spells vaginal aperture penetrated by a finger. Characteristically, Chaucer gives us a body, or a body part, where we may least expect to encounter it. I argued in the Introduction that the Virgin Mary sticks her arse out of a window in a fabliau. In the Squire's aristocratic romance, the daughter of a king masturbates privately in her chamber and then parades the sign of a finger in a vulva in the public court. By the Squire's standards of narration, the Miller's occluded narration of Alison's 'hole' is positively decorous, encoding as it does the mystery of the Virgin birth. The Knight's 'curteis' and 'servisable' son, however, discloses mysteries of anatomy that Galen may not have had in mind when he praised the wonderful articulation of the fingers and joints as the noble work of the hand. In *The Squire's Tale*, as elsewhere in *The Canterbury Tales*, the work of the hand unfixes the normative discourses that discipline the roles it is thought to be able to play. Through puns, collocation and narrative focalisation, discursive etiquette is inseparable from the revelation of tabooed sexual practice.

The work of the hands unravels aristocratic display elsewhere in the *Tales*. Chaucer draws on a rich tradition of visual iconography in which hands functioned as publically recognised emblems. Saints, biblical persons and historical figures were identified by signs that they carried.[46] Allegorical figures were defined by objects that they touch or hold.[47] The hands of Classical figures bore objects that told a defining exploit from their lives.[48] In *The Canterbury Tales*, members of the nobility who bear an object in their hands expose violent faultlines in aristocratic culture. In *The Manciple's Tale*, Phoebus, 'flour of bachilrie, / As wel in fredom as in chivalrie' bears 'in his hand a bowe' (IX.125–9) in sign of his victory against Phitoun the python. It is with this bow that he kills his wife in a paroxysm of jealousy. In *The Knight's Tale*, a story in which erotic passion disorders the cosmos, Mercury, the messenger of the gods, has '[h]is slepy yerde in hond' (I.1387).[49] In the sumptuous pre-tournament pageant, Emetreus bears a tame eagle on his hand, white as any lily (I.2177–8). Suggestive of Marian purity and innocence, the lily-white symbol of aristocratic control over a beast presages a staged knightly combat in which violence cannot be contained. When Arcite's body is laid out on his funeral bier, hands are mentioned several times. A 'swerd ful bright and kene' is placed into his hand (I.2876). One of his mourners bears his shield, and another 'his spere up on his hondes heeld' (I.2893–4). Theseus himself clothes Arcite's hands in white gloves (I.2874). Arcite's dead hands perform a chivalrous display of vanquished knighthood that masks the grisly details of his actual demise: vomiting up black bile after being brained by the aristocratic pommel of his own horse. The exhibition of Arcite's hands gives him a staged visual identity that attempts to veneer the chaotic violence of the tale. In Chaucerian narrative, what a person bears in their hands is not simply a distillation of their symbolic meaning, or a token of a famous exploit; it signs a body that cannot be contained in its discursive place.

Chaucer's verbal hands are recognisable from the kinds of hands about which other medieval authors wrote. But Chaucer revels in the unruly opportunities that arise from the unsettled place of the hand in medieval cultural thought. Chaucer's hands are as deft as the physiologists praised them to be; only the matter of which those hands speak or the actions they perform are not necessarily what such writers might want to own up to have said. The sacramental hand is touched with queer company and excrement; it exposes the uncomfortable silences of pastoralia and it performs perverted church ritual. The hand that should quest after knowledge seeks financial remuneration and carnal adventure. The aristocratic hand of 'gentil' conduct displays the brutality of senseless death and parades erotic taboo. When the manuscript illustrators created pictures of the Canterbury pilgrim tellers, those itinerant hands, like those told in *The Knight's Tale*, carry crucial identifying information. As I now go on to argue, translated in time, place and media, they magnify the discursive transgressions that so characterise the verbal hands of *The Canterbury Tales*. There are six pilgrims only in *The General Prologue* whose hands are described. From these, only the Yeoman and the Parson carry an object. But when the pilgrims are seen riding their horses, all of them display hands that supplement the already discursively wayward hands that are narrated through words.

## Illustrated hands

The visual pilgrims in Ellesmere and CUL MS Gg.4.27 are shown literally in transit; they all ride horses on the move from Southwark to Canterbury. They are also materially and figuratively transported from their place in the narrative. None of the illustrations appears beside the pilgrims in *The General Prologue*. They are depicted beside the tales that they tell on the journey.[50] The pilgrims are transported from being characters that the narrator sees in the Tabard to narrators themselves. With one exception, no medieval manuscript of *The Canterbury Tales* illustrates a pilgrim-teller in the prologues to their tales, nor in any other links between them.[51] Told in one place, they become tellers in their journey to another. The six surviving illustrated figures in the Cambridge manuscript are all placed in the centre of the page: either above or below the rubric of the tale that they are about to tell. Four of the figures intrude into the rubrication; they become absorbed into the words of the text.[52] The Ellesmere figures also become part of the ordinatio of the text; not in the centre, but in the demivinets of the page. With the exception of the Miller, a pilgrim illustrated on a recto folio is placed to the right of the text, and, if on a verso, they are placed on the left.[53] Their positioning is functional; it marks the place in the manuscript where they start to speak their tale.[54]

That ordinational role does not exhaust the interpretative potential of these illustrated pilgrims. Resulting from the new physical place that they occupy, the Canterbury pilgrims take shape intermedially between visual and verbal representation, and between place and time. The physical appearance of the pilgrim teller beside their tale shuffles narrative chronology with illustrative memory, instruction and/or invention. Some of the personal details narrated in *The General Prologue* travel with the pilgrim to their new visual position beside their tales. Other details are supplied either from the tales that they themselves are about to narrate and/or from those already yet to be told by their fellow pilgrims. In some instances, visual details have no obvious cue from any textual detail in *The Canterbury Tales*. They would appear to be the creative response of the illustrator and/or his supervisor.[55]

While previous studies have explored the illustrated pilgrims through codicology, through costume and through props, so far no systematic attention has been paid to the pilgrims' hands.[56] The provision of horses for all the pilgrims can be seen to be the fruits of an active creative choice. Representing the pilgrims with hands is a rather different issue. Simply to place a person on a horse creates an expectation that they might take hold of the reins (though, as we shall see, this was obviously not felt to be mandatory in all instances).[57] The majority of the pilgrims acquire hands in their visual mediation for which there is no mention anywhere in the text. But, as no pilgrim, so far as we are told, lacks hands, or has endured a mandectomy (the severance of that body part is a non-issue even for the Pardoner), it transpires that all the pilgrims will have had hands all along. Once hands are supplied to the pilgrims' bodies, whether or not hands have been mentioned in any textual appearance, they compromise the ordinational role of the illustrations. These hands ruffle the neat markings of time and place that ordination is meant to provide. In translation between the Tabard and St Thomas of Kent, these pilgrims' hands make available to the eye information which the reader may not yet have read. Once they come to be seen, hands, and the bodies to which they are attached, become more and more out of narrative bounds.

Since the appendix to this chapter lists details of all the illustrated hands, my discussion here will be selective.[58] In the *General Prologue* the Parson visits on foot those at the furthest reaches of his parish whatever the weather, 'and in his hand a staf' (I.495); a sign of the spiritual care for the flock of his own parish. The Ellesmere Parson assumes an even greater degree of selfless-ness. His hands are crossed over his chest in a gesture of penance. So detached is he from secular interests and the affairs of this world that in his prayerfulness he does not even make contact with the reins of his horse. The Parson's spiritual hands stand in contrast to those of the Ellesmere Friar. Although the *General Prologue* makes no mention of Huberd's hands, his visual self holds a staff that is tipped. The detail recalls the friars in *The Summoner's Tale* which has not yet been told. The friar who suffers so uncomfortably at the hands (or arse) of Thomas carries a 'scrippe and tipped staf' (III.1737), and his fellow friar has 'a staf tipped with horn' (III.1740).[59] What the Friar carries in his hand invests him with the professional mercenariness of characters whom the Summoner has yet to narrate. What an Ellesmere reader sees is a reminder of mendicant corruption drawn from the perspective of the Friar's bitterest narrative rival.

The Monk's hands *are* described in *The General Prologue*. The narrator can see them. The Monk's habit is 'purfiled at the hond / With grys, and that the fyneste of the lond' (I.193–4). Ostensibly just a casual observation, the detail of the squirrel fur at the monk's wrists, is of course, a sign of the monk's violation of monastic habit, and his disregard for sumptuary laws: why he should 'swynken with his handes, and laboure / As Austyn bit?' (I.186–7). The animal skin that hugs his wrists shows the assembled pilgrims and the narrative audience that the hands of this monk are far too finely dressed to toil in the earth. However, the story told by the hands of the monk in his visual appearance in illustrated manuscripts appears to trade in the jolly Monk of the Prologue for the dour speaker of his Tale. The right hand of the Ellesmere monk is placed upon his upper chest. Emmerson sees him to hold the hood of his Benedictine habit.[60] As such, the deferential gesture points to a devotion to monastic rule that appears at odds with the hands of *The General Prologue*, but in keeping with the memory of the gloomy tragedies of the tale upon which the Monk is about to embark. Whether the Monk created by the Cambridge artist is even more sober and unworldly, or is in defiance of rules governing the amount of cloth allowed for a Benedictine habit is hard to determine.[61] Turned away from the viewer, the whole body is the monastic reverse of aristocratic display of manliness or squirrel fur. The cloth of this cloak is ample, perhaps to a fault, but it so encompasses his body that the back of his one hand showing is all that is visible. Lowered hands, especially with their backs turned have been interpreted as a sign of humility. Covered hands are seen in representations of priests who dare not touch a scared object, a holy book or Christ's body, for example, with their hands.[62] Because the

Monk's hands are described in *The General Prologue*, a reader who has not yet read his tale may be surprised by their representation in Ellesmere and Cambridge. Anyone who has textual memory both of the Tabard pilgrim and his 'clowdy' tale will recognize that in his transit between being told about and becoming a teller himself, the Monk is become divested of some of the secular manliness that made him attractive in the first place.

The Prioress is the only other illustrated pilgrim assembled in the Tabard whose hands the narrator claims to be able to see. Like the hands of the Monk, those of this religious lady are hard to call, for some of the same (and for different), reasons. This is what the narrator tells us in *The General Prologue*:

> At mete wel ytaught was she with alle;
> She leet no morsel from hir lippes falle,
> Ne wette hir fyngres in hir sauce depe;
> Wel koude she carie a morsel and wel kepe
> That no drope ne fille upon hire brest.
> In curteisie was set ful muchel hir lest.
> Hir over-lippe wyped she so clene
> That in hir copp ther was no ferthyng sene
> Of grece, whan she dronken hadde hir draughte.
> Ful semely after hir mete she raughte.

(I.127–35)

The narrator describes a religious woman in terms that could have been borrowed straight out of a courtesy book. The work of the hands in the delicate ferrying of food and drink to avoid spillage, the wiping, restrained dipping and reaching, are all signs of 'clean' civility. The explicit focus on the fingers rather than the whole hand is suggestive of delicacy and finesse; their exquisite articulation being, of course, a sign of the work of civilisation that Galen so praised. But the negative persistence with which the fingers are not too deeply wet in the sauce, their dabbing at the mouth to remove the patina of grease, which once suggested is difficult for the audience to wipe from the Prioress's face, the tiny pieces of food in the hands, invite a narrative focus on lips, mouth, breast and meat flesh which brings the audience rather more close to the Prioress's own body than decency ought to permit. Wetness, stains and spillage mark what the business of the hands attempts to wipe away, and in following the course of the fingers, the audience partakes in the touches and the flesh of what is meant to be a holy woman. Drawn by the narrator with such tasteful tact, fingers of lechery reach out to snare the onlooker's drooling gaze. The hands of the Prioress are produced through a crimping of ecclesiastical, aristocratic and sexual discourses.

When her hands are told visually, they do not, at first glance, appear to draw attention to her person; and certainly not in the synaesthasic orgy of sense perception that they orchestrate in her *General Prologue* appearance (see Plate 5). Her left hand, back facing, seems to rest decorously on the reins. Her right hand is raised in what looks like a holy speaking gesture. Both hands suggest a self-effacing religious woman until we see that the position of her 'modest' left hand draws open the skirts of her habit and her prayerful right hand daintily parts her mantle. The purpose of a nun's cloak (we might remember that the Prioress's is '[f]ul fetys', I.157), was to keep the woman's body well and truly covered.[63] Both the Prioress's hands invite the onlooker to see the woman's white tunic beneath the nun's dark clothing.[64] Drawn in by the white paint of the undergarment, the eye travels from breast to groin. While the pose is not wholly dissimilar to that of an illustration of St Gertrude, Benedictine Nun and Visionary, preserved in a fifteenth-century Book of Hours, there is a crucial difference. In one hand St Gertrude holds a book and in the other a gold staff.[65] The only holy object that comes anywhere near Sister Eglentyne's hand is the rosary just above her left wrist; pictured beads whose *General Prologue* inscription runs 'amor vincit omnia' (I.162). Transported to Ellesmere, the Prioress's hands reprise the coy sexual exhibitionism of her appearance in a Southwark public house even as she is on the verge of a tale of Marian devotional piety.[66]

Many of the illustrated Canterbury pilgrims have hands for which there is no cue in *The General Prologue*. But in the case of the Man of Lawe, memory of the Sergeant's legal learning can be seen to have informed how his hand gets to be seen. There is a detail that is almost invisible to the naked eye, and which is obscured in digital reproduction (see Plate 6). Examination of the physical manuscript through 3D binoculars, however, shows that there is a black ligature wrapped around the thumb and first two fingers of the lawyer's flamboyantly raised right hand. He wears a memory aid. Mary Carruthers notes that *nota bene* hands in manuscripts are often shown with string attached.[67] The illustrator has produced a visual quip at the expense of the Man of Lawe's prodigious legal memory. The lawyer's claim to be able to recite all the statutes and terms from the time of William the Conqueror 'by rote' (I.323–7) boasts of a memorial recall that is both mechanistic and scarcely credible.[68] The string tied round the visual fingers cues either a figure with learning that relies on a prompt and/or a figure who is so proud of his legal 'learning' that he sports a reminder of it for his fellows to see; digital shamming that is in keeping with the furnishing of the Man of Lawe with a 'coif' towards which his stringed hand waves.[69] This visual hand transports the lawyer's statutory self-importance to the start of the piously repetitive tale that he has yet to tell.

When his hands become intermediated, the Man of Lawe emerges as an especially ingenious composite of text and image. So too does another of the 'professionals' as he is transported from Southwark. The Physician carries a huge urinal above his head. One hand supports the base; the other rests close to the neck of the flask as if he is taking its temperature; an action that suggests that the Physician is in mid-diagnosis. He is looking upwards as he rides, maybe in recall of his consultations of astronomical configurations (I.415–18). The illustrator has produced a generic image of a doctor in which his *General Prologue* prognostications catch up with the Host's taunt about the Physician's 'urynals' and 'jurdones' in the Introduction to *The Pardoner's Tale* (VI.305).[70] Medieval hands can produce profoundly moving acts of healing in their searching of wounds, but the Doctor's hands, unmentioned in the verbal text of *The Canterbury Tales*, are visually preoccupied with a huge artefact of medical fraudulence.[71] In the tale for which this image is an ordinational placeholder, the hand of Virginius 'compassionately' slaughters his only child.

The Doctor is not the only pilgrim whose hitherto silent hands acquire visual accessories that create a character composite between text and image and between different fragments of the *Tales*. Neither the Ellesmere Knight nor the Squire carries anything. But they do have costumed hands: both wear gloves. It has been observed that the fingerless mittens worn by the Knight resemble those of the aristocratic characters in the illustrations in the *Pearl*-poet manuscript. Close inspection, however, reveals that the gloves are not fingerless. Nor are they mittens. The reddish brown paint extends right to the fingertips and matches the colouring of his chaperon. As previous critics have noted, the fashionable costume of the Ellesmere Knight is at odds with the travel-stained garments described in *The General Prologue*.[72] As teller, this well-dressed Knight fits the outward show of his chivalric narrative, even as his apparently handless self in the *General Prologue* tells a different story.

The fashionable dress of his son, the Squire, matches the verbal portrait in *The General Prologue*, but a significant detail has been added. The sole hand visible sports a white glove (see Plate 7). The only character in the written text of *The Canterbury Tales* who has gloved hands is Arcite.[73] It is Theseus, an avatar of the Knight, who places them on Arcite's hands in the aristocratic display of noble death he orchestrates.[74] Gloved in white, the Squire becomes the lover who has died in an earlier *Canterbury Tale*. Textual and visual memory play back and forth. At this point in Ellesmere, the Squire's white glove reminds us that the Knight has told a story that will narrate the death of his own son. But this does not exhaust the intermediated hands of the Ellesmere Squire. There is one other Chaucerian character who wears white gloves: Idleness in *The Romance of the Rose*. In both the French and Middle English versions of the poem she wears them to stop her hands going brown: '[a]nd for to kepe hir hondis faire / Of gloves white she had a paire' (571–2).[75] As is well known, the verbal portrait of the Squire draws some of its details from *The Romance of the Rose*; his May morning associations are shared with the figure of Idleness. For a reader of Chaucer who is familiar with the Squire's intertextual companion, it is hard not to see his Ellesmere white glove as a marker of feminisation. The memory of a woman's white gloves that protect her hands from weathering serves to contrast the Squire with the Yeoman who rides in his company; brown-faced, and with a sturdy bow in his hand. The memory of the martial prowess of the Yeoman's hand becomes available as a contrast to the dandy hands of his feminised social superior.[76] The Ellesmere Squire sports the white glove of a knight whose father lays him out in an aristocratic pageant even while the bitter taste of his wasteful death lingers on the tongue. And the Squire/Arcite sports the white glove of a fictional woman who disdains profitable occupation.

The Squire's hand also cues other gendered associations. The white paint on the fourth finger of his right hand is interrupted between the second and third metacarpals. The distension in the outline of the finger suggests that the Squire wears a ring under his glove.[77] For a reader who already knows what the Squire is about to say, the ring prompts anticipated memory of the ringed fingers in his tale. The Squire's visual ring is both a marker of aristocratic finery and a bit of costume jewellery caught up in temporal drag. Temporal drag is a phrase that Elizabeth Freeman uses to describe how retro clothing that is worn with performative transgression mobilises bodies across time. Costume remembered from the past that is ostentatiously worn in the present destabilises and transforms how bodies come to signify in time and place. Moving back and forth across historical, present and future planes of representation, the body is like the wave whose forward movement is always accompanied by the undertow that drags it back to where it came from.[78] Flaunting his ring, the Squire is Canace in drag. He precipitates and recalls the masturbating princess whose 'queynte' ring is a body part about which his fine romance ought not properly to speak. The text-image Squire gets caught up in annular narration that is beyond his control. He becomes narrated proleptically in memorial time.

No other hand of a Canterbury pilgrim that is illustrated solely in Ellesmere is as densely intermediated as the Squire's. But the hands of some of the other pilgrims have more than one visual incarnation.[79] Between Ellesmere and Cambridge, the Pardoner's hands are intermediated differently. Both the Ellesmere hands are occupied in carrying a cross covered with jewelled stones which recalls the 'croys of latoun ful of stones' that the Pardoner carries from *The General Prologue* (I.699). Familiarity with the dense textual layering of testicles and religious objects in the future epilogue to *The Pardoner's Tale* makes the superabundance of stones in the visual Pardoner's cross available for a visual pun; an ocular quip at the testicular plentitude that he is presumed to lack, and which is so recursively and endlessly transacted in the lines between the Host and the Pardoner. Whether the illustrator was consciously aware of the potential figurativeness of his illustration or not, what he shows in the Pardoner's hands mediates selves of the Pardoner dispersed in time and place between *The General Prologue* and the aftermath of his tale.

In the Cambridge manuscript, the Pardoner holds a jawbone. In the *General Prologue*, the bones in his jar are those of a pig (I.700). The Cambridge artist draws on the iconography of religious history to judge the Pardoner's status within community. While Chaucer's Monk recounts how Samson slew thousands with a jawbone (Judges 15:15–16), more likely as a source of inspiration for the Cambridge illustration is the story that Cain slew his brother Abel with the cheekbone of an ass.[80] While the murder weapon is not mentioned in the biblical account, the jawbone tradition, both pictorial and verbal, is well attested from the ninth century onwards. It is illustrated in the Holkham picture bible and in a stained glass window in York Minster[81] and features in medieval drama.[82] Cambridge's iconographical hand translates the Pardoner into Cain; a figure available to be read in a number of ways. He is aligned with the first homicide and exile. Lollard writers used the sign of Cain to brand the friars as members of the devil's church.[83] Viewed through this cultural association, the Pardoner becomes branded as a demonic, fraudulent church official; one outside the apostolic orders of the 'true' Church. His relics are a murder weapon. As the first outsider, a monster marked in feud with God, Cambridge's jawbone could also be seen to reference the Pardoner's abnormative sexuality. Whichever strain of the Cain legacy one attaches to the Pardoner, he is stamped as aberrant; destined for damnation. A pilgrim shown with a cheekbone in his hand has no place in an acceptable – or blessed – assembly of human companions. Cain is mentioned once in *The Canterbury Tales*. Alongside Judas, the Parson names him as a figure of despair, unavailable for God's mercy (X.1015). The Cambridge illustrator creates an impression of the Pardoner that anticipates the Parson's condemnation. The Pardoner's body is already confected from a tissue of French and English texts. It is a body touched by the hand of the Pope. The hand of the Cambridge Pardoner, however, transports him back in time through biblical history and contemporary cultural reference to sentence him to everlasting perdition.

## Chaucer's hand

Even as the Pardoner's Cambridge hand can be seen to assign him a place in Hell, because different versions of his hands are dispersed throughout the textual fragments of *The Canterbury Tales*, and in more than one illustrated manuscript, they produce a pilgrim who won't fit easily back into the place where he appears to have started. The Pardoner's ongoing displacement is exceeded only by one other pilgrim: Chaucer. The final part of this chapter examines the discursive unruliness of Chaucer's 'own' hand. Its waywardness is generated both from the iconic manuscript in which Chaucer's hand is pre-eminently located, and also from its appearance in other places. I begin with an aspect of how hands come to be seen and read which, so far, I have addressed only intermittently: gesture. Hand gestures may be thought to relay significant information about the subjectivity of a person and their expressive intent. But as the Pardoner teaches us, the signing of hands is not a reliable gauge of sincerity. Gestures may be learnt and performed. Further, to calibrate the expressiveness of gestural hands in early surviving literary texts is fraught with difficulties.

Studies of the history of gesture jump swiftly from the classical
period to the early modern. Recourse to figural art stumbles on two
problems: the extent to which gestural representation is mediated
by aesthetic rules, and how far the gestures of persons assembled
in populated scenes are available for transfer to situations where,
as in the Canterbury illustrations, pilgrims appear by themselves.[84]
Very few references to gesture are made explicit in the texts of
*The Canterbury Tales*, and those that do exist are not specifically
relevant to the gestural hands of illustrated pilgrims. Many of the
visual gestures are without obvious counterpart in any of Chaucer's
oeuvre, or beyond.[85]

More useful an approach is to think of gesture less as a guide to
a person's subjective expressivity and more as an objective sign of
how a person takes up position in space. Freed from a requirement
to express interior thoughts or emotions, the hand gestures of the
illustrated pilgrims can be seen to function deictically. They sign
their bodies into spatial relationships of various kinds. Hands can
direct the gaze of an onlooker to the body of the person signing,
and/or to other objects on the page where the pilgrims are placed,
including its words.[86] The appendix to this chapter collates the
gestural hands of each illustrated pilgrim. It charts the morphology
of deixis across the whole Canterbury assembly as depicted in
Ellesmere, Cambridge and the Oxford fragments. No pilgrim in
either Cambridge or Oxford is in gestural relationship with the
text that they ordinate. The majority of the pilgrims' hands in
Ellesmere are also without deictic relationship to the text that they
are beside. The Clerk is busy with his books, for example, the
Physician with his urinal and the Summoner with his riding crop
and his summons. The Second Nun has one hand on the reins, the
other rests modestly in her lap. In both Cambridge and Ellesmere,
the Manciple has one hand on the reins and the other holds up a
drinking gourd. The Franklin and the Reeve each have one hand
on the reins and the other resting close to their chest. The hands
of the Man of Law and the Squire, raised flamboyantly in the air,
draw attention to their costumed accessories not to the words that
they are beside.[87] Their hands have their backs showing; a gestural
position that does not draw the gaze of an observer to anything
beyond the pilgrim's own body. The Prioress's hands, as we have
seen, also direct the gaze to her body, even while the hand that
pulls aside her gown is raised with an open palm in what appears
to be a holy speaking gesture.[88] Neither of her hands is in explicit
deictic relationship to the tale that the Prioress rubricates, even if

they can be seen to reproduce how the figure of the nun is crimped between secular and ecclesiastical discourses.

There are three pilgrims in Ellesmere, however, whose hands are extended towards the text with their palms facing outwards. These open hands draw the Knight, Friar and Shipman into relationship with their tale. The hands of this somewhat unlikely trio offer the tales which they are about to speak for the consideration of the onlooker.[89] The deixis of open hands differs significantly from that of closed, pointing hands. An open hand shows a person guiding or inviting the attention of their addressee. It creates traffic back and forth between person and object. A closed hand singles out external phenomena whose significance exceeds that of the person who points.[90] There is only one illustrated pilgrim whose hand unambiguously points, rather than invites, the gaze towards the adjacent tale. That hand is Chaucer's left. His is the only hand with a fist and an extended horizontal index finger. In contrast to the deixis of all the other pilgrims' hands it singles out an object separate from the pilgrim's body for the observer's attention.[91] No other hand takes the same shape or appears to direct the gaze in such a way. Of all the digits of the hand, it is the index finger that is the most imperative.[92] Only in Chaucer's case, predictably, there is a complication (see Plate 8). While the hand is beside the rubric 'heere bigynneth Chaucer his tale of Melibee', that is not exactly to what it points. An imperative index hand ought to draw an invisible line between the tip of the finger and the particular object towards which the observer's eye is drawn. In Ellesmere, Chaucer's hand runs out of conviction. It points to an empty space. This may be an accident of design. The top-heavy proportions of Chaucer's body in relation to the size of his horse suggest that the artist may have had trouble fitting the figure into the space that was left for him. Figures on verso folios are painted in between the outer edge of the page and the demivinet border. Even though the edge of the border has been moved to accommodate Chaucer, the decorative foliage on fol. 153v blocks the line to specific wording in the text.[93] Were the start of *Melibee* to have fallen on a recto folio, Chaucer's pointing hand would have been unimpeded. Even though the prose lines of *Melibee* take up more room than verse, the artist would have had more space with which to play. In the margin on fol. 153v, Chaucer and his pointing hand seem not quite to fit with where they are supposed to belong.

The placement of the Chaucer miniature has been the subject of considerable debate. While it appears next to *The Tale of Melibee*,

this is not the first tale that Chaucer as pilgrim delivers. His first
tale is *Sir Thopas*. Critical discussion has argued back and forth
as to why Chaucer was placed next to *Melibee* rather than *Thopas*.
The dominant answer to this apparent truancy (after all, his position flouts proper sequencing of narration) is that the placing more
befits Chaucer's literary standing. Chaucer's 'portrait' is deferred
from the first place in the manuscript where he tells a tale because it
would frame him as a hack rhymester rather than a serious writer of
prose morality. His future reputation would have been damaged.[94]
This may, or may not be, a critical reversal of carts and horses. Did
practical considerations determine the choice? *Melibee* begins early
in quire 20 whereas *Thopas* begins at the end of quire 19 (fol. 151v).
Emmerson argues that Artist 2 may have painted Chaucer's portrait
in quire 20 next to *Melibee* because quire 19 was still in the hands of
Artist 1 still at work on the portrait of the Prioress (fol. 148v).[95] If
this scenario is correct, Chaucer's hand fetches up in the margin of
quire 20 because his preordained place was unavailable at the time.

It is appropriate that Chaucer's left hand points to a space. Later
readers and critics of Chaucer have wanted to have him positioned
where they think he should properly belong. In asking whether
that ordinational left index finger is where it was destined to be,
readers have wanted to see Chaucer's hand settled once and for all.
The majority of them have made the hand bear the weight of one
aspect only of Chaucer's future reputation: an author who should
command serious attention. As I shall go on to show, this critical
direction is driven as much by appearances of Chaucer's hand elsewhere as what it looks like and what it does in Ellesmere.

Chaucer's left hand, wherever it ought to have been placed, does
not solely mark out an author, hack or wholesome. On fol. 153v,
the figure of Chaucer is a pilgrim speaker. As such, his hand performs the gesture of one of Chaucer's characters. Like the hands of
the other pilgrim tellers, Chaucer's hand is intermediated between
image and word, voice and text. Unlike any other hand, however,
Chaucer's hand is a sign of intermediation itself. The hand of
Chaucer is the hand of a fictional character that Chaucer the poet
wrote into being. Chaucer's creation points to a tale that he is about
to deliver orally that has been written by Chaucer the poet and
which an illustrator visualised on the Ellesmere page. Chaucer's
hand unsettles the roles of author, character, illustrator and scribe.

The appearance of Chaucer's left hand is unsettling in itself. It is
a manicule.[96] Manicules, little text hands, are commonly associated
with teaching authority, especially in academic texts, where, as

marginal annotation, they draw attention to material that either the scribe or a later reader thought to be especially important. They take their place alongside the ordinatio of rubrics, capital letters, running titles, introductory paraphs and flourishes.[97] As Sanger has shown, these forms of punctuation grew more frequent in proportion to the rise of the practice of private reading.[98]

But the pointed authority of manicules is compromised by their very form. In contrast to many other *nota bene* marks, a manicule is not an arbitrary sign; it is anthropomorphic. Because it looks the part of the body pre-eminently associated with agency, a little text hand mimes human action.[99] Even when manicules are drawn severed they are macabre remains of a once full human form. A text hand chopped at the wrist sporting a frilly cuff cues the memory of a hand that is dressed ready for action.[100] Manicules embody presence and absence at the same time: both organic and prosthetic, they disturb the ontological certainties of the living and the dead.[101] Sherman argues that manicules take the text in hand.[102] They do. But they also let the text get out of hand: attention drifts between the specific words to which a manicule points and the indeterminacy of the sign itself. Little text hands also blur the lines between textual participants. Manicules are not usually the signs of an author; more often they mark the contributions to a text by a reader or scribe. Irrespective of who supplies them, including the author of the text, manicules re-predicate the words on the page to which they point.[103] Even as they endorse an assertion, they qualify its authority because their contribution to the text is tautologous; they act out command and subordination in equal measure. Because these lively dead hands intervene in hierarchies of responsibility for the production of textual matter, the words of an author compete for attention with visibly intrusive signs that direct the eye to the views of fictional characters, the work of scribes and illustrators, and the interpretations of readers.[104]

A manicule may come to usurp the role of the author, much as a gloss can sometimes take the place of what an author appears to have said.[105] Joined to human bodies in a manuscript, manicules can tell stories that go beyond what an author thought his words to have compassed. As is well known, the copy of the C version of *Piers Plowman* in Bodleian Library MS Douce 104 is plentifully illustrated with human figures whose margined hands gesture towards the text. As Kathryn Kerby-Fulton and Denise Deprès have shown in great detail, these hands form part of a physical discursive space between author and audience that is contested between the visible

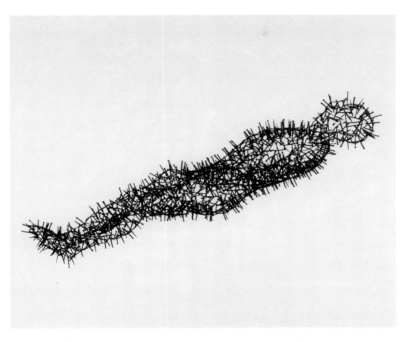

1 Antony Gormley, *Transport*, 2010. Iron nails, 210 × 63 × 43 cm. Collection of Canterbury Cathedral. Photograph by Stephen White. © the artist

2 Eilward castrated by the townsfolk of Westoning. Stained glass panel, north ambulatory, Canterbury Cathedral n III 19

**3** St Thomas Becket heals Eilward's castration and restores his sight. Stained glass panel, north ambulatory, Canterbury Cathedral n III 11 R

**4** Pilgrim as vulva. Reproduction of medieval secular badge courtesy of Fettered Cock Pewters

5 The Prioress piously opens her cloak. Ellesmere manuscript EL 26 C 9, fol. 148v

**6** The Man of Law with string around his hand. Ellesmere manuscript EL 26 C 9, fol. 50v

7 The Squire parades his ring. Ellesmere manuscript EL 26 C 9, fol. 115v

**8** Chaucer points into an empty space. Ellesmere manuscript EL 26 C 9, fol. 153v

**9** The lawyer's hands in *Piers Plowman* from Bodleian Library MS Douce 104, fol. 41r

Howe he þat was mayden marie
And sit his sone floure and fruitife

Al thogh his lyfe be queynt þe resemblaunce
Of hym hath in me so fressh lyflynesse
þat to putte othir men in remembraunce
Of his persone I haue heere his lyknesse
Do make to þis ende in soothfastnesse
þat yei þt haue of him left þought & mynde
By this peynture may ageyn him fynde

The ymages þt in þe chirche been
Maken folk þenke on god & on his seyntes
Whan ye ymages yei beholde & seen
Were oft vnsyte of hem causith restreyntes
Of þoughtes gode Whan a þing depeynt is
Or entailed if men take of it heede
Thoght of þe lyknesse it wil in hym brede

Yit somme holden oppynyoun and sey
þat none ymages schuld I maked be
yei erren foule & goon out of þe wey
Of trouth haue yei scant sensibilite
Passe ouer þt now blessid trinite
Vpon my maistres soule mercy haue
ffor him lady eke þy mercy I craue

Othir þing Wolde I fayne speke & touche
Heere in þis booke but such is my dulnesse
ffor þt al voide and empty is my pouche
þat al my lust is queynt wt heuynesse
And heuy spirit comaundeth stilnesse

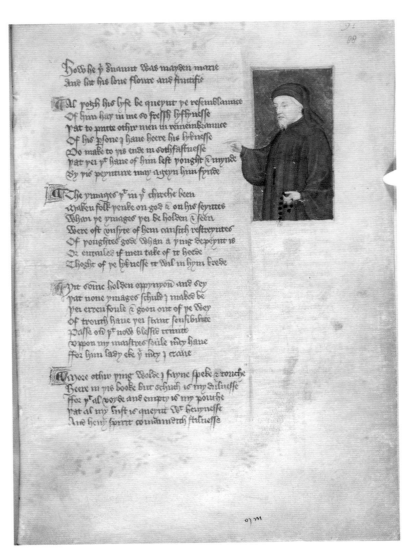

**10** Chaucer points at 'soothfastnesse' in Thomas Hoccleve's *De Regimine Principum* from British Library MS Harley 4866, fol. 88r

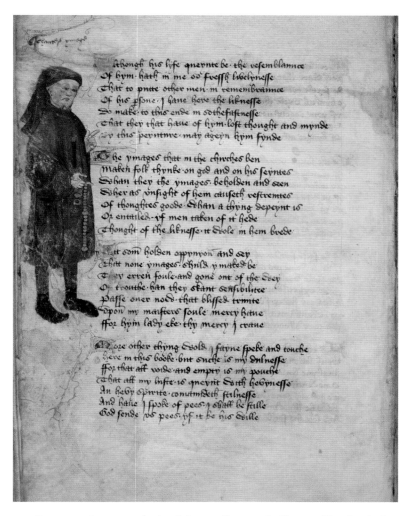

Althogh his life qwenche be · the resemblance
Of hym · hath in me oo fressh liflynesse
That to putte other men in remembrance
Of his persone · I haue heere the liknesse
Do make · to this ende in sothfastnesse
That they that haue of hym lost thoght and mynde
By this peynture may ageyn hym fynde

The ymages that in the chirches ben
Maken folk thynke on god and on his seyntes
Whan they the ymages · beholden and seen
Where as vnsight of hem causeth restreintes
Of thoghtes goode · whan a thyng depeynt is
Or entailled · if men taken of it heede
Thoght of the liknesse it wole in hem breede

Yit som holden oppynyoun and sey
That none ymages · sholde ymaked be
They erren foule · and goon out of the wey
Of trouthe · han they skant sensibilitee
Passe ouer now · that blessed trinitee
Vpon my maistres soule mercy haue
ffor hym lady eke · thy mercy I craue

Moore other thyng wolde I fayne speke and touche
Heere in this booke · but swiche is my dulnesse
ffor that al voide · and empty is my pouche
That al my lufte is quenyt with heuynesse
In heuy spirite conntmeth fulnesse
And haue I spoke of pees · I shal be stille
God sende vs pees · if it be his wille

**11** Chaucer points towards the defence of images in Thomas Hoccleve's *De
Regimine Principum* from British Library MS Royal 17.D.VI, fol. 93v

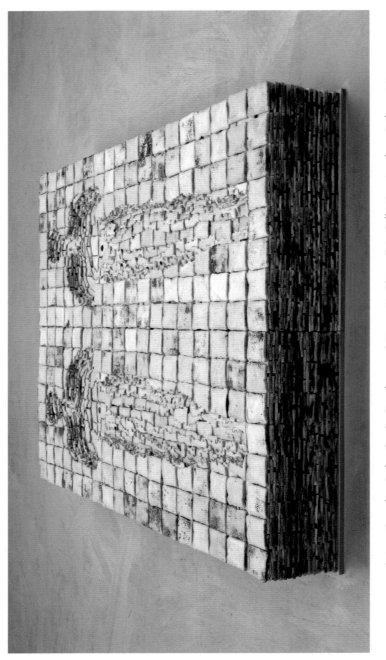

**12** Antony Gormley, *Bed*, 1980–81. Bread, wax, 28 × 220 × 168 cm. Tate Collection, London. © the artist

marks of those who created the manuscript and the words and voices of those persons in the poem composed by Langland. The maniculed figures of Douce are visual signs of the argumentative play of voices in the poem. Sometimes they act as silent witnesses to the words of the narrators; sometimes they perform the actions of a fictional character. Sometimes they appear at loggerheads with the text they are beside.[106] A great number of these figures in Douce perform many roles simultaneously. On folio 41v, for instance, a figure of a lawyer stands beside a passage that accuses 'men of lawe' of refusing to plead for common people unless they are paid beforehand 'pre manibus' (9.45) (see Plate 9). Lawyers are warned that they will be excluded from salvation unless they live by 'here hands / Lellyche and lauhfollyche' (9.58–9). The hands of the illustrated lawyer, prominently and disproportionately large to the rest of his body, pun on the reference to hands in the text. The left hand is a *nota bene* hand. It points to the words '[s]hal haue grace of a good ende and greet ioye aftur' (9.46–50). But its line to this happy foretelling of lawyer's future is compromised by the raised right hand which blocks direct access to the text. The thumb of the right hand touches the index finger of the left. The right hand bars access to the felicitous message of salvation towards which the left hand points. It mimes the verbal accusation that the acceptance of payment 'pre manibus' excludes lawyers from salvation.[107] Each hand tells a slightly different story. Together, they repredicate the Latin/English textual play with the significance of a lawyer's hands.[108]

This unruly play is not simply the preserve of fictional texts, even one as earnest as *Piers Plowman*. Manicules heedless of discursive lines of command also orchestrate works that we might think wholly instructional. The encyclopaedia *Omne Bonum* in BL MS Royal 6.E.VI and 6.E.VII was compiled by James le Palmer, a Treasurer's scribe in the Exchequer of Edward III. Attached to hybrid, fantastical creatures, Palmer's manicules often bypass the text to point to the compiler's annotations. There is a marginal figure of a Pope whose manicule points to the gloss 'nota hic qualia papa potest facere'. The Papal manicule glosses a gloss.[109] Not quite the undermining of papal authority that we saw earlier in Chaucer's treatment of the Pope's hand, but unsettling all the same. In a Psalter in Trinity College Cambridge MS B.V the figure of Augustine stands beside one of Peter Lombard's glosses. In one hand Augustine carries a scroll which says 'nego' and in his other, a barbed arrow which he points at the text.[110] Augustine's testy

manicule dynamises an authorial spat between influential commentators.[111] Animated manicules can also rearrange the word of
God by correcting the work of a distracted scribe. An illustration
in the margins of a French Psalter shows a man scrambling up the
side of the text, pulling into place with his pointing left hand the
fourth verse of Psalm 127 which the scribe has omitted. This ludic
manicule nimbly intermediates the Word of God and the work
of a scribe. An annotating hand makes truthful correction from a
mobile marginal position.[112]

And here, I turn back to Chaucer's pointing hand in Ellesmere.
Recognition of Chaucer's left hand as a manicule tempers some of
the commanding authority with which it has come to be charged.
Seen in the company of other manicules at large, Chaucer's
Ellesmere hand takes its place in a material manuscript culture
whose various systems of 're-presentation' – annotations, glosses,
rubrics, miniatures and interpolations – are time and time again
the work of little text hands, full-bodied or severed.[113] Chaucer's
left hand, apparently hemmed in by foliage, can be seen to be just
as wayward as those other little hands the shape of his own replicates. It has not usually been seen to be so. Chaucer's left hand has
become legible not as a sprightly manicule but as a teacherly sign of
authority. This is not just because it appears besides *Melibee* rather
than *Thopas*, but because discussion of that issue itself is influenced
by where that hand is thought to have been before making its
appearance in Ellesmere. The significance of Chaucer's pointing
hand has become bound up with the anticipated memory of a hand
from another manuscript. The sight of Chaucer's Ellesmere hand
has become conditioned by the hand in the image of Chaucer in
the copy of Hoccleve's *Regiment of Princes* in British Library MS
Harley 4866, fol. 88r (see Plate 10).[114] Hoccleve's narrator pre-
pares the reader for Chaucer's image by framing him as 'the firste
fyndere of our fair langage'. He claims his 'worthy maistir Chaucer
as 'fadir' (4978–83). These are the lines besides which the image of
Chaucer appears:

> Althogh his lyf be qweynt, the resemblance
> Of him hath in me so fressh lyflynesse
> That to putte othir men in remembrance
> Of his persone, I have heere his liknesse
> Do make, to this ende, in soothfastnesse,
> That they that han of him lost thoght and mynde
> By this peynture may ageyn him fynde.

(4992–8)[115]

Chaucer is dead. But the narrator provides a textual and visual gloss to take the edge off that finality. To immortalise his living presence the 'liknesse' of Chaucer is put 'heere'. The figure of Chaucer appears to the right of the stanza. He wears a long black gown and has a rosary that hangs looped from his wrist. He points his right finger at the word 'soothfastnesse'. It has been argued that Chaucer's Harley hand assumes a role that appears authoritative and advisory, a gesture of teaching and instruction.[116] Chaucer appears in Harley as a revered author. His counsel and guidance shore up the credentials of the younger author Hoccleve who has commissioned his image to sanction the worth of his own poem and his own poetic reputation. It is hard to disagree with that view. The figure is garbed in religious sobriety; his indexical figure points unequivocally at a word of high moral seriousness.

It is also hard to disagree with the view that this image of Chaucer stands in relationship to the one that appears in Ellesmere. While the Ellesmere Chaucer rides a horse and has a penner round his neck, and the Harley Chaucer carries a rosary, one portrait appears to have been modelled upon the other, or on a common exemplar, now lost.[117] The facial appearance, clothing, posture and hand gesture of the two portraits are remarkably similar. Given the ill-fitting proportions of the Ellesmere Chaucer on the folio where it appears, it seems more likely that this was not the figure that was created first. Chaucer's Ellesmere hand must come after Harley, or after what preceded Harley and Ellesmere both. The resemblance between the two Chaucers has made it all the more plausible to sustain the argument that Chaucer ought to appear beside *Melibee* rather than *Thopas* in Ellesmere. Chaucer's hand in Harley is a sign of instruction and moral guidance; *Melibee* is a tale about moral teaching. So the portrait from Harley was imped into Ellesmere beside *Melibee* because the counsel and guidance indicated by Chaucer's Harley hand indicate the importance of those issues in the tale that Chaucer the pilgrim is about to recount. Putting 'this' Chaucer beside *Thopas* would not have been suitable. The authority of Chaucer's Harley hand guarantees the authenticity of its placement in Ellesmere. So, in recreating the Harley image for the border space in Ellesmere, Artist 2 presents us with the figure of an author whom Hoccleve had earlier shaped into a wise father of English vernacular poetry.

Given the frequency with which Chaucer's Ellesmere hand is discussed in relation to his hand in Harley, and the effect of seeing the two images reproduced out of context side by side, it is hard

to resist this explanation for the course of textual events. When
we encounter that iconic pointing gesture either in Ellesmere or
in its frequent reproduction elsewhere in a variety of media, it is
hard not to bow to the weight of tradition that teaches us to see
the sage hand of the founder of English poetry. I am not trying to
argue that it is somehow 'wrong' to see Chaucer's Ellesmere hand
in this way. It is no more wrong than Honest John of Wakefield
seeing Antony Gormley's body in a membrane of nails hanging
from the crypt in Canterbury Cathedral. And that is precisely the
point. Intriguingly, the text that hangs beside Gormley's sculpture
sounds hauntingly Hocclevean. Gormley argues that the body is
a place through which thought, memory and anticipation filter.[118]
Chaucer's Ellesmere hand is just such a place. It has become
inseparable from the anticipated memory of Hoccleve's Chaucer
hand; the hand of the author placed next to Hoccleve's own text
to establish the place of the younger poet in literary history. But
neither Hoccleve nor the Harley illustrator can hold a monopoly on
how bodies come to be seen.

Pointing at 'soothfastnesse' from its Harley margin – its prede-
termined place of 'heere' – Chaucer's manicule does the serious
work with which manicules are associated in texts of teaching and
moral instruction. And yet, the grave hand that Hoccleve's text
directs us to imagine disturbs ontology and sequential temporality.
Like the signs of manicules in other texts, it refuses distinction
between the deceased and the living. Dead Chaucer's hand takes
an animated interest in a poem he has been made posthumously
to father. Between text and image, and between quick and dead
versions of his person, Chaucer's marginal hand rewinds temporal
succession even as it authors an influential scene of literary history.
For all of the imperative singularity with which Chaucer's Harley
hand has become invested, it is not untouched by the discursive
waywardness of those hands that Chaucer initially wrote into
being, or by the continuing intermediations of their illustrated
forms.

It is not only in Harley and in Ellesmere that a version of
Chaucer's belatedly fathering hand appears. While the text of
Hoccleve's poem tells us that he has Chaucer's likeness 'heere',
the *place* of his pointing hand is not entirely in the younger poet's
control. Another version of Chaucer's image appears adjacent
to Hoccleve's homage in a different manuscript of *De Regimine*.
In British Library MS Royal 17.D.VI, fol. 93v, an image of
Chaucer appears adjacent to the stanza I have already quoted,

but its significance is extended to lines in the stanza that follows
(see Plate 11):

> The ymages that in the chirches been
> Maken folk thynke on God and on his seintes
> Whan the ymages they beholden and seen,
> Where ofte unsighte of hem causith restreyntes
> Of thoghtes goode. Whan a thyng depeynt is
> Or entaillid, if men take of it heede,
> Thoght of the liknesse it wole in hem breede.
>
> (4999–5005)

The Royal portrait gives Chaucer two manicules. The left points at
the line '[b]y this peynture may ageyn hym fynde' (4998), and the
right, looped with a rosary, at '[w]han the ymages they beholden
and seen' (5001). The conjunction of 'ymages' and the finger
from which the rosary beads are suspended in a long line down
Chaucer's gown, almost like a *nota bene* annotation in themselves,
directs the gaze to the commentary on orthodox Church ritual
between lines 4999 and 5005. Chaucer's Royal hands draw attention to the poet's posthumous authority not solely to legitimate
Hoccleve's literary standing but to mount a contemporary defence
of church liturgy and images. Chaucer's hands are once again
co-opted to perform serious work, but their role is not identical
to that in Harley MS 4866. This is not just because of Hoccleve's
agenda or that of the compiler; Chaucer's hands become intermediated differently between Harley and Royal because of the
position on the page where they appear. The lines in Royal appear
on a verso. The margin is on the left, and that is where Chaucer is
placed. His hands are close to the words 'peynture' and 'ymages'
simply because of where Chaucer stands. In Harley the lines fall
on a recto. From his marginal place on the right hand side of the
page, Chaucer is standing at the end of the lines, not at their beginning. His hand can point to 'soothfastnesse' simply because the
word is within his reach. In Royal, 'soothfastnesse' lies beyond his
grasp. An author may have no control over the precise deixis of a
pointing hand, even if he has commissioned an illustrator to place
it 'heere'. Despite their imperative deixis, Chaucer's hands do not
command interpretative stability. They are composite between
text, voice and image. From their respective positions in Ellesmere,
Harley and Royal, Chaucer's hands perform the work of a deceased
author in the making, a fictional narrator who is about to speak and
an annotator who speaks on another person's behalf. When their

codicological truancy is assembled in full, the significance of
Chaucer's little text hands exceeds any determined attempt to pen
them into a stable discursive formation.[119]

That is not the end of the story of Chaucer's hands.[120] Remembered
with Harley, his Ellesmere hand raises issues about location in time
and space more profound than representational variation between
manuscripts. The Chaucer hands are mirror images of each other;
the Harley right hand becomes Ellesmere's left – or should that
be the other way round?[121] What significance does that 180 degree
turn hold for viewers? The deixis of left and right, so beguilingly
attractive in the production of the apparent same, deserves pause
for thought. A mirror image does turn a left hand into a right,
and right into a left, but in two dimensions only. The trick works
only on a surface plane. The perception of similarity extends only
to shape. Right and left hands are what Kant called incongruent
counterparts.[122] In three dimensions, hands take up volume in
space. They become essentially different mass with characteristics
that cannot be identically mapped. The truth of Kant's argument
becomes irritatingly apparent when you lose one glove of a pair. A
left one won't fit a right, and vice versa. The Harley right hand,
for all its uncanny resemblance to Chaucer's Ellesmere left, might
look the same, but it cannot fill its place. The mirror's reflection is
misleading. The argument that the authority of Harley is there in
Ellesmere works only on the surface. Between them, those right
and left hands are signs of a neat symmetry which volume and mass
disarrays. Ellesmere Chaucer cannot embody his Harley hand.

That left and right conundrum, however, does offer an opportunity to think in a different way about how the body of Chaucer gets
moved around. The axis of left and right does not hold a monopoly
on positioning in time and place. It may seem to – only because,
in Western culture, it is so ubiquitous. But the co-ordinates of left
and right are not human universals. They are determined by the
position of an observer for whom those directions in relationship to
their own sense of body place are meaningful, and according to the
space where an object is placed.[123] The happenstance of Harley's
and Ellesmere's left and right hands confronts us with fundamental
issues of how we determine our own position in relationship to
something else in space and time. After all, the reason why one of
the Chaucers points with his right and the other with his left is a
byproduct of how far the text has reached; determined by the leaf
of the page where the hands border the text. Those hands prompt
us to think about deixis itself. They prompt us to think about what

is going on when we are attracted to mirror images. A reflected image gives us only one version of the facts. Trying Chaucer's hand on a body facing the opposite direction can make us question how those facts come to be framed.

To turn a right hand into a left in more than two dimensions can be done. But the result is disorientation; dislocation from positions in time and space that are familiar because acculturated. Antony Gormley's sculpture *Bed* (1981) shows how (see Plate 12). Gormley made a mould (in many senses) of two human forms in bed by biting through two slices of bread at a time to fit a template he had made of his own body mass. Each pair of slices was identically indented. But one slice of each of the hundreds of pairs ended up on the left half of the body mould, and the other on the right. Both sides of the bread body were then flipped over. The result was that the co-ordinates of left and right failed to signify in the way that we are accustomed to think that they do. They could not be seen as opposites; nor could they give an observer back their comfortable bearings. The 'universal' of perceiving left from right was confounded because Gormley made an enantiomorph. Because the sculpture disrupted the phenomenology of left/right apprehension, intuitions about how we place our bodies, and those of others, were dislocated. The play between left and right in the puzzle of the body of bread disoriented the recognition of a body in space.[124]

There is, of course, a very long tradition of producing bodies from bread that disturbs human sense of ontology and the discrete placement of historical and transcendent bodies in time and place, but it is not the Eucharistic resonances of Gormley's sculpture that I want to pursue here. Like the *Transport* body in Canterbury Cathedral, *Bed* asks questions about how we locate bodies in time and place, and how we invest ourselves in their apprehension. The scrambling of co-ordinates apparently so familiar and so necessary for orientation as left and right makes us see that they need not have an imperative hold on how bodies come to be encountered. Losing our bearings makes us more aware of how the positions from which objects have been customarily viewed are not sovereign but conditional. The play between left and right Chaucer hands in Ellesmere and Harley provides an opportunity to rethink not only their relationship to each other but their relationship to the positioning of Chaucer and ourselves. We may want to have Chaucer confirmed in the iconic place to which Hoccleve helped to guide him. We may want those Chaucer manicules to bear the authority of definitive teaching and instruction. What I hope to have shown in this chapter is that Chaucer's hands are also figures of narrative truancy. It is fitting that Chaucer's most iconic hand cannot be said entirely to belong to him.

## Appendix: Illustrated Manuscript Hands

### 1. Ellesmere, Huntington MS EL 26 C 9

| Pilgrim | Reins | Object | Appearance | Gesture | Folio/ Artist |
|---------|-------|--------|------------|---------|---------------|
| Knight | Left | | Gloves | (R) Open palm, slightly raised, thumb vertical. Presenting/ offering | 10r (1) |
| Miller | | Bagpipes | (L) Gold thumb | Holds bagpipes with both hands | 34v* (1) |
| Reeve | Right | | | (L) Back of hand, horizontal, thumb raised | 42r (1) |
| Cook | | (L) Meathook (R) Bowl of blood | | (R) Offers bowl | 47r (1) |
| Man of Lawe | Left | | (R) String wrapped round fingers | (R) Back of hand raised, thumb pointing upwards and slightly left | 50v (1) |
| Wife of Bath | Left | (R) Riding whip | | | 72r (1) |
| Friar | | (R) Tipped staff | | (L) Open palm, horizontal, thumb slightly raised. Presenting/ offering | 76v (1) |
| Summoner | Left | (L) Riding crop (R) Summons | | (R) Holds out summons | 81r (1) |

| Clerk | | (R) Book (L) Stack of books | | (R) Supports book from underneath and holds outwards (L) Misdrawn bearing bookstack | 88r (1) |
|---|---|---|---|---|---|
| Merchant | Left | | (R) Hand on the wrong way round | (R) Open, palm facing. Hand raised, and pronated awkwardly at shoulder height | 102r (1) |
| Squire | | | White gloves; 'ring' underneath on fourth finger | (R) Back of hand, raised between shoulder to clavicle. Thumb pointing slightly left | 115v (1) |
| Franklin | Right | | | (L) Back, self-referential across chest. Thumb pointing slightly left | 123v (1) |
| Physician | | Urinal | | (R) Supports urinal (L) back of hand rests against neck of urinal | 133r (1) |
| Pardoner | | Jewelled cross | | (R) Holds stem of cross (L) Supports its top | 138r (1) |
| Shipman | Right | | | (L) Open palm, hand raised, thumb vertical. Presenting/greeting | 143v (1) |

| Pilgrim | Reins | Object | Appearance | Gesture | Folio/ Artist |
|---------|-------|--------|------------|---------|---------------|
| Prioress | Left | | (R) Rosary on wrist | (L) Back of hand visible. Rests on top of reins (R) Raised, palm facing. Speaking/ preaching. Both hands draw back the outer gown from the habit | 148v (1) |
| Chaucer | Right | | | (L) Index finger points horizontally from closed fist | 153v (2) |
| Monk | Left | | | (L) Touches bells on reins (R) Back of hand resting between shoulder and sternum. Self-referential/ pious? Touches habit | 169r (3) |
| Nun's Priest | Left | | (R) Badly drawn and smudged | (R) Loosely cupped; index finger raised, pointing upwards crookedly | 179r (3) |
| Second Nun | Right | | | (R) Between thumb and forefinger (L) Rests on lap, back facing. Thumb not visible | 187r (3) |

| Canon's Yeoman | Left | (R) | | (R) Loosely cupped, raised. Palm tilting upwards | 194r (3) |
|---|---|---|---|---|---|
| Maniciple | Left | Drinking gourd | | (R) Holds up gourd (L) Jerks the reins, pulling round horse's head | 203r (3) |
| Parson | | | | Backs facing; both arms folded penitentially across chest | 206v (1) |

## 2. Cambridge CUL MS Gg.4.27

| *Pilgrim* | *Reins* | *Object* | *Appearance* | *Gesture* | *Folio* |
|---|---|---|---|---|---|
| Reeve | Left | | | (R) Back, fingers closed, palm upwards. Welcoming? | 176r |
| Cook | Left | (R) Two-thonged whip | | (R) Holds whip over right shoulder | 182v |
| Wife of Bath | Left | (R) Three-thonged whip | | (R) Raises whip aloft | 222v |
| Pardoner | Right | Jawbone | | (R) Displays jawbone | 290r |
| Monk | Left | | | (L) Back showing, thumb not visible (R) Totally occluded by cloak | 332v |
| Maniciple | Left | Drinking gourd | | Hand cupped upwards. Reins held between thumb and fingers. Movement follows that of eyes | 372v |

**3.** John Rylands University Library MS English 63

| Pilgrim | Reins | Object | Gesture |
|---------|-------|--------|---------|
| Miller | | (L) Hand supports end of flute and touches rope halter (R) Holds two-pronged whip pointing downwards | |
| Cook | Left | (L) Rope halter looped over wrist (R) Meat cleaver | (R) Brandishes meat cleaver |
| Man of Lawe | Left | (R) Rolled document | (R) Back showing, holding document across chest |

## Notes

1  The work of the Pardoner's hands to secure remuneration for his preaching contrasts with his disdain to live by the virtues of apostolic poverty. He claims that he will not make baskets, nor 'do no labour with myne handes' (VI.444). In MS Cotton Nero A.x, fol. 86v, Jonah is illustrated preaching in Ninevah. His eyes look at his disproportionately large hands as he makes preaching gestures. The illustration is reproduced in R. J. Blanch and J. N. Wasserman, *From Pearl to Gawain: Forme to Fynisment* (Gainesville: University Press of Florida, 1995), p. 99, figure 25.

2  I use the term 'intermediated' as a verbal form of 'intermediality': a particular form of intertextuality in which there is an interpenetration of words and image. In my reading of the visual texts of *The Canterbury Tales*, the figures that accompany the text are not visual illustrations of text, but a realisation of available responses to text both from the place where that illustration appears and from textual and cultural knowledge further afield. For discussion of this term, and the related concept of 'iconotext', see Peter Wagner, *Reading Iconotexts: From Swift to the French Revolution* (London: Reaktion, 1995), pp. 11–13.

3  Blanch and Wasserman, *From Pearl to Gawain*, pp. 65–110. This chapter is an extremely rich study of the iconographical and gestural position of the work of the treatment of hands both in the *Gawain*-poet's works and in wider manuscript illustration.

4  For instance, he dries all the flood water from the earth (*Confessio* 7.547), smites a false knight dead as he swears perjuriously on a book (2.874), and enables Constance to conceive a child in the land of the Saracens (2.1124), John Gower, *Confessio Amantis* in *The English Works of John Gower*, ed. G. C. Macaulay (EETS ES 81, 1900).

5 References to *Piers* in this chapter are taken from *Piers Plowman: A Parallel-Text Edition of the A, B, C and Z Versions*, ed. A. V. C. Schmidt (London: Longman, 1995).

6 Margaret Tallmadge May, ed. and trans., *Galen on the Usefulness of the Parts of the Body* (Ithaca: Cornell University Press, 1968), p. 69.

7 'The soul is as the hand is; for the hand is a tool of tools', Aristotle, *De Anima: Books II and III with Passages from Book I*, ed. and trans. D. W. Hamlyn (Oxford: Clarendon Press, 1993), 3:8, p. 65.

8 Gower's account of the Nebuchadnezzar's punishment captures this dichotomy through verbal parallelism: 'In sted of handes long cles / In sted of man a bestes lyk' (*Confessio* I.2994–5). Hands make a man: claws mark a beast.

9 *On the Properties of Things: John Trevisa's Translation of Bartholomaeus Anglicus*, ed. M. C. Seymour et al. (Oxford: Oxford University Press, 1975), 2 vols, II.221.

10 *The Institutio Oratoria of Quintilian*, ed. H. E. Butler (Loeb Classical Library, Cambridge, MA: Harvard University Press, 1922), Book XI, iii.85–7.

11 Augustine, *De Doctrina Christiana*, ed. and trans. R. P. H. Green (Oxford: Clarendon Press, 1995), II.5.

12 *The Digby Poems*, ed. Barr. Hands as worthy instruments of travail feature prominently also in *Piers Plowman* (A.7.235, 291, 8.63; B.6.306; 7.60; 15.291, 15.454; C.Pr.223; 8.259, 261; 8.330; 9.58, 198; 17.18). They contrast to the leisured aristocratic ladies with their 'longe fyngres' (B.6.10).

13 A good officer who serves his lord must be 'handles' to ensure that he does not steal (Poem 4/214); Poem 18 warns monks of the dangers of lechery if the hand's capacity to grip is misdirected towards sin: make sure '[þ]at ȝe grype not hand in honde, / When ȝe take leue, loke not ȝe kys' (18/83–4).

14 The hand has been described as the pre-eminent bodily metaphor for human action: Katherine Rowe, *Dead Hands: Fictions of Agency, Renaissance to Modern* (Stanford: Stanford University Press, 1999), p. x. In *Piers Plowman* the work of the hands is reckoned, as in *Digby*, within a scheme of Christian judgement: 'the harm that y haue do with hand and with tonge' (C.6.109) and '[b]e ware what þi riȝt hond werchiþ or deliþ' (A.3.56). A praiseworthy man is one who is true of his tongue and of his 'handes' (A.9.72, B.5.287 and B.8.80).

15 The narrator imagines gazing on his lady's hand (*Confessio* 4.2781), and dreams of embracing his lady and taking her hand (4.2783). Compare Chaucer's Wife of Bath who comments that desire sends men to the devil as a result of fantasising either about hands or small arms (III.261–2) and, in *Piers*, the alluring Mede with fingers 'fetisliche ... fretted with gold wyr' (B.2.11).

16  Virginius is described as a worthy knight with his sword in his hand, but, when he has killed his daughter, the narrative pauses with a suspended focus on the blood of Virginia dripping from the weapon in his hand (*Confessio* 7.5259). Tarquin's rape of Lucrece is focalised through the action of his hands (7.4676, 7.4966 and 7.4986), as is Orestes's murder of his mother Clytemnestra (3.2091, 3.2011, 3.2095, 3.2110).

17  Pirrus kills Penthesilea with his own hand (*Confessio* 4.2164), Iphis is commanded to wreak vengeance with her own hand (4.3615), Jupiter severs Saturn's genitals with his own hand (5.854) and Absolon slays his brother with his own hand (8.221). Conversely, heretics sow cockle in corn that has been sown by Christ's 'oghne hond' (5.1883).

18  See Richard Newhauser, *The Early History of Greed* (Cambridge: Cambridge University Press, 2000), p. 82 and pp. 135–6.

19  Covetousness is explicitly associated with the hands of the mighty (5.2008), simoniacal priests (Prol.205), and judges (7.2755–8). Covetousness has a keeper in his house called Skarsete (parsimony), who is so avaricious 'that he no good let out of his honde' (5.4677). False Semblant empties the goods of the land with a 'subtil hond' (2.2125), Neptune reaches out with his hand to a coffer to plunder it (5.6177), and Micherie (thievishness) puts his hand under a man's coat to cut his purse (5.6519). In *Piers Plowman* the personification of Coueitise has 'hondes and armes of a long lengþe' (B.14.242), fraudulent regraters have 'riche handes' (C.3.118), and those that live unlawfully have hands that are large (C.3.289).

20  A hypocrite is one who has no worldly goods in his hand (*Confessio* 1.659).

21  The paradox of the senses in medieval thought is discussed acutely in Gabrielle M. Spiegel's essay 'Paradox of the Senses', in Stephen G. Nichols, Andreas Kablitz and Alison Calhoun (eds), *Rethinking the Medieval Senses: Heritage, Formations, Frames* (Baltimore: Johns Hopkins University Press, 2008), pp. 186–93.

22  *The Book of Vices and Virtues*, ed. F. W. Nelson (EETS OS 217, 1942), pp. 89–90.

23  Susan Stewart, 'Remembering the Senses' in David Howes (ed.), *Empire of the Senses: The Sensual Culture Reader* (Oxford and New York: Berg, 2005), pp. 59–69 (p. 88).

24  As discussed by Carla Mazzio, 'The Senses Divided: Organs, Objects and Media in Early Modern England', in *Empire of the Senses*, pp. 85–105 (p. 88).

25  *Myrc's Instructions for Parish Priests*, ed. E. Peacock (EETS OS 31, 1868), p. 44/1439–41. *The Book of Vices and Virtues* explicitly lists the 'five wittes' – eyes, ears, mouth and nostrils only tellingly – then to fail to name an available organ to calibrate touch: 'or to fele vnclene and vnhonest þinges as in hemself in here wyues' (p. 180/16–17).

26 *Handlyng Synne*, ed. F. J. Furnivall (EETS OS 123, 1903), lines 83–4.

27 In *Piers* the Ark of the Covenant is to be kept sacred from the hand of any 'lewed man' (B.12.114), and in Richard de Bury's *Philoblon* the touching of holy books by the unclean hands of priests is akin to the defilement of the vestments and vessels of the Lord's body, *The Philobiblon of Richard de Bury*, trans. Andrew Fleming West (New York: P. C. Duschnes, 1945), ch. 17.

28 As discussed by David Wallace, '*Cleanness* and the Terms of Terror', in R. J. Blanch, M. Youngerman Miller and J. Wasserman (eds), *Text and Matter: New Critical Perspectives on the Pearl-Poet* (New York: Whitston Publishing Co., 1991), pp. 93–104.

29 *The Babees Book* in *Education in Early England*, ed. F. J. Furnivall (EETS OS 32, 1867), lines 135–54; *The Lytylle Childrenes Lytil Boke*, ibid., lines 144–5; quotation from *Lytle C's Book*, ll. 71–2.

30 For discussion of oaths and handpledge, see Richard Firth Green, *A Crisis of Truth: Literature and Law in Ricardian England* (Philadelphia: University of Pennsylvania Press, 1999), pp. 57–9; John Burrow, *Gestures and Looks in Medieval Narrative* (Cambridge: Cambridge University Press, 2002), pp. 11–15. In *Confessio* Florent makes a pledge to the loathly lady who will be his wife by taking her hand (1.1587), and the False Bachelor violates the practice whereby the hands is a sign of a contract when he fraudulently lays 'to wedde' the ring of his betrothed into her father's hand (2.2663).

31 *Confessio* 5.2889 and 5.2.874. The hypocrisy of hands in public show is seen when Hypocrisy rides in a barge that is steered by Envy. False Seeming (one of Chaucer's Pardoner's avatars) rows the barge with the oar in his hand (2.1904).

32 In *The Merchant's Tale*, for instance, January is repeatedly described as having his hand on May (V.2091 and 2103).

33 In the tale of the three questions, the daughter leads her father by the hand (*Confessio* 1.3225). Before Jason betrays her, Medea takes him softly 'be the hond' (5.3374). After her betrayal, the narrative describes her standing holding the hands of their children, only to slay them four lines later (5.4211). Gower's story of Constance tells how she takes her child in hand in order to suckle it (2.1078), and, in a change from *Filostrato*, when Troilus and Criseyde part before Criseyde is given over to the Greeks, Troilus gazes at his departing love and for once takes the initiative in their intimacy as he take Criseyde's hand (*Troilus and Criseyde* V.79–81). See B. Windeatt, 'Gesture in Chaucer', *Medievalia et Humanistica* 9 (1979), 141–61, p. 151.

34 Malory, *Complete Works*, ed. E. Vinaver (Oxford: Oxford University Press, 1971), 2nd edn, p. 668.

35 The Parson speaks of God's mighty hand in confession (X.985–90), and quotes St Augustine's moving description of how Christ suffered

so keenly in the Passion that his blood 'brast out at every nayl of his handes' (X.265–70). Prudence counsels Melibee that mortal victories are not to be attributed to the agency of human beings, but 'lith in the wyl and in the hand of oure Lord God Almyghty' (VII.1656). The Monk mentions twice the biblical armless hand that so terrifies Belshazzar with its writing on the wall (VII.3393/3421), and states also that Adam was created '[w]ith Goddes owene fynger' (VII.3198). The friar in the *The Summoner's Tale* tells the bedridden Thomas that Moses received the law 'that was written / With Goddes fynger' (III.1889–90), but, as we shall see, the hand that receives most prominent attention in that tale belongs not to God but to a grasping human being.

36  Richard Newhauser discusses the sources of this image in 'The Parson's Tale', in Robert M. Correale and Mary Hamel (eds), *Sources and Analogues of the Canterbury Tales* (Cambridge: D. S. Brewer, 2002–5), 2 vols, 1.529–615. See also Gregory M. Sadlek, 'The Image of the Devil's Five Fingers in the *South English Legendary's St Michael* and Chaucer's *Parson's Tale*', in Klaus P. Jankofsky (ed.), *The South English Legendary: A Critical Assessment* (Tübingen: Francke, 1992), pp. 49–64.

37  *Melibee* opens with an allegory in which the daughter Sophie (wisdom) is wounded in five places: feet (eyes in the French source); hands, ears, nose and mouth (VII.2160–5). In the Parson's catalogue of the Seven Deadly Sins, the envious man 'bereth hym on hond thyng that is fals' (X.505) while the man guilty of undevotion is unable to 'travaille with his handes in no good werk' (X.720–5). Intriguingly, the Parson's treatment of avarice contains no mention of the hand that was its presiding iconographical symbol. Psalm 75:6 is quoted to warn that the rich shall find nothing in the hands of all their treasure, not to condemn avarice as such, but dangers of worldly honour (X.190–5).

38  In *The Franklin's Tale* Stymphalides takes refuge in the temple of Diana to preserve her virginity and will by no means be separated from the image of the goddess that she grasps in her hands (VI.1391–3). In *The Second Nun's Tale* Cecilia tells Almachius that the gods to whom he commands her sacrifice are idolatrous blocks: 'lat thyn hand upon it falle / And taste it wel, and stoon thou shalt it fynde' (VIII.502–3). In *The Man of Lawe's Tale* Constance 's hand is 'ministre of fredam for almesse' (II.168). Donegild's hand writes a letter full of venom (II.891). When Canace takes the pen in her hand in *Confessio*, the plight of which she writes arouses pity (3.271), but when Damien, in *The Merchant's Tale,* writes his adulterous 'bille' of love to May, he puts it slily 'into hire hand' (IV.1937), together with his 'purs'.

39  Samson slays a lion with no weapon 'save his handes tweye' (VII.2024); and with the jawbone of an ass, kills a thousand men 'with his hond' (VII.2037). Neither Roman emperors nor leaders of any other race

dare face Odenake in the battlefield '[l]est that she wolde hem with hir handes slen' (VII.3531).

40 R. G. Benson, *Medieval Body Language: A Study of the Use of Gesture in Chaucer's Poetry* (Copenhagen: Rosenkilde and Bagger, 1980), notes that the friar should be groping Thomas's conscience, not his buttocks, p. 75.

41 See for instance, Brunne's *Handlyng Synne*, 'Maner þer ys of foule kyssyng, / As ys of dede and of handlyng, / Þat falleþ ofte yn pryuyte, / But þat shal nat be tolde for me' (8119–22).

42 For discussion of the efforts of the church to deal with the practice of sodomy, see William E. Burgwinkle, *Sodomy, Masculinity and Law in Medieval Literature: France and England 1050–1230* (Cambridge: Cambridge University Press, 2004), pp. 19–45. The *Prologue to the Summoner's Tale* proleptically, and imaginatively, associates friars with damnable sodomy with the image of the mendicants as stinging bees swarming in and out of Satan's arse (III.1693–8).

43 The majority of the illustrative quotations for *MED* 'hond-brede' (n.) are from chivalric romance tales, though there is also a reference to c. 1425 *Arderne Fistula*, 2/21: 'Some holez was distant fro the towell by the space of the handbrede of a man'.

44 The sodomitical inflection of the encounter is more explicit in the Dutch analogue, *Heile van Beersele*. Hugh the smith kisses the priest's 'bottom mouth' with such burning desire that his nose shoots inside. When the priest puts forth his 'hindest hole', the smith promptly sticks 'the red-hot iron into his arse', Peter G. Beidler, 'The Miller's Tale', in Correale and Hamel, *Sources and Analogues*, II.249–76 (p. 270).

45 With its unique grasping and rotating position, the thumb is the hand's most powerful digit according to *Isidore of Seville: The Medical Writings*, ed. and trans. William D. Sharpe, *Transactions of the American Philosphical Society* n.s. 2 (1964), 1, 66–71. *MED* 'purs(e (n) 4a)' lists senses with references to the male body: 'the scrotum; nethere ~, ballok ~, ~ of the ballokes (codde, prive stones, testicles)'. But sense (b) 'a bladder or pouch-like membrane' is more suggestive of female genitalia even if the *MED* does not acknowledge so. *MED* 'ring' 3a) lists anatomical references, but all to the cartilaginous tissue of the trachea.

46 As on the left panel of the Wilton Diptych, where Edward the Martyr, who stands to the left, holds the arrow which killed him in 869, Edward the Confessor, at the centre, holds the ring he gave to a pilgrim who turned out to be the disguised John the Evangelist and John the Baptist (right) holds the Lamb of God, see Dillian Gordon, Lisa Monnas and Caroline Elam (eds), *The Regal Image of Richard II and the Wilton Diptych* (London: Harvey Miller, 1997), plate 2.

47 In *Confessio* Aquarius carries a water spout in each hand (7.1193); Virgo carries measuring scales (7.1105) and Sagittarius has

a bow (7.1145). Lechery in *Piers Plowman* bears a bow and a sheaf of arrows (B.20.117). In Cambridge MS Gg.4.27 the visual images of the Sins and Virtues that accompany *The Parson's Tale* hold symbolic objects. Lechery, for instance carries a sparrow, and Charity a winged, flaming heart, see M. B. Parkes and Richard Beadle, *Poetical works: A Facsimile of Cambridge University Library MS GG.4.27* (Cambridge: D. S. Brewer, 1980), fol. 433r. Phillipa Hardman discusses these illustrations, 'Presenting the Text: Pictorial Tradition in Fifteenth-Century Manuscripts of the *Canterbury Tales*', in William K. Finley and Joseph Rosenblum (eds), *Chaucer Illustrated: Five Hundred Years of the Canterbury Tales in Pictures* (London: British Library, 2003), pp. 37–72 (pp. 61–3).

48  Paris with an apple (*Confessio* 5.7414), or Diana with her bow (5.1267).

49  *MED* 'yerd' 2 (n). 5. (a) A penis.

50  See Ralph Hanna, *The Ellesmere Manuscript of Chaucer's Canterbury Tales: A Working Facsimile* (Cambridge: D. S. Brewer, 1989), p. 14.

51  Bodleian MS Rawlinson poet.223, fol. 143r, shows the Friar beside the prologue to this tale. He stands in a pulpit with his left hand raised and carries a springil in his right. Phillipa Hardman suggests that the presence of the miniature is to clear up speaker confusion between the Summoner narrating a story about a Friar and vice versa, 'Presenting the Text', p. 50. I discuss the running titles in this MS along with the issues concerning representations of 'Chaucer' below, n. 120.

52  The heads of the Reeve (fol. 186r), and the Manciple (fol. 395r); the Cook's hat (fol. 192r), and the hooves of the Monk's horse (fol. 352r).

53  Schulz argues that, wherever the beginning of a tale falls on the verso of a leaf, the illustrator appears to have reduced the amount of decoration alongside the opening four-line capital letter which otherwise would have been filled with border ornamentation. No such space was left at the start of *The Miller's Tale* (the first tale to begin on a verso – the Knight's starts on a recto folio). To have included the figure would have destroyed the aesthetics of the border illustration, and so the Miller is placed to the right of the text rather than in the margin. By the time the next such verso is reached (*The Man of Lawe's Tale*), a suitable niche has been left for the painting, Herbert C. Schulz, *The Ellesmere Manuscript of the Canterbury Tales* (San Marino, CT: Huntington Library, 1990), p. 20. When the manuscript was prepared for digital reproduction in 1994, study with a binocular manuscript showed that the painter of the illustrations followed the work of the scribe. For instance, the portrait of the Summoner was painted over the final letters of the word 'gesse' (fol. 81r). This is a detail obscured by the 1911 facsimile of Ellesmere which retouched the portrait and moved it slightly to the right to clear the text, Martin Stevens, 'Introduction', in Martin Stevens and Daniel Woodward

(eds), *The Ellesmere Chaucer: Essays in Interpretation* (San Marino, CA: Huntington Library and Yushodo Co. Ltd, 1997), p. 20 and p. 26. Malcolm Parkes argues that some of the portraits appear to have been inserted before the decoration, e.g. the Prioress (fol. 148v) and Chaucer (fol. 153v), where the borders have been modified to avoid the portraits. With the Man of Law (fol. 50v) and the Shipman (fol. 143v), the details of the horses have been covered by the decoration, 'The Planning and Construction', in Stevens and Woodward, *The Ellesmere Chaucer*, pp. 41–7 (p. 45). Anthony G. Cairns argues that examination of the pigments when the manuscript was unbound shows that the text was written before the decoration was applied, 'The Bindings of the Ellesmere Manuscript', special issue 'Reading from the Margins: Textual Studies, Chaucer and Medieval Literature', ed. Seth Lerer, *Huntington Library Quarterly*, 58 (1996), 127–57, p. 129. Maidie Hilmo suggests that, while the position of the Miller may be an accident of the production process, the unique placement of the Miller – both tales starting with an W – is a visual representation of 'quiting' since the Miller occupies the same position as the Knight, Maidie Hilmo, *Medieval Images, Icons and Illustrated English Literary Texts from the Ruthwell Cross to the Ellesmere Chaucer* (Ashgate: Aldershot, 2004), p. 192.

54  M. B. Parkes, 'The Influence of the Concepts of *Ordinatio and Compilatio* on the Development of the Book', in *Scribes, Scripts and Readers: Studies in the Communication, Presentation and Dissemination of Medieval Texts* (London: Hambledon, 1991), p. 65. Mary C. Olson argues that the choice of pilgrims and their positioning draws attention to the fictional orality of the tales, *Fair and Varied Forms: Visual Textuality in Medieval Illuminated Manuscripts* (London and New York: Routledge, 2003), pp. 154–76, and 'Marginal Portraits and the Fiction of Orality' in Finley and Rosenblum, *Chaucer Illustrated*, pp. 1–36.

55  Rick Emmerson discusses the different artists at work in 'Text and Image in the Ellesmere Portraits of the Tale-Tellers', in Stevens and Woodward, *The Ellesmere Chaucer*, pp. 143–70 (pp. 151–4).

56  Writing before Ellesmere was digitalised, Martin Stevens discussed the portraits as realistic representations of figures from *The General Prologue*, 'The Ellesmere Miniatures as Illustrations of Chaucer's Canterbury Tales', *Studies in Iconography* 7–8 (1981–82), 113–34. He has subsequently revised his views in 'Introduction', Stevens and Woodward, *The Ellesmere Chaucer*, Maidie Hilmo argues for an aristocratic agenda in the presentation of the miniatures in 'Framing the Canterbury Pilgrims for the Aristocratic Readers of the Ellesmere Manuscript' in Kathryn Kerby-Fulton and Maidie Hilmo (eds), *The Medieval Professional Reader at Work: Evidence from the Manuscripts of Chaucer, Langland, Kempe and Gower*, English Literary Studies

(Victoria, BC: University of Victoria, 2001), pp. 14–72. This argument is echoed in Joseph Rosenblum and William Finley, 'Chaucer Gentrified: The Nexus of Art and Politics in the Ellesmere Miniatures', *Chaucer Review* 38 (2003), 140–57. It will be seen from my discussion that I disagree with their conclusion that in the illustrations 'the ambiguities and criticism of the text disappears', p. 153. Closer to my approach to the miniatures are Laura F. Hodges in *Chaucer and Costume: The Secular Pilgrims in The General Prologue* (Cambridge: D. S. Brewer, 2000), Emmerson's 'Text and Image in the Ellesmere Portraits of the Tale-Tellers', pp. 143–70, and Elizabeth Scala, 'Seeing Red: The Ellesmere Iconography of Chaucer's Nun's Priest', *Word and Image* 26 (2010), 381–92, who argues that the illustration reflects how the character of the Nun's Priest came to be seen.

57  In all the surviving illustrations, including those in MS English 63, John Rylands University Library of Manchester, the pilgrims have at least one hand visible. All the Cambridge pilgrims, and thirteen in Ellesmere, have at least one hand on the reins. Only once does this action appear in the verbal text of the *Tales*. Signalling that his stay at Cambuyskan's court is over, the anonymous knight in *The Squire's Tale* 'leyde hand upon his reyne, / And seyde, "Sire, ther is namoore to seyne"' (V.313–14). The appendix to this chapter lists all the illustrated pilgrims in Ellesmere, Cambridge and Oxford and details of their hands.

58  Neither the Host nor the Plowman is realised visually because they are not tale-tellers. Nor is the Yeoman, so the 'mighty bowe' he bears in his hand (I.108) creates a figure whose martial potency is tellingly absent from those figures who are illustrated, Hodges, *Chaucer and Costume*, pp. 127–8.

59  Rosenblum and Finley suggest that he carries a staff like that of the Parson's to suggest that ordinarily he travels on foot, 'Chaucer Gentrified', p. 145.

60  Emmerson, 'Text and Image in the Ellesmere Portraits', p. 62.

61  Laura F. Hodges, *Chaucer and Clothing: Clerical and Academic Costume in the General Prologue to the Canterbury Tales* (Cambridge: D. S. Brewer, 2005), pp. 112–25.

62  See Moshe Barasch, *Giotto and the Language of Gesture* (Cambridge: Cambridge University Press, 1987), p. 47, and p. 98.

63  As stipulated in a fifteenth-century sermon, see V. M. O'Mara, *A Study and Edition of Selected Middle English Sermons* (Leeds Texts and Monographs, n.s. 13 (1994)), pp. 199–203. William of Wykeham's 1387 injunctions to the convents of Romsey and Wherwell forbade even openings in the seams of the outer mantle. Hodges writes, 'we shall never know whether Madame Eglentyne wears a russet or a white tunic because Chaucer offers no glimpse beneath her cloak', *Chaucer and Clothing*, p. 79. True: but the artist did.

64 Stevens, 'The Ellesmere Miniatures', argues that the Prioress opens her gown daintily with an outstretched hand, and describes her memorably as the 'lively fashionable nun who is as open as her gown shows her to be for the admiration of the world', p. 120. Stevens's reading (which he does not link back to *The General Prologue*) is more persuasive than that of Rosenblum and Finley, who argue that the artist has created an 'archetypal Benedictine Nun', 'Chaucer Gentrified', p. 146. The hands of the Second Nun are actually more decorous than those of the Prioress since they both have only their backs showing. There is no suggestion that her hands part her religious habit.

65 *Horae Beatae Virginis cum Calendario orationibus ad sanctos & aliis*, British Library MS Harley, 2962, fol. 41 (reproduced in Hodges, *Clerical Clothing*, opposite p. 146).

66 Bill Burgwinkle and Cary Howie, *Sanctity and Pornography in Medieval Culture: On the Verge* (Manchester: Manchester University Press, 2010), argue that being on the 'verge' articulates time though space: '[t]he verge tries to give co-ordinates to something that, strictly speaking, escapes co-ordination', p. 165.

67 Mary Carruthers, *The Book of Memory: A Study of Memory in Medieval Culture*, 2nd edn (Cambridge: Cambridge University Press, 2008), p. 314 and p. 450. Quintilian lists string tied around the fingers as a mnemonic in his *Institutiones Oratoriae*, XI.II.30.

68 For discussion of the specious ability of the lawyer to know all the legal terms by rote, see Helen Barr, 'Religious Practice in Chaucer's *Prioress's Tale*: Rabbit and/or Duck?', *Studies in the Age of Chaucer* 32 (2010), 39–66, p. 53

69 The illustrator also adds a detail not in the verbal portrait by showing the lawyer wearing a coif, which as Laura Hodges has argued, singles out a lawyer as above the rank and file because of its denotation of extensive education which grants such a figure both ceremonial and learned authority, *Chaucer and Costume*, pp. 106–9. Rosenblum and Finley interpret the coif as a sign that the Sergeant at Lawe is a bastion of the establishment of a kind that the patron of the manuscript would have supported, 'Chaucer Gentrified', p. 142.

70 Stevens suggests that the Physician uses his right hand to shield his eyes from the sun, 'The Ellesmere Miniatures', p. 115.

71 In Douce 104, the last illustrated figure is of a friar holding a urinal, fol. 111v. Other manuscript illustrations of this iconographical representation are listed in Kathryn Kerby-Fulton and Denise L. Deprès, *Iconography and the Professional Reader: The Politics of Book Production in the Douce Piers Plowman* (Minneapolis and London: University of Minnesota Press, 1999), p. lxxx, n. 185.

72 Stevens, 'The Ellesmere Miniatures', pp. 123–4; Hilmo, *Medieval Images*, pp. 168–80; Emmerson, 'Text and Image in the Ellesmere Portraits', p. 154, and p. 159 where he notices the gloves.

73   In her aristocratic reading, of the portrait, Maidie Hilmo likens the Squire to a victorious Arcite, *Medieval Professional Reader*, p. 32.

74   Stevens likens the illustrated Knight to Theseus, 'The Ellesmere Miniatures', p. 124. Hilmo argues that 'as storyteller, he is the Knight of the *Prologue*, as subject of the story, he is Theseus', *Medieval Images*, p. 176.

75   'Et pour garder ses mains blanches / Ne halaissent ot uns blans gans' (*Le Roman de la Rose*, 562–3).

76   Hodges discusses parallels between the Squire's costume and that of the God of Love in *The Romance of the Rose, Chaucer and Costume*, pp. 162–73. On pp. 128–9 she notes the contrast between the Yeoman's bow and arrows and the lack of weapons carried by the Knight and the Squire.

77   Hilmo draws attention to the ring, *Medieval Professional Reader*, p. 32, and in *Medieval Images* she connects it to the marginal annotation adjacent to *The Squire's Tale* on fol. 118v, 'of the vertu of the ring', p. 183. She argues that the Squire models an alternative to violence and licentious sexuality, p. 186.

78   Elizabeth Freeman, *Time Binds*, pp. 59–65.

79   The Manciple has no description in *The General Prologue*, but his hands are illustrated in both Ellesmere and Cambridge. They raise a drinking gourd. The illustration reprises an incident of professional rivalry that the Manciple has just narrated in the Prologue to the Tale he is about to speak. He tells the Cook, 'I have heere in a gourde / A draughte of wyn' (IX.82–3) and forces him to drink so deeply from it that he falls from his horse. The Wife of Bath, with a whip in her hands, appears in both Ellesmere and Cambridge. Hardman suggests that the Wife's whip was generated from the memory of a figurative expression she uses in her own *Prologue*, '[o]f tribulation in marriage / Of which I am expert in al myn age – / This is to seyn, myself have been the whippe' (III.173–5), 'Presenting the Text', p. 55. The Cook appears in Cambridge, in Ellesmere and in the Oxford fragments. The bowl of blood that he carries in Ellesmere may have been prompted by the Host's taunt that he has drawn off the blood from many a 'pastee' (I.4346).

80   Hardman suggests that the artist may have been influenced by the pictorial topic of Samson with a jawbone, 'Presenting the Text', p. 56.

81   Michelle P. Brown, *The Holkham Bible Picture Book: A Facsimile* (London: British Library, 2007), fol. 5b. York Minster, East Window; main light 14a.

82   'Mactatio Abel', 324 in A. C. Cawley (ed.) *The Wakefield Pageants in the Townley Cycle* (Manchester: Manchester University Press, 1958). Cawley's note observes that the tradition is seen also in *Cursor Mundi* 1073, and the *Ludus Coventriae*.

83 Helen Barr, *Socioliterary Practice in Late Medieval England* (Oxford: Oxford University Press, 2001), pp. 146–9. In *Beowulf*, Grendel is twice associated with Cain, lines 107 and 1261.

84 For discussions of the history of gesture, see Adam Kendon, *Gesture: Visible Action as Utterance* (Cambridge: Cambridge University Press, 2004); Rowe, *Dead Hands: Fictions of Agency*; Claire Richter Sherman, *Writing on Hands: Memory and Knowledge in Early Modern Europe* (Washington, DC: Folger Shakespeare Library, 2000); David McNeill, *Hand and Mind: What Gestures Reveal about Thought* (Chicago: University of Chicago Press, 1992). John Bulwer's *Chirologia, or, The naturall language of the hand* (1644), accessed via EEBO is an alphabet of the natural gestures of the hand that draws on Classical texts. It contains two illustrated tables of hand gestures which give some help to the Ellesmere gestures, but there are none that are exactly identical. Correspondences between Bulwer and individual Ellesmere miniatures are listed *in situ*. In their analysis of Bodleian Library MS Douce 104, *Iconography and the Professional Reader*, Kerby-Fulton and Deprès make extensive use of Barasch, *Giotto and the Language of Gesture*, as do Blanche and Wassermann, *From Pearl to Gawain*, in their rich study of hands in the *Pearl* manuscript. I have used Barasch's work more cautiously in relation to the Ellesmere miniatures partly because he discusses another medium in a different culture, but also because his discussion of gesture is based on populated scenes rather than individual images of persons.

85 The penitential Parson, with his hands folded across his chest in Ellesmere, performs a gesture for which the verbal tales provide no counterpart. It is recorded elsewhere, however; a hypocrite lays his hand 'ful ofte upon his brest' to say 'mea culpa' (*Confessio* 1.663). Barasch discusses this gesture, *Giotto and the Language of Gesture*, pp. 72–87. Hand gestures used elsewhere in *The Canterbury Tales* are often straightforward, but they offer little help in decoding those of the Ellesmere pilgrims. In *The Merchant's Tale*, May makes secret signs to Damien with her fingers to arrange their secret sexual liaison (IV.2209); the constable in *The Man of Lawe's Tale* wrings his hands and weeps when he finds the bloody knife in the Constance's bed (II.606), and the clerk in *The Franklin's Tale* claps his hands to indicate that his projection show is over and it is time for supper (V.1203–4). Studies specifically devoted to gesture in medieval texts have little that is relevant to the Ellesmere hands.

86 Adam Kendon discusses the distinction between objective gestures that refer to something in the external world, and subjective gestures that refer to the speaker's state of mind. He provides visual illustrations of seven available shapes, positions and directions of the hand which create gestural relationships between speakers, and

between speakers and objects, *Gesture: Visible Action*, pp. 207–8.
The deixis of those gestures is discussed on pp. 199–224.

87  Hilmo notes how the Squire's self-referential hand position displays
the ring, *Medieval Images*, p. 182. Hodges, *Chaucer and Costume*,
notes that the Ellesmere Squire wears a costume designed to draw
attention to the body, p. 60.

88  This preaching or praying gesture appears in the verbal text of
*The Canterbury Tales*. Aurelius raises his hands to heaven to begin
his delirious prayer to Apollo (VI.1024). Urban lifts his hands to pray
to Christ in *The Second Nun's Tale* (VIII.189). In *Melibee*, before
the wise man speaks, he 'made contenaunce [with his hand] that men
sholde holden hem stille and yeven hym audience' (VII.1041–2).
These meaning of these gestures is corroborated by their appearance
in *Confessio*: Medea raises one hand to pray (5.3980); Constance
raises both when she prays to God (2.1055), and the blind man
raises both hands to Hermengild and prays her to give him his sight
(2.761). Bulwer illustrates a gesture that is a raised hand which he
labels 'Benedico', Image 90. Barasch discusses the gesture he calls
'adlocution' where a character raises their right hand, request-
ing quiet and attention, *Giotto and the Language of Gesture*, p. 17.
He distinguishes this from 'acclamatio' which is more like addressing a crowd. A vertical hand can also be an announcing hand, p. 25.
He notes that it is quite hard in the frescos to establish whether a hand
is announcing, speaking or blessing, pp. 28–30.

89  The gesture is close to that which Bulwer identifies as 'Protego'.
Hilmo has suggested that the Knight's hand suggests the aristocratic
grace of the Knight, serving as formal greeting to the audience and
as a courteous introduction to the text, 'Framing the Canterbury
Pilgrims', p. 20.

90  Kendon, *Gesture: Visible Action*, pp. 201–16.

91  Bartholomaeus, as Isidore of Seville before him, makes the link
between indexing and the pointing work of the index finger:
Bartholomaeus, *De Proprietatibus Rerum*, pp. 224–5.

92  The Nun's Priest's raised hand shows some similarities, though
partly because the portrait is badly executed its precise deixis is
hard to determine. The greater thickness of the arms and hand
suggests repainting, and the miniature is smudged. The Priest's
hand is cupped with an index finger slightly raised towards the text
underneath the word 'tale'. Its shape resembles that of the Canon's
Yeoman's. The hand of the Canon's Yeoman is raised in front of
him. The palm is horizontal, and the fingers cupped loosely above
it; the thumb nearly touching the ring finger. This is a semi-closed
hand position, which resembles what modern theorists of gesture call
the ring position or the 'grappolo' (Kendon, *Gesture: Visible Action*,
p. 223); a demonstrative gesture that gives emphasis to the Canon's

Yeoman as speaker. His eyes look towards his hand, which in turn directs the onlooker's gaze to the gesture itself; there is no objective reference. Quintilian argued that the most common speaking gesture was that 'in which the middle finger is drawn in towards the thumb, the other three fingers being open', *Institutio Oratoria* XI.3.92. It also resembles the gesture that Bulwer identifies as 'Invito', Image 90. Placed morphologically alongside the hand of the Canon's Yeoman, it is clearer to see that the deixis of the Nun's Priest's hand lies somewhere between self-referentiality and reference to his tale.

93 The border has also been moved for the Prioress miniature. On fol. 206v a daisy bud has been erased to allow room for the miniature of the Parson, see H. C. Dutschke, *Medieval and Renaissance Manuscripts in the Huntington* (San Marino, CA: Huntington Library, 1966), p. 147.

94 Stevens, 'The Ellesmere Miniatures', p. 116. Alan T. Gaylord, 'Portrait of a Poet', in Stevens and Woodward (eds), *The Ellesmere Chaucer*, pp. 121–42, suggests that the placing is due to the incompleteness of *Thopas*, and perhaps because the makers of Ellesmere wanted the picture to be associated with Chaucer's 'more serious contribution', *The Ellesmere Chaucer*, p. 121. Schulz notes the absence of a decorative border on the folio which *Thopas* begins; the opening lines are marked only by a two-line initial. All this, in Schulz's view, points to 'a feeling on the part of all concerned – the scribe, the illuminator, the stationer – that a minimum of attention should be drawn to *Sir Thopas*, for the tale was destined to be a disappointment', pp. 26–7. I discuss the portrait adjacent to *Melibee* in Bodleian MS Rawlinson poet.223 below, n. 120.

95 Emmerson, 'Text and Image in the Ellesmere Portraits', p. 152.

96 This is the term used by William H. Sherman, first in 'Toward a History of the Manicule', www.livesandletters.ac.uk, posted online: March 2005, and subsequently in *Used Books: Marking Readers in Renaissance England* (Philadelphia: University of Pennsylvania Press, 2008). He observed in 2005 that the history of the manicule, the little text hand, had yet to be written, p. 1. His 2008 monograph writes that history, but chiefly from the early modern period forwards. There is still no sustained discussion of the manicule in medieval texts. My treatment of its appearance and functions is merely a brief synopsis of some of its salient features.

97 Lucy Freeman Sandler, '*Omne Bonum*: Compilation and Ordinatio in an English Illustrated Encyclopedia of the Fourteenth Century', in L. L. Brownrigg (ed.), *Medieval Book Production: Assessing the Evidence* (Los Altos Hills: Anderson-Lovelace; London: The Red Gull Press, 1990), pp. 183–200 (p. 189). A copy of Gregory's *Decretals* in Oxford Bodleian MS lat.th.6.4. has a cuffed pointing hand in the right inner margin between the text and the gloss, reproduced in

Christopher de Hamel, *A History of Illuminated Manuscripts* (London: Phaidon, 1994), p. 139. See also Carruthers, *The Book of Memory*, p. 135 and p. 314, and Michael Clanchy, *From Memory to Written Record: England 1066–1307*, 2nd edn (Oxford: Basil Blackwell, 1995), p. 172.

98  Paul Sanger, 'Silent Reading', *Viator* 13 (1982), 367–414, pp. 392–413.

99  Sherman, *Used Books*, p. 47. Their gesture differentiates them from other anthropomorphic signs, for example, the head.

100  Carruthers, *The Book of Memory*, p. 314.

101  Rowe, *Dead Hands*, p. xiv; Sherman, *Used Books*, p. 29, and pp. 35–40.

102  Sherman, *Used Books*, p. 41.

103  Stephen G. Nichols, 'On the Sociology of Medieval Manuscript Annotation', in Stephen Barney (ed.), *Annotation and Its Texts* (Oxford: Oxford University Press, 1991), pp. 43–73, p. 56.

104  In Cambridge Gg.4.27, one of three manicules points to the lines at the end of *The General Prologue* (fol. 144v/A.725–6), where the pilgrim narrator Chaucer asks his audience to excuse his 'vileynye' for speaking plainly, and for rehearsing the words of the pilgrims as they spoke them, however coarse. Readers are given a command to note the speaking voice of a fictional pilgrim who impersonates the words of other characters. The hand points not to written authority but to vocal mobility. The author's own voice and presence is replaced first by his own writing, and then by the written sign of an annotator who, with a severed hand (cuffed), points successively to the projection of voices of intermediated characters.

105  For instance, in both the Ellesmere and Hengwrt copies of *The Shipman's Tale*, the question 'Qy est la', words supplied by the annotation of a scribe, becomes part of the text. The annotation elbows its way into a space that it challenges from the margins. Author is presented as gloss and a scribal glossator as Chaucer's text, Ralph Hanna III, 'Annotation as Social Practice', in Barney, *Annotation and Its Texts*, pp. 178–91 (p. 182).

106  Kerby-Fulton and Deprès, *Iconography and the Professional Reader*, argue that the Douce illustrations pay little heed to the clerical world; the cycle is full of an almost defiant, reformist, absence of representations of Christ and the saints. Tom Stowe is depicted, but Christ never. Kerby-Fulton and Deprès see the artist to 'out-Langland Langland', pp. 25–31. They cite a pertinent example (p. 32) of the artist's willingness to bypass the words of the text when Pride, named in the text as 'Pernele proud herte', falls contrite to the earth but is illustrated as a man wearing the bells of a minstrel (C.6.3), Douce 104, fol. 24r.

107  My reading differs slightly from that of Deprès, *Iconography and the Professional Reader*, pp. 144–5, which does not observe the blocking of the hands, nor that they touch.

108 Douce 104 is not an isolated example of this play with meaning, either in *Piers Plowman* or in other texts. The copy of *Piers Plowman* contained in BL MS Add.35157 has nine pointing hands alongside copious underlining, notae and verbal annotations, see Carl James Grindley, 'Reading *Piers Plowman* C Text Annotation: Notes Towards the Classification of Printed and Written Marginalia in Texts from the British Isles 1300–1641', in Kerby-Fulton and Hilmo, *Medieval Professional Reader*, pp. 73–142.

109 Sandler, '*Omne Bonum*', p. 189. Palmer also copied a set text version of William of Nottingham's early fourteenth-century Gospel commentary. He drew a vigorously spotted leper who points a scrofulous finger at the marginal commentary on the text of Luke 17:16 (Bodleian Library MS Laud Misc.165, fol. 364). Via James, a diseased hand points not to God's word but to the human commentary that mediates it. The red ink annotator in *The Book of Margery Kempe* in BL MS Add.61823 draws a host of symbols in the margins to act as notae, including tears, faces, Our Lady's smock, a bleeding heart and a snowcloud. There are two pointing hands. The first points to God's words 'I am that I am' with its middle finger (fol. 11v/ch. 10, p. 23/3). The second manicule wittily points its index finger at God's words 'with mine own hand' (fol. 25v/ch. 22, p. 51.30). The hand of God is a hand drawn by an annotator who supplements God's handiwork with his own. For discussion of these annotations, see Kelly Parsons, 'The Red Ink Annotator of the Book of Margery Kempe and His Lay Audience', in Kerby-Fulton and Hilmo, *The Medieval Professional Reader at Work*, pp. 143–216. My line references are to *The Book of Margery Kempe*, ed. H. E. Allen (EETS OS 212, 1940).

110 Camille, *Image on the Edge*, p. 21.

111 We might compare this to an illustration in a copy of Thomas Netter's *Doctrinale*, Oxford Merton College MS 31, fol. 41r, where, from a roundel, the figure of Netter points accusingly at the figure of Wyclif. The historiated initial illustrates the elevation of the Host.

112 Psalter and Book of Hours in Walker Art Gallery, Baltimore, MS 102, fol. 33v. This is illustrated in Camille, *Image on the Edge*, p. 24.

113 The notion of 're-praesens' – re-presenting the work – is discussed in Kerby-Fulton and Deprès, *Iconography and the Professional Reader*, p. 103. See also the collection of essays *Annotation and Its Texts*, ed. Barney, and Stephen G. Nichols, 'Philology in Manuscript Culture', *Speculum* 65 (1995), 1–10.

114 For discussion of the Harley portrait, see James H. McGregor, 'The Iconography of Chaucer in Hoccleve's *De Regimine Principum* and the *Troilus* Frontispiece', *Chaucer Review* 11 (1977), 338–50; Jeanne E. Krochalis, 'Hoccleve's Chaucer Portrait', *Chaucer Review* 21 (1986), 234–45; David R. Carlson, 'Thomas Hoccleve and the Chaucer Portrait', *Huntington Library Quarterly* 54 (1991), 283–300; Derek

Pearsall, 'The Chaucer Portraits', in *The Life of Geoffrey Chaucer: A Critical Biography* (Oxford: Blackwell, 1992), pp. 285–305; Pearsall, 'Thomas Hoccleve's *Regement of Princes*: The Poetics of Royal Self-Representation', *Speculum* 69 (1994), 386–410, and Ethan Knapp, *The Bureaucratic Muse: Thomas Hoccleve and the Literature of Late Medieval England* (University Park, PA: Pennsylvania State University Press, 2001), pp. 119–24.

115 Thomas Hoccleve, *The Regiment of Princes*, ed. Charles R. Blyth (Kalamazoo, MI: Medieval Institute Publications, 1999).

116 Nicholas Perkins, *Hoccleve's Regiment of Princes: Counsel and Constraint* (Cambridge: Brewer, 2001), p. 119. Perkins also draws attention to the pointing finger used in other manuscript illustrations which shows a figure in an advisory role. There is a manicule on Thomas Hoccleve's personal seal attached to a document that confirms receipt of his annuity. It points upwards to an equilateral cross on the topmost edge of the red wax, see Linne Mooney, 'Some New Light on Thomas Hoccleve', *Studies in the Age of Chaucer* 29 (2007), 293–340, pp. 317–18, and Richard Firth Green and Ethan Knapp, 'Thomas Hoccleve's Seal', *Medium Ævum* 77 (2008), 319–21. Perkins compares the pointing hand in Hoccleve's seal with that of Harley, arguing that if the maniculum is Hoccleve's personal device it directs viewers back to Hoccleve's own claims to intimate knowledge or preoccupation with Chaucer's personal and poetic corpus, 'Haunted Hoccleve?: *The Regiment of Princes*, the Troilean Intertext, and Conversations with the Dead', *Chaucer Review* 43 (2008), 103–39, p. 138, n. 50.

117 The rosary may be a result of recalling the influence of Gower as Hoccleve's other 'maisttir' even though he is not mentioned in the stanzas beside which the figure points. Penitential beads suggest those given to the moral poet John Gower (*Confessio* 8.2907), see Charles R. Blyth, 'Thomas Hoccleve's Other Master', *Medievalia* 16 (1993), 349–59.

118 See above, p. 1.

119 The availability of roles for Chaucer cued by his left hand exceeds the conflation of author and narrator as argued by Mary C. Olson, *Fair and Varied Forms*. His unruly manicules conflate the two dominant strains of Chaucerian memory that have been posited as the chief ways in which he materialises in works and artefacts produced after his death: remembered presence and lost absence. In the first, his guiding personal presence is vividly fresh, and in the second, the philological model, he is definitely absent; only his textual remains survive, see Lerer, *Chaucer's Readers*, pp. 147–75, and James Simpson, 'Chaucer's Presence and Absence, 1400–1550', in Piero Boitani and Jill Mann (eds), *The Cambridge Companion to Chaucer* (Cambridge: Cambridge University Press, 2004), pp. 251–69. Perkins

argues that Chaucer is sometimes a painful absence and sometimes a revenant presence, 'Haunted Hoccleve', p. 120.

120 Other manuscripts of *The Canterbury Tales* show hands that could be seen to belong to 'Chaucer'. On folio 1 of the Devonshire manuscript of *The Canterbury Tales* a man is seated on a grassy plot. His inclined head rests upon his raised right hand and he points to the ground with his left. The pose resembles that in which a contemplative author is shown dictating his work. In Bodleian Library MS Lansdowne 851, fol. 1r, a man wearing a penner is positioned in a three-quarters facing pose with a serious facial expression. Both hands hold an open book as if he were an author presenting its contents for his audience. In Bodleian Library MS Bodley 686, fol. 1r, a young man who embodies the exuberant spring setting both of *The General Prologue* and of the Squire's physical description, inhabits the decorated initial in which we might expect an author portrait. His manicule points through the lively foliage to the 'drouth of march'. If this is Chaucer's hand as author, it is also the hand of the narrator of *The General Prologue* dressed up like one of his characters. The historiated initial adjacent to *The Tale of Melibee* in Bodleian Library MS Rawlinson poet.223, fol. 183v, shows a man seated with his left hand on his knee. He points to the text of *Melibee* with his right. This could be a portrait of Chaucer as author in his study, an illustration of Chaucer as pilgrim teller (the historiated initial on fol. 143r shows the Friar in a pulpit at the start of the *Prologue* to his *Tale*), or a representation of a character within the tale itself. The right hand points towards the line 'A yong man called Melibee'. Hardman discusses these illustrations, 'Presenting the Text', pp. 46–50.

121 Indeed, when the two portraits are placed on the verso and recto pages of a full-page opening, as they are in Stevens and Woodward, *The Ellesmere Chaucer*, pp. 22–3, figures 28 and 29, the mirror image effect is made all the more apparent.

122 Immanuel Kant, 'On the First Ground of the Distinction of Regions of Space' [1768], in James Van Cleve and Robert E. Frederick (eds), *The Philosophy of Left and Right* (Dordrecht: Kluwer Academic Publishers, 1991), pp. 27–33.

123 For discussion of the relativity of 'left' and 'right', see Stephen C. Levinson, 'Space and Place', in Antony Gormley, *Some of the Facts* (Exhibition: Tate St Ives, 2001), pp. 69–109 (pp. 81–7).

124 Robert E. Frederick, in his discussion of Kant's 1768 work on left and right, argues that a 3D hologram of a left hand would be a 3D image of the hand that is left – right reversed. It would look like an ordinary right hand, 'Introduction to the Argument of 1768', in *The Philosophy of Left and Right*, pp. 1–14, pp. 4–5. For further discussion of Gormley's *Bed* see Levinson, 'Space and Place', pp. 100–5.

# 4

# 'Wrinkled deep in time': Emily and Arcite in *A Midsummer Night's Dream*

When Theseus is offered the show of a drunken mob of women tearing the poet Orpheus limb from limb for his nuptial celebrations he dismisses it thus:

> That is an old device, and it was played
> When I from Thebes came last a conqueror.
>
> (*A Midsummer Night's Dream* 5.1.50–1)[1]

How old and when? Theseus's allusion to his own backstory presents a temporal puzzle. In Chaucer's *The Knight's Tale*, Theseus returns in triumph from his conquest of Thebes, *after* he has married his Amazonian bride Hippolyta. In *Two Noble Kinsmen*, he interrupts his wedding (at what point in the play it happens is unclear) to wage war against Thebes *before* he returns to Athens with the two knights Palamon and Arcite he has taken prisoner. How, in *A Midsummer Night's Dream*, can Theseus already have witnessed a worn celebration in honour of his last victory against Thebes when his marriage to Hippolyta is not yet a day old? This long since event ought not yet to have happened. In the 'past source' of *The Knight's Tale* and the 'play yet to be written' that is *Two Noble Kinsmen*, Theseus's conquest of Thebes, foretold as past in *A Midsummer Night's Dream*, is plot-crucially present, along with its catastrophic aftermath.[2]

Theseus's faux-casual dismissal of the frenzied Maenads is a 'wrinkle, or fold in time' in the story of *A Midsummer Night's Dream*. It is, as Paul Strohm says of Petrarch's sonnet in Chaucer's *Troilus and Criseyde*, 'a doubling back or superimposition; a nonsynchronous intimation of past and future at the heart of the present'.[3] It contains a prediction, a hint, of the not-yet thing that has already occurred. *A Midsummer Night's Dream* contains the story that was *The Knight's Tale* and the story it will have been: *Two Noble Kinsmen*. It contains them in both senses, for it is imperative that *A Midsummer Night's Dream* does not fully tell the story to which it keeps alluding.[4]

If Theseus has already conquered Thebes in *A Midsummer Night's Dream*, then where are his prisoners, Palamon and Arcite? And where too, is Emelye, Hippolyta's sister?[5] 'We are not here' says Quince/Prologue (5.1.115). But the craftsmen are 'here' at Theseus's court, both as 'themselves' and the parts that they 'present/disfigure' (3.1.56). Differently, and yet likewise, Palamon, Arcite and Emelye are 'here' in *A Midsummer Night's Dream*; their parts in *The Knight's Tale* and *Two Noble Kinsmen* enfolded between Theseus's first worded 'Now' and the 'amends' (Amen/ends) with which *A Midsummer Night's Dream* 'properly' concludes.[6] While previous studies of the relationships between *A Midsummer Night's Dream*, *The Knight's Tale* and *Two Noble Kinsmen* have produced some dizzying textual intercourse[7] which perforate their temporal boundaries, the sequence of their composition is left largely intact: *The Knight's Tale* begets *Dream* begets *Two Noble Kinsmen*.[8] What I propose here, chiefly by examining the roles of Emelye and Arcite, is an intervention into the relationships of these plays that disobeys linear chronology. If we disaggregate the temporalities of *Dream* we reveal its stories of Emelye and Arcite that are predicted in *Two Noble Kinsmen* by the story that *The Knight's Tale* itself contains. Emelye and Arcite are always already 'here' in *Dream*.

## Emily[9]

It is well known that time in *Dream* doesn't submit to arithmetic. References to the moon don't add up. At the start of the play it is waning four days off its end, and yet when Quince consults his almanac in the wood (3.1.43–54), he triumphantly tells the craftsmen that the moon will shine brightly enough on the night of their performance to illuminate their play through an open casement window. The 'four days' which Theseus wishes to hurry in order to consummate his marriage unaccountably shrink to a single night.[10] Theseus may be determined to tell the time: '[n]ow' is his first word, but the present is not his to determine. Hippolyta immediately contradicts his observation that the moon's time is 'slow'; her reiterated 'quickly' stages early opposition to Theseus's version of events.[11] Midsummer is the season of the year suggested by the play's title, but Theseus, on finding the lovers asleep in the wood in Act 4 remarks, '[n]o doubt they rose up early to observe / The rite

of May' (4.1.131–2). His quip at the expense of the lovers betrays
the fragility of his own hold over time. His reference to May wrinkles the temporality of *The Knight's Tale* and *Two Noble Kinsmen*
into *Dream*. In *The Knight's Tale*, May is the month when Palamon
and Arcite fall fatally in love with the same woman, and it is May
when Palamon and Arcite are discovered by Theseus fighting in
the grove. In *Two Noble Kinsmen*, the rites of May are dramatised
on stage; with Emilia at the heart of their festivities and strife. May,
according to Arcite:

> is a solemn rite
> … and the Athenians pay it
> To th'heart of ceremony. Oh, Queen Emilia,
> Fresher than May, sweeter
> Than her gold buttons on the boughs.
>
> (3.1.2–6)

May is a metonym for Emily,[12] for violence between men, and
for impediment to arranged marriage. Theseus's temporal slip
folds the trouble of Emily into *Dream*: Hippolyta's sister becomes
available to the play's temporal imagination. In *The Knight's
Tale* Emelye is inseparable from Hippolyta: where Hippolyta
appears, 'and Emelye' is next in line.[13] As in *Two Noble Kinsmen*,
Emelye and Hippolyta attend Theseus when he catches Arcite and
Palamon fighting. With Emily present, the wood contains violence
between two men over one woman, so, when Theseus finds the
four lovers asleep on the ground of the wood in *Dream*, their
love-triangles straightened into two neat pairs, he presumptuously
and hastily directs them into marriage.[14] For the normative – and
dynastic – couplings in *Dream* to work, Emily must be prevented.
That is, she must be both stopped and seen coming. Her presence
is rendered impossible by the exigencies of the plot of *Dream*, but
her absence is supplied by familiarity with the story of *The Knight's
Tale*. Once known, a recollection of Emily presents her role in
the plot of *Dream* in which she must not be seen. But Theseus's
attempts to rule time in *Dream*, to speed over what prevents his
purpose, are overridden by the play's polysynchronicity. Neither
Theseus nor *Dream* can define the play's own moment; its variable
'now' unfolds future and past 'Emily's inside its bounds.

   *Two Noble Kinsmen*, *Dream* and *The Knight's Tale* are
intratemporal; they contain each other's stories. Like Theseus,
Chaucer's Knight prevents them. This is how he introduces the
temple of Diana:

Now to the temple of Dyane the chaste
As shortly as I kan, I wol me haste,
To telle yow al the descripsioun.

(I.2051–3)

Ther saugh I many another wonder storie,
The which me list nat drawen to memorie.

(I.2073–4)

His reluctance to tell us what he sees introduces a scenario absent
from the *Teseida*, the story from which his narration is supposed
to be drawn,[15] but present in the story of *Two Noble Kinsmen* and
*Dream*. He tells us he sees Diana in the temple, seated high on a hart,
dogs at her feet, and underneath them a moon: '[w]exynge it was
and sholde wanye soone' (I.2079). He sees a series of lovers forced
into sex against their will, all metamorphosed into something else,
including Daphne, following her ordeal with Apollo. And he sees
Lucina, Diana's other self, the goddess of childbirth, protector of
women in travail (I.2055–85). The Knight fills a silence in *Teseida*
with the desire for chastity and with desire between women which
excludes men; a desire stated in emphatically in Emelye's prayer to
the 'chaste goddesse of the wodes grene' (I.2297):

Desire to ben a mayden al my lyf,
Ne nevere wol I be no love ne wyf.
I am, thow woost, yet of thy compaignye,
A mayde, and love huntynge and venerye,
And for to walken in the wodes wilde,
And noght to ben a wyf and be with childe.
Noght wol I knowe compaignye of man.

(I.2305–11)

And whil I lyve, a mayde I wol thee serve.

(I.2330)

Emelye is a votaress to Diana and her moon, devoted to the
'compaignye' not of men, but of a chaste goddess. Theseus wants
none of her, 'the pale companion is not for our pomp' (1.1.15). But
Emily keeps on turning up. As here:

Flying between the cold moon and the earth
Cupid, all armed. A certain aim he took
At a fair vestal thronèd by the west,
And loosed his love-shaft smartly from his bow
As it should pierce a hundred thousand hearts.
But I might see young Cupid's fiery shaft
Quenched in the chaste beams of the wat'ry moon,

And the imperial vot'ress passèd on,
In maiden meditation, fancy free.
Yet marked I where the bolt of Cupid fell.
It fell upon a little western flower –
Before, milk-white; now, purple with love's wound.

(A Midsummer Night's Dream 2.1.156–67)

Oberon's 'fair vestal', so often associated with Elizabeth I,[16] the absent, excluded woman upon whom *Dream* depends,[17] etches the memory of Emily. Emily is the woman the play needs to exclude in order to reach its dynastic end, but the labour of this erasure is indelible. Especially in these lines. While she has no throne, Emily is literally, not metaphorically, a votaress of the Amazonian empire, devoted to Diana, goddess of the moon. Dedicated to chastity, she wishes no part of Cupid's fiery shaft to pierce her maiden heart. But Emily, like the milk-white flower, cannot escape becoming empurpled with the bloody wound of ruptured maidenhead.[18] Oberon's speech in *Dream* will have been Emily's prayer to Diana in her temple in *The Knight's Tale*:

Syn thou art mayde and kepere of us alle,
My maydenhede thou kepe and wel conserve,
And whil I lyve, a mayde I wol thee serve.

(I.2328–30)

And Diana's inability to grant her request:

    sodeynly she saugh a sighte queynte,
For right anon oon of the fyres queynte
And quyked agayn, and after that anon
That oother fyr was queynt and al agon;
And as it queynte it made a whistelynge,
As doon thise wete brondes in hir brennynge,
And at the brondes ende out ran anon
As it were blody dropes many oon.

(I.2333–40)

Emelye's desperate desire to remain chaste speaks 'mayde' three times in three lines, only to be answered by the assonance of four 'queyntes' in the vision. Glossing 'queynte' always grammatically and chastely) as 'extinguished/curious', editors gloss over the sense of its dysphemism: cunt.[19] The translation of 'mayde' into 'queynte' batters home the impact of Emelye's 'enforcèd chastity', while Diana's moon with every little flower 'looks on with wat'ry eye, and weeps' (*Dream* 3.1.188–90).[20] The erotic burning of the wet brands dripping blood will have been Oberon's white flower, source of erotic mayhem, swollen red. The Knight's failed attempt at courteous narration is not less but more grotesque than the single rose (the bloodied flower) that falls in the temple when Emilia is discharged from Diana's service in *Two Noble Kinsmen*.[21]

Emily's frustrated desire courses through *Dream*'s endemic splittings, and metamorphoses. *Dream* contains, of course, not just one votaress but two: the mother of the Indian changeling boy was 'a vot'ress' of Titania's order (2.1.123); she will have been of the unnamed woman in Diana's temple:

> A womman travaillynge was hire biforn;
> But for hir child so longe was unborn,
> Ful pitously Lucyna gan she calle
> And seyde, 'Help, for thou mayst best of alle!'
>
> (I.2083–6)

Just as Diana cannot preserve Emelye's white flower, so she cannot prevent Titania's votaress from dying in childbirth. Diana's inability to protect women in her service will also have been the death of Emilia's beloved Flavina who 'took leave o'th'moon / (Which then looked pale at parting)' (*Two Noble Kinsmen* 1.3.52–3). Emilia's love for Flavina is Emelye's denied desire to cling to her maiden Amazon life and the future perfect of the childhood devotion between Helena and Hermia 'with two seeming bodies and one heart'; who 'grew together / Like to a double cherry: seeming parted / But yet an unison in partition' (*Dream* 3.2.209–12).[22] The strength of all these gynocentric bonds will have impeded the heteronormative conclusion that is so vital to Theseus's dynastic plans.[23] It has been argued that these female attachments must be placed in the past, so that they can be succeeded, got over.[24] Viewed within linear time, that is correct. But in the wrinkled time of these consynchronous stories this powerful female block is never succeeded. Female – female attachment might be 'got over' at the level of diachronic plot, but it remains available and possible within 'folded' time.

Emily keeps turning up and back; like all those metamorphoses. Take the story of Apollo and Daphne as Chaucer's Knight tells it in Diana's temple:

> Ther saugh I Dane, yturned til a tree –
> I mene nat the goddesse Diane,
> But Penneus doughter, which that highte Dane.
>
> (I.2062–4)

The assonance of Danae, Diana and Dane chimes the metamorphoses with which *A Midsummer Night's Dream* teems. The Knight does not mean to mention the goddess Diana, but he can't help himself. The doubling of names is doubled back in Helena's description of her chase for Demetrius:

> The story shall be changed:
> Apollo flies, and Daphne holds the chase.
>
> (2.1.231)

Helena rewinds the transformation rather as Theseus gets Diana's moon back to front: '[w]exynge it was, and sholde wanye soone' (*Knight's Tale* 2078); '[h]ow slow / This old moon wanes' (*Dream* 1.1.4–5). The moon, symbol of Diana, to whom Emily is votaress, crosses the Knight's – and Theseus's – desires, and neither man can subject the changes of the moon to his control. The shrinking moon with which Theseus is so impatient in *Dream* endangers the production of healthy progeny that is so vital to his marital plans.[25] Theseus's anxiety about Diana and her followers dogs his preoccupation with the moon. Joining forces with Egeus to exert his will over Hermia's desires; to dispose of her virginity, like Emily's, to the 'right' man, he threatens Hermia that she will be forced, 'to abjure/For ever the society of men' (1.1.65–6). But the continuation of his threat speaks his own anxieties:

> To live a barren sister all your life,
> Chanting faint hymns to the cold fruitless moon.
>
> (1.1.72–3)

While Chaucer's Knight and Theseus speak Emily's desire to force it to their patriarchal will, their narrative determination towards a marital conclusion whose progeny will reproduce healthy versions of themselves must contain Emily and the childless moon to which she is avowed: sign of chastity, untimely menstruation and sisterly devotion. Once spoken, Emily's desire is let loose. The expressed will to its coercion or banishment unleashes its expression. Neither Emily nor her cold fruitless moon will be so easily packed up.[26]

The moon appears more often in *Dream* than in any other Shakespeare play. Even when the lovers are safely out of the wood and married at Theseus's palace, just at the point when Theseus might have felt in control, the craftsmen stage his worst nightmare: not perhaps the play of Pyramus and Thisbe, whose tragedy of lovers divided by parental will dramatises the plot that *Dream* must not fulfil, but their arduous attempts to bring the moon back

into Theseus's court. The efforts of the craftsmen prompt much
ribaldry amongst the 'gentle' characters, but Theseus's contribution has a particular edge. Ostensibly commenting on staging, he
quips that 'the man should be put in the lantern. How is it else
the man i'th'moon?' (5.1.241–3). This is not just a jape about a
male-punctured moon: there is play on the proverbial expression:
to 'be in the lantern', which means to be 'hanged from the post'.[27]
Theseus's 'joke' threatens death by execution for the actor who has
had such temerity to bring into his court, on the craftsmen's own
terms, Theseus's dreaded moon, symbol of chastity, and female
bonding. Moonshine, as the craftsmen call the moon, contains even
further horror. The word has the sense not only of 'the light of the
moon' but also 'an appearance without substance; something insubstantial or unreal'.[28] The very thing, or name, of 'moonshine' that
the craftsmen strain to produce for Theseus encapsulates *Dream*'s
preoccupation with presences/absences, substances/shadows, and
actors/roles which Theseus attempts to explain away through 'cool
reason' (5.1.6). 'I am invisible' says Oberon (2.1.186), standing on
stage for all to see. The craftsmen, like the moonshine, both are and
are not here: present/absent, substances/shadows and actors/roles.
In dramatic figure they body forth the shape, if not the name, of
prevented Emily; the intratemporal threat to the play that insists
on turning up.

Theseus's mockery of the moon prevents the grotesque mer-
riment in *Two Noble Kinsmen*. The Second Queen, appealing
to Hippolyta, 'most dreaded Amazonian' (I.1.77–8), to show
Theseus her warlike strength to persuade him to wage war
against Thebes, urges her to imagine her not-yet husband swollen
'i'th' blood-sized field / Showing the sun his teeth, grinning at
the moon' (1.1.99–100). *Two Noble Kinsmen* dramatises, hor-
rifically, what *Dream* and *The Knight's Tale* contain: Amazonian
brutality; monstrosity, infanticide. The First Queen beseeches
Theseus 'by warranting moonlight' to imagine 'rotten kings or
blubbered queens' (1.1.177–80) when he kisses the sweetness of
the 'twinning cherries' of Hippolyta's lips that will have been the
kissing cherries that Demetrius sees in Helena's visage (*Dream*
3.2.140), and Helena's and Hermia's 'double cherry' (3.2.209).
The dove, that according to Helena will chase the griffin (2.1.232),
or the term of endearment which Flute (as Thisbe) addresses
to the dead Bottom/Pyramus (5.1.324), will have been the brief
kneeling gesture of an Amazonian woman which lasts no longer
than 'a dove's motion, when the head's plucked off' (*Two Noble*

*Kinsmen* 1.1.98). The promise of healthy progeny at the close
of *Dream*, unharmed by the vagaries of the moon, are the babies
which Hippolyta and her Amazonian soldiers 'broach ... on the
lance', broil in the brine of their tears and devour (*Two Noble
Kinsmen* 1.3.20–2). *The Knight's Tale* and *Dream* contain the story
of Amazonian Emily to which *Two Noble Kinsmen* gives full rein.

In *Two Noble Kinsmen*, while Emilia is handed in marriage first
to Arcite, and then to Palamon, her primary allegiance remains
to Diana: to the company of women rather than the company of
men.[29] *Two Noble Kinsmen* gives full dramatic expression to the
Emilian desire that is prevented in *The Knight's Tale* and *Dream*,
and not only in Emilia's speech about Flavina. When Palamon and
Arcite spy Emilia in the garden she is engaged in sexy banter with
her female attendant. 'Thou art wanton' Emilia tells her woman.
'I could lie down, I am sure' she replies. 'And take one with you?'
asks Emilia (2.2.147–52). Whether the 'bargain' on which the two
women 'agree' (2.2.153) is the punchline to a verbal sparring, or
as it has been read, a mutual invitation to bed, the scene gives to
Emilia a gynocentric scenario that makes a mockery of the two
knights' rivalry as they gaze on her from their prison.[30]

Theseus forces Emilia to look at these two men to choose
between them, but when asked for her opinion of Arcite, she
replies:

> His mother was a wondrous handsome woman;
> His face, methinks, goes that way.
>
> (2.5.20–1)

In Act 4, when Emilia reluctantly compares the kinsmen's pictures, she again looks beyond the men to women:

> Two such young, handsome men
> Shall never fall for me; their weeping mothers
> Following the dead cold ashes of their sons,
> Shall never curse my cruelty.
>
> (4.2.3–6)

> Palamon ...
> He's swart and meagre, of an eye as heavy
> As if he had lost his mother ...
>
> (4.2.25–8)

> Two greater and two better never yet
> Made mothers joy –
>
> (4.2.62–3)

Emilia may be forced to choose between men, but she sees through them to women. She remains unassimilated to the dynastic resolution, the 'concord from discord', which *Dream* must produce.

Emily's insouciant desire, prevented and unmoored in *Dream* and *The Knight's Tale*, is refracted in *Two Noble Kinsmen* through the role of the Jailer's Daughter. Unnamed, she is the woman who in performance steals the play. In her pursuit of Palamon through the wood and her wish to have him 'do / What he will with me ... [f]or use me so he shall' (*Two Noble Kinsmen* 2.6.28–30), the Daughter is Helena's contemporary, racing after Demetrius, begging him that, as she is his spaniel, to use her as he would his dog (*Dream* 2.1.203–10). The Daughter's desire for Palamon and her rejection of her Father's sanctioned wooer will have been Hermia's love for Lysander despite Egeus's preferment of Demetrius. Hermia's chastity must be preserved for a legitimate marriage bed, not taken on the dank and dirty ground, but the Daughter's chastity has no such protection. It is flaunted in the wood when – literally in the RSC 1986 production – she was caught up in the phallic exuberance of the countrymen's Morris.[31] And in her later mad scene, when she imagines she hoists a sail up on a ship, the 'nautical' commentary of the Jailer, Wooer and his brother disguises but very thinly what they see up the Daughter's skirts and what they desire to do there:

> BROTHER Let's get her in.
> JAILER Up to the top, boy ...
> DAUGHTER What kenn'st thou?
> 2 FRIEND A fair wood
> DAUGHTER Bear for it, master;
>   Tack about!
> [*Sings*] When Cynthia with her borrowed light.
>
> (4.1.148–52)

Once more, Diana/Cynthia is unable to protect a woman. The men imagine gang sex as the Daughter exposes her pubic hair ('[a] fair wood'), and instructs them to 'tack'.[32] Emilia's desire, thwarted and refracted, stages an unlicensed display of sexuality which would have Theseus howling at the moon in despair. The Daughter is not Emilia, nor Emelye. She is their unruly, prevented part, dispersed in wrinkled time amongst her contemporaries: Hermia/Helena/Diana/the fair vestal/Emilia/Votaress/The Maid/ Titania/Flavina/Emelye. All these parted women. What's in a name? Moonshine?

Arcite

Moonshine: a name without a substance. Theseus may attempt to
police the powers of the imagination which give to 'airy nothing /
A local habitation and a name' (5.1.16–17), but the proliferation
of names and persons to whom they attach are out of his reach.[33]
*Dream* is full of 'airy nothings': Nedar; the changeling boy; Thisbe's
mother; Titania's votaress and Lysander's widowed aunt.[34] And
one whose role has been less discussed: Philostrate, Theseus's
Master of the Revels. Shakespeare, we are told, takes the 'name'
of Philostrate from Chaucer's *Knight's Tale*.[35] In a play where
there is so much sport with names and roles, what does it mean
for Shakespeare to take the 'name' of Philostrate from Chaucer?
Philostrate is the name which Arcite assumes when he defies his
banishment by Theseus and returns to Athens. According to the
wrinkle in time of the performed play of Orpheus, Philostrate
ought to be somewhere at court, either in prison or acting as
Emelye's squire. Philostrate is not just a name, but a role, and its
player is Arcite. Philostrate's intratemporality marks the erasure of
Arcite's history. The sounding of the name of Philostrate makes his
'other' self (Arcite as Palamon), available to the temporal imagination of a knowing audience. And Arcite, like Emily, threatens the
felicity of dynastic marriage. In *The Knight's Tale*, and *Two Noble
Kinsmen*, Arcite is the odd lover out – and he dies. Which is why he
must be prevented in *Dream*.

   In a play already filled with changelings, disfigurings and
role-playing,[36] the craftsmen's amateur dramatics foreground the
process of producing and transacting roles from names. Quince's
pairing of 'disfigure' and 'present' (3.1.56) exposes the queasy
relationship between name and person. In Act 5, the craftsmen's
blatant exposure of the insubstantial relationship between name
and thing confronts Theseus, rather like their efforts with the
moon, with a prevented truth that is staring him in the face. They
repeat their concern not to frighten the court with their assumed
roles: 'I, Pyramus, am not Pyramus, but Bottom the weaver. This
will put them out of fear' (3.1.19–20), and:

> You, ladies, whose gentle hearts do fear
> The smallest monstrous mouse that creeps on floor,
> May now perchance both quake and tremble here
> When lion rough in wildest rage doth roar.
> Then know that I as Snug the joiner am
> A lion fell, nor else no lion's dam;

> For if I should, as Lion come in strife
> Into this place, 'twere pity on my life.

(5.1.217–24)

Snug is both Lion and Snug, not one or the other, and he is both 'Lion' and 'a lion'.[37] L[l]ion worries he might terrify the court, but he also fears for his own life should he come in strife as Lion Proper. Wrinkled into Snug's speech are the terms of the threat of Philostrate's assumed role exposed: Philostrate presented in Theseus's palace as an 'Arcite' or Arcite *in propria persona*.

In *The Knight's Tale* Arcite is banished from Athens. He returns illicitly, and when he turns up at Theseus's court, he introduces himself presciently like one of the craftsmen in *Dream*, 'Philostrate he seide that he highte' (I.1428),[38] but, when the Duke catches him 'at strife' with Palamon in the grove, 'real' names are emphatically pronounced:

> This is thy mortal foo, this is Arcite

(I.1724)

> For this is he that cam unto thy gate
> And seyde that he highte Philostrate.
> Thus hath he japed thee ful many a yer.

(I.1727–9)

> And this is he that loveth Emelye.

(I.1731)

> I am thilke woful Palamoun ...
> I am thy mortal foo, and it am I
> That loveth so hoote Emelye the brighte.

(I.1734–7)

The revelation of true identity is compulsively pathological. Palamon's use of the familiar 'thy' pronoun taunts Theseus with the identities of the men standing before him. Philostrate may have japed Theseus, but Palamon's brutal unmasking is tantamount both to suicide and fratricide. Revealed as 'themselves', both men are under Theseus's sentence of death.

Theseus's attempt to civilise this savagery by restaging the unlicensed brawl in the woods as a bloodless tournament in his exquisitely constructed amphitheatre is powerless to prevent Arcite's death (I.1851–62; I.1881–913). In curbing the autonomy of the kinsmen to stage their own fight, he merely postpones the inevitable tragedy. The unmasking of Philostrate as Arcite can lead only to death in *A Midsummer Night's Dream*. The craftsmen's fear for their own lives, which they project on to their audience, contains the fear of the consequences of exposing Arcite before Theseus. Philostrate must not be unmasked, for, if Arcite is revealed as himself, the mathematical couplings do not work, and mortal confusion will have followed. Like Emelye, he must be prevented for he will have wrecked the procreative couplings on which Theseus's dynastic plans depend. But wrinkles of time unfolded, Philostrate has been 'here' all along; stalking the boards, the wings and the audience with the threat of his disclosure.[39]

Philostrate/Arcite's presence on, or off, stage is textually complex. In Act 1, the stage directions have Philostrate enter along with Theseus and Hipployta, and at line 11 Theseus commands him by name '[g]o Philostrate' to stir up 'the Athenian youth to merriments' (1.1.11–12). That neither the Quarto or Folio marks his exit perhaps matters less (though intriguing all the same) than it remains unclear when he re-enters the play. [40] He could come back in Act 4, Scene 1. According to the Folio's stage direction Theseus enters the wood with Egeus, Hippolyta and all his train. The Duke's Master of Revels could reasonably be expected to be included in Theseus's retinue, but it would be difficult to stage; the speeches which are assigned to Philostrate in Q1 of *Dream* are, in the Folio, given to Egeus: 'Call Philostrate' (Q); 'Call Egeus' (F).[41] Tantalisingly, the role of the revels master is parted in this play between the two 'names' which Shakespeare took from Chaucer but not, ostensibly, their persons: Egeus is not Hermia's father in *The Knight's Tale*, but the father of Theseus (I.2838). The implications for patriarchal and social order depending on whether Egeus is present or absent in Act 5 of *Dream* have been brilliantly analysed.[42] Philostrate has not received the same attention. If the speech prefixes of the Folio text are faithfully observed, then he is excised from the text; he becomes 'simply a name invoked in Act I'.[43] Nothing, though, becomes simply a name in *Dream*. Even as the Folio systematically purges his name, a 'part' of him remains; one 'ghost' prefix: 'Phi' at the head of a page (sig. 2v). As Holland rightly observes, 'we can reasonably assume that the Folio version was intended to turn Philostrate into a mute in this scene, if indeed he is on stage at all'.[44] But perversely, if we court 'unreasonableness' instead, and give full play to the imagination that Theseus equates with irrational fear, then Philostrate/Arcite becomes one of Holland's 'men on the stair who refuses to go away'.[45] His presence lingers on even after the Folio tries to cut him out.

The textual redistribution of the parts of Philostrate wrinkles names from *The Knight's Tale* into a scene in which names and roles are most fearfully in question. This is, after all, the scene in which Theseus lets slip his conquest of Thebes. Q1 has Theseus overbearing the will of Philostrate/Arcite in the choice of entertainments; the Folio attempts to banish Philostrate as Arcite; but not only does half his name hang at the top of a verso, the conversation he has with Theseus gets split: not in two, but three. Theseus and Egeus share the warm-up act for the craftsmen's play with a new speaker: Lysander. Philostrate's role is shared out between two wandering Chaucer names, and one of the lovers. Unless Lysander is Philostrate/Arcite? The suggestion is fanciful but not without substance. The Folio's collaboration between Lysander, Theseus and Egeus doubles a three-hander in the first scene of the play when Theseus calls Egeus and Demetrius to some offstage business in preparation for his nuptials (1.1.123–6). But in Act 5, one lover's part is replaced by another on stage: Lysander replaces Demetrius. The plot of *Dream* requires the exchange of one male for another to secure the proper pairings of lovers; an exchange secured not by reason but because Demetrius's eyes are still coated with the magic love juice of the milk-white flower. In Act 5, Lysander takes Demetrius's place alongside Theseus and Egeus in a mirror image of Demetrius's replacing Lysander as the husband of Hermia.

The splitting of the lovers, stalked by Philostrate's on/off presence, contains Arcite's replacement by Palamon in *The Knight's Tale* and *Two Noble Kinsmen*. It prevents the triangular love entanglement of Arcite, Palamon and Emily which *Two Noble Kinsmen* and *The Knight's Tale* brutally contract into Jack-marries-Jill because Arcite is killed by his horse.[46] To regularise the asymmetrical surplus of lovers Theseus determines that Palamon take Arcite's place and marry Emily. No one dies in *Dream* (apart from Titania's votaress) and the play closes with three pairs of lawful, heteronormative couplings. But the name games, the textual uncertainty and the role reversals around Philostrate wrinkle Arcite, who, like Emily, will have impeded dynastic resolution, into the play. Puck's sweeping behind the door (5.1.380–1) to secure *Dream*'s happy ending is a figure for the play's mechanisms of prophylaxis. 'Now are frolic' he declares (378). Nothing is allowed to 'disturb this hallowed house': not hunger, weariness, woe, wild animals, death or gaping graves (361–72). Puck (whose stage double is Philostrate) speaks a catalogue of dangers in the compulsory 'now-frolic' which his broom may tidy, but cannot remove. Puck speaks and sweeps what *Dream* prevents: the death

of one of the lovers in *The Knight's Tale* and the intensification of
divisions, splittings and refractions in *Two Noble Kinsmen*.

In *Two Noble Kinsmen*, there are either not enough parts for
Jack and Jill pairings or too many.[47] The subplot multiplies
arithmetic confusions. The Daughter, Emilia's parted self, is
co-opted into the Morris dance in Act 3 because the male players
find they are a woman short: '[h]ere's a woman wanting' (3.5.39),
causing the players to fear that their business has become a 'nullity
/ Yea, and a woeful and piteous nullity' (3.5.55–6). Unmatched
numbers of men and women bring all to naught. The play cannot
go on. Mercifully, for the men, the Daughter wanders on stage,
singing in madness, and is inveigled into the dance: 'we are made,
boys!' (3.5.77), and the entertainment is saved. The Countryman's
delight at resolution belies the textual confusion around normative
pairings in this scene. The Quarto stage direction calls for 'Gerrold
and 4 countrymen', which as Waith notes, is insufficient both for
the names of the men whose names are called out and for them to
partner the number of women expected.[48] Five countrywomen are
named in the scene but the Quarto stage direction calls for only '2
or 3 wenches'. The textual asymmetry of men and women parallels
the numerical complications of the Arcite/Palamon/Emilia plot.
But, Theseus-like, editors must sort out the pairings. So Waith
supplies six countrymen and five women in his stage direction.
Lois Potter gives us five of each which means that the figure of the
Daughter, seized upon with glee, is then surplus to requirements.
There are either too many or two few men and women. For all the
efforts to sort them out, someone is still left without a partner.

*Two Noble Kinsmen* proliferates the ill-matched and superfluous
couplings that *Dream* contains. To whom is Hippolyta married?
Theseus is split into Pirithous, and, if there is any marital rite in
the temple in Act 1, Pirithous must stand in for his friend.[49] For the
rest of the play, the two men are inseparable: there are three people
in Hippolyta's marriage. The textual crux at the close of Emilia's
lament for Flavina encapsulates the obstacles to normative pairings.
Emilia exalts the true love 'tween maid and maid' ... 'more than in
sex dividual' (1.3.82). 'Dividual' is an emendation for the Quarto
reading 'individuall'; partly on metrical grounds (a line with not
enough stresses) but also to improve the sense. But is it bettered or
diminished? The sense of the word has been claimed as 'divided',
'singular', 'not able to be severed'.[50] Confusion over whether this
term is a marker of individuality, division or inseparability, is writ
large in the dramatisation of the roles of Palamon and Arcite.

When Arcite is banished and subsequently discovered in the grove, there is no mention of his assumed name Philostrate. In keeping with many other roles in the play, Arcite-as-Philostrate has no Proper Name. The 'common' name of Arcite, however predicates many different roles, including that of his rival Palamon. Here is Arcite, having just spied Emilia:

> I am as worthy and as free a lover,
> And have as just a title to her beauty,
> As any Palamon
>
> (2.2.182–4)

> ... am not I
> Part of your blood, part of your soul? you have told me
> That I was Palamon and you were Arcite.
>
> (2.2.187–9)

The exchanges between 'Arcite' and 'Palamon', between a Proper and a common name, and between 'part's, produce changelings whose roles are recursively transacted. Earlier in the scene when Arcite argues that their 'imaginations' can make their prison a space of freedom, he realises Bottom's desire in *Dream* to play as many parts as possible (1.2.45, 62, 75).

> We are an endless mine to one another;
> We are one another's wife, ever begetting
> New births of love; we are father, friends, acquaintance,
> We are in one another, families;
> I am your heir, and you are mine.
>
> (2.2.79–83)

The extratemporal slippage between roles that are erotic, familial and social, and between singular and plural personal pronouns, makes the names of these two lovers endlessly available to play almost any part, and to exchange them at will. As an endless 'mine' to one another (79), they are both possessed of each other outside normative chronology, and they are also a limitless supply of each other's parts.[51] Arcite, the lover who cannot be married to Emily, imagines the intratemporal danger he poses to the story which contains him in *A Midsummer Night's Dream*. In its disturbing obsession with 'parts', *Two Noble Kinsmen* is prescient of the role of 'dividual' Philostrate it dramatises.

The triangle of Arcite, Emilia and Palamon is mirrored by Theseus, Hippolyta and Pirithous and doubled by the threesome of the subplot. While the Jailer's Daughter is courted by her nameless

Wooer, she is madly in love with Palamon. Her unlicensed passion impedes Father's plans to marry her to Wooer. So the two men, assisted by a Doctor, undertake to 'cure' her. Their strategy to unstraighten the triangle has horrifying implications for the roles of Arcite, Palamon and Emilia, and all their contemporaries in *Dream*. The Doctor as Arcite convinces the others that the Daughter will be restored to sense if she has sex with the Wooer, and that she could be persuaded to do this if the Wooer plays the part of Palamon. The men succeed both in their fore-role-play, and in the act which follows. 'Are you not Palamon?' asks the Daughter of the Wooer (5.2.82) to which he replies, '[d]o you not know me?' 'Is this not your cousin Arcite?' she asks, pointing to the Doctor:

> Yes, sweetheart,
> And I am glad my cousin Palamon
> Has made so fair a choice.
>
> (5.2.89–92)

The generic characters of Doctor and Wooer assume the name – and parts – of 'Arcite' and 'Palamon' to purge the Daughter of erotic desire that doesn't fit into their plans. The sight trick of *Dream*, achieved through the juice of the milk-white flower, turns bloody here. Parted I/eye gives way to parted thighs. Three men, working in collaboration, untangle the problem of one woman with two male lovers through a play, dreamt up and co-acted by 'Arcite,' in which 'Palamon' coerces the Daughter to his sexual will. Arcite's part in *Dream* and *The Knight's Tale* will have been an accessory to rape of a woman he is unable to possess himself. It is a sick remedy that still doesn't solve the Jack and Jill problem.[52] Names, *Dream* teaches us, must be taken seriously. 'Palamon', in this play, gets the girl twice: first the Daughter, and then Emilia.[53] For all his interchangeability with Palamon, and timeless supply of parts, Arcite fetches up with nothing: death; the failure of the Countryman short of a wench for his play. The Daughter, Emily's parted self, ends up with two men: Palamon and the Wooer. There are no happy nuptials in the story that *Dream* prevents.

## Time

This chapter imagines the parts of Emily and Arcite in *A Midsummer Night's Dream* without fixing three texts in the sequence of their historical composition; that is, without setting them in hierarchically bounded time. If no text 'can be temporally self-consistent, for the very reason that it does not own its own words and cannot specify their prehistories'[54] (or post-, for that matter), then no text can be temporally self-sufficient. 'Source' study, so often a kind of reading which stabilises an earlier text as a fixed point and leads to the inevitable conclusion of its latest avatar, is far more wrinkled. It may crinkle backwards, or sideways; in starts, or in-conclusions. Of the three works under consideration here, arguably *Two Noble Kinsmen* is the 'earliest' in one sense. Its scene of Palamon and Arcite in Thebes (1.2) is 'before' *The Knight's Tale* except that the temporal sequence of *The Knight's Tale* confounds 'before' and 'after'. Set in 'adventure time', its all-purpose temporal joiners of 'whanne/thanne' string out its many episodes.[55] Told and glossed over; they lie like assortedly shaped beads on a necklace wanting spacers. With the absence of sustainedly specific co-ordinates of time and space, 'events' sort of follow on, or maybe have already happened some time. Before which, quite how long since when is not spelled out. Which makes *Dream*'s variable 'now' presciently historical.

Narrative's closure lies at its end. Nor, of course, is it possible to set bounds on that end. *The Knight's Tale* 'ends' much later than *Two Noble Kinsmen* or *A Midsummer Night's Dream*. Emelye and Palamon are happily – and endlessly – married:

> Hath Palamon ywedded Emelye.

(I.3098)

> For now is Palamon in alle wele,
> Lyvynge in blisse, in richesse, and in heele,
> And Emelye hym loveth so tenderly,
> And he hire serveth so gentilly,
> That nevere was ther no word hem bitwene
> Of jalousie or any oother teene.
> Thus endeth Palamon and Emelye;[56]
> And God save al this faire compaignye! Amen.

(I.3101–8)

The conclusion to *The Knight's Tale* contains its own temporal inconsistency. '[N]ow' in line 3101 sets the ending in the historic present; a tense conjoined snugly between now and then. '[N]evere was' in line 3105 reaches back into the endless past and points towards an unfulfilled future. And in whose time? The Knight's who speaks the words, Chaucer's who wrote them, or the 'compaignye's' who hears them; the Canterbury pilgrims, or a later audience? The temporal gap between lines 3107 and 3108 yawns between the some time of ancient Athens and the now of the Canterbury pilgrims.[57] Crucially, however, the last verb in the tale ('save', 3108) is in the subjunctive. Hovering somewhere between the jussive and optative, this final verb, following on from the interrupted sequence of historic presence, is a sign of incompleteness, a marker of vulnerability. The relationship of 'when' and 'now' floats somewhere in eternal time out of human reach. The Knight's attempt to use God to staple his story closed is a failure.

When the Royal Shakespeare Company opened the Swan Theatre in 1986, they chose *The Two Noble Kinsmen* as the premiere. *A Midsummer Night's Dream* was also part of that season's repertoire. What might a member of the audience on the Swan's first night have made of a later performance of *A Midsummer Night's Dream*? Some of the cast played roles in both performances, some were missing.[58] There were no parts assigned to Emily and Arcite. Not yet.

Or, at least not in 2010 when I wrote the first version of this chapter. In 2012, however, the Movement Theatre Company staged a production of *A Midsummer Night's Dream* 'to rediscover and chart the wonders of the imaginative process; that which lies off the edge of the map'.[59] In order to suggest a world beyond and before the events of the play, it was decided to cast Puck as a throwback to an earlier age: a guardian of the ancient world of the forest in an England almost vanished. At times, especially at moments of high tension, Puck delivered versions of his lines in Middle English as if he had temporarily reverted to speaking in his native tongue. A former age irrupted into the already unstable temporalities with which the play disports. In Shakespeare's playtexts Puck concludes the play. In this production, he began it. Only not with Shakespeare's words but with Chaucer's. Puck opened the play with the first twelve lines of *The Knight's Tale*. As a consequence, he unpuckered the wrinkle of time that is disclosed by the Orphic entertainments in Act 5 Scene 1. The last lines of Puck's intratemporal Prologue were:

> And weddede the queene Ypolita,
> And broghte hire hoom with hym in his contree
> With muchel glorie and greet solempnytee
>
> (I.868–70)

Puck stopped just short of full disclosure. Had he continued with the next line of Chaucer's Knight, he would have announced the presence of the woman that *Dream* must contain: '[a]nd eek hir yonge suster Emelye' (I.871). Even so, Emily became present by prophylactic omission; heard in loud silence.

At the end of the play Puck's Shakespearean epilogue was replaced by the final lines of *The Knight's Tale*. The entire play of *Dream* was thus wrinkled into the time of the first *Canterbury Tale*. Some dramatic sleights of hand with names were called for:

> And thus with alle blisse and melodye
> Hath Theseus ywedded Hippolyta.     [Palamon ywedded Emelye]
> And God, that al this wyde world hath wroght,
> Sende hym his love that hath it deere aboght;
> For now is Theseus in alle wele,                          [Palamon]
> Lyvynge in blisse, in richesse, and in heele,
> And Hippolyta hym loveth so tendrely,                 [Emelye]
> And he hire serveth so gentilly
> That nevere was ther no word hem bitwene
> Of jalousie or any oother teene.
>
> (I.3097–106)

Those 'harmless' substitutions contain huge repercussions. In a play that teems with doubles and absent presences, Theseus and Hippolyta do not replace Palamon and Emelye; they re-place them. The sounds of their names' erasure call attention to persons not properly admitted. In summing up one marriage, Puck added another. He produced a nuptial quartet; a reprisal, perhaps of his mischief-making in the wood when he appears to be incapable of telling Athenian couples apart.

And Puck, of course, is a double himself. His theatrical avatar is Philostrate, the ghostly name whose presence as Arcite stalks the play. So at the end of this 2012 production, Arcite spoke the words of the plot of a play that Theseus is determined to stop him from entering. There is more: Puck as Philostrate as Arcite publically deletes the names of the two persons who have taken his place in the Athenian wedding festivities. Standing there, broom in hand, Arcite sweeps the dust of *The Knight's Tale* behind the door in plain sight. His parting shot produced another nominal excision of the couple happily married in his place. This is how *The Knight's Tale* ends:

> Thus endeth Palamon and Emelye;
> And God save al this faire compaignye! Amen.
>
> (I.3107–8)

And this is The Moment Theatre Company's version:

> Thus endeth now oure queynte fantasie
> And God save al this faire compaignye.

Palamon and Emily become a communally owned sexual 'derk ymaginyng' (I.1995). The horrors that lurk in the immaculately constructed amphitheatre of Theseus's Athens turn out to have been the play of *A Midsummer Night's Dream*.

But still no parts for Emily or Arcite. Were there?

## Notes

1  This chapter has drawn upon material from Helen Barr, '"Wrinkled deep in time": Emily and Arcite in *A Midsummer Night's Dream*', *Shakespeare Survey* 65 (2012) © Cambridge University Press, reproduced with permission. William Shakespeare, *A Midsummer Night's Dream*, ed. Peter Holland (Oxford: Clarendon Press, 1994). In *Two Noble Kinsmen* the Jailer's Daughter's fantasy about the sexual threat posed by Palamon's imagined four hundred children – '[t]hey must be all gelt for musicians / And sing the wars of Theseus' – is also out of sync with the time-scheme of the play, William Shakespeare, *The Two Noble Kinsmen*, ed. Lois Potter (London: Methuen, 1997), 4.1.132–3.

2  Chaucer's *Knight's Tale* provides the chief source for *Two Noble Kinsmen*, while it is one of the Chaucerian 'elements' in composite sources for *A Midsummer Night's Dream*, Shakespeare, *A Midsummer Night's Dream*, ed. Harold F. Brooks (London: Methuen, 1979), p. lviii; Ann Thompson, *Shakespeare's Chaucer: A Study in Literary Origins* (Liverpool: Liverpool University Press, 1978), pp. 88–92, and Cooper, *Shakespeare and the Medieval World*, pp. 211–19. Both Thompson and Cooper note Chaucerian influences on *Dream* beyond *The Knight's Tale*.

3  Paul Strohm, 'Chaucer's *Troilus* as Temporal Archive', in *Theory and the Premodern Text* (Minneapolis: University of Minnesota Press, 2000), pp. 80–98 (p. 91).

4  There are parallels here (though inflected with a different temporality) to ways in which *A Midsummer Night's Dream*, through the naming of Theseus, brings the whole baggage of his notorious Classical history into the play, see Peter Holland, 'Theseus's Shadows in *Dream*', *Shakespeare Survey* 47 (1994), 139–52, and Laurie Maguire, *Shakespeare's Names* (Oxford: Oxford University Press, 2007), pp. 78–90.

5  What is not now clear is the extent to which Richard Edwards's *Palamon and Arcite* (premiered at Oxford 1566 and now lost) could have been used as source material for both *A Midsummer Night's*

*Dream* and *Two Noble Kinsmen*. Also now lost is the 1594 *Palamon and Arcite*, Thompson, *Shakespeare's Chaucer*, p. 17; Cooper, *Shakespeare and the Medieval World*, pp. 208–11.

6  Nicolas Tredell, *Shakespeare: A Midsummer Night's Dream: A Reader's Guide to Essential Criticism* (Basingstoke: Palgrave Macmillan, 2010), draws attention to the framing of the play between 'now' and 'ends', p. 1. (The 'amen' is my own.)

7  Jeffrey Masten, *Textual Intercourse: Collaboration, Authorship and Sexualities in Renaissance Drama* (Cambridge: Cambridge University Press, 1997), pp. 42–55.

8  See, for example, E. Talbot Donaldson, *The Swan at the Well*; Susan Green, 'A mad woman? We are made boys! The Jailer's Daughter in *Two Noble Kinsmen*', in Charles H. Frey (ed.), *Shakespeare, Fletcher and the Two Noble Kinsmen* (Columbia: University of Missouri Press, 1989), pp. 121–32; Alan Sinfield, 'Cultural Materialism and Intertextuality: The Limits of Queer Reading in *A Midsummer Night's Dream* and *Two Noble Kinsmen*', *Shakespeare Survey* 56 (2003), 67–78; Hugh Richmond, 'Performance as Criticism: *Two Noble Kinsmen*', in Frey, *Shakespeare, Fletcher*, pp. 163–85; Helen Cooper, 'Jacobean Chaucer: *Two Noble Kinsmen* and Other Chaucerian Plays', in Theresa M. Krier (ed.), *Refiguring Chaucer in the Renaissance* (Gainesville: University Press of Florida, 1998), pp. 189–209; Glynne Wickham, '*Two Noble Kinsmen* or *A Midsummer Night's Dream*, Part II?', in G. R. Hibbard (ed.) *The Elizabethan Theatre* VII (Ontario: University of Waterloo, 1980), pp. 167–96, and James R. Andreas, 'Remythologising *The Knight's Tale*: *A Midsummer Night's Dream* and *Two Noble Kinsmen*', *Shakespeare Yearbook* 2 (1991), 49–68.

9  I use the name Emily when I refer both to Emelye in *The Knight's Tale* and to Emilia in *Two Noble Kinsmen*. If referring to each character in their respective works, the difference of spelling distinguishes them.

10  Helen Hackett, *William Shakespeare: A Midsummer Night's Dream* (Plymouth: Northcote House in association with the British Council, 1997), p. 10, p. 14. Richard Wilson, 'The Kindly Ones: The Death of the Author in Shakespearean Athens', in Richard Dutton (ed.), *A Midsummer Night's Dream* (Basingstoke: Macmillan, 1996), pp. 198–222 (p. 208).

11  Philip C. McGuire, *Speechless Dialect: Shakespeare's Open Silences* (Berkeley: University of California Press, 1985), pp. 2–4.

12  In *The Knight's Tale* the description of Emelye in the garden more resembles that of a literary May morning description than the portrait of a human being. May is mentioned four times (I.1033–55).

13  Priscilla Martin, *Chaucer's Women: Nuns, Wives and Amazons* (Basingstoke: Macmillan, 1996), p. 42.

14  *A Midsummer Night's Dream*, ed. Stanley Wells (London: New Penguin Shakespeare, 2005), introduction by Helen Hackett, p. lxiii.

15  The 'derke ymaginyngs' of the temple of Diana in which Emelye
    prays are those of Chaucer's Knight; in Boccaccio the temple is simply
    clean and adorned with hangings, Giovanni Boccaccio, *Teseida*, ed.
    Salvatore Battaglia (Florence: G. C. Sansoni, 1938), 7.72.

16  The association between this passage and Elizabeth I is reviewed in
    Helen Hackett, *Shakespeare and Elizabeth: The Meeting of Two Myths*
    (Princeton: Princeton University Press, 2009), pp. 114–24.

17  Louis Adrian Montrose, '"Shaping Fantasies": Figurations of Gender
    and Power in Elizabethan Culture', *Representations* 2 (1983), 61–94,
    p. 81.

18  Hackett, *A Midsummer Night's Dream*, explores the sexual symbolism
    of the milk-white flower, and its purpling as a sign of female bleeding:
    menstruation, and ruptured maidenhead, pp. 17–31.

19  For discussion of the issue, and the argument that 'queynte' is not a
    homophone, see Larry D. Benson, 'The Queynte Puns of Chaucer's
    Critics', *Studies in the Age of Chaucer* 1 (1984), 23–47.

20  Cf. the scenario imagined in Michael Hoffman's film of *A Midsummer
    Night's Dream* (Fox Searchlight Pictures, 1999) when Norma's aria to
    the chaste moon, 'Casta diva', from Bellini's opera *Norma* is played
    during the coupling of Bottom and Titania.

21  Gordon McMullan emphasises Emilia's misinterpretation of the sym-
    bolism in this scene, and the agony of recognition in being 'discharged'
    from Diana's service. He argues that the 'rose becomes a symbolic
    palimpsest: at once a symbol of virginity, menstruation and deflora-
    tion, and thus a sign of the heterosexual path a woman is obliged to
    tread if she is to mature in Theseus' Athens', 'A Rose for Emilia:
    Collaborative Relations in *Two Noble Kinsmen*', in Gordon McMullan
    (ed.), *Renaissance Configurations: Voices/Bodies/Spaces, 1580–1690*
    (London: Palgrave Macmillan, 2001), pp. 129–47 (p. 143).

22  Andreas, 'Remythologising *The Knight's Tale*', argues that Chaucer's
    Emelye is 'doubled' in *Dream* and *Two Noble Kinsmen* as Hermia and
    Helena and the Jailer's Daughter, p. 53.

23  Laurie Shannon, *Sovereign Amity: Figures of Friendship in
    Shakespearean Contexts* (Chicago: University of Chicago Press, 2002),
    pp. 103–22.

24  Valerie Traub, 'The Insignificance of Lesbian Desire in Early Modern
    England', in Susan Zimmerman (ed.), *Erotic Politics: Desire on the
    Renaissance Stage* (London: Routledge, 1992), pp. 150–69 (pp. 158–9),
    and Richard Mallette, 'Same-Sex Erotic Friendship in *Two Noble
    Kinsmen*', *Renaissance Drama* 26 (1995), 29–52, p. 34.

25  For the waning moon as a threat to healthy progeny, see Hackett,
    *A Midsummer Night's Dream*, pp. 17–31, and Wilson, 'The Kindly
    Ones', p. 209.

26  Mark Taylor argues that Helena's preservation of her chastity in
    the wood is a product of the play's need for virginal and hence

marriageable heroines at the end of the play. To have surrendered to desire before marriage would subvert the 'kind of play *A Midsummer Night's Dream* is trying to be, in which marriage is the fitting reward for chastity, faithfully preserved. It is only when the play's middle seems to forget about its end, so to speak, that this subversion seems capable of being actualised', 'Female Desire in *A Midsummer Night's Dream*', *Shakespeare Yearbook* 2 (1991), 115–31, p. 129.

27 Wilson, 'The Kindly Ones', p. 210.

28 *OED* 'moonshine' n.2a. It is used in this sense in *Love's Labour's Lost*, 5.2.207, '[t]hou now requests but Mooneshine in the water'.

29 Barry Weller, '*Two Noble Kinsmen*, the Friendship Tradition and the Flight from Eros', in Frey, *Shakespeare, Fletcher*, pp. 93–108, p. 95.

30 Mallette 'Same-Sex Erotic Friendship', discusses the erotic potential of flirtation in what he calls this 'crucially and usually overlooked exchange', pp. 33–4. Shannon, *Sovereign Amity*, also argues that this scene has been completely neglected, pp. 118–19.

31 The equation between Morris dancing and sexual prowess is spelled out in the Daughter's fantasy of Palamon's stamina, '[h]e'll dance the morris twenty mile an hour – / And that will founder the best hobby-horse' (5.2.51–2).

32 'Tack' is not glossed in this play in a sexual sense, but cf. the reference to sexual activity in *Measure for Measure* 1.2.180–1 'lost at a game of tick-tack'. The verb 'tack' describes driving pegs into holes, E. Partridge, *Shakespeare's Bawdy* (London: Routledge, 1968), p. 262. The Prologue to *Two Noble Kinsmen* has the two dramatists 'tack about' (Prol.26) their business, which, given that new plays are likened to new maidenheads (Prol.1), has clear sexual resonance.

33 Maguire, *Shakespeare's Names*, p. 88.

34 As discussed by Terence Hawkes, 'Or', in *Meaning by Shakespeare* (London: Routledge, 1993), pp. 11–43, especially with reference to Nedar, Lysander's widowed aunt; Ania Loomba, 'The Great Indian Vanishing Trick: Colonialism, Property and the Family in *A Midsummer Night's Dream*', in Dympna Callaghan (ed.), *The Feminist Companion to Shakespeare* (Oxford: Blackwell, 2000); Blackwell Reference Online [accessed 27 July 2010]. Michael Hoffman's film introduces a wife for Bottom; the 1909 Vitagraph silent film transforms Oberon into a woman and calls her Penelope. Kalyan Ray's *Eastwords* (London: Penguin, 2004) reimagines the play across ages and continents with a host of metamorphoses, and additional and reinvented characters (from a range of Shakespeare's plays and other stories) and includes Sheikh Piru/Bardshah (Shakespeare).

35 See Thompson, *Shakespeare's Chaucer*, p. 88; note the subsection entitled 'mere names', pp. 63–75. In glossing *A Midsummer Night's Dream* 1.1.11, Holland notes that Philostrate is Arcite's 'assumed name when disguised', p. 132.

36  Patricia Parker, *Shakespeare from the Margins: Language, Culture, Context* (Chicago: University of Chicago Press, 1996), pp. 100–6.

37  Maguire, *Shakespeare's Names*, discusses the craftsmen's uncertainties as regards the difference between a proper noun and a name, p. 89. The confusion between actor, name and role is wonderfully preserved in the stage direction to the Folio version of 5.1.125 'Enter Tawyer with a trumpeter before them'; William Tawyer was an actor with the King's Men. This SD is absent from the Quarto.

38  Overt reference to being 'highte' Philostrate occurs also at line I.1558. Palamon accuses Arcite of falsely changing his name at I.1586.

39  Cf. Philostrate's 'double' Puck, who, overwatching the craftsmen's play in the wood, states that he will be an actor and an auditor too, i.e. visible to the audience, on and off stage at the same time (3.1.74–5)

40  The stage direction [Exit] is Theobald's.

41  Holland (ed.), *Dream*, p. 31 and p. 38 (5.1.37; 5.1.123–6).

42  Philip C. McGuire, 'Egeus and the Implications of Silence', in Marvin and Ruth Thompson (eds), *Shakespeare and the Sense of Performance* (London and Toronto: Associated University Presses, 1989), pp. 103–15, and Barbara Hodgdon, 'Gaining a Father: The Role of Egeus in the Quarto and the Folio' *Review of English Studies* 37 (1986), 534–42.

43  Holland (ed.), *Dream*, p. 266.

44  Holland (ed.), *Dream*, p. 266.

45  Holland, 'Theseus' Shadows', p. 150.

46  Boccaccio's *Teseida* at least grants Arcite the dignity of an apotheosis. In his textual afterlife, he ascends to the eighth sphere and looks down on the futility of human experience. Chaucer – or his Knight – cuts this. In Chaucer's *Troilus and Criseyde* Arcite's role is given to Troilus and he is granted an afterlife perspective that has no counterpart in Boccaccio's *Filostrato*, the major source for *Troilus*.

47  Masten, *Textual Intercourse*, draws attention to the fact that both plots lack an available woman to shore up the cultural imperative on monogamous marriage, p. 49.

48  *The Two Noble Kinsmen*, ed. Eugene Waith (Oxford: Clarendon Press, 1989), p. 143.

49  As noted by Shannon, *Sovereign Amity*, p. 103.

50  Peter Stallybrass, 'Shakespeare, the Individual and the Text', in Lawrence Grossberg, Cary Nelson and Paula A. Treichler (eds), *Cultural Studies* (New York: Routledge, 1992), pp. 593–610.

51  *OED* 'mine' n. 1c.

52  Weller, '*Two Noble Kinsmen*', argues that the Daughter is 'worked into a marriage with a surrogate Palamon just as Palamon himself becomes, in effect, a surrogate Arcite for Emilia', p. 104.

53  Cooper, 'Jacobean Chaucer', p. 199.

54  Strohm, 'Chaucer's *Troilus*', p. 81.

55 The term is Bakhtin's: 'all the days, hours, minutes that are ticked off within the separate adventures are not untied into a real time series, they do not become the days and hours of a human life. These hours and days leave no trace and therefore one may have as many of them as one likes', 'Forms of Time and of the Chronotope in the Novel', in *The Dialogic Imagination*, ed. and trans. M. Holquist (Austin: University of Texas Press, 1981), pp. 84–258, p. 94.

56 What 'ends' here? The story of Palamon and Emelye, or the characters' lives?

57 A situation akin to the presence of 'English' craftsmen and Greek nobility in *Dream*. Paul Menzer notes how the play's ostentatious heterogeneity reaches an absurd peak in Act 5 where a group of early English craftsmen present the Classical tale of Pyramus and Thisbe for a duke and duchess at their Athenian palace, after which a rural English fairy named 'Robin Goodfellow' sweeps up, 'The Weavers' Dream: Mnemonic Scripts and Memorial Texts', in Regina Buccola (ed.), *A Midsummer Night's Dream: A Critical Guide* (London: Continuum, 2010), pp. 93–111 (p. 95). Adrian Noble dramatises temporal and locational discontinuity by dressing the craftsmen in costumes which recall the British TV comedy about the British Home Guard, *Dad's Army* (1968–77) while the Athenians wear exotic Indian-influenced costume, *A Midsummer Night's Dream* (Channel Four Films, 1996).

58 Jailer (*Two Noble Kinsmen*); Egeus (*Dream*); Emilia/Hermia; Wooer/Snout; Palamon/Oberon. Roberta Taylor played Hippolyta but did not perform in *Dream*; likewise Hugh Quarshie as Arcite and Imogen Stubbs as the Jailer's Daughter, *The Two Noble Kinsmen by William Shakespeare and John Fletcher* (RSC: Methuen, 1987), p. iii.

59 The Moment Theatre Company, *A Midsummer Night's Dream*, Courtyard Theatre Hoxton, London, 18 September – 14 October, 2012, dir. Ben Fairfull. George Collie played Puck.

# 5
# Bones and bays: on with *The Knight's Tale*

The Prologue to *The Two Noble Kinsmen* dubs Chaucer a learned author whose fame stretches from Italy to England. He also gets a speaking role. Dead Chaucer decries the imped vulgarity of the noble play he is said to have bred:

> How will it shake the bones of that good man
> And make him cry from under ground, 'Oh, fan
> From me the witless chaff of such a writer
> That blasts my bays and my famed works makes lighter
> Than Robin Hood' ...

$$(Prol.17-21)^1$$

If the bones of Chaucer shake at these words, rattling around under the slabs of Westminster Abbey, then they will have done so more from laughter than from poetic rage. Chaucer tilted at bays, but he did not claim them. In the third book of *The House of Fame*, in a hilarious restaging of Dante's poetic vaunting at the start of *Paradiso*, the narrator promises Apollo that the next time he passes his laurel tree he will bestow a kiss on its bark (1106–9). Its leaves are beyond him. Lydgate might have invested Chaucer with laureate prestige but such earnestness is very different from the game with fame that *Two Noble Kinsmen* continues to play.[2] Although Chaucer is made to protest at witless chaff and light fare, his speech would not look out of place beside another of his staged apologies for indelicacy. In *The Canterbury Tales* Chaucer apologises in advance for the 'harlotrie' (I.3184) of *The Miller's Tale*, reassuring us that, if we don't want to hear it, we can turn over the leaf of the book and choose another 'storial thyng that toucheth gentillesse' (I.3179). Chaucer elides oral storytelling with bookish literacy to whet our appetites for a tale that makes nobility a dirty story. Although the Miller swears:

> by armes, and by blood and bones,
> I kan a noble tale for the nones,
> With which I wol now quite the Knyghtes tale

> (I.3125–7)

his challenge does not simply come after *The Knight's Tale*. Robin the Miller exposes the 'harlotrie' that the 'gentillesse' of *The Knight's Tale* already contains. Even as it purports to lay the foundations for storytelling order, *The Knight's Tale*, as its first audience recognises, teems with social and narrative indecorum. While the 'gentils' claim it for a 'noble storie' (I.3111), Harry Bailey has heard a different tale:

> Oure Hooste lough and swoor, 'So moot I gon,
> This gooth aright; unbokeled is the male.'

> (I.3114–15)

If you gloss Harry's riposte decorously as 'the game is well begun', you miss a crucial part of what he has actually said. The pun on 'male' as 'pouch' and 'genitalia' has been well-established by the teasing testicles of the Pardoner in *The General Prologue* (I.694).[3] So the Host's delight at how the storytelling competition has opened up also expresses his joy at the prospect of an untrussed scrotum. The audience japery at the start of *Two Noble Kinsmen* restages the ribaldry that the 'storyal thyng' of *The Knight's Tale* has already provoked.

Although Chaucer is described as a 'noble breeder and a pure' (10), the play that he is made to spawn is likened in the very first line not just to a maidenhead but a maidenhead that is in commercial demand:

> New plays and maidenheads are near akin:
> Much followed both, for both much money gi'en.

> (1–2)[4]

The claim that Chaucer is a noble laureate progenitor is undermined even before it is said. While the *Prologue*'s Robin Hood is not Robin the Miller, as previous chapters have argued, the shuttling of names between works has the uncanny knack of introducing persons into texts that we might not have realised are there.[5] 'Robin' and 'chaff' prompt recall of more than a little milling in the knight. I argue in the first part of this chapter that *Two Noble Kinsmen* continues the Miller's exposure of *The Knight's Tale*'s shaky nobility. The Jacobean play mingles the matter of Thebes and Athens with the licentious holiday world of England.[6]

The Prologue's faux-apology for witlessness replays a joke on the inseparability of 'chaff' and 'grain' that is legendary in Chaucer's ouevre.[7] The noble grain of *The Knight's Tale* and Chaucer's learned breeding are the chaff of playhouse 'harlotrie'.

*Two Noble Kinsmen* was one of a number of plays that Sir William Davenant adapted for the Restoration stage. It opened in the Duke of York's theatre, London, in 1664. Davenant gave the play a new title – *The Rivals*. As I shall discuss in the second part of this chapter, he also changed the names of the characters and its plot in ways that disfigured them. *The Rivals* is a thinly disguised, but by no means servile, celebration of the restoration of Charles II and the fall of Oliver Cromwell. To restore nobility to the English stage, and to banish the turbulence of recent political events, Davenant tempers the licence of *Kinsmen*'s more outrageous moments. But this seventeenth-century knight proves no more successful at controlling his story than Chaucer's did. Through altering the Chaucerian names of his characters, Davenant's drama contains another challenge to the Knight's version of events: one that is both inside and outside *The Canterbury Tales* sequence – *The Siege of Thebes* told by the fifteenth-century Benedictine monk John Lydgate. In telling *his* Knight's Tale, Lydgate restores one aspect of narrative decorum: it ought to have been the Monk that told the story after Chaucer's Knight. Only Robin the Miller gets in the way. At the same time, however, Lydgate devastates the temporal and narrative foundations of *The Knight's Tale* that its teller had rendered so fragile. So when Davenant incorporates names used in Lydgate's version of *The Knight's Tale* into *The Rivals*, his own project of theatrical and social restoration becomes threatened. It is only through altering the course of Theban history, and the outcome of *The Knight's Tale*, that *The Rivals* staves off a restaging of noble annihilation. But Davenant's dynastic diversions still create room for royal licentiousness.

Davenant worked with John Dryden in adapting Shakespearean drama for the Caroline stage. It would have been impossible for Dryden not to have known that his former colleague, fellow knight and predecessor as Poet Laureate had dramatised a version of Chaucer's *Knight's Tale*. And yet when Dryden comes to produce his own telling of that tale, 'Palamon and Arcite' in his 1700 *Fables and Poems*, Davenant's version disappears without trace. Dryden reinstates the Chaucerian names of the characters, and in his prefatory materials he also restores a different poetic

and political line of succession. *The Knight's Tale* is detached
from Caroline restoration and severed from Lydgate's entailment.
Dryden courts a different monarch for the English throne and
puts himself next in place to Chaucer's assumed bays – and his
Westminster bones. As I shall argue, however, there is no direct
line back to Chaucer.

## 'Harlotrie' in *Two Noble Kinsmen*

When Robin the Miller swears by bones to 'quite' *The Knight's
Tale* with a noble tale of his own, an audience alert to the verbal
chiming between the two tales will remember that bones have
already figured prominently in the rivalry between two men:

> We stryve as dide the houndes for the boon;
> They foughte al day and yet hir part was noon.
> Ther cam a kyte, whil that they were so wrothe,
> And baar awey the boon bitwixe hem bothe.
>
> (I.1177–80)

Noble competition is a dogfight. And it is a vulture (a ravening
bird which *Parlement of Foules* dubs a coward, 349) that gets the
spoils. The Miller's vaunting bones pay back contentiously those
of the Knight's on their own terms. Robin's 'literary peasants'
revolt' stages a narrative insurrection that is already present in *The
Knight's Tale*.[8] Saturn, the architect of chaos whom the Knight
introduces into his tale (he has no role in Boccaccio's *Teseida*),
tells us that he presides over the 'cherles rebellyng' (I.2459).
Saturn is the source of aristocratic 'ruyne': he causes high halls,
towers, and walls to fall on those that helped to make them,
including (significantly) 'the carpenter' (I.2464–5).[9] So, when
John the carpenter tumbles from the roof of his house at the end
of *The Miller's Tale* in a contraption he has made with his own
hands, the fabliau recast of *The Knight's Tale* tells of what was
already there in the first place.

   *Two Noble Kinsmen* continues the Miller's enlargement of what
*The Knight's Tale* pens in. As E. T. Donaldson recognised, 'the
characters themselves seem to have come down from the Knight's
temple walls'.[10] The temple of Mars contains a pickpurse (I.1998);
a cook (I.2020); a carter (I.2022); a barber; a butcher and a smith
(I.2025). *Kinsmen* gives us a jailer, his daughter, a doctor, countrymen and wenches, an executioner, a schoolmaster and a taborer.
I argued in the previous chapter that the Jailer's Daughter is

an avatar of Theban Emelye from *The Knight's Tale*. She also
embodies the raw sexual energy of the Miller's English Alison.[11]
Nothing of Emelye's physical body is seen in *The Knight's Tale*
save her head and her back; she is fairer than a lily, and she sings
like an angel (I.1035–50). The Miller directs his gaze straight
to Alison's loins (I.3237). A series of similes compare her to a
weasel (I.3234); a sheep (I.3249); a swallow (I.3258); a kid or a
calf (I.3260); and a flower, whose name, 'piggesnye' (I.3268), suggests rather the eyes of a sow than the Virgin Mary's lily. Alison
is an aristocratic Emelye, roughcast. She is a wench that 'any *lord*'
can 'leggen in his bedde', but only a 'good *yeman*' can 'wedde'
(I.3269–70). *Kinsmen*'s Daughter reprises Alison's marital stock.
She points out that, because she is base and Palamon is a Prince,
he will never 'affect' her (2.4.1–4).

Alison and the Jailer's Daughter are repeatedly associated with
animals. The Miller compares Alison to a 'colt' that springs out of
the frame where it is contained (I.3282), and, when she completes
Absolon's sexual humiliation at the window, she cries '[t]ehee'
(I.3740) like the stallion that chases the wild mares in *The Reeve's
Tale* (I.4066). Horses feature prominently in the sexual fantasies
of the Jailer's Daughter.[12] She identifies herself as a chestnut
mare 'horribly in love' with Palamon (5.2.62). But even though
her dowry is '[s]ome two hundred bottles / And twenty strike
of oats', he will never have her for '[h]e lisps in's neighing, able
to entice / A miller's mare. He'll be the death of her' (5.2.66–7).
The Daughter's sexual imagination reprises Alison's horseplay.
Palamon is become a virile stallion, whether his 'tail' is long or
docked (5.2.49), and when he dances the Morris 'twenty mile an
hour', he outperforms the best 'hobby horse' and 'gallops to the
tune of "Light o' love"' (5.2.51–4).

The Daughter's sexual fantasies are repeatedly freighted with
reference to popular songs. After Act 1, she performs all the songs
in the play, and they have much more in common with Alison's
singing 'loude and yerne' (I.3257) than with Emelye's angelic
voice. 'Light o' love' (5.2.54), the tune to which Palamon 'gallops',
is a term for a prostitute.[13] 'Bonny Robin' (4.1.108) is a cant
word for penis.[14] *Kinsmen*'s vocal register reprises the unbridled
sexuality of Robin the Miller.[15] These vulgar English songs set in
Ancient Greece replay how the aristocratic jousting tournament in
*The Knight's Tale*'s amphitheatre contains entertainment of a ruder
kind. Grecian lords are degraded into base anonymity '[a]nother
*lad* is on that oother syde' (I.2620). Chivalry 'roll[s] … under

foot as dooth a bal' (I.2614). Nobility bites the dust and jousting
becomes holiday football. *The Miller's Tale* springs open the noble
cracks in the narration by 'quiting' the tournament that takes place
in Thebes 'al that Monday' (I.2486) with the 'disport and pleye'
on the 'Monday' at 'Oseneye' (I.3659–60). Theseus's three exquisitely crafted temples are transformed into the three kneading tubs
which, hung in the carpenter's roof, create a visual image of male
genitalia.[16]

Sexual frolic runs rife in *Two Noble Kinsmen*. When the
Daughter first catches sight of Palamon and Arcite, she declares
'[i]t is a holiday to look on them' (2.1.56). The Maying games in
the wood substitute for the workaday world of labour '[l]et the
plough play today; I'll tickl't out / Of the jades' tails tomorrow'
(2.3.29–30). '[C]ountry sport', as Pirithous aptly terms the festivities (3.5.96), is insistently sexualised.[17] The Bavian, a human actor
dressed as half-ape, half-baboon, has a long tail and 'eke long tool'
(3.5.131), and the sexual charge of the maypole and Morris dancing
is bolstered with references to the coupling games of 'barley-break'
(4.3.31) and playing at 'stool-ball' (5.2.74).[18] The holiday world
that *Kinsmen* and *The Miller's Tale* spring from *The Knight's Tale*
has its seeds in *The General Prologue*. We learn that Robin is a
seasoned winner of holiday games:

> Ful byg he was of brawn, and eek of bones
> That proved wel, for over al ther he cam,
> At wrastlynge he wolde have alwey the ram.

> (I. 546–8)

But while *this* wrestler always gets his ram, *Kinsmen*'s Arcite
misses his chance. Although he sees the countrymen's preparations
for their sport of '[w]restling and running' (2.3.70) as an 'offered
opportunity' to be close to Emilia:

> Well I could have wrestled –
> The best men called it excellent – and run
> Swifter than wind upon a field of corn.

> (2.3.78–80)

he ends up without his prize. He fulfils Palamon's description
of him as a 'chaffy lord', '[v]oid of appointment' (3.1.40–1).
*Two Noble Kinsmen* does not stage the tournament in which Arcite
is killed; aristocratic pageantry is upstaged by the rough games of
the middle of the play. But Pirithous's extensive commentary on
what happens off stage in Blackfriars reproduces the ignobility

with which Arcite's death is narrated by the Knight on the road to
Canterbury.[19] Pirithous suspends the account of Arcite's death in
mid-action:

> He kept him, 'tween his legs – on his hind hoofs
> On end he stands,
> That Arcite's legs, being higher than his head,
> Seemed with strange art to hang
>
> (5.4.76–9)

Before the horse falls backwards, crushing Arcite beneath its
weight, the 'his' of the 'horse' and the 'his' of the man become
confused. Remembering perhaps his own terrible encounter with
such man-beasts, Pirithous's tangle of legs and pronouns produces
the suggestion of a centaur.[20] Furthermore, Pirithous tells how
Arcite's 'hot horse, hot as fire' (5.4.65) rears up on his hind legs.
'[P]ig-like he whines' (5.4.69) at the spur and 'seeks all foul means /
Of boist'rous and rough jad'ry to disseat / His lord' (5.4.71–3). The
aristocratic pageant of Arcite's death retold becomes a nightmare
of animal brawn in which man, horse and pig are not easily told
apart. Through his images of conjoint man and beasts, Pirithous
brings nobility far closer to the level of fabliau than epic romance.
In *The General Prologue*, Robin the Miller is compared to a fox,
and twice to a pig. His beard is as red as a sow, and the hairs on the
wart on the top of his nose are as red as the bristles inside a sow's
ears (I.552–6).

Released from *The Knight's Tale*, Pirithous takes delight in low-
ering the tone of elevated conversation. His obsessive commentary
on male body parts reproduces the sodomitical comedy of the end
of *The Miller's Tale*. As we have already seen in the discussion of
Chaucer's hands, the denouement of *The Miller's Tale* has one man
borrowing a coulter from another which leaves the handprint of
flayed flesh on a third man's arse. The Miller turns the Knight's
chivalric weapons into labouring tools that score the flesh between
men. In *Kinsmen*, Pirithous blazons the bodies of Palamon and
Arcite in homoerotic puns which equate chivalric accomplishment
with penile pageantry.[21] Arcite has 'on his thigh a sword, / Hung
by a curious baldrick, when he frowns / To seal his will with'
(4.2.85–7). This arch description of Arcite's 'sword' attracts warm
commendation from Theseus, '[t]hou hast well described him' (89).
Pirithous's reply, '[y]et a great deal short, / Methinks, of him that's
first with Palamon' (4.2.89–90), sets up a competition between the
two noble kinsmen's penises. He observes that '[Palamon's] nose

stands high, a character of honour' (4.2.110). Pirithous's syntax
elides honourable standing with erectile one-upmanship.[22]

Pirithous and his companion Theseus take part in a three-
handed homoerotic exchange that occupies the middle of *Two
Noble Kinsmen*. Choreographed by Gerrold the Schoolmaster,
the Prologue to the Morris dance peddles a series of sodomitical
innuendoes directed to Theseus.[23] Gerrold goes by the title of
*'pedagogus'*, one

> that let[s] fall
> The birch upon the breeches of the small ones
> And humble with a ferula the tall ones,
> Do here present this machine, or this frame,
> And dainty Duke, whose doughty dismal fame
> From Dis to Daedalus, from post to pillar,
> Is blown abroad, help me, thy poor well-willer.

(3.5.109–15)

Dainty Theseus's slaying of the Minotaur, and his descent into
hell to rescue Pirithous, are relayed through the phallic diction of
'post', 'pillar', 'blown abroad' and 'well-willer'.[24] That the blazon
of Theseus's legendary fame should refer teasingly to his sexual
exploits is not, perhaps, surprising. More shocking is that they are
embedded in a sodomitical focus on the instruments of Gerrold's
own profession: the 'birch' that falls on small boys' breeches and
the 'ferula' with which he humbles 'the tall one'. Part confession,
part boast, these paedophiliac puns preface Gerrold's offering up
his 'penner' at Theseus's great feet (3.5.123). The great 'noble'
hero of Ancient Greece becomes the butt of homoerotic banter
with an English country schoolmaster.

The dance over, Gerrold begs Theseus that, if they have done
'as good boys should do', then he will give them a tree or two for a
maypole (3.5.142–5). Given the relentless play between maypoles,
Morris, and penile performance, there is a subtext of sexual
invitation. Theseus hands over some money; Pirithous offers 'something to paint your pole withall' (3.5.151). Does he offer to enhance
Gerrold's 'pole', or to coat it?[25] Irrespective of the particular sodomitical practice to which Pirithous alludes, his daring quip seals
homoerotic banter between two nobles and a schoolmaster. Their
equal participation in sexually loaded exchange erodes difference
in social rank. In its persistent exposure of unlicensed sexuality
and social levelling, *Two Noble Kinsmen* rolls *The Knight's* and
*The Miller's Tales* into one. Chaff and grain are indistinguishable.

## Restoring nobility

Sir William Davenant's *Rivals* strips *Two Noble Kinsmen* of its 'harlotrie'.[26] The status of its participants is enhanced and its unbridled
sexuality is tempered. The Jailer's Daughter, now named Celania,
is the daughter of a noble General. She still imagines herself as the
chestnut mare (p. 46), but without mention of the miller.[27] When
she compares herself to a nightingale she replaces the Daughter's
'prick ... to put my breast against' (*Kinsmen*, 3.4.25–6) with a
'hawthorn' (p. 31). Her fantasises of Palamon dancing the Morris
and playing with her at barley break happen not in the rough and
tumble of an English forest but in the Classical literary landscape
of Elysium 'where blessed spirits walk' (p. 46). In *The Rivals* the
wood is a pastoral Arcadia that bears more than a passing resemblance to the Forest of Arden in *As You Like It*. It is a place where
princes may repair 'to entertain their courts' with 'various pleasures
of delight'; 'where one might sit down'... 'in dainty arbor / Where
trees are trimmed as perriwig is by Barbor' (p. 37).[28] Country games
are socially repositioned. Arcite, now named as Theocles, is still
associated with wrestling, but in dialogue which makes persistent
references to gentlemanliness: more Orlando than Robin (p. 23).

A Morris is still danced but the First Countryman assures the
audience it is no 'mad Morris' (p. 33), and Celania is not forced
to take part. The Entertainment here is provided not by a paedophiliac schoolmaster but by a First Countryman whose title
is 'master of the Revels' (p. 34). Although the Bavian's tail is
mentioned as carrying the potential to scandalise the ladies (p. 32),
his 'long tool' passes without comment. The Morris is no longer
framed by homoerotic exchange between three men. No money
changes hands, and there is no offering, whether of augmentation
or coating, towards a new maypole. Instead, the scene removes to a
musical interlude which tops the country entertainment with noble
spectacle of the kind at which Davenant's productions excelled.[29]
And for which the stage machinery and ensemble of the Duke of
York's Theatre, Lincoln's Inn Field, was so well equipped.[30]

Arcadia becomes the setting for a masque. A consort of instruments and song stages the death of a stag. The offstage hunting
scene from *Two Noble Kinsmen* is transformed into a wonder
of stagecraft. Its low humour is banished. While, in *Kinsmen*,
Gerrold tells Theseus and Pirithous that the ladies will enjoy the
stag's 'dowsets' – its testicles – as a delicacy (3.5.156), the humiliation of the stag in *The Rivals* is more concerned with its antlers.

Testicular sport is transformed into an Arcadian masque which stages a celebration of the death of Harpacus, the 'unbounded tyrant'.[31] Harpacus is a version both of Theban Creon and English Cromwell. The ten-branched stag is brought down in a musical 'tragedy' in which horns play a commanding role in the musical accompaniment. Phallic jokes are bypassed to focus on the destruction of Cromwell's claims to power. Hounded by dogs that recall those that Ariel conjures up in *The Tempest* to bait the would-be usurping trio of Trinculo, Stephano and Caliban, the stag is killed in a tempestuous finale.[32] Foresters command the audiences, both on stage and off, to '[s]ee the Stag's head which so did spread his bream / The small trees did seem to envy him'.[33] The antlers of the dead stag are a political and theatrical trophy. Envied by the small trees, the ten-branched antlers form a puny contrast to the emblem of Charles II as the Royal Oak.[34] *The Rivals* creates a version of *The Knight's Tale* in which Theseus's victory against Thebes and Creon is become the royalist triumph over the Commonwealth. The noble masque in the forest stages a civil war that is over.

Theseus, now named Arcon, is a figure for Charles II. While, in *Kinsmen*, the celebrations in the forest are for Emelia's birthday, and in honour of Theseus's marriage, Hippolyta has no part in *Rivals*. Instead the sylvan festivities subordinate the marking of Emelia's/Heraclia's birthday to celebration of Charles's/Arcon's nativity and his reinstatement as lawful king. Charles was born on 29 May 1630. He returned from exile to London to reclaim his throne on his thirtieth birthday in 1660. By reminding the audience that Charles's birth and restoration happened on the same day, *The Rivals* can rejoice in the return of England's legitimate king and the rebirth of the theatre that Cromwell had suppressed. Caroline audiences would have been familiar with overt parallels between the restoration of the Stuart monarchy and the London stage before *The Rivals* premiered. Charles II had already figured in one of Davenant's plays. In the revival of his *Love and Honour* Thomas Betterton appeared costumed in the King's coronation robes. In 1660 Davenant had contributed the Prologue to the Restoration court's first dramatic command performance. It explicitly celebrated the close connection between the political objectives of the restored monarchy and the activities of the reopened theatres:[35]

Greatest of *Monarchs*, welcome to this place
Which *Majesty* so oft was wont to grace
Before our Exile, to divert the Court,
And balance weighty Cares with harmless sport.

This truth we can to our advantage say,
They that would have no KING, would have no *Play*,
The *Laurel* and the *Crown* together went
Had the same *Foes,* and the same *Banishment*.[36]

Four years later, Davenant's *Rivals* continues to dramatise the celebration that his Prologue announces. The commercial bawdry of *Kinsmen*'s Prologue has no place. The play opens with Cromwell's defeat, '[t]he Tyrrant's high designs found ill success' (p. 1). The 'noble breeder' of Davenant's version of *The Knight's Tale* is no longer Chaucer with his shaking bones and blasted bays but Charles II. Theatrical laureation and legitimate monarchy have triumphed over the Commonwealth and weighty cares.

While *The Rivals* is not without some unruliness (as I shall go on to discuss), the play's most graphic representation of social discord is dramatised in Celania's fantastical ramblings:

> CELA. They lead a fore life in the other Place,
>     Burning, Frying, Boyling, Hissing, Cursing,
>     There some are put in Cauldrons full of Lead,
>     And Usurer's grease amongst a Million
>     Of Cutpurses, and there boyle like a Gammon
>     Of Bacon that will never be enough.
> PROV. Alas, will the Cordial never Work?
> CELA. O 'Tis fine sport to hear a Citty wife
>     And a proud Lady howle together there:
>     One Cryes out! O! this Smoke! th'other this Fire!
>     One Curses the day-bed and Garden-walks.
>     The other all her Husbands Customers.
>     But in the other place we dance and Sing.
>
>                                                        (pp. 46–7)

Celania contrasts the Arcadia of *The Rivals* with 'the other Place'; a place whose heat and howling conjures visions of hell. Its low-life usurers, cutpurses, 'Citty wife' and 'Customers' with their greasy food are far removed from the Court and its 'harmless sport'. What Davenant has conjured here, through Celania's distraction, is a version of the Commonwealth that figured in a different kind of theatrical enterprise: the city comedies that satirised the Interregnum.[37] In casting his version of *The Knight's Tale* as a pastoral comedy, Davenant positions commercial theatre and Commonwealth satire as the hellish distractions of a woman temporarily removed from her gentlewoman's sanity. In travelling between Thames-side and the Duke of York's Theatre, Lincoln's Inn Fields, *The Knight's Tale* appears to have parted company with unruliness. The social and sexual contumacy that the Miller and the Host saw in it is consigned to another time and place. *Kinsmen*'s ribaldry and the commercial audience that its Prologue had courted are transported to a theatre with very different social tastes.

That, however, is not the whole story. For reasons that pertain to its production history, and also to Davenant's meddling with the poetic ancestry of his plot, *The Rivals* does not quite manage to banish past contention, or to escape from the presage of future revolution. None of the characters in *The Rivals* has the same names as those in Chaucer's *Knight's Tale*, or *Two Noble Kinsmen*.[38] It has been noted that the names of Davenant's *dramatis personae* are drawn from Classical legend.[39] Davenant renames Pirithous as Polynices and Arcite becomes Theocles. What has not been noticed hitherto (so far as I am aware) is that Polynices and Theocles are key actors in a medieval work that presents a very different social vision of *The Knight's Tale*: Lydgate's *Siege of Thebes*. Caroline audiences could have known Lydgate's *Siege*: it was included in all sixteenth- and seventeenth-century editions of Chaucer's *Canterbury Tales* from Stow's 1561 edition onwards.[40] Lydgate's version of *The Knight's Tale* digs out its prehistory to chronicle the destruction of Thebes. Lydgate's 'prequel' to the Knight's story of Palamon and Arcite focuses extensively on the roles that Polymite and Etheocles played in that annihilation. Polymite is the medieval spelling of Polynices; lose the initial 'E', and Etheocles is Davenant's Theocles.

Polymite/Polynices and Etheocles/Theocles were the sons of Oedipus; fruit of his incestuous union with his mother Jocasta. Lydgate spares no attempt to draw attention to the atrocities that these unlawful offspring perform. When Oedipus tears out his own eyes because his sons despise him they trample the ruptured jellies underfoot (1008). When their father dies, they throw him into a pit in an act of cruelty worse than any serpent or wild tiger: 'of Cursid stok cometh vnkynde blood' (1014). Having fallen into emulous contention as to which of them should succeed their father, each brother strengthens his own party to sustain his proud discord, '[f]ully worchyng into destruccioun / And Ruyne of this noble toun. / So hoote brente the hatred and envie / Of bothe two' (1073–5). To fill the vacuum left by her husband's death, Jocasta arranges that each brother shall rule Thebes for a while in rotation, beginning with the first-born Etheocles. Neither brother honours the agreement: each continues in deeds of unspeakable atrocity. Polymite is full of 'malys and hegh pride' (1323); Etheocles is

'wilful', 'indurat' and full 'of malyce obstynat' (4007–8). Thebes
is destroyed 'for doublenesse of Ethiocles' (1778); 'rote of vnreste
and causer of vnpes' (4260). When the brothers meet in battle,
the envious fire burns their hearts so intensely with the cankered
hatred of 'unkynde blood' (4273) that they kill one another.
Polymite rives Etheocles through the heart, but then is suddenly
smitten with compassion and attempts to save his life by pulling
out his spear. Driven to envious fury, Etheocles 'the felle' (4289)
stabs his brother to death even as Polymite tries to save him. At
the conclusion of this battle, all the worthy knights of the land
(4344), and 'al the blood Royal' (4342), are slain. The mutual
slaughter of Etheocles and Polymite is a palimpsest of total royal
wipeout.

This catastrophic tale of aristocratic contention overwhelms the
portion of *Siege* that retells *The Knight's Tale*. Lydgate eventually
begins the Knight's story of Theseus, Palamon and Arcite after
4500 lines on the destruction of Thebes. His gigantic 'prequel'
creates a spectacular 'ruyne' of nobility out of the not-quite buried
unruliness of *The Knight's Tale*. By prefacing *The Knight's Tale*
with the warring brothers of Thebes, Polymite and Etheocles
become the narrative progenitors, and indeed the avatars, of
Palamon and Arcite.[41] The first Canterbury Tale and its conten-
tious cousins become overtaken by disaster.

Lydgate the monk can be seen to be picking some old narrative bones. In *The Canterbury Tales*, the Monk is prevented
from telling his tale before he has had a chance to open his mouth
because of the Miller's irruption into the socially normative order
of narration. When the Monk does finally get his say, the Knight
stops his series of gloomy tragedies in their tracks (VII.2766).
Far from claiming Chaucer's *Knight's Tale* as a 'noble breeder',
Lydgate, himself a monk, speaks over both Knight and Miller.
In the Prologue to *The Siege*, the company of pilgrims are riding
back from Canterbury to London. Lydgate unwinds the narrative trajectory of the whole Canterbury sequence even as he rolls
back *The Knight's Tale* in time. While Lydgate is amongst the
returning pilgrims, self-narrated as a 'monk of Bery' (line 93),
there is no place for the Knight – or indeed for Chancer.[42] The
origins of *The Knight's Tale* are re-founded temporally, socially,
and narratively.

Lydgate's 'knight's tale' comes last.[43] After 4501 lines of narration, the story of Thebes finally joins up with an event near the
beginning of the Knight's: Creon's refusal to bury the slaughtered

warriors of Athens. Lydgate assures his audience that he is telling the tale exactly as the Knight – and Chaucer – did: '[a]nd as my mayster Chaucer list endite' (4501). With a sly appropriation of the apologia for *The Miller's Tale* (I.3176–7), Lydgate reminds his pilgrim audience that they have already heard what Chaucer wrote: '[ʒ]if ʒe remember ʒe han herde it toforth / wel rehersyd at Deptforth in the vale, / In the begynning of the knyghtys tale' (4522–4). Lydgate proves a good narrative match for Chaucer's Miller's sleight of hand. The pilgrims have not yet reached Deptford when the Knight starts to speak; they have only just set off from Southwark.[44] And far from narrating *The Knight's Tale* exactly as Chaucer did, Lydgate abandons the first Canterbury Tale before it has seriously got under way.

Having rehearsed only a hundred lines of the longest story in *The Canterbury Tales*, Lydgate excuses himself from continuing any further, '[t]o tellyn al, it wer to gret a charge' (4602). Not content with speaking over the Miller, Monk Lydgate reprises a narrative tic of the Knight's delivery: his use of 'occupatio'. But while the Knight is constantly apologising for all the stories that he does and does not manage to cram into his tale, Lydgate hijacks the rhetorical device to feign regret for failing to deliver the substance of *The Knight's Tale* at all. Irrespective of how satisfactory one finds the end of *The Knight's Tale*, it does stage reconciliation between Athens and Thebes through Palamon's marriage to Emelye. Lydgate's 'knight's tale' gets nowhere near. It stops at the point where Theseus razes the walls of Thebes. Even more audaciously, the end of *Siege* confuses beginnings with ends. It embeds an episode at the finish of *The Knight's Tale* into one at its opening. *Siege* narrates how the 'worthy duk [Theseus] restoryd hath agayn' (4564) 'the bonys of the lordys that were slayn' (4563). There is no pressing reason why the restoration of these Theban bones should be told in an extended 'occupatio' of funeral rites (4565–94). But that is exactly how Lydgate tells it, and, in telling us what he is not going to tell us, he focuses our attention on ashes and burning. The restoration of one set of Theban bones, an act of 'remembraunce' (4581) close to the beginning of the Knight's narration, is described through recall of the description of another funeral: Arcite's at *The Knight's Tale*'s close.

*Siege* turns the precarious order of *The Knight's Tale* inside out. The Knight's source of 'ruyne' is Saturn, but his far-reaching malign chaos is outlined only after 2453 lines of the story have been told. Given the length of the tale, and the Knight's wayward

narrative threads, it is entirely possible to miss how Saturn's crucial
role in the plot gets drowned out by Theseus's staged Boethian
'make do and mend' account of the workings of Providence at the
tale's conclusion. Theseus's encomium to the 'Firste Moevere'
and the 'faire cheyne of love' (I.2987–8) glosses over the fact that
Saturn has already spoiled the party. You can't miss Saturn in
Lydgate's *Siege of Thebes*. Saturn is plucked from the bowels of
the Knight's story and placed right at the start. Replacing the
rejuvenation of the spring opening of the start of the Canterbury
pilgrimage, the return to London is heralded by the astrological
movement of 'old' Saturn, who with 'his frosty face' takes the place
of the 'virgin' (Virgo), with melancholy and decrepitude (1–6).
The beginning of the returning 'Knight's Tale' springs open the
destructive cankerousness that the Knight had tried so very hard
to contain. Saturn prefaces – and prefigures – the deadly unlawful-
ness that the warring brothers Etheocles and Polymite exemplify.
Their father Oedipus is born when the constellation of Saturn
has entered the Scorpion (388). At Oedipus's wedding to Jocasta,
which was '[v]nhappy' and 'passing odious', '[i]nfortuned and
vngracious' (821–82), the guest lists include Herebus, the father
of hatred; Night, the Furies, Dread, Fraud, Treachery, Treason,
Poverty, Indigence, Nede, Death, Cruel Mars; '[b]rennyng Ire
of unkynde blood' and deep-seated '[f]raternal hate' (868–7).
Etheocles and Polymite do not exactly get off to a good start.

Inaugurated by Saturn, riddled with temporal upheaval, filled
with the darkest treacheries and betrayals, and closed with a
reminder of the envy in heaven which caused Lucifer to rebel
against God (4660–89), Lydgate's version of *The Knight's Tale*
presents a relentlessly dismal picture of noble discord. While there
is some evidence to suggest that Lydgate wrote *The Siege of Thebes*
to coincide with the Treaty of Troyes between France and England
in May 1420, the events of the poem foreshadow very much more
clearly the internecine wars between the House of York and
Lancaster that followed on from Henry V's death in September
1422.[45] Surely the catastrophe of noble factionalism that Lydgate's
version of Theban history expounds would have been the last thing
that Davenant would have wanted to afford any space in his dramatised version of *The Knight's Tale*? And yet, whether he knew it or
not, Davenant's use of the names Theocles and Polynices trails into
his play reverberations of another 'knight's tale' in which there is
no possibility of political restoration on earth. Only in its very final
lines does *Siege* offer a glimmer of hope for the dreadful history

it has unfolded. That hope rests not with human beings but with God (4681–716).

So – what *are* Theocles and Polynices doing in *The Rivals*? If unruliness and discord were so alien to Davenant's project that he purged his play of *Kinsmen*'s most egregious offences, why invest two of his characters with names that spark recall of contentiousness and disaster much more potent and far-reaching?[46] Because *The Rivals* creates roles for them that transform the history of Thebes, England's recent past – and *The Knight's Tale*. Polynices and Etheocles become something other than 'themselves', and, in so doing, they enter into a new relationship with their avatars Palamon and Arcite. They become part of a different story. Lydgate's monkish tragedy of *The Knight's Tale* becomes Sir William's stage play of 'A Comedy'. Lydgate's 'olde Tyraunt þat callyd was Creon', made king of Thebes, '[a]lthogh he had no title by discent / But by free choys made in parlement' (4389–90), is a Harparcus/Cromwell that *The Rivals* immediately consigns to history. The play's opening celebrates the return of pastoral that had been threatened by the 'tragedies' of 'tyranny and war'. While the soft Arcadians had been forced to 'quit the Sheep-hook to assume the Sword', with Harpacus dead, '[a] grave contains him, that usurp'd a throne' (p. 1), regeneration is possible. There is no Saturn in Davenant's 'knight's tale'. Arcon/Charles heralds a new reign. '[Harpacus's] blackness makes your Glory shew more bright / Thus darkness alwayes ushers in the Light' (p. 1). Arcon's birthday celebrations are 'day-break to all the Year' (p. 5), and 'fields of Blood may us to Gardens bring / As furious Winter ushers in the Spring' (p. 5).[47]

While in *Siege*'s Theban history, Polymite and Etheocles foreshadow what Palamon and Arcite will have become, Davenant prevents them. Davenant reassigns the names of the rivalrous brothers so that parallels between Polynices and Palamon and Theocles and Arcite no longer work. Theocles still plays the role of Arcite, but Polynices becomes somebody else: Pirithous. Recalling the loyalty of Seyton from Davenant's earlier *Macbeth*, Polynices/ Pirithous is Arcon/Theseus's faithful General. There is a new name given to the lover who corresponds to Palamon: Philander (I discuss the significance of this choice later). With this redistribution of names and roles *The Rivals* transposes deadly enmity into co-operation between generations and factions. At the start of the play, Polynices persuades Arcon to be merciful towards the two Theban prisoners who have been captured from Harpacus's

defeated army. His reason, and one that is reiterated throughout
the play, is that one of the prisoners, Arcite/Theocles, saved his life:

> POLYN. This is that *Theocles*, who in reward
>   Of what he pleas'd to praise in me as Valour,
>   Rescu'd my Life when I was Pris'ner tane
>   By his own Troop, and gave me liberty,
>   A debt which I will strive to pay.

(p. 2)

Athenian pleads for Theban in mutual indebtedness of life
and freedom. Royalist Polynices pleads for the life of roundhead
Theocles. Audacious liberties are taken with history, both historical and legendary, in order to heal up the implacable rivalry
that the names of these two characters encapsulate. While in both
Chaucer's *Knight's Tale* and *Two Noble Kinsmen*, it is through
the intervention of Pirithous that Arcite is released from prison,
Davenant's reassignment of names changes completely the roles of
Pirithous and the two cousins.

Although in *Kinsmen* the character of Pirithous is an obstacle
to nobility, in the *Rivals* he is a constant source of the desire for
noble rapprochement. Polynices facilitates the resolution of the
love rivalry between two knights through his love and care for
the distracted Celania, now *his* daughter rather than the offspring
of an anonymous Jailer. Staging a paternal concern of a very different kind from the solution to the Daughter's predicament in
*Kinsmen*, Polynices's solicitation for Celania's health convinces
the court that the most amicable resolution to the love triangle is
for Theocles/Arcite to marry Arcon's niece Heraclia (Emilia), and
for Palamon/Philander to marry Celania. In *The Siege*, Polymite
refuses allegiance to Etheocles during his brother's tenure of
the Crown, resulting in a civil war that annihilates the nobility.
Davenant's Polynices, now neither a warring brother nor a jealous
lover but Arcon's right-hand man, secures reconciliation between
father and daughter, between emulous cousins and between
king and subjects. He fulfils the pledge he makes to Arcon in the
opening scene:

> Supported by the Justice of your Cause,
> I might do things perhaps beyond my age,
> But ne're out-doe my duty. I owe more,
> To this my Country and your Sacred Person;
> Then my exhausted blood or life can pay.

(p. 2)

The services of a dutiful subject, loyal to Arcon's sacred person, heal up the implacably destructive rivalry of ancient and recent past.

*The Rivals* banishes the ugly solution of *Kinsmen* by rewriting Theban history. Restoring mathematical and social decorum to the close of the play, Celania/Jailer's Daughter is no longer raped both by the nobility and by a nameless man from a lower social estate. Her distraction is no longer the disorderly focus of a play riddled with unbridled sexuality. Rather, it is through royal care for the situation of the daughter of a loyal subject that restoration is made of both Celania's distracted wits and amorous gridlock. Heraclia/Emilia realises that only if she rights what she sees as a '[w]rong' toward Celania, and gives up any claim on Philander/Palamon, can her dear friend be restored to health. This show of gentle amity teaches Arcon how to proceed. In the rhyming couplets to which Davenant resorts at particularly solemn moments of his drama, he decrees that both Philander/Palamon and Theocles/Arcite shall live. Heraclia shall marry Theocles, and Celania shall marry Philander.

Deadlock is resolved. No cousin need die. Since there is no need for a tournament there is no call for horses, Saturnine or scandalous. No one suffers even so much as a broken arm, and there is no jiggery-pokery with maypoles. Honour prevails, and the 'emulous Philomels' (*Kinsmen* 5.3.124) are restored to manly love:

> THEO. My Admiration and my Love Contest,
>   Which shall out-vy the other in my breast.
> PHIL. My quarrel here with *Theocles* shall end,
>   I loose a Rival and Preserve a Friend;
>   *Celania* does our Cause of strife remove,
>   We onely shall contend which most shall love.

> (p. 55)

Davenant turns contest into admiration, strife into friendship, and rivalry into resolution. To anyone who remembers the more dismal denouements of any of the other 'Knight's Tales', the strain of these forced verbal chimings is perfectly obvious. But they ease the passage of the play towards its comedic closure. Given the spectacular capabilities of the Restoration stage, it is surprising that Davenant did not seize the opportunity to dramatise the tournament part of the plot. Instead, in a move that counters criticism of restoration plays for drowning words with sight and noise, he opts for introducing some verbal dramatic tension.[48]

Heraclia sees each cousin brought into the court with their followers. Philander's man denounces Theocles in the blackest terms, and vice versa. Davenant writes new speeches for Philander and for Theocles in which each defends the other from slander:

> PHIL. These thy black aspersions are
>     As false as *Theocles* to honour true.
>     He offer violence? O! Heavens can you
>     Permit this Blasphemy? can you endure
>     To see so black a cloud his worth obscure?
>     Which wou'd (but that he does unjustly Love)
>     So bright appear, as wou'd all envy move.
> PHIL. From such designs I'me sure he is exempt.
> ARCON. Will you your Rival vindicate?
> PHILA. I must; else to his honour I shou'd be unjust.
> THEO. Cousin you are too Civil ...
> THEO. Detracting Villaine, could *Philander* fly
>     Each motion of his Sword gives thee the lye,
>     Whose lighting took perhaps thy light a way,
>     As Bats and Owls are dazl'd with the day:
>     That Sword which brandish'd made all others quake,
>     Blinded thy Eye-sight into this Mistake.
> POLYN. How equally these Miracles of men do
>     Share in Honour?
>
>                                                           (pp. 52–3)

Lest the repeated exchange of the word 'honour' between cousins be lost, it is the reformed rival Polynices who drives home the message. Former strife is become a display of equivalent honour.

For all the strain to present a noble story purged of harlotry and political discord, however, Sir William's honourable marital resolution is not quite the end of the story. Davenant may have been able to steer his plot to a favourable outcome, but he is unable to control its succession; either on stage or off. The noble strife trailed into the play by his choice of names, even if it is derailed through redistribution of their roles, does not vanish. The Arcadian jubilation with which *The Rivals* opens is tempered by the legacy of the future:

> ARCON. I much rejoice in that felicity
>     Our Subjects from the Victory derive;
>     But that exempts me not from discontent
>     Whilst I foresee the posture of my Throne,
>     When I Expire. No remnant of my blood

Shall ere survive th' Interrment of my bones
Or Solemnize my burial with a Tear
Of Kin to those my aged Eyes let fall.
Had I a child, my Joyes would then be full,
Which now prove Empty and not worth a Smile.

(p. 4)

In a replay of how *Siege* conflates Theseus's restoration of the
Thebans' bones with Arcite's funeral, the beginning of *The Rivals*
imagines Arcon's interment on the threshold of his birthday
celebrations. Unquiet bones have a knack of resurfacing in these
wayward 'knights' tales'. When Charles II and his subjects heard
those words on stage, even in 1669 when *The Rivals* was revived,
the King still had no legitimate heir. In *The Knight's Tale*, and *Two
Noble Kinsmen*, Emelye is the sister of Theseus's wife Hippolyta,
but there is no part for Arcon's wife in Davenant's play. None of
the three marriages at the end of *The Rivals* guarantees royal succession through Charles II.[49] Celania is the daughter of General
Polynices, and Heraclia is Arcon's niece. With Arcon as a figure
for Charles II, Heraclia becomes Mary, the daughter of the king's
brother, James, Duke of York.[50] Only there is no part either for
Arcon/Theseus's brother in the re-forging of noble dynasty in
*The Rivals* – or in any of the 'knight's tales'. The exclusion of
Arcon's brother in *The Rivals* turns out to have been prescient.
James II acceded to the throne in 1685 because Charles had died
with no legitimate heir. But, having survived the political crisis
of 1678–83, during which a bill in 1681 attempted to exclude him
from any claim to the throne on the grounds that he was a Roman
Catholic, James lasted as king for only three years before he fled
to France.[51] In the Glorious Revolution of 1688, through the
invitation of Parliament, he was replaced by his daughter Mary
and her husband, William of Orange. So although *The Rivals*
stages the hope of royal succession through marriage, it is not, as
Arcon rightly predicts, through a 'remnant of [Charles's] blood'.
Heraclia/Mary does end up as a Royal Queen, but the Stuart line
that Davenant's play celebrates is preserved by the intervention of
another William entirely.

Charles II did produce children, of course, but none of them
legitimate. His 'unkynde blood' proved to be a recurrent source of
trouble during his reign. The Duke of Monmouth was a contender
to the throne during the Exclusion Crisis.[52] *The Rivals* is not the
only play by Davenant that ribs the King for his promiscuity but
his philandering has particular edge in a play that registers anxiety

over his future childlessness.[53] At the end of Act 4, Arcon imparts
this avuncular advice to Heraclia:

> You cannot Marry both, and when I save
> But one, You can no more from *Hymen* Crave;
> By Love's great Law you can but one Enjoy:

(p. 44)

If Charles II recognised his own counsel, he did not heed it. The
unruly sexuality of *Two Noble Kinsmen* is not wholly purged from
Davenant's staging of aristocratic resolution. In a curious reprisal
of how the Jailer's Daughter has sex off stage both with Palamon
and her Wooer, Celania fetches up on a promise to two men. Her
onstage future husband is Palamon renamed Philander. It would
beggar belief to think that Davenant was unaware of the etymol-
ogy of Palamon's new name. In a joke that must have tickled the
fancy of those merry theatregoers at the Duke of York's, 'Serial
Womaniser' has star billing. Philander was played by Thomas
Betterton – the leading man of the Restoration stage who wore
Charles II's coronation robes in the revival of Davenant's *Love
and Honour*. Contemporary commentators on *The Rivals* do not
mention Betterton, but they do have something to say about regal
philanderers who enter into alliances with actresses. Mary (Moll)
Davis played the part of Celania.[54] Promised to Philander on stage,
she was bedded by Charles II off it. One of the songs she sang in
*The Rivals*, 'My lodging it is on the Cold ground' was such a great
success that it was quickly parodied in a new show starring Nell
Gwynn, and became lodged in one of the few anecdotes about *The
Rivals* that has achieved anything like popular currency.[55] John
Downes quipped that Moll Davis's performance of this song raised
her from the cold ground to a royal bed.[56] Davenant's 'knights'
tale' prompts new emulation – only this time between two women –
as Moll Davis and Nell Gwynn vie for attention as mistresses of
Charles II.[57] Davenant's restoration of nobility to 'The Knight's
Tale' did not last.

### Back to bays

In 1699, John Dryden returned to the story that his theatrical colleague had dramatised twenty-five years earlier. With Davenant
now in a cold ground of his own, Dryden restores *The Knight's
Tale* to Chaucer in his *Fables*.[58] Palamon and Arcite return to

'themselves'; in name and fortune. Arcite dies and Palamon gets the girl. Only, this time, there is a new arena for the story of lineage and succession: both royal and poetic. The 'noble breeder' of this story of Athenian rivalry is no longer a king. Dryden dedicated his *Fables* to James Butler, second Duke of Ormond. He wrote a dedicatory poem and preface to 'Palamon and Arcite' which he addressed to Ormond's wife, Mary, daughter of the Duke of Somerset. Butler is explicitly compared with Palamon and, passing up the opportunity to continue the Heraclia/Mary Stuart identification, Emelye is compared to Mary Ormond. Tracing her lineage back to the Plantagenets, Dryden declares her a 'Daughter of the Rose ... Red and White' (151–2).[59] From her father's side, Mary could trace her lineage back to Lancastrian John of Gaunt. Her father's mother claimed descent from the Yorkist Earls of Salisbury. Mary/Emelye is celebrated as a symbol of unbroken royal lineage, and a promise of its continuation: 'the precious Mould / Which all the future Ormonds was to hold' (142–3). Even more, she promises the restoration of the nation and the race: '[a]n Heir from You, who may redeem the failing Kind' (145). In praising the sanctity of line and the virtue of name through the history of the Ormonds Dryden withholds the attribution of noble descent to his current monarchs William III and Mary. For Dryden, the Glorious Revolution of 1688 had violated royal lineage and estate.[60] And so these honourable virtues are displaced from the King on to a subject who had been loyal to William in his wars, but who had recently been passed over for naval honour. Dryden uses the dying Arcite as an occasion for a speech which extols the virtues of Palamon/James Ormond:

> Nor holds this Earth a more deserving Knight,
> For Vertue, Valour, and for Noble Blood,
> Truth, Honour, all that is compriz'd in Good;
> So help me Heav'n, in all the World is none
> So worthy to be lov'd as *Palamon*.

('Palamon and Arcite' 823–7)

But *this* knight can no more contain his tale's history than any of the others. After Dryden's death, James Butler embraced the Jacobite cause and died in exile in France.

Arcite's praise of his rival recalls the speeches that Davenant gave to his Theocles and Philander. But if Dryden had any memory of *The Rivals*, he suppressed it. He collaborated with Davenant on their version of Shakespeare's *The Tempest, The Enchanted Isle*,

in 1667; the year in which *The Rivals* was revived. Dryden com-
mended his erstwhile collaborator in these words:

> I could never have receiv'd so much honour in being thought
> the Author of any Poem how excellent soever, as I shall
> from joining my imperfections with the merit and name of
> *Shakespear* and *Sir William Davenant*.[61]

Such high regard for Davenant and Shakespeare is conspicuous
by its absence from the extensive preface that Dryden wrote to
his *Fables and Poems*. The poetic lineage to which the Preface lays
claim omits both Davenant and Shakespeare. William-bred stories
of Palamon and Arcite are bypassed. With a breathtaking pucker of
temporalities, Dryden puts himself next in line to Chaucer 'in the
first place' (*Preface* line 342).

In preparing his translation of Chaucer's *Knight's Tale*, Dryden
worked from a reprinting of Speght's 1598 edition. It would
have included Lydgate's *Siege of Thebes*. But Dryden overlooks
the Benedictine monk in his story of succession. While 'Lidgate'
is named as a contemporary of Chaucer's, the *Preface* ignores
Lydgate's presence. Dryden goes right back to the start of the
Canterbury pilgrimage and to the Tabard. With a creative mingle
of present and future past, he writes: 'I see ... all the Pilgrims in
*The Canterbury Tales*, their Humours, their Features, and their
very Dress, as distinctly as I had supp'd with them at the tabard in
Southwark' (lines 282–5). Picturing himself as eating and drinking
with the pilgrim band at the start of their journey, Dryden excludes
Lydgate from their company. And the Ormond descent from the
Plantagenets is matched by Dryden's tracing of his own lineage
as Poet Laureate directly back to Chaucer 'my Country-man and
Predecessor in the Laurel' (line 55).[62] Lydgate is doubly edged out
of the picture. Dryden manoeuvres himself into the moral high
ground that the monk Lydgate had staked out in *his* version of
*The Knight's Tale*. Dryden's jockeying through poetic history to
end up in first place beside 'laureate' Chaucer is accompanied by a
determination to tell of no 'harlotrie'. Distancing himself from the
fabliau ribaldry that is very gross, obscene and 'undecent', Dryden
declares 'such tales shall be left untold by me' (541–2). Dryden sol-
emnises his position by speaking through the accents of Chaucer's
Parson, 'thow gettest noon fable ytoold for me' (X.31). Chaucer's
laureate successor sounds like a man of the Church.

But Dryden's immediate poetic 'Predecessor in the Laurel'
was not Chaucer. It was his erstwhile 'honoured' collaborator Sir

William Davenant, the knight that attempted to restore nobility to his version of *The Knight's Tale* by tempering *Kinsmen*'s vulgarity. Davenant was created Poet Laureate in 1638, and held on to the title until his death in 1667. The leafy succession of Davenant and Dryden was not lost on contemporary wags. What did 'parsonical' Dryden make of this quatrain, I wonder?

> 'tis wit in him, if he all Sense oppose,
> 'Twas wit in D'avenant too to lose his Nose;
> If so, then Bays is D'avenant's wisest son
> After so many claps to keep his on.[63]

Dryden's predecessor in the laurel contracted syphilis so badly that he lost most of his nose. To compensate for his deficiency, so contemporary ribalds quipped, Davenant inserted an apostrophe between the 'D' and 'a' of his name in order to restore dignity to his person.[64] 'Bays' was Dryden's nickname. The pun on 'claps' as both 'syphilis' and 'acclaim' suggests that Dryden is heir not only to the laurel but to 'the incurable bone ache' as well.[65]

For all the jestering about laureate succession however, Davenant and Dryden were both buried in the same place as Chaucer's bones: Poet's Corner in Westminster Abbey. Only, Chaucer was interred there not because he was a poet but because he was Clerk of Works. So he gets the last laugh when, in a final act of green-eyed emulation, 'John Bayes' asked to be buried, not just 'near Mr Chaucer's Monument' but actually in Chaucer's grave with his 'noble breeder''s bones.[66] But as this chapter has attempted to argue, for all of the claims to it (in game, and in earnest), there is no direct line back to Chaucer. The past imperfect narration of the first Canterbury Tale has seen to that. Its narrative incontinence licenses a telling free-for-all that zigzags back and forth in between temporalities, lineages, social rank and generic decorum. The spillage from *The Knight's Tale*'s unbuckled pouch is become a motley collection of 'knight's tales' through which clear lines of propriety cannot be told.

## Notes

1  Unless specified otherwise, all quotations from *Two Noble Kinsmen* are to the edition by Lois Potter.

2  This is Lydgate's tribute: 'Chaucer is deed, that had suche a name / Of fayre makyng, that without[en] wene / Fayrest in our tonge, as

the laurer grene', *Floure of Courtesye* 236–38 in *Minor Poems of John Lydgate*, ed. H. N. MacCracken (EETS OS 192, 1934), vol. II.

3  *The Riverside Chaucer* glosses the line 'as the pouch is opened i.e. the game is well begun', p. 66.

4  Abrams explores the tensions in the Prologue between the worlds of heroic endeavour and trade, '*Two Noble Kinsmen* as Bourgeois Drama' in Frey, *Shakespeare Fletcher,* pp. 145–62 (pp. 145–7). Thompson notes that 'Chaucer the philosophical poet and Chaucer the teller of bawdy stories were confused in the often ambiguous references to him in the literature of the time', *Shakespeare's Chaucer'*, p. 171 and p. 211. An early commentator on *The Two Noble Kinsmen* recognises the crude sexual licence of the noble rivalry of Palamon and Arcite: 'Two wooers for a wench were each at strife, / Which should enjoy her to his wedded wife: / Quoth th'one, shee's mine, because I first her saw, / Shee's mine, quoth th'other, by *Pye-corner* law: / Where, sticking once a *Prick* on what you buy / It's then your owne, which no man must deny.' Henry Parrot, *Laquei ridiculosi* (1613), no. 3, B1v, quoted in Potter, p. 69.

5  The mention of Robin Hood may be a reference to a preoccupation with Robin Hood plays between rival theatre companies at the turn of the seventeenth century. The Earl of Huntingdon plays written by Nicolas Munday were performed by the Admirals' Men in 1598–99. Shakespeare's *As You Like It* (1599), with its reference to Robin Hood (ed. Juliet Dusinberre (London: Methuen, 2006), 1.1.109–11), combines the outlaw tradition of *The Tale of Gamelyn* with the Italianate gentrifications superimposed on the story by Thomas Lodge in his *Rosalynde* (1590). The anonymous *Looke Aboute You* produced in 1600 is a particularly zestful mingling of nobility and 'lighter fare'. See, for example, the wonderful stage direction 'Enter Robin Hood in the Lady Faukenbridge's gown, night attire on his head'. *Looke About You*, ed. W. W. Greg (London: Malone Society, 1913), line 1747.

6  Andreas, 'Remythologising the Knight's Tale', compares Puck in *A Midsummer Night's Dream* to Robin the Miller, p. 55. So far as I am aware, no critic has yet outsourced *Two Noble Kinsmen* to *The Miller's Tale*.

7  The grain and chaff metaphor is used in Chaucer's work to poke fun at the idea that one can separate meaningful corn from surrounding narrative draff. Where this metaphor is used, the context elides the apparent opposition, e.g. *The Nun's Priest's Tale* VII.3443; *Legend of Good Women* F.74–5; G.62–3. Lydgate reprises the Chaucerian pseudo-separation of grain and chaff as a joke in the Prologue to his *Siege of Thebes*. He praises Chaucer for 'keping in substance / the sentence hool / with-oute variance, / Voydyng the chaf / sothly for to seyn, / Elumynyng the trewe piked greyn / Be crafty writing / of his sawes swete', *Lydgate's Siege of Thebes*, ed. Axel Erdmann (EETS ES,

108, 1911), ll. 53–7. As I argue below, Lydgate exercises more than his fair share of 'crafty writing' in this text.

8 For discussion of *The Miller's Tale* as a 'literary peasant's revolt', see Lee Patterson, *Chaucer and the Subject of History* (London: Routledge, 1991), pp. 244–79, and Peggy Knapp, *Chaucer and the Social Contest* (London: Routledge, 1990), pp. 32–44.

9 Thompson, *Shakespeare's Chaucer*, pp. 199–200, notes echoes of Saturn's speech in the Arcite's prayer to Mars in the Temple in *Two Noble Kinsmen* 5.1.49–56.

10 E. T. Donaldson, 'The Swan at the Well', pp. 53–4.

11 Piero Boitani, 'The Genius to Improve an Invention: Transformations of *The Knight's Tale*', in Ruth Morse and Barry Windeatt (eds), *Chaucer Traditions: Studies in Honour of Derek Brewer* (Cambridge: Cambridge University Press, 2006), pp. 185–98, argues that the image of the Jailer's Daughter 'as mad as a march hare' is an animal image that stands at the very centre of the play 'although the epic context has been completely eliminated and replaced by popular, proverbial wisdom which points to starkly naked eros, if not to actual lechery', p. 190.

12 As noted by Abrams, '*Two Noble Kinsmen* as Bourgois Drama', p. 155. Roberts observes that the sustained references to horses function as a 'leitmotif' of the play, 'Crises of Male Self-Definition', p. 143.

13 Potter, p. 303.

14 Waith, p. 171.

15 Potter provides extensive discussion of the songs and music in the play, pp. 360–3.

16 Kendrick, *Chaucerian Play*, pp. 1–19.

17 Richard Underwood's extensive commentary on the sexual innuendoes of the play brings out the force of the sexual licence in the Maying games, *Two Noble Kinsmen and Its Beginnings* (Salzburg: Salzburg University Press, 1993), pp. 34–86.

18 Frey notes that beneath the nobility of kinship and quite independent of its aims, lies the sheer, blind, mad, drive for sex itself, 'Grinning at the Moon', p. 119.

19 The title page of the 1634 Quarto text states that the play had been presented by the King's Men at Blackfriars. It does also appear to have played to courtly audiences. The Morris dance in 3.5 was presented as an antimasque in *The Masque of the Inner Temple and Gray's Inn* on 20 February 1613 at Whitehall as part of the festivities for the marriage of King James's daughter Elizabeth to Frederick, Elector of Palatine. The play may also have been revived at performance at court in 1619, see Waith, pp. 1–3.

20 Ovid's *Metamorphoses* relates that Pirithous invited centaurs to his marriage feast. Eurytus, the fiercest of them, becomes so inflamed with lust for Pirithous's wife that he seizes Hippodame by the hair and runs off with her. Coming to the rescue of his friend, Theseus kills Eurytus

with an antique goblet, causing the centaur to fall backwards and to lie drumming his heels on the sodden ground, vomiting gobbets of blood and wine and brains from his shattered mouth. Ovid, *Metamorphoses*, ed. R. J. Tarrant (Oxford: Oxford University Press, 2004), XII.210–44. Abrams argues that in Pirithous's speech 'all that chivalric man stigmatizes as base ... returns in this beastly incarnation to wreak revenge', '*Two Noble Kinsmen* as Bourgois Drama', p. 159.

21   Richard Mallette draws attention to the homoeroticism of the blazons, 'Same-Sex Erotic Friendship', p. 42.

22   That well-worn pun on nose anticipates Pirithous's appraisal of Palamon's 'lineaments', including his axe with its 'staff of gold', as 'strong and clean' as a man could wish them (4.2.113–15). The comparison between the two parts of the body has a long history, see Alfred David, 'An Iconography of Noses: Directions in the History of a Physical Stereotype', in Jane Chance and R. O. Wells, Jr (eds), *Mapping the Cosmos* (Houston: University of Rice Press, 1985), pp. 76–97.

23   Paul Bertram notes that Gerrold, as the 'rectifier of all', is a country version of Theseus, the Knight's 'ministre general', *Shakespeare and Two Noble Kinsmen* (New Brunswick, NJ: Rutgers University Press, 1965), p. 275.

24   Cf. *A Midsummer Night's Dream* 5.1.275 where Bottom's 'O dainty duck' refers to Thisbe. Gerrold's narration bears more than a passing resemblance to the style of Bottom's narration here. Theseus's rescue of Pirithous is one of the many stories which the Knight mentions but does not have time to tell (I.1191–201).

25   *OED* 'paint' (v.1) 2a and 5.

26   *The Rivals* was first printed anonymously in 1688, but John Downes, *Roscius Anglicanus or an Historical Review of the Stage from 1660–1706* (1708), ed. Judith Milhous and Robert D. Hume (London: The Society for Theatre Research, 1987), p. 55, and Gerard Langbaine, *An Account of the English Dramatick Poets* (Oxford, 1691), p. 547, both attribute it to Davenant. The play ran for nine days in September 1664, Mary Edmond, *Rare Sir William Davenant* (Manchester: Manchester University Press, 1987), p. 188. It was revived in January 1665, and November 1667, W. Van Lennep (ed.), *The London Stage, 1660–1800*, Part I: 1660–1700 (Carbondale IL, 1960), pp. 83, 85, 86 and 124.

27   All references are to *The Rivals: A Comedy* (William Cademan, at the Pope's Head in the Lower Walk of the New Exchange, 1668).

28   As in *As You Like It*, there are songs by male nobles in the wood, for instance, Palamon's willow song in Act 3, p. 29.

29   Katherine West Scheil discusses the added spectacle and novelty to his theatre productions in his first Shakespeare adaptation, 'Sir William Davenant's Use of Shakespeare in *The Law Against Lovers* (1662)', *Philological Quarterly* 76 (1997), 369–86 (p. 372).

30 The extensive designs and mechanical capabilities of Davenant's theatre are discussed in Edmond, *Rare Sir William Davenant*, pp. 171–8, including a reproduction of the plans for Leslie Hotson's conversion of the tennis court at Lincoln's Inn Fields, p. 178. See also Mongi Raddadi, *Davenant's Adaptations of Shakespeare* (Uppsala: Almqvist & Wiksell International, 1979), pp. 23–48. John Downes records that Davenant opened his theatre 'with the said Plays, having new Scenes and Decorations, being the first that e're were Introduc'd in England', *Roscius Anglicanus*, p. 51. Charles II's 1660 grant mentions the '[g]reat expences of Scenes, musick and such new Decorations as Haue not bin formerly used', quoted from State Papers in Edmond, *Rare Sir William Davenant*, p. 143.

31 Davenant had already produced his version of *Macbeth* with the titular hero as a figure (more complicatedly than in *The Rivals*) for Cromwell. His head is not displayed at the close; Macduff brings on Macbeth's sword as the sign of his victory. Christopher Spencer, '*Macbeth* and Davenant's *The Rivals*', *Shakespeare Quarterly* 20 (1969), 225–9, argues that first scene of *Rivals* contains imitations of *Macbeth* – sometimes from Shakespeare's, sometimes from Davenant's version of the Scottish play.

32 *The Tempest*, ed. Stephen Orgel (Oxford: Oxford University Press, 1987), 5.I.253–8. There are other echoes of *The Tempest* (the play that Davenant would rework into *The Enchanted Isle* with John Dryden in 1667). Celania's song in the next act 'I'le sweetly ring his Knel / With a pretty Cowslip Bell / Ding, ding etc.', p. 39, splices Ariel's 'Full fathom five', 1.2.403–5, with 'Where the bee sucks', 5.1.89.

33 There are echoes here of the killing of the deer in *As You Like It* (4.2.1–16).

34 Dryden's Prologue to *The Enchanted Isle* compares Shakespeare to an image of the Royal Oak of Charles II: 'As when a Tree's cut down the secret root / Lives under ground and thence new Branches shoot / So, from old Shakespear's honour'd dust, this day / Springs up and buds a new receiving Play', *The Enchanted Isle*, London, Printed by F. M. for *Henry Herringman* at the *Blew Anchor* in the *Lower-walk* of the *New-Exchange*. MDCLXX, p. 6.

35 Richard W. Bevis, *English Drama: Restoration and the Eighteenth Century 1660–1789* (London and New York: Longman, 1988), p. 34. Prospero also wore the robes of Charles's brother, the Duke of York, Michael Dobson, *The Making of the National Poet: Shakespeare, Adaptation and Authorship, 1660–1769* (Oxford: Clarendon Press, 1992), pp. 18–20.

36 *The prologue to His Majesty at the First Play Presented at the Cockpit in Whitehall; Being part of that Noble entertainment Which Their Majesties received Novemb. 19 from His Grace the Duke of Albemarle* (London, 1660).

37  Jonsonian comedies that depicted the commonwealth as caricatured humours-infested cozenors included Abraham Cowley's *Cutter of Coleman Street* (1661) and George Etherege, *The Comical Revenge or Love in a Tub* (1664).

38  The difference in names is one explanation for the surprising neglect of *The Rivals* in discussions of versions of *The Knight's Tale*. Although he traces versions of *The Knight's Tale* through to Dryden's *Fables*, Boitani does not mention *The Rivals* in his 'The Genius to improve an Invention'. Cooper briefly contrasts the lack of resolution in *Two Noble Kinsmen* with Davenant's ameliorated version, 'Jacobean Chaucer', p. 199. Waith notes Davenant's chief alterations to the story, pp. 31–4, as does Potter, pp. 75–6. In the only book-length study of Davenant's Shakespearean adaptations, Mongi Raddadi excludes *The Rivals* from major consideration, noting only incidental parallels to those works that Davenant adapted which she considers to have been solely authored by Shakespeare. Because *Two Noble Kinsmen* is co-authored by Fletcher she excludes the play from her discussion: 'there seems indeed to be no adequate reason to treat *The Rivals* here in detail', p. 15. This argument ignores the issue of Middleton's contributions to *Macbeth* and to *Measure for Measure*. Raddadi discusses Davenant's versions of both plays in full (the latter is mixed with *Much Ado about Nothing* to become *The Law against Lovers*).

39  Potter, noting that Pirithous is called Polynices, observes that Davenant obviously knew the Classical background to Chaucer's tale, 'but he deliberately detached the play both from *The Knight's Tale* and from legend, changed all the names of the characters, and set it in Arcadia', p. 75.

40  Rosamund S. Allen, '*The Siege of Thebes*: Lydgate's Canterbury Tale', in Julia Boffey and Janet Cowen (eds), *Chaucer and Fifteenth Century Poetry* (London: King's College London, 1991), pp. 122–42 (p. 131). Thompson, *Shakespeare's Chaucer*, p. 177, notes that Shakespeare probably read *The Siege of Thebes*, which may account for the political accounts of Creon and Thebes in the new scene in *Two Noble Kinsmen*, 1.2.

41  Andreas likens Palamon and Arcite in *The Two Noble Kinsmen* to the warring brothers Etecoles and Polynices in Statius's *Thebaid*, but he does not mention either Lydgate or Davenant, 'Remythologising *The Knight's Tale*', p. 57.

42  As noted by Trigg, *Congenial Souls*, p. xv, and Hardman, 'Presenting the Text', p. 37.

43  The temporal dislocations are discussed by James Simpson, '"Dysemol daies and fatal hours": Lydgate's Destruction of Thebes and Chaucer's *Knight's Tale*', in Helen Cooper and Sally Mapstone (eds), *The Long Fifteenth Century* (Oxford: Clarendon Press, 1997), pp. 15–34 (p. 33).

44 The changes in the time sequence of the journey are discussed by John M. Bowers, 'Alternative Ideas of *The Canterbury Tales*'.

45 Signed on 21 May 1420 in the French city that bears its name, the Treaty of Troyes was an agreement that Henry V of England and his heirs would inherit the throne of France upon the death of King Charles VI of France. Under its terms, Henry would marry Catherine, Charles's daughter. Their sons were to be successors to the French throne. There may be a citation of the terms of this treaty in *Siege* 4690–3 and 4702–3.

46 Potter argues that 'once its Chaucerian and classical sources are forgotten', the story has more potential for tragedy than for comedy', p. 75; a statement that may be true, but who is it that does the forgetting? As Patterson notes, writing on the Theban-ness of Chaucer's short poem 'Anelida and Arcite', 'the Theban story is itself about disordered memory and fatal repetition, about the tyranny of a past that is both forgotten and obsessively remembered, and about the recursive patterns into which history falls', *Subject of History*, p. 75.

47 Davenant had already used this imagery to signal Charles's victory over Cromwell in his version of *Macbeth*. Macduff's last words in the play, addressed to Malcolm are: 'So may kind Fortune Crown your Raign with Peace, / As it has Crown'd your Armies with success; / And may the Peoples Prayers still wait on you, / As all their Curses did *Macbeth* pursue: / His Vice shall make your Virtue shine more Bright, / As a Fair Day succeeds a Stormy Night' (London: P. Chetwin, 1674), p. 65.

48 By 1664 Richard Flecknoe was warning the public that whereas old theatres had been 'plain and simple ... ours now for cost and ornament are arriv'd to the heighth of Magnificence; but that which makes our Stage the better, makes our Playes the worse perhaps, they striving now to make them more for the sight then hearing', 'A Short Discourse of the English Stage' (1664), quoted in Bevis, *English Drama*, p. 34.

49 In addition to the noble marriages, Celania's maid Leucippe marries the Provost's man Cunopes.

50 In the list of *dramatis personae*, Heraclia is unequivocally labelled 'neece to the prince'. Potter calls her Arcon's sister, and therefore the only heir to the unmarried Arcon, p. 75.

51 Nahum Tate's version of *King Lear* was one of a number of Shakespearean adaptations that can be seen to respond to the events of this crisis, see Sandra Clark (ed.), *Shakespeare Made Fit* (London: J. M. Dent, 1997), pp. lxv–lxvii.

52 Charles's eldest – and Protestant – bastard son was created Duke of Monmouth in 1663. The character who corresponds to Edmund in Tate's *King Lear* is consistently named 'Bastard' and may have been fashioned for resemblance to Monmouth's part during the Exclusion Crisis.

53  His first Shakespearean adaptation was *The Law Against Lovers* in which *Measure for Measure* is spliced with *Much Ado about Nothing*. Like *The Rivals*, it celebrates the restoration of the Stuart monarchy and its theatre. But into the mouth of Beatrice, a character who was a particular favourite of Charles II's, Davenant gives a speech which makes a joke at the expense of Charles's marriage to Catherine of Braganza by wooing through ambassadors and wedding by proxy: 'O Sir! you are a very princely Lover! / You cannot woo but by Ambassadors / And may chance to marry by Proxy', William Davenant, *The Law Against Lovers* in *Measure for Measure: The Text of the Folio of 1623, with that of 'The Law against Lovers' by Sir William D'Avenant, 1662*, ed. B. Frank Carpenter (New York: The Shakespeare Society of New York, 1908), p. 105.

54  Winifred Gosnell played the role of Celania in the September 1664 run of the play, Edmond, *Rare Sir William Davenant*, p. 189. Mary Davis took over the role when the play was revived.

55  'My Lodging it is on the Cold ground' from *The Rivals* was so well known it was parodied in James Howard's *All Mistaken* performed as early as 1665, Scheil, 'Sir William Davenant's Use of Shakespeare', p. 378.

56  'She perform'd that so Charmingly, that not long after, it Rais'd her from her Bed on the Cold Ground to a Bed Royal', *Roscius Anglicanus*, p. 55.

57  Katharine Eisaman Mauss, 'Playhouse Flesh and Blood: Sexual Ideology and the Restoration Actress', *English Literary History* 46 (1979), 595–617, notes how the 'opportunities' for female actresses did not change perception of their role in society. She quotes Downes's anecdote to support her argument that audiences showed an obsessive concern with the sexuality of the actors newly admitted to the stage, p. 601.

58  *Fables Ancient and Modern; Translated into Verse, from Homer, Ovid, Boccace, and Chaucer: with Original Poems* was published in 1700, but Dryden had finished writing them in 1699.

59  'To her Grace the Duchess of Ormond', in *The Works of John Dryden: Volume VII, Poems 1697–1700*, ed. Dearing. This edition prints 'Palamon and Arcite' adjacent to Speght's text of Chaucer. C. D. Reverand argues that Mary Ormond is compared not to Joan, Countess of Kent, an allusion that would position her as the prize for three contending husbands in succession, but to John of Gaunt's wife Blanche, in memory of whom Chaucer had written *Book of the Duchess*, 'Dryden's "To the Duchess of Ormond": Identifying her Plantagenet predecessor', *Notes and Queries* 54:1 (2007), 57–60.

60  This is the argument of Steven N. Zwicker, *The Arts of Disguise: Politics and Language in Dryden's Poetry* (Princeton: University of Princeton Press, 1984), pp. 158–67.

61 Preface to the *Enchanted Isle*, p. 6.

62 As I mentioned at the start of this chapter, Chaucer was never Poet Laureate in his own time. Lydgate, however, invests Chaucer with the laurel in *Siege* and he writes in 'The Lyf of Oure Lady' that Chaucer 'worthy was the laurel to haue', *Minor Poems*, ed. MacCracken (lines 757–8). Paul Hammond and David Hopkins (eds), *The Poems of John Dryden, vol. 5 1597–1700* (Harlow: Pearson, 2005), draw attention to Lydgate's verse in the Speght edition that Dryden used, p. 51, note to line 59. Robert J. Meyer-Lee brings out the subtlety and finesse of Lydgate's laureate positioning in *Poets and Power from Chaucer to Wyatt* (Cambridge: Cambridge University Press, 2007), pp. 65–87.

63 *The Tory Poets: A Satyr*, cited in James Kinsley and Helen Kinsley (eds), *John Dryden: The Critical Heritage* (London: Routledge, 1995), p. 156 and for discussion, see Jane Spencer, *Literary Relations: Kinship and the Canon 1660–1830* (Oxford: Oxford University Press, 2005), p. 24.

64 Edmond recounts the stories about his nose and surname, *Rare Sir William Davenant*, p. 37, and pp. 45–6.

65 This is the name that is given to syphilis in *Troilus and Cressida* 5.1.21. The line does not appear in Dryden's reworking of the play. The phrase is still used in the later seventeenth century, see Gordon Williams, *Shakespeare's Sexual Language: A Glossary* (London: Continuum, 2006), pp. 129–30.

66 John Downes records that William Davenant was 'Bury'd in Westminster Abbey near Mr Chaucer's Monument', *Roscius*, p. 66. None of the other contenders for 'The Knight's Tale' (Lydgate, Beaumont and Fletcher) is buried in the abbey. Shakespeare is buried in the parish church at Stratford-upon-Avon. His splendid memorial in Westminster Abbey does not contain his body.

# 6

## Reverberate Troy: sounding *The House of Fame* in *Troilus and Cressida*

In Shakespeare's *Troilus and Cressida*, Achilles prompts a lecture on fame and oblivion by asking Ulysses what he is reading. 'A strange fellow', Ulysses replies (3.3.95).[1] In a play that resounds with the declamation of names, the name of Ulysses's author is never said. Like Nature, critics 'abhor a vacuum', but, while they have suggested plenty of authors to fill this tantalising lacuna of nomenclature, chiefly Plato, Seneca, Davies, Cicero and Montaigne, no critical consensus has been reached on christening the 'strange fellow'.[2] It would be fanciful, of course, to suggest that he is the chimerical 'man of gret auctorite' whom the narrator cannot name at the end of Chaucer's *House of Fame* (2157–8):[3] Chaucer's dream vision poem rarely features in studies of the relationships between any of Shakespeare's plays and Chaucer's works;[4] the Chaucerian 'source' for the plot of *Troilus and Cressida* is *Troilus and Criseyde*,[5] and neither of Shakespeare's eponymous characters appears in *The House of Fame*. And yet, while this chapter will not seek to claim that Shakespeare *must* have used the poem as a textual source for his play, in no other early modern work does the soundscape[6] of *The House of Fame* receive such acute replay as in *Troilus and Cressida*.[7] In both works, aurality dissolves discrimination between fame and honour, and ignominy and oblivion. Classical legend becomes suburban clamour, distinction between voice(s) is eroded and meaningful sound is percussed into airy space.

Between 1553 and 1625 it is clear that the poem was read – and heard – in this much more anarchic fashion. In William Baldwin's *Beware the Cat*, Gregory Streamer, one of the many internal narrators of the piece, takes part in a debate about whether there is any difference between words and noise.[8] He conducts an experiment. Having swilled down a cocktail of potions distilled from disgusting parts of various beasts, he clothes himself in

animal pelts, and furnishes himself with ears made from those
of a cat. Thus accoutred, he is miraculously able to hear every
kind of sound from his Aldgate house: the music of the spheres,
and this:

> While I harkened to this broil, laboring to discern both voices and
> noises asunder, I heard such a mixture as I think was neuer in
> Chaucer's House of Fame; for there was nothing within an hundred
> mile of me done on any side (for from so far, but no farther, the air
> may come because of obliquation) but I heard it as well as if I had
> been by it, and could discern all voices, but by means of noises
> vnderstand none. Lord what ado women made in their beds – some
> scolding, some laughing, some weeping; some singing to their
> sucking children, which made a woeful noise with their continual
> crying. And one shrewd wife a great way off (I think at St. Albans)
> called her husband 'cuckold' so loud and shrilly that I heard that
> plain and would fain haue heard the rest, but could not by no means
> for barking of dogs, grunting of hogs, wawling of cats, rumbling of
> rats, gaggling of geese, humming of bees, rousing of bucks, gaggling
> of ducks, singing of swans, ringing of pans, crowing of cocks, sewing
> of socks, cackling of hens, scrabbling of pens, peeping of mice,
> trulling of dice, curling of frogs, and toads in the bogs, chirping of
> crickets, shutting of wickets, shriking of owls, flittering of fowls,
> routing of knaues, snorting of slaues, farting of churls, fizzling of
> girls, with many things else as ringing of bells, counting of coins,
> mounting of groins, whispering of louers, springling of plouers,
> groaning and spewing, baking and brewing, scratching and rubbing,
> watching and shrugging – with such a sort of commixed noises as
> would deaf anybody to haue heard; much more me, seeing that the
> pannicles of mine ears were with my medicine made so fine and stiff,
> and that by the temperate heat of the things therein, that like a tabor
> dried before the fire, or else a lute string by heat shrunk nearer, they
> were incomparably amended in receiuing and yielding the shrill-
> ness of any touching sounds. While I was earnestly harkening, as I
> said, to hear the woman, minding nothing else, the greatest bell in
> St. Botolph's steeple, which is hard by, was tolled for some rich body
> that then lay in passing, the sound whereof came with such a rumble
> into mine ear, that I thought all the deuils in Hell had broken loose,
> and were come about me, and was so afraid therewith, that, when
> I felt the foxtail under my foot (which through fear I had forgot),
> I deemed it had been the Deuil indeed.[9]

The tract replays both the aurality of Chaucer's *House of Fame* and
its learned debate on the mechanics of sound. Textual fame becomes
inflated sonic mayhem. And yet, a marginal note placed adjacent to
the description mock-glosses it as 'poetry': '[Here the poetical fury

came upon him]' (p. 32). Learned marginalia sound the same notes as urban din.[10]

Ben Jonson's response to *The House of Fame* shows that appreciation of Chaucer's soundscape did not die out with Edward VI. It might seem that the 1609 *Masque of Queens* pays respectful homage to Chaucer's poem. Jonson states that, in building the House of Fame for the dance of the ladies of the court of James I, Inigo Jones 'professed to follow that noted description that Chaucer made of the place'.[11] Brass pillars hold up the illustrations of famous classical poets (360–1; 452). Lady Fame, the daughter of Heroic Virtue, has a trumpet of peace in one hand and an olive branch in the other (426).[12] The virtuous reputation of noble ladies is celebrated with stately dance and verse, and their names are recorded in the textual version of the masque's conclusion to preserve their honour for posterity (529–34). But Jonson does not spaniel *The House of Fame* at heels. The aristocratic masque is preceded by the cavorting of twelve hags who proclaim that they are the antithesis of virtuous fame. They are associated not with gracious music but with the sound of every instrument playing at once (334): with thunder, barking dogs, howling wolves, clouds of pitch and chaos (260–309): noise that sounds 'black-mouthed execration' (111). While Baldwin made no distinction between animal noise and human words, poetry and brabble, Jonson preserves the oppositions only to polarise them – as he must do for his occasion – between the masque and anti-masque. But that enforced parallelism recognises that Chaucer's *House of Fame* is as much about black-pitched rumour and animal discord as majestical notes of glory. Fourteen years later, when Jonson wrote *The Staple of News*, 'the House of Fame' is the office that circulates texts of unsourced gossip and baseless propaganda for financial gain.[13]

*Troilus and Cressida*, written in the years between *Beware the Cat* and *The Staple of News*, replays the acoustic profile of *The House of Fame* even more precisely. Shakespeare's play rehearses the keynotes of the poem's collapse of sonic distinction. Trumpets, so prominent in both works, proclaim eminence and abasement with insouciant caprice; silence undermines the oppositions between famed authority and unspoken abjection, and, crucially, both works share an identical sound topography.[14] Both dramatise the fiction that holds up the Legend of Troy, and by extension, the fiction that supports the translation of Trojan epic to narrate contemporary civic identity, medieval or early modern. Ulysses's 'strange fellow' and the unnamed 'man of gret auctoritee' are anonymous textual authors spoken in a soundworld of Troy that is situated in Southwark. Rerouted from swelling the pomp of the city of London, the classical legends of 'reverb'rate Troy' sound suburban. Sounds that exceed legislature are mapped on to an area of London that is without the city's jurisdiction.[15]

## Troynovant Southwark

For Chaucer and Shakespeare and their contemporaries, Troy was the perfect unreal city:[16] a name from a tissue of Classical texts ungrounded by the material remains of any city in Turkish place. Without foundation, Troy was supremely well fitted to serve as authority for civic fiction-making. Medieval and early modern London capitalised richly on the connections, but not without strain.[17] Myth doctors in both ages were faced with a fractured legacy: the history of Troy as a foundation myth for a succession of great civilisations that move increasingly westwards until they settle conclusively on Londinium / New Troy. And the destruction of Troy as a warning of civic and moral dissolution.[18] It was hard to invoke one without summoning up the other. In *The House of Fame* and *Troilus and Cressida* Trojan glory and ashen ruin are as inseparable as the lie and the truth that fly 'compouned' out of the same window (2108–9) at the close of Chaucer's dream vision. Not solely because of the Jekyll and Hyde legacy of Trojan history, but because of where their soundscapes are located in (sub)urban space.

In the Folio version of *Troilus and Cressida*, the Prologue declares '[i]n Troy, there lies the scene' (Prol.1).[19] The Grecian ships have disgorged their soldiers and they are encamped in tents outside six-gated Troy. The precise geographical referent of 'there' has been a matter of dispute. From the evidence of the prefatory epistle to Quarto 2, 'there' did not exist; the play was never 'clapper-clawed' in live performance.[20] And if the theatre of Troy *was* performed on stage, was 'there' the Inns of Court or the Globe in Bankside?[21] Whether *Troilus and Cressida* was ever performed or not, either for lawyers in the City or for the public on the South Bank, the speeches of some of its dramatis personae situate it in Southwark. In the final act, Thersites relocates the combat between Greeks and Trojans to the arena which staged bear-baiting and bull fights next door to the Globe. Commenting on the fighting between Menelaus and Paris:

The cuckold and the cuckold-maker are at it! Now, bull, now,
dog! 'Loo Paris, 'loo! Now my double-horned Spartan!
'Loo Paris 'loo! The bull has the game: ware horns, ho!

(5.8.9–12)

Thersites impersonates the noise made by cheering on the hounds
and bulls at Paris Gardens; a site of entertainment deplored even
more thoroughly than its neighbouring theatre.[22] The soundscapes
of the two venues must often have overlapped and were satirised
as loci of unbearable din. Morose in Jonson's *Epicoene*, desperate
for sanctuary from civic hullabaloo, declares that he would rather
do penance in the belfry at Westminster Hall, or the cockpit at
the fall of a stag ... or Paris garden.[23] In *Troilus and Cressida*,
Thersites snorts the name of Trojan Paris and Menelaus's legendary cuckold's horns in the bays of suburban sport. Even if *Troilus*
were being performed in the city, the conducting of the Trojan war
sounds the bullish bark of Bankside.

The last words in the play, according to most editors and directors,[24] are those of Pandarus. While the start of the play tones
declamations of Troy, it concludes in the seething of Southwarkian
stews:

Brethren and sisters of the hold-door trade,
Some two months hence my will shall here be made.
It should be now, but that my fear is this:
Some galled goose of Winchester should hiss.
Till then I'll sweat and seek about for eases,
And at that time bequeath you my diseases.

(5.11.49–54)

The audience are directly addressed as pimps and prostitutes.
Southwark prostitutes worked from the stews which were on land
that was regulated by the Bishop of Winchester; the grounds of his
palace adjoined the theatrespace of the Globe. A galled goose is
both an infected prostitute and a syphilitic sore. A prostitute who
hisses like a goose offended by the sight of Pandarus's 'will' is also
a member of the audience who boos the performance of the play.[25]
Acoustically, Pandarus ends the play in an extended hissy-fit.
There is sustained sounding of the phoneme closest to voiced
air [ð] ('this', 'then', 'that', 'then'). The last four lines are rich in
internal sibilance ('is', 'this', 'some'; 'goose', '-chester', 'should',
'sweat', 'seek', 'ease' and 'dis'), and the rhymes of unvoiced [s]
in 'this' and 'hiss' are chimed by the disyllabic sounding of [z] in
'eases' and 'diseases'. Located in Southwark, the heroic sounds

of Troy and its onlookers are indistinguishable from animal noise. The resounding rhetorical gymnastics at the start of the play (whether the Prologue's declamation or Troilus's anguished histrionics) are become the beastly friction of air.[26]

While Chaucer's *Troilus and Criseyde* undoubtedly provides materials for Shakespeare's play, its sound geography is not amongst them. As critics have observed, the urban Troyscape of Chaucer's *Troilus* is London, not Southwark,[27] and the end of the poem leaves all earthly cities behind as Troilus ascends to the hollowness of the eighth sphere and looks down mockingly at the 'litel spot of erthe' he has left so far down below. Earthly ties are ruptured as the city of men yields to the city of God.[28] The insistent anaphora of the severance from earthly pleasure and pagan experience that resounds in the repetition of '[s]wich fyn' (V.1828–34), and '[l]o here' (1849–54) in the final stanzas of this poem is tonally worlds apart from the suppurating sound-sleaze at the end of Shakespeare's play. Closer by far in sound and location is the conclusion to *The House of Fame*. The structure and trajectory of their soundscapes map closely. Like Shakespeare's *Troilus*, *The House of Fame* moves from the proclamation of classical Troy to the boisterous snurting of contemporary Southwark trade.

The prefatory materials of the dream vision over and done with, the narrator of *The House of Fame* finds himself in a temple of glass that contains the story of Troy engraved on brass tablets. The narrator mediates this history through the sonority of Virgil's opening line of the *Aeneid*, 'I wol now synge, if I kan, / The armes and also the man' (143–4). Even if the epic Latin 'cano' is muffled by English translation and diffidence, the initial sound of Troy is one of grandiloquent empire-building. By contrast, the end of the dream fetches up in the territory of Ovidian counter-culture; in the suburb that has been described as 'London's scrapheap'.[29] The story of Troy ends abruptly in the House of Rumour. Ovid introduces the figure of Rumour into Book 12 of his *Metamorphoses* just before narrating how the Greek ships set sail bent on the destruction of Troy (coincidentally, the place where Shakespeare's Prologue starts). Rumour lives in a brazen house where every voice is audible. Its innumerable entrances, a thousand openings, have no doors. Open night and day, it rustles with noise, echoing voices, and repeating what it has heard. While it knows neither peace nor silence, there is no clamour, only the subdued murmur of voices, like the waves of the sea, or the sound of distant thunder when Jupiter makes the dark clouds rumble. Crowds fill the hallways:

a fickle populace comes and goes, truth mingles randomly with fiction, a thousand rumours wander and confused words circulate.[30]

The materials of Chaucer's house are very different; the house is not brazen, but:

> Was mad of twigges, falwe, rede,
> And grene eke, and somme weren white,
> Swiche as men to these cages thwite,
> Or maken of these panyers,
> Or elles hottes or dossers;
> That, for the swough and for the twygges,
> This hous was also ful of gygges,
> And also ful eke of chirkynges,
> And of many other werkynges.

(1936–44)

Resounding brass is become several different kinds of basket ('panyers', 'hottes', 'dossers'): baskets for bread, baskets to be carried on the back or baskets to be carried on the backs of horses. The noise that rattles through the house is likened not to the sea or to thunder, but to magnified wind whistling through the woven panniers that would contain a victualler's goods, or provisions for a journey. The choice of diction in lines 1938–44 is acoustically dense. Internal sibilance is emphasised by all six lines ending in plurals. The di- and poly-syllables of the rhymes 'twygges', 'gygges', 'chirkynges', and 'werkynges', together with their medial velar stops and alveolar fricatives, produce the sounds of whooshing, chocked air.[31] While I am anxious not to fall into onomatopoeic fallacy,[32] the persistence of the sibilant plurals in Chaucer's description of the wicker house scarcely seems accidental:

> Ne never rest is in that place
> That hit nys fild ful of tydynges,
> Other loude or of whisprynges;
> And over alle the houses angles
> Ys ful of rounynges and of jangles
> Of werres, of pes, of mariages,
> Of reste, of labour, of viages,
> Of abood, of deeth, of lyf,
> Of love, of hate, acord, of stryf,
> Of loos, of lore, and of wynnynges,
> Of hele, of seknesse, of bildynges,
> Of faire wyndes, and of tempestes,
> Of qwalm of folk, and eke of bestes;

Of dyvers transmutacions
Of estats, and eke of regions.

(1956–70)

The insistent accumulation of sibilance, medially and terminally,
makes the wicker house one whose primary sense is auditory. The
description is one of echo and repetition; the multiply anaphoric
verse conducts an indiscriminate catalogue of plural nouns with
amplified susurration. An unregulated whispering soundtrack is
not, in itself, of course, evidence of a Southwark location.[33] The
topography of the never silent house is revealed partly by its
inhabitants:

And, Lord, this hous in alle tymes
Was ful of shipmen and pilgrimes,
With scrippes bret-ful of lesinges,
Entremedled with tydynges,
And eek allone be hemselve.
O, many a thousand tymes twelve
Saugh I eke of these Pardoners,
Currours, and eke messagers,
With boystes crammed ful of lyes
As ever vessel was with lyes.

(2121–30)

Boatmen, pilgrims, Pardoners, couriers and messengers would
all have been conspicuous in the business of Southwark. The
first staging post out of the city towards the port of Dover, along
Watling Street (mentioned line 939), Southwark provided tran-
sient lodging for Pardoners hot foot to Rome, and for pilgrims
(including, of course, those fictional persons of Canterbury assembled at the Tabard), at one of the numerous inns that lined both
sides of Southwark High Street.[34] Boatmen were ubiquitous:
ferrying passengers to and from the city across the Thames, or
working at other riverside trades – stamping on eels, perhaps, like
those persons frantic for news in the last few lines of the poem
(2154). As a centre of communication, the business of news and
gossip would have kept messengers and couriers well occupied: the
rime riche of 'lyes' as lies and wine dregs a fitting aural pun on the
economies of truth in tavern trade and narrative exchange.[35]

Not just its inhabitants but the very materials of the house of
Rumour recall the commerce of Southwark; all those wicker baskets.
In a place of transitory passage, a hub of the service industry, huck-
sters, those female street pedlars who sold ready-to-eat-food from

baskets, were plentiful. Hucksters feature prominently in the Poll
Tax return for Southwark in 1381.[36] The entrances to the house also
sound a Bankside note not heard in Ovid's account:

> And eke this hous hath of entrees
> As fele as of leves ben in trees
> In somer, whan they grene been;
> And on the roof men may yet seen
> A thousand holes, and wel moo,
> To leten wel the soun out goo.
> And be day, in every tyde,
> Been al the dores opened wide,
> And by nyght echon unshette;
> Ne porter ther is noon to lette
> No maner tydynges in to pace.
>
> (1945–55)

Added to Ovid are the details in the description of the holes,
the doors opened wide at every hour, and each door kept unshut at
night.[37] The house of female Rumour is a house of easy access. Its
innumerable holes and unbarred doors connote prostitution; the
trade of the stews as prominent a service industry in Southwark
as victualling, hostelry and water transport. Doors stood open
on the holidays were a trade sign for sex.[38] All those open 'o'
sounded anaphorae I discussed above take on further seething
resonance when we remember some other details unheard in Ovid.
Right at the start of Chaucer's description we hear that Rumour's
house is 'queyntelych ywrought' (1923), and '[t]his queynte hous'
(1925) turns about unceasingly. The sounding of 'queynte' in this
context, especially 'queynte' in open supply, calls up the sense of
Bankside brothels. The sound topography of the narrative structure of *The House of Fame* turns the epic city of Troy into a giant
stew: a babbling, windy tinderbox of promiscuous traffic. Though
Faustus was referring to her face, it was, after all, a traded woman
who 'launched a thousand ships and burnt the topless towers of
Ilium'.[39]

## Voys, or noyse, or word or soun
## What's aught but as tis valued?

In *The House of Fame* and *Troilus and Cressida*, we hear the ruin
of Troy into Southwark as part of an encompassing soundworld in
which 'degree', so vaunted by Ulysses, is deregulated into chaos.[40]
Sound that is attributed meaning by the mind is indeterminable

from noise that enters the body.[41] The preservation of fame by the reverberation of name is returned to first principles; nothing more than physical air. Chaucer's eagle puts it better. While his portly auditor dangles, terrified, from his talons in (significantly) mid-air, he tells him that sound is nothing more than 'eyr ybroken' (765). Every speech, loud or secret, foul or fair, '[i]n his substaunce ys but air' (766–8).[42] As Martin Irvine has shown, this definition of sound is found in grammatical treatises and commonplace books, and repeated in encyclopaedias of natural history.[43] Explication of its sense followed logical niceties of distinction. Grammarians argued that the 'substance', the material form, of sound was air. But the accident of that material substance was conceptual: hearing. Sound as material air was not the same as sound that was heard: voice, or utterance. Every voice was a sound, but not every sound was a voice. In a further distinction, voice was divided into discrete categories: sound that could not be heard as distinct phonetic units (i.e. noise); animal sounds without meaning, like crowing or screeching which could be represented by letters, and inarticulate human sounds like groaning which are meaningful but lack discrete phonetic units. All three of these categories were distinct from 'vox articulata literata'; articulate speech and literary language. The eagle's discourse swallows up all such classification. During a very long lecture, to which the narrator can answer only in monosyllables, the eagle argues that *every* speech, *every* sound, be it foul or fair,[44] has its natural place in air, and *every* 'voys, or noyse, or word, or soun' (819) is moved by the reverberation of the air until it comes to the House of Fame. Voice, noise, word and sound are rattled out indiscriminately as if one were the equal of another. Word has no more weight than noise, and the categories in between are scrambled: the eagle's list has no ascending or descending order. Value is neutralised.

The poem slyly dissolves the matter and substance of the eagle's speech itself. In drawing attention to 'telling' – pretending that he has used no 'subtilite / Of speche', philosophical terms, poetic figures, or rhetorical colours (853–63) – the eagle keeps reminding his audience that a non-verbal bird is capable of philosophical discourse.[45] According to the narrator, the eagle speaks 'in the same vois and stevene, / That useth oon I koude nevene' (561–2), only with a kindness to which the dreamer is not accustomed. While the supply of a misogynist domestic backstory in the form of a scolding Mrs Chaucer fills the silence, the creation of a hen-pecked husband misses the more salient point that the voice that scrambles all distinctions of sound is a voice that is unanchored.[46] It is beyond naming – and the physical characteristics of the eagle's voice are beyond framing. Philosophical discourse merges with bird shriek; 'he gan to crye, / That never herde I thing so hye' (1019–20). Is this an animal or a human? Intelligible sound, or unrepresentable noise? The eagle's speech is one long-winded epistemological conundrum.[47]

Description in *The House of Fame* is consistently pitched towards the recreation of sound. As here:

Mo discordes, moo jelousies
Mo murmures and moo novelries,
And moo dissymulacions,
And feyned reparacions,
And moo berdys in two houres
Withoute rasour or sisoures
Ymad then greynes be of sondes;
And eke moo holdynge in hondes,
And also moo renovelaunces
Of olde forleten aqueyntaunces;
Mo love-dayes and acordes
Then on instrumentes be cordes;
And eke of loves moo eschaunges
Then ever cornes were in graunges.

                                                            (685–98)

In amongst the clash of registers: 'dissymulacions', 'berdys', 'renovelaunces' and 'sondes', the unvoiced sibiliance of plurals and polysyllables hiss insistently through the rhythmic pulsing of an anaphoric list. No clear hierarchy of sound and sense emerges. The sonic texture of the verse is an acoustic realisation of the eagle's words, as repeatedly, the verse demands attention to its aurality:

'Maistow not heren that I do?'
'What?' quod I. 'The grete soun,'
Quod he, 'that rumbleth up and doun
In Fames Hous, full of tydynges,
Bothe of feir speche and chidynges,
And of fals and soth compouned.
Herke wel; hyt is not rouned.
Herestow not the grete swogh?'
'Yis, parde,' quod y, 'wel ynogh.'
'And what soun is it lyk?' quod hee.
'Peter, lyk betynge of the see,'
Quod y, 'ayen the roches holowe,

> Whan tempest doth the shippes swalowe,
> And lat a man stonde, out of doute,
> A myle thens, and here hyt route;
> Or elles lyk the last humblynge
> After the clappe of a thundringe,
> Whan Joves hath the air ybete.'

(1024–41)

'Do you not hear it as I do?' asks the eagle. Listen to it well. Do you not hear the great 'swogh' – the sound of the wind? What sound is it like? Forced to supply a description of what pounds his ears, the narrator reaches for similes drawn not from Virgil's account of Fame but from Ovid's account of the House of Rumour: the beating of the sea or the rumbling of the beaten air after Jove has thundered. Virgil is silently spliced with Ovid in lines which emphasise the physical reverberation (percussed air) of sound: 'betynge', 'route', 'humblynge', 'clappe', 'thundringe' and 'bete'.[48]

The poem plays a persistent medley of sound games with grandiloquent texts. Taking full advantage of the tripping sound of octosyllabic couplets, the dominant rhyme pattern in the poem plays off name and fame with name and shame and name and game.[49] The repetition of the phoneme [ɑ:mə] is a dogged acoustic reminder that name, fame and shame are, at first base, simply sounds. Virgil, Ovid, Dante – even the Book of Revelation, perhaps – are a series of pat chimes whose acoustic echo dins discrete written names into endlessly similar sound. The narrator, acting less like a teller, and more as an overhearer, simply amplifies the confusion. It is well known that the version of Virgil's *Aeneid* that he starts to speak from the multimedia images on the wall in the Temple of Glass slides imperceptibly into Dido's complaint from the *Heroides*. But, as mediated by the dreamer, Dido's speech is ontologically unhinged through the random distribution of speech acts and sounds:

> O woful Dido, wel-away!
> Quod she to hirselve thoo.

(317–18)

> 'O, wel-awey that I was born!
> For thorgh yow is my name lorn,
> And alle myn actes red and songe
> Over al thys lond, on every tonge.'

(345–8)

> '"Loo, ryght as she hath don, now she
> Wol doo eft-sones, hardely;" –
> Thus seyth the peple prively.'
> But that is don, is not to done;
> Al hir compleynt ne al hir moone,
> Certeyn, avayleth hir not a stre.

(358–63)

As so often in this poem, when the issue of textual authority is being debated, au/orality comes to the fore. The text and sound of Chaucer's *House of Fame* are themselves the 'actes' of Dido that the narrator reports Dido speaking to herself in the voices of those speaking after her (358–9). Is 'welaway' a recognised bit of written lexis or the transliteration of a human sound of grief that lacks distinct phonetic units? Does Dido *say* ('quod') 'welaway', or does the narrator's writing/speaking for her create a graphematic representation of the sound of strangulated sobs? Dido's speech is both a 'compleynte', a recognised aristocratic verse form, and a 'moan', a sound that can be given recognisable shape in lettered form, but meaningless. Both will be both 'red' and 'songe', on every physical 'tongue' – a pun that is heard in rhyme.[50] Dido may complain (or should that be moan?) that her 'name', that is, her reputation, has been lost as a result of Aeneas's betrayal, but since all the air sounds come up to the House of Fame, and since the letters of the names on the ice can scarcely be told because they have been blown around so widely (1137–41), her name, or the lack of it, is immaterial.

Dido's predicament becomes Cressida's: between empires, between men, between text and voice, between words and noise. Cressida re-cites her reputation that has already been written through anonymous future voices:

> ... when they've said 'as false
> As air, as water, wind or sandy earth,
> As fox to lamb or wolf to heifer's calf,
> Pard to the hind or stepdame to her son'
> Yes, let them say to stick the heart of falsehood,
> 'As false as Cressid'

(3.2.171–6)

The substance of Cressida's resounding litany of similes is reportage, unnamed and plural: Cressida's name is become the stuff of proverbial gossip. Her own last words in the play are unheard. When Pandarus gives Troilus her letter, he tears it into pieces without rehearsing its contents:

> Words, words, mere words, no matter from the heart.
> Th'effect doth operate another way.
>                   [*Tearing and scattering the letter*]
>
> Go, wind, to wind, there turn and change together.
>                                              (5.3.107–9)

Cressida's written words are become air; as immaterial as Dido's words in the House of Fame.[51] While the stage direction appears neither in the Folio nor in the Quarto versions of the play, its action on stage produces the sound of the destruction of words into noise. In Mendes's production (1990) the audience heard the ripping of the paper as Anton Lesser scattered the fragments over Pandarus's head. In Judge's (1996) production, the shredding of paper chimed with the sounding of the bassoon notes associated with the lovers in Act 4 Scene 2.[52]

Performance realises the collapse of textuality into sound that Chaucer's poem describes through acoustic mime. It is not only Cressida's letter that is shredded. Achilles can crumple the letter sent to him from Queen Hecuba (5.1.36) (Judge (1990)); or Patroclus can retrieve it after he has thrown it down and rip it apart in frustration (BBC (1981)). In either action, the tearing of words leaves its mark on the soundtrack. Ajax's impatience to learn the proclamation (2.1.20–9) exposes the gaps between the graphematic letters and words as sound as Achilles enunciates each of the letters slowly, and points at the words with his fingers (Mendes (1990)). Peter Hall's (2001) production dramatised even more fundamentally the orality/textuality question that haunts the whole play: was it ever performed, or only read? With the house lights still on, the actor playing the Prologue brought out a copy of David Bevington's Arden edition and read the lines from the epistle to Quarto 2 which claim that the play was never 'clapper clawed' (the phrase itself alluding to the abrasion of sound) by performance.[53]

The polyvocality of the play, its heteroglossia and its discordant mingling of registers and strains have been much noted.[54] In the theatre, or on soundtrack, it is much heard. Voices are strung out in the sinewy suspension of rhetorical bravura, exchanges are rapped out with venomous rapidity and reverberant polysyllables deflated by monosyllabic slurs. An arsenal of words for different kinds of sound batters the ears of the audience. The most frequently articulated of these is 'O';[55] a letter whose name is the same as its sound but whose meaning and shape suggests nothingness, or at least something untranslatable into a full-bodied word.

'O' is one of those human emotion sounds which can be registered in graphematic form, but whose sense exceeds taxonomic classification. It is both a sound shared with beasts, particularly the howls of wolves and dogs, and a sound whose function is often to serve as a discourse marker, a signal to call attention to the act of speaking rather than have anything very specific to say for itself.[56] *Troilus* groans under the weight of words that call attention to its soundscape. They include: 'applause'; 'bay'; 'brabbler'; 'brag'; 'chide'; 'clamour'; 'cough'; 'croak'; 'curse'; 'discourse'; 'ho'; 'laugh'; 'music'; 'passion'; 'peace'; 'praise'; 'rail'; 'rhyme'; 'shriek'; 'sigh'; 'sob'; 'threat'; 'thunder'; 'tune'; 'vow'; 'weep' and 'whisper'. Cassandra's truthful prediction of the fall of Troy is a 'noise': a 'shriek' (2.2.97). The person who dares bring news to Priam or to Hecuba that 'Hector's dead' will for evermore be called a 'screech-owl' (5.11.16). On the day that morning brings Troilus and Cressida's consummated love to a close with the news that she must be exchanged for Antenor, 'the lark' hath 'roused the ribald crows' (4.2.10).

Performance intensifies this verbal acoustic discord. The 'orgulous' sonority of the Prologue is dispersed, for instance, if the actor speaks it when blowing his nose.[57] Ulysses's own grand monologues can sound like a 'bellowing pedant and schoolmaster', Regents Park (1998), or compete for attention with the sound of a harmonica and Nestor's very noisy eating of grapes, Hands (1981).[58] A reviewer of Davies (1985) wrote that Ralph Koltai's set, a decaying mansion, was a 'family pile ... full of noises', in which the actors were busy 'playing tunes on wine glasses'.[59] In the Greek camp scenes (BBC (1981)), barking dogs are continuously audible alongside the speeches; and in Act 5, when the drunken Greeks and Trojans clamber their noisily inebriated way through the tents, canine howling is accompanied by the crowing of cockerels and the murmuring of insects.[60] The scope for martial dissonance in the play is huge, encompassing the heroic ringing of weapon on armour[61] and wailing bombs, shells and sirens.[62] In Judge (1996), Hector beat the metal bin which stored the wooden staves used for the fight against Ajax. When he threw it against Ajax's chest, the improvised 'weapon' (Hector had dropped his stave) bounced off and rolled around the stage like a clamorous dustbin. As in many productions stentorian grunts, heavy breathing and wild cheering accompanied the fight.[63] At the slaughter of Hector (Davies (1985)), Thersites let out a high-pitched scream, while, in 1963, a production by the Birmingham Repertory

Theatre sounded to the noise of wrenches and chains as Achilles led a gang of leather-jacketed motorbike thugs. In Canada in 1987, one of the Myrmidons was heard to utter 'vroom vroom' as they moved in for the kill.[64]

Performance history reveals that these pugilistic sound effects were heard alongside a cacophony of incidental noise: Patroclus hitting Thersites over the head while he is wearing a saucepan and Cressida playing a teaspoon on Pandarus's head (Mendes (1990)); the stage resounding to the heroic tread of the Greeks, the roar of a bull, the rattling of bottles in a crate (Davies (1985)); stamping and heel-clicking; the sizzling of meat on crackling flames; a proleptic sound effect of burning Troy (BBC (1981)); birdsong in the orchard as Troilus and Cressida declare their love (Pelican audio recording); the insistent thump of Aeneas's knocking as he comes to deliver the news of Cressida's imminent exchange (Judge (1996)); Pandarus whistling; the crumpling of paper; and the loud scrub, scrub, scrub of washing against a board as camp-sibilant Thersites lisps out a string of curses (BBC (1981).[65] In the collaboration between The Wooster Group and the RSC as part of the World Shakespeare Festival 2012, North American Indian chant, pipes and the rattle of beaded charms kept stage with buzzing aeroplanes, party whistles and ear-splitting rock drums. In a play where there is so much overhearing, perhaps we should add the gasp of audience disgust as Simon Russell Beale/Thersites drooled painstakingly into the meal he had just prepared for Achilles/Alan Rickman (Mendes (1990)).[66]

Of course, to play emcee with the history of production sounds of *any* play has the potential to produce a brabble, not all of which can be argued to have deliberate thematic significance.[67] It is striking, however, how often directorial and/or actorly decision is concerned to emphasise acoustic dissonance. Reflecting on his performance as Thersites (Mendes (1990)), Simon Russell Beale speaks of the decision to use a conventional joker's stick with bells: the more jolly the sound of the stick the more painful a reminder to this intelligent and cynical entertainer of his exclusion from the circle of protagonists.[68] The section on sound in the 1968 Barton promptbook cues for Trojan theme, Greek theme and discord theme, and the opening prompts for Davies (1985) call for 'scream, typewriter, noise, cry, drone, ticker tape, bangs, bugles, piano, fan, wind and papers blowing'.[69] Words are whirred by wind, military sounds merge with noise and music with the clatter of mechanical objects.[70] Human utterance emerges from shrieks and bombilation.

The windy plains of ringing Troy reverberate 'voys, and noys, and word, and soun' in untuned degree.[71]

As in Chaucer's *House of Fame*, the whole business of legendary stories and names is conducted within a turbulent soundscape in which discrimination is lost. Characters in *Troilus* incessantly tell either their own names or those of others. While the name/fame/game rhyme of Chaucer's poem has no exact audio replication; the constant sounding of names and the saying of names creates a similar sound effect. Names need to be told and retold because no one seems to know who anyone else is. All the talk of fame and opinion needs the continuous substantiation through talk to establish any correlation between name and personhood.[72] The Trojans have heard of the Greeks and vice versa, but in battle, covered with armour, especially helmets, one man could be anyone. Hence all the comic confusion when Aeneas delivers his challenge to the Greek council in Act 1 Scene 3 and needs to have the leader's identity spelt out for him.[73] When Hector arrives in the Greek camp, he asks to be told '[t]he worthiest of them ... name by name' (4.5.160). The names of Achilles and Hector are sounded with particular repetition in the play,[74] but when they finally meet, Hector has to ask '[i]s this Achilles?' (4.5.233). To which Achilles has to sound his own name/fame, 'I am Achilles' (4.5.234).[75] In the same scene Menelaus moves to greet the warlike brace of brothers Troilus and Aeneas, only for Hector to enquire after the identity of the cuckolded husband in whose cause the Trojan war is fought (4.5.174–5). Agamemnon tells Troilus he is a 'well-famed lord of Troy' (4.5.173); but he has learnt (informed by Ulysses) who Troilus is only seventy lines earlier (4.5.95ff). Ulysses tells him that '[t]hey call him Troilus' (108). Rather appositely, this is a line that is repeated in the Folio version of Ulysses's speech, though critical editions strike out the addictive fit of repetitive name-telling.[76]

Confusion over identity is not confined to cross-camped males. In Act 1, Scene 2 when the Trojan warriors pass over the stage, ostensibly so that Pandarus can tell out their names and attributes to Cressida, the overall dramatic effect is a name call and identity parade. One which is presented rather ironically if there are no warriors physically present on stage, and/or if the sequence of questions and answers in the scene make it quite clear that Cressida already knows the identities of the men with whom she is presented.[77] Pandarus's role as nomenarch is thus redundant. In the warm-up act before the entrance of Paris and Helen, a servant asks Pandarus who is in the palace, 'the mortal Venus, the heart-blood of beauty, love's invisible soul'. 'Who?' asks Pandarus, 'My cousin Cressida?' 'No sir, Helen. Could you not find out that by her attributes?' (3.1.32). Helen or Cressida. What does it matter? After all, as Troilus finds out to his cost, 'this is, and is not, Cressid' (5.2.145).

The resounding of names, so crucial to the founding of fame, is undone by its staged sounding off. A serio-comic version of the dissolution of name into sound is enacted with the playful punning on the pronunciation of legendary names. Ajax's name is sounded as 'a-jakes';[78] 'Aeneas' becomes a word that the Greeks can't get their tongues around. In Mendes (1990), Mike Dowling injuredly corrected the wilful pronouncing of his name as 'any arse' (1.3.246–7). Modulation of voice also has the potential to deflate Classical celebrity. Thersites's spitting image tribute to the elder statesmen of Greece in Act 5 compares Agamemnon to a whole carnival of paltry beasts, but, when he comes to compare him with Menelaus, there is the dramatic potential for the pitch of the voice to do the work of defamation: '[b]ut to be Menelaus, I would conspire against destiny ... Ask me not what I would be if I were not Thersites, for I care not to be the louse of a lazar, so I were not Menelaus' (5.1.56–9). Russell Beale in 1990 whispered the word 'Menelaus' as if even to mention it were an act of ignominy. Richard McCabe (Judge (1996)) spat it out in a conspiratorial hiss to the audience.

With so much talking about each other and speaking of names, the legendary fame of Troy sounds like Chaucerian gossip. Antique praise is spoken into a whirligig of tidings. Characters are constantly reporting on each other, or asking for news or asking them to tell them what their opinion is, or who they are. Here is an earshot of what is heard again and again: 'what says my sweet queen (3.1.77; 81); '[w]hat says Achilles? (3.3.57); 'what says she there?' (5.3.105–6); 'tell him from me' (1.3.296); '[t]hen tell me, I pray (2.3.40); '[t]hen tell me, Patroclus' (2.3.42); 'And tell me, noble Diomed, faith, tell me true' (4.1.52); '[t]ell me, sweet uncle' (4.2.80); '[m]y Lord Ulysses, tell me I beseech you' (4.5.277); '[c]ome, tell me whose it was' (5.2.88); '[y]ou understand me not that tell me so' (5.10.11); 'would somebody had heard her talk yesterday, as I did' (1.1.42–3); '[b]ut if I tell how these two did co-act' (5.2.117); 'I'll tell you what I say of him' (2.1.65–6).[79] Thersites is often characterised as the running commentator on the action of the play, but he is not a lone voice in this regard; it is a dramatic technique that extends to the whole ensemble.[80]

Individual voices fail to command their own singularity. Ulysses impersonates Patroclus's impersonations of Agamemmon and Nestor, and impersonates Achilles's responses to the series of impersonations he has heard second hand. In performance, the set piece gives great scope to the actor to play charades in different voices (1.3.164ff).[81] Sources of utterances are brought repeatedly into question as characters speak the words of others. In critical editions, speeches are spattered with internal quotation marks.[82] Although these embedded speech marks afford great scope for showboating – Pandarus's narration of the story of the hairs on Troilus's chin (I.2.139–44), for instance, or Thersites's recitation of his conversation with Ajax (3.3.251–67) – these psychomachic mini-dramas are not always available to the ear, and, even then, not always with consistency.[83] It is not only Ajax who is 'dress[ed] ... up in voices' (1.3.381); Agamemnon's unsuccessful refusal to be addressed in 'second voice' (2.3.139) draws attention to the sustained rupture between voice and its origins.[84]

These re-citations are tonally dissonant. Achilles imagines the future trumpeting of his fame in the voices of 'all the Greekish girls', who 'tripping sing: / "Great Hector's sister did Achilles win"' (3.3.212–13). Cassandra's impassioned prophecy of Hector's death:

> Look how thou diest, look how thy eye turns pale,
> Look how thy wounds do bleed at many vents,
> Hark how Troy roars, how Hecuba cries out,
> How poor Andromache shrills her dolours forth ...
> And all cry 'Hector, Hector's dead! O Hector'.
>
> (5.3.81–7)

finds no matching answer. Hector dismisses her prediction with a glib couplet '[g]o in and cheer the town. We'll forth and fight, / Do deeds worth praise and tell you them at night' (5.3.92–3). Achilles also speaks in consecutive rhyming couplets when he proclaims the death of Hector:[85]

> How ugly night comes breathing at his heels;
> Even with the vail and dark'ning of the sun
> To close the day up, Hector's life is done ...
> So Ilium, fall thou next, come, Troy, sink down.
> Here lies thy heart, thy sinews and thy bone.
> On Myrmidons, and cry you all amain:
> 'Achilles hath the mighty Hector slain'.
>
> (5.9.6–14)

The jubilant echo rings out a lie. Heard by an audience who has watched the cowardly gruesomeness of Hector's slaughter, Achilles's vaunt is an ignominious jingle chorused by a hit squad.[86] The discordant report of the death of a hero whose name is sounded more often than any other in the play is continued in the next scene:

| | |
|---|---|
| Agamemnon | Hark, hark, what shout is that? |
| Nestor | Peace, drums. |
| Soldiers (*within*) | Achilles! Achilles! Hector's slain! Achilles! |
| Diomedes | The bruit is Hector's slain and by Achilles. |
| Ajax | If it be so, then bragless let it be |
| | Great Hector was as good a man as he. |

(5.10.1–6)

This martial press release creates huge potential for noise.[87] The speeches function as sound cues: 'hark'; 'shout'; 'peace'; 'drums'; 'bragging', 'noise' which merge with the baying of Achilles's name by anonymous soldiers. Neither the sound nor the sense of Ajax's tame rhyme seems in character with this man of elephantine locution. Only Diomedes gets it right. A close homophone of 'brute', 'bruit' is noise or clamour.[88]

It is left to Pandarus with his fretwork of half-song, half talking, half-whisper, to close up the play with his rheumy coughing and spluttering hisses.[89] In ending the play with air fighting to word itself from gargling lungs, we *hear* the reverb'rate fame of Troy as Ulysses has earlier spoken it: 'airy' (1.3.145). All the speeching, the naming, the rhyming and the legendary booming: broken air fighting for words.[90]

## Trumping

When Aeneas delivers his challenge in the Greek camp, he explains to Agamemnon that the only pure praise is that which comes from the enemy; that 'breath fame blows' (1.3.245). Aeneas's words are truer than he knows, but not necessarily in the sense which he intends. Both *The House of Fame* and *Troilus and Cressida* dramatise, with considerable force, that fame blown by breath is a far less stable, 'sole', 'pure' and 'transcendent' phenomenon than Aeneas would wish. And there is no better medium to dramatise it than the loud and unpredictable sound of the trumpet. It is through trumpets that reputations are blown both in *The House of Fame* and in *Troilus and Cressida*, the Shakespeare play that features trumpets more often than any other.[91]

Resulting in part from the role of the trumpet as harbinger of Judgement on the Last Day, its sound is associated with reputation; with being summatively assessed. The sheer loudness of the trumpet also associates it simply with getting noticed, and/or commanding attention. This is one reason why it was used in battles and also for proclamations. It could be heard above the racket of warfare or civic noise.[92] Three trumpet blasts alerted the populace of London to the start of a performance at the Globe on the south bank.[93] As heralds of majesty or other significant persons, trumpets conferred importance by the volume of their fanfare. The sound of a trumpet was not only loud, however, but volatile, especially before it acquired valves, slides or crooks.[94] Unless carefully controlled by an experienced performer, it was as likely to issue forth a stentorian fart as a fanfare; one reason for its association with the gutsiness of the body.[95] This bipolar temperamentality further helps to explain the oppositional values with which the trumpet is invested as an agent of judgement. Proclamations could give notice of news that carried royal or civic significance, but trumpets were also used to broadcast shame, as the reporting of the treatment of the unfortunate John Kakford makes clear. Convicted of false conspiracy, he was ordered to come out of Newgate, without hood or girdle, barefoot and unshod, with a whetstone hung by a chain from his neck which was marked with the words 'a false liar'. '[A]nd there shall be a pair of trumpets trumpeting before him on his way to the pillory'.[96] In searching the collocational patterns of the word 'trumpet' in dramatic texts from 1550 to 1610, I found equal scores for its association with words of shame and disgrace as with virtue and praise.[97] The perception of the symbolic sound of the unpredictably noisy trumpet embraced ignominy and honour in equal measure. The trumpet is the musical equivalent of [o:]: its sound produces the loudest decibels but within an indeterminate range of pronouncing that encompasses angels and devils alike.

Trumpets are an especially brazen example of the way that *House of Fame* and *Troilus and Cressida* mix up the world of music as they have jangled words and noise; what gets sounded by the trumpet is heard in a musical soundworld that has lost its bearings.[98] Ulysses's music of the spheres has only an oblique counterpoint in Chaucer's poem. In contrast to *The Parliament of Fowles* (60–3), description of the celestial harmony of the planets is conspicuously absent where it might have been expected. At the highest point in the poem, the narrator looks behind him to see the earth as no more than a 'prikke' because the air is so 'thikke' (907–8). He hears nothing.

What he sees is a fug of 'ayerissh bestes', 'mystes', 'tempestes', and 'snowes hayles' (965–7). Behind his 'bak', he sees only 'cloude'; a word placed sonically – and mischievously – in trochaic position at the start of the line (978). We have learnt already that the narrator is as deaf as a block to sounds in his earthly life (648–51); Chaucer extends the joke to his obliviousness to the celestial concord that ought to have accompanied his astral flight.

Music played by humans rather than planets had a clear hier-archy: strings, wind, brass and percussion. Stringed instruments, especially the harp and the lyre, were associated with the soul; with concord and with intellect. Woodwinds were the domain of amour or gentle plaint; brass was body; and percussion was noise.[99] That is not exactly how the eagle tells it. He illustrates his maxim that sound is nothing but 'eyr ybroken' with two analogies: flame from lighted smoke (a tell-tale Troy nudge/wink); and this, drawn from music:

> But this may be in many wyse,
> Of which I wil the twoo devyse,
> As soun that cometh of pipe or harpe.
> For whan a pipe is blowen sharpe
> The air ys twyst with violence
> And rent – loo, this ys my sentence.
> Eke whan men harpe-strynges smyte,
> Whether hyt be moche or lyte,
> Loo, with the strok the ayr tobreketh;
> And ryght so breketh it when men speketh.
> Thus wost thou wel what thing is speche.
>
> (771–81)

Music ought to act as a mediator between sound and speech.[100] Here there is no distinction between music, speech and noise: 'sentence' rhymes with 'violence' and the taxonomy of pipe or harp is collapsed into itself, and into percussion: 'twyst'; 'smyte'; 'tobreketh'; 'strok' and 'breketh'. This description precedes, and undermines, the bands of musicians that the narrator sees in the House of Fame itself. Appropriately, the harpists, led by Orpheus, their famed performer, are placed first. Woodwind follows; trum-pets bring up the rear (on which more later). But within the lists, decorous placement is abandoned. Gleemen with small harps counterfeit classical harpers like apes. Bagpipes, whose vulgarity is all too familiar from the Miller, precede the delicate pipes of the shepherd. The finale of the whole ensemble is an English trickster playing a windmill under a walnut shell (1280–1).

Music is no more orderly in *Troilus*. An acoustic contrast could be available between the music of love and the martial clamour of military instruments.[101] Music is cued explicitly in Act 3 Scene 1 as a prelude to the only scene with Helen and Paris (3.1.16–27). Productions have equipped Pandarus with a series of 'amorous' instruments to accompany his later 'serenade' to love.[102] Pandarus had no instrument to play in Judge (1996), but a contrast was set up with the oboes, clarinets and bassoons of this scene and the almost incessant brass of the rest of the production.[103] Even within the scene as Shakespeare scored it, however, such tonal contrast is muffled. The jokes on 'parts' (17); 'fits' (49); 'performance' (44), and 'broken' music (41–4) introduce raucous sexuality rather than dulcet courtship; and the charivari of rough music rather than epic love. A consort of music brings musical instruments of different families together;[104] but the potential for harmony here is undone by filthy punning and sound echo.[105] The potentially Lydian interlude in Act 3 is dumbed not just by the verbal cues for music in 'parts' but by the obscene soundscape of the song that Pandarus sings in it:

These lovers cry O, O, they die!
Yet that which seems the wound to kill
Doth turn O O to ha ha he,
So dying love lives still.
O O a while, but 'ha ha ha'
O O groans out for 'ha ha ha'.

                                                            (3.1.105–10)

Anticipating Pandarus's solicitation for 'groans' from the audience in the final act, the sounds here score the familiar pun on dying and orgasm with aural accompaniment. All those 'o's of the Southwarkian bawdy house that feeds Chaucer's House of Fame are here realised acoustically by the prolonged repetition of tickling laughter: coitus that subsides into exhausted, giggling, gulps of air.

It is from within these unruly musical soundworlds that trumpets sound their parts.[106] Chaucer lists 'trumpe', 'beme' and 'claryoun' after the harps and pipes, as those instruments that make 'blody soun' in a 'large space' (1238–40). The fanfare of military trumpeters that follow makes it clear that brass wind is the sound of warfare. Combative clariouning, however, is undercut, not only by the female sorceresses and trance-inducers who frame the player of 'an uncouth thyng to telle' (1279), the windmill in a walnut shell, but by how trumpets are the medium of fame itself. The narrator recounts how groups of petitioners approach Lady Fame to beseech her to announce their glory throughout the world. Each group has its worth proclaimed by the blast of a trumpet; but the choice between the trumpet of praise or the trumpet of shame is unpredictably unmotivated. Eolus, the god of winds, has a 'clarioun' that is 'ful dyvers of his soun' (1573–4). Irrespective of the merits or disgrace of the suitors, Eolus blows 'Clere Laude' or 'Sklaundre' with absolute caprice (1575–80). But even the antynomy is blown to smithereens: Eolus holds all the winds under his control and compresses them so violently that they roar like bears (1589). The trumpet sound of human worth is indistinguishable from animal roar and wind. One example of the extended trumpet ritual must suffice. The first group that approaches claim that they are of 'good name' in honour and 'gentillesse' and deserve good fame. Fame dismisses their suit out of hand, telling them that she is not disposed 'as of now' to grant them good fame. Even though they have deserved 'good loos' they shall have 'a shrewed fame', 'wikkyd loos, and worse name' (1615–21). She commands Eolus to take his trumpet 'Sklaundre' and to 'trumpe alle the contrarye / Of that they han don wel or fayre' (1625–30). So Eolus takes his black trumpet of brass, and blows so hard that it seems that the whole world should come to an end. The blast sounds like the firing of a cannonball and smoke bursts out of 'his foule trumpes ende' (1646):

> Blak, bloo, grenyssh, swartish red,
> As doth where that men melte led,
> Loo, al on high fro the tuel ...
> And hyt stank as the pit of helle.
> Allas, thus was her shame yronge,
> And gilteles, on every tonge.

(1647–56)

Thus are the praiseworthy heralded. Military cannonfire sounds suburban smelting; a trumpet *rings* out shame on every *tongue*. Sonic distinction is confounded further by the conflation of the Last Judgement wake-up call with what must surely rank as the stinkiest fart in all Middle English literature.[107] A set-piece which nearly overwhelms the whole poem, the recording of Eolus's capricious trumpet voluntary takes nearly three hundred lines. Its indiscriminate noteworthiness is made all the more frangible by the post-dated revelation that all sounds which enter the House of

Fame have been wafted from the wicker house of Rumour. Eolus does not even blow his own trumpet.

An analogue to this Chaucerian scenario is realised succinctly in a single line in *Troilus and Cressida*: '[t]he Trojans' trumpet' (4.5.64). Read on the page, the aural pun on trumpet/strumpet[108] disappears with the grammatical authority of the modern apostrophe.[109] It is a joke, tellingly, that is fully available only when it is heard. If it is sounded in performance the collapse of value between 'laus' and 'sklaundre' is proclaimed by the whole company on stage; a cheer, or a jeer, that can be accompanied by laughter and/or shouts.[110] In all its glorious confusion the trumpet pun epitomises the sonic mayhem that is the soundscape of Troy.

Even while directors and editors provide more trumpets than the Folio and the Quarto of *Troilus* explicitly cue, no other Shakespeare play replicates both the volume of trumpet references and their association with reputation.[111] Antiochus is anxious lest Pericles's divination of the riddle should 'trumpet forth' his 'infamy' (*Pericles* 1.1.146), but this is the only appearance of the 'trumpet' in the play. Likewise, Benedick's witty excursus on praising himself, 'the trumpet of his own virtues', contains the only instance in *Much Ado* (5.2.77). Twice, in *Troilus*, vagaries of reputation are discussed with reference to the figurative sense of 'trumpet'. In the scene in which the Greek leaders ironically beef up the reputation of Ajax before his blockish ears, Agamemnon says:

> He that is proud eats up himself; pride is his own glass, his own trumpet, his own chronicle, and whatever praises itself but in the deed devours the deed in the praise. (2.3.141–3)

Blown by a narcissist who does not match the opinion of his self-worth with action, the trumpet of 'laud' proclaims honour that self-consumes even as it pronounces. The second figurative use of 'trumpet', significantly, occurs in Ulysses's lecture to Achilles. Ulysses invites Achilles to consider his future reputation. How would he rather be remembered? As a man who threw down Hector? Or a sissy who bedded Polyxena? How Pyrrhus, Achilles's son, must grieve at home:

> When fame shall in our islands sound her trump,
> And all the Greekish girls shall tripping sing:
> 'Great Hector's sister did Achilles win
> But our great Ajax bravely beat down him'.

(3.3.211–14)

Performed by Ulysses, Fame's mighty trumpet sounds a slur. Composing Achilles's shameful epitaph before his ears, the wily politician turns the legendary proclamation of a Classical goddess to a tripping ditty by Greekish girls. Even as they dangle the enticement of a glorifying trumpet before Achilles and Ajax, Ulysses and Agamemnon make it speak of oblivion and shame. Like Eolus with his capricious blasts they confound memorial praise with abjection.

The literal trumpeting of reputation in the play is just as unstable. Despite the wording of trumpets, and the presence of so many 'legendary' figures on stage, there are fewer calls in *Troilus* for a 'flourish' than are heard in most productions,[112] and fewer than in many other Shakespeare plays.[113] The role of trumpeters in heralding elevated persons is itself called into question. Although Agamemnon welcomes Hector to the Greek camp with a call for sounds of celebration that combines applause with martial clamour – '[b]eat loud the tabourins, let the trumpets blow, / That this great soldier may his welcome know' (4.5.274–5) – neither Folio nor Quarto has a stage direction. If Agamemnon's command is performed, then it is supplied by editors and/or directors, not by the playtext.[114] And while the call for a trumpet cues a grand welcome for a legendary figure, the men from both sides of the great argument of war simply go off to have supper together. When battle does take place, martial trumpets are noticeably reticent.[115] A cue for a trumpet that follows Achilles's boast of slaying Hector is glossed as a 'retire upon our Grecian part' (5.9.15). No other cue for sound is given in either Quarto or Folio, but editors supply '[Another retreat sounded]' to make sense of the next line '[t]he Trojan trumpets sound the like, my lord' (5.9.16).[116] If two trumpets are indeed heard, are their sounds different? Is it possible to tell Trojan and Greek trumpets apart? While other contexts show that it is possible to identify for whom the trumpet blows, this distinction is not preserved in *Troilus*.[117] Notably, the first reference to trumpet in the play asks whose it is: '[w]hat trumpet?' (1.3.214). The sound that ought to proclaim singular prominence goes unrecognised.

Trumpets are cued for the fight between Ajax and Hector in Act 4 Scene 5.[118] This is the scene which has the greatest number of references to trumpets, worded or sounded, in the whole play. In addition to the fight, this is the scene that contains the 's/trumpet' pun, Ajax's directions to the trumpeter and Agamemnon's call for trumpets and drums. All these trumpets

clamour for attention during exchanges in which obscurity and
personal slighting are showcased to the maximum. This is the
scene in which groups of Trojans meet with Greeks for the first
time without any armour and so everyone has to ask everyone
else who everyone is.[119] Plentiful trumping heralds naming and
anonymity without discrimination.

Trumpets that accompany challenges challenge reputation
itself.[120] Prefaced by a trumpet call, Aeneas's words attempt to
assume its brazen voice:[121]

> Trumpet, blow loud,
> Send thy brass voice through all these lazy tents
> And every Greek of mettle let him know
> What Troy means fairly shall be spoke aloud.

> (1.3.257–60)

Martial rhetoric redounds: the polyptoton of 'loud/aloud' equates
powerful sound with broadcast words; the transferred epithet of
'brass voice' conflates trumpet and speech with words and war, and
the paronomasia of a 'mettle' as hard material and courage yokes
the brass metal of the trumpet with the intransigence of Greek
resolve. Hard tropes sound trumpet might. Forcefully, or forced?
Memorial brass or swartish fart? Aeneas's trumpet challenge in
Act 1 is trumped by that of Ajax in Act 4:

> Thou, trumpet, there's my purse:
> Now crack thy lungs and split thy brazen pipe,
> Blow, villain, till thy sphered bias cheek
> Outswell the colic of puffed Aquilon;
> Come stretch thy chest and let thy eyes spout blood,
> Thou blowest for Hector.

> (4.5.6–11)

Ajax wants his trumpet to be bigger and better than the trumpet
of legend. Urging a 'villain' to 'outswell' Aquilon imagines a
nameless slave outperforming a Greek god. Unfortunately, Ajax's
verbal brio is let down by poor word selection, 'colic' and 'puffed',
while his forceful imperatives, 'crack', 'split', 'blow' and 'spout
blood', strain high rhetoric into painful flatulence. Unsurprisingly,
directors have milked the scene for comedy: Barton (1976) had
the trumpeter raise and lower his trumpet three times before Ajax
finally stopped speaking. In Mendes (1990), after the deflationary
silence that followed 'no trumpet answers' (4.5.11), Ajax blew a
raspberry. The trumpet answered after all: with the 'breath' that
'fame blows' (1.3.245).[122]

## Silence

Without silence, articulate sound cannot be heard. As the audible boundary of speech, silence also predicates the perception of music and noise. The soundscapes of *House of Fame* and *Troilus and Cressida* share significant – and crucial – silences that reveal the abysmal oblivion into which the legend of Troy is destined to be evermore spoken. In Chaucer's poem, those silences are constituted by voices whose names are never sounded. In *Troilus*, one character who is named repeatedly on stage utters not a single word.

In *The House of Fame*, 'the man of gret auctorite' neither speaks in the poem nor has a name.[123] He is the only figure who has some escape route from the economy of fame in which the poem operates, and the poem breaks off with nothing more to say after his description is told. Other figures in the poem do have voices, even if their Proper origins are suppressed: in addition to the voice of the eagle, the voice of the 'frend' that appears in the House of Rumour and the voice of the narrator himself. While the 'friend' is simply 'oon' (1869), his first words are to ask the narrator what he is called '[f]rend, what is thy name? / Artow come hider to han fame? (1871–2). The narrator replies, '[s]ufficeth me, as I were I ded, / That no wight have my name in honde' (1876–7). He withholds his name from his nameless interlocutor and pleads for anonymity. He does not wish any person to deliver him up by name: 'I wot myself best how y stonde' (1878). The narrator lays claim to his *own* 'art' (1882); not a version of it that will be spoken in his name by somebody else. He simply wants to come to listen, not to speak; and certainly not to be memorialised. These are amongst the best truthful lies in the whole poem; the narrator has already been characterised as someone who is deaf even to the tidings that his neighbours bring him on his own doorstep (648–51), and he has already been named: the eagle addresses him as 'Geffrey' (729).

'Geffrey' is not 'Chaucer'.[124] There are other 'geoffreys' whose oeuvre might better fit the famous names that have already been recounted in the poem: Geoffrey de Vinsauf, who is named in the mock-Trojan heroics at the end of *The Nun's Priest's Tale* (VII.3347), and Geoffrey of Monmouth, who starts his monumental history with the translation of empire story from Troy to Britain. A first name is not even a proper name for a famous poet; Virgil is not called Publius; neither is Ovid; and not only because they would then be indistinguishable. A first name does not lay

the same claim to literary fame as a name that is public. Through
silencing 'Chaucer', the poet reserves for his own Troy work an
idiosyncratic place in the hall of fame: one that is exceptional
because it refuses to be told and it is too multiple to be contained.
Because he has been telling all the stories of all the famous writers
in his 'own voice', he is all their names and none of them. His is
a voice without stable origins that can sound the Classical past,
a philosophical bird and the babble of contemporary gossip. His
voice is ultimately the more telling than all of those he speaks for.
Significantly, the withholding of names happens in a conversation inside the house of Rumour. In writing his exceptional claim
to fame, Chaucer the poet repositions Trojan textuality within
vernacular speech. It is a translation of literary empire story with
a twist. In an act of breathtaking brazenness, the emperor who has
no clothes speaks back through the texts that would dress him up in
foreign voices. Through playing the name game of literary history
by changing its rules of participation, silent Chaucer lays suit to a
vernacular fame of legendary Troy.

The name that *Troilus and Cressida* dramatises without a voice is
Antenor. It's a name that is never sounded in *The House of Fame*.[125]
None of the other mute characters in Shakespeare's plays has the
stature of Antenor; eminence afforded both by the frequency with
which he is named and also by his importance to the story.[126]
Antenor appears in four scenes and is named twelve times in the
dialogue. Reported, though not seen in the course of the play, he is
taken prisoner by the Greeks, and it is his ransom for Cressida that
prompts the swift reversal of the love plot. Nothing in the appara-
tus of the play – or production materials I have seen – draws attention to Antenor's pivotal role in the destruction of Troy itself.[127]
Antenor was the traitor who brought the metal horse into Troy
from which the Greek warriors disgorged to sack the city. Of this
infamy, the play is silent. Both Cressida and Antenor are on stage
at the moment when Troilus delivers up Cressida to the Greeks
'for Antenor'. Neither Cressida nor Antenor speaks (4.3). The
most crucial action for the love plot, and for the future reputation
of Troy, is accomplished without a word from those who are traded
between the words of others around them.[128]

With no knowledge of the Trojan story but that which the play
supplies, an audience can know Antenor only through what is
said *about* him;[129] the exact opposite of reputation the narrator of
*The House of Fame* desires. This is Pandarus's assessment when
Antenor files past in the parade of Trojans in Act 2 Scene 1:[130]

That's Antenor. He has a shrewd wit, I can tell you, and he's
a man good enough, he's one o' the soundest judgements in Troy
whosoever, and a proper man of person. (1.2.162–4)

When he is named in the play again, he is a prisoner of the Greeks.
In Act 3 Scene 3, Calchas strikes a bargain for Antenor to be
returned to the Trojans in exchange for his daughter. Troy holds
him very dear, says Calchas (3.3.19), and calls him such:

> a wrest in their affairs
> That their negotiations all must slack
> Wanting his manage, and they will almost
> Give us a prince of blood, a son of Priam,
> In change of him.

(3.3.23–7)

Since Calchas, by his own admission, has 'incurred a traitor's
name' (3.3.6), one should not, perhaps, take his words at face value.
But nothing that is spoken out loud in the play ever suggests that
Antenor is anything but vital to Troy's stability. As a 'wrest', a
device for maintain the tuning of a stringed instrument, Antenor is
the preservation of harmonious political order.

Once news of his exchange for Cressida reaches Pandarus's ears,
however, earlier praise changes into a thrice-uttered curse: '[t]he
devil take Antenor' (4.2.74–5) and 'plague upon Antenor! I would
they had broke 's neck' (4.2.75–6, and cf. 4.2.84–5). Even though
he never draws attention to Antenor's future infamy, Pandarus,
the speaker for those who 'trade' in Pander's hall, and speak with
the triteness of 'painted cloths' (5.11.43–5),[131] trafficks the name of
Antenor between admiration and denunciation. The name of the
silent traitor who went behind Trojan backs to bring Greeks back
into Troy is heard more often in Pandarus's voice than in that of
any other character.[132] The sounding of silent Antenor's worth is
recursively transacted between 'traders'.

In a play whose casting requirements are already expensive, it
would be extraordinarily extravagant to pay an actor to come on
stage in four scenes with nothing to say, and, to the ears at any
rate, no other business in the drama. In performance, Antenor
has simply been deleted, so after the first act any mention of his
name is simply a sound without substance.[133] But there are other
ways of handling this persistent 'supposed' non-entity. While the
dramaturgy allows for very little doubling between the principal
roles, there is plenty of scope for doubling, or tripling , of actors in
the minor ones.[134] Absent throughout Acts 2 and 3, and between

Act 4 Scene 3 and Act 5 Scene 1, Antenor could also play the servants of Paris (3.1), Troilus (3.2) and Diomedes (5.5). Noticed or
not, 'Antenor' is free to come and go between Greek and Trojan
camps, following those men most strongly associated in the play
with the traffic of women. He could also be Calchas. In 5.2, he
does not even need to be seen. Prompted by Diomedes's line
'Calchas, I think' (5.2.3), editors add the stage direction 'within'
to the two lines that Calchas speaks in this scene.[135] Played thus,
silent 'Antenor' becomes just a voice. When Calchas praises him in
3.3, Antenor is not present. With the doubling of roles, the traitor
'Antenor' praises himself through the voice of another treacherous
go-between: 'Antenor' becomes the voice of both men's duplicity.

The voice of the actor playing Antenor is available to sound a
variety of roles that sneak his future reputation into the play under
cover.[136] Barton (1968) and Barton/Kyle (1976) had 'Antenor'
play a Myrmidon in the scene where Hector is killed.[137] It is a
Myrmidon who has the final say on trumpets in the play: line 5.9.16
'[t]he Trojan trumpets sounds the like, my lord', or, as the Quarto
has it, 'the Troyans trumpet sound'. The unfixed, unrecoverable
textual trumpet(s) of Troy, existing in no-man's-land somewhere
between 'laud' and 'sklaundre', are said in the voice of the traitor
which the playtext silences. It would require a nimble wardrobe
function for 'Antenor' to change from Myrmidon to the part of the
'one in sumptuous armour' (5.6), but it would be fitting. 'Antenor',
future guardian of the metal Trojan horse, as the unnamed, unseen,
'mettle'-clad figure whose glittering outside and 'putrified core' so
distracts Hector from the business of epic fighting, that caught
unmetalled, he is vulnerable to Achilles's slaughter.

But perhaps most salient of all of the roles that Antenor has
played in performance was that in the final scene in Barton/Kyle
(1976).[138] The speech prefix at 5.11.3, 'Hector? The gods forbid!'
is 'ALL'. In 1976, this line was spoken by 'Antenor' alone. The
silent traitor was everybody's spokesman. 'All' is a keynote in the
voicescape of this play.[139] Agamemnon identifies himself as leader
of 'all the Greekish heads which with one voice / Call Agamemnon
head and general' (1.3.222–3) but the series of impersonations by
Achilles, Patroclus and Ulysses suggest otherwise. In the debate
over the return of Helen in the Trojan council Troilus reminds his
fellows that they 'all' must avouch for the wisdom of Paris's abduc-
tion of Helen for 'you all cried 'Go, Go' (2.2.85); 'you all clapped
your hands / And cried "Inestimable"' (2.2.87–8). Troilus's
omniventriloquism, is of course, motivated by his private desire for

another woman. The unisonance of the Trojans' rehearsed opinion of Helen is countered by her appearance in the play as 'Nell', and Thersites's reduction of her to a 'placket' (2.3.16).

'All' has particular sonic resonance at the end of Act 3 Scene 2. Troilus, Cressida and Pandarus proclaim their own future legends in presumed voices. Pandarus has a choric refrain:

> Let all pitiful goers-between be called to the world's end after my name: call them all panders. let all constant men be Troiluses, all false women Cressids, and all brokers-between panders. Say Amen. (3.2.180–2)

Assuming the sound of the last trump ('be called to the world's end'),[140] Pandarus summons up fame and infamy by commuting Proper Names into common generic nouns. 'All' subsumes individual value into public reputations, the truth of which the audience may already know, even though the play has not yet dramatised it. With its confounding of origins and scrambling of voice, the repetition of subjunctive 'All' speaks for one and for all in the voice of Pandarus speaking for three.

When 'Antenor' spoke for 'ALL' in Act 5 on the Stratford stage in 1976, the audience would not have heard the speech prefix; nor without a text in front of them could they necessarily have been aware that there is only one other cue for 'ALL' to speak in the entire play. It's at 4.5.64, '[t]he Trojan/s/trumpet'. The line which makes no distinction between trumpeting 'laud' and 'sklaundre' is spoken by everyone: the glory and infamy of the Trojan world is common speech. In 1976, the unheard chime between the speech prefixes in Acts 4 and 5 equated silent 'Antenor' with the Eolian trumpet of 'reverb'rate Troy'. 'Antenor's' textual role is that of a name for others to speak out of the silence of his future treachery. When performance lets 'Antenor' be heard in the voices of other textual names he is available to play, he becomes the incongruent counterpart of 'Chaucer' in *The House of Fame*.[141] Antenor speaks for all of Troy as a name without a voice: 'Chaucer' speaks for all of Troy as a voice without a name.

## Notes

1 William Shakespeare, *Troilus and Cressida*, ed. Anthony B. Dawson (Cambridge: Cambridge University Press, 2003).
2 Colin Burrow notes that absent or occluded sources are a particular feature of stories about Troilus and Cressida, and that the story of

Troy for Shakespeare was akin to the book that Ulysses is holding; not a single heroic narrative thundered out by Homer to preserve the fame of Troy, but many texts which might carry different significances for different characters on different occasions, 'Introduction', in *Troilus and Cressida*, ed. R. A. Foakes (Harmondsworth: Penguin, 1967), revd edn, 1987, p. lx, and p. lxiii.

3 This mysterious figure has generated even more speculation than Ulysses's author. The identity parade of suspects includes Richard II, John of Gaunt, Boethius, Christ, the Constable-Marshal of the Christmas Revels at the Inner Temple, Amor, a messenger from Cardinal Pilea da Prato, Chaucer and The Reader. I return to the 'man of gret auctorite' in the final section of this chapter.

4 The poem is unmentioned by Talbot Donaldson, *The Swan at the Well*, and does not feature in Cooper's *Shakespeare and the Medieval World* (2010). Thompson, *Shakespeare's Chaucer*, p. 74, mentions *The House of Fame* as a source for the Prologue spoken by Rumour in *Henry IV, Part Two*, and critical editions cite the poem as a possible source for *Titus Andronicus*, 2.1.126–7, '[t]he emperor's court is like the House of Fame, / The palace full of tongues, of eyes and ears' (pointing out, simultaneously that the image could have come directly from Ovid's *Metamorphoses* without Chaucer's mediation). For Heather James's discussion of *The House of Fame*, see n. 17 below. The poem was printed by Caxton (1483), and Pynson (1526). Both editions also contain *Troilus and Criseyde*.

5 Alongside Chaucer's *Troilus and Criseyde*, the major sources are George Chapman's translation of seven books of Homer's *Iliad* (1598) and William Caxton's *Recuyell of the Historyes of Troy* (1474). John Lydgate's *Troy Book* and Henryson's *Testament of Cresseid* may also have been influences.

6 Bruce R. Smith, *The Acoustic World of Early Modern England: Attending to the O-Factor* (Chicago: University of Chicago Press, 1999), is a compelling account of soundscapes, both conceptually and as a record of early modern culture. I thank Emma Smith for telling me about this book; the thought of this chapter is deeply indebted to it.

7 For all that, there are many instances where locutions have uncanny resonance with Chaucer's poem, not least in the speech where Ulysses claims that he is quoting from his 'author's drift' (3.3.113): 'some men creep in skittish Fortune's hall' (3.3.134); 'reverb'rate / The voice' and 'gate of steel' (3.3.120–1).

8 William Baldwin, *Beware the Cat*, ed. William A. Ringler Jr and Michael Flachman (San Marino: Huntington Library, 1988). In keeping with the anti-Catholic quippery throughout, Streamer is named 'Gregory' in the closing, parodic paean. Named only here, the narrator is jokingly distinguished from the Pope who sent the first Roman missionaries to England, p. 55. Intriguingly, Smith, in

his quotation from the tract consistently names Gregory 'Geoffrey', thus subconsciously investing the channel of voices with the name of 'Chaucer', pp. 30–1.

9  *Beware the Cat*, pp. 31–3. The editors date the text to 1553, just before Edward VI's death, pp. xvi–xix. The work seems not to have been printed until 1570 and was reissued in 1584. The passage quoted, and indeed the rest of the work, is clearly also indebted to *The Nun's Priest's Tale* and *The Manciple's Tale*. The thoroughgoing Chaucerian playfulness of this work deserves fuller treatment than I can make space for here.

10  Baldwin had evidently read the eagle's disquisition on sound in *The House of Fame* (see discussion below) with great attentiveness. Not only does he find his own equivalent to the collapse of sound into noise, he also continues the joke of deflating textual birds. A crow, who has been sitting on the roof, listening to the sounds of London, falls down the chimney. He lands, talons first, on Streamer's head and further terrifies the 'catman' by addressing him in human language as 'knave', p. 33.

11  *The Masque of Queens* in Ben Jonson, *The Complete Masques*, ed. Stephen Orgel (New Haven and London: Yale University Press, 1969), lines 457–8. The masque was performed at Whitehall on 2 February 1609.

12  Jonson wrote *Epicoene: or The Silent Woman* in the same year as the masque. Trumpets are anything but peaceful. Morose, who cannot stand any kind of noise, is roused in his own house by unwelcome visitors. He chases them out with these words: 'Rogues, Hellhounds, Stentors, out of my dores, you sonnes of noise and tumult, begot on an ill May-day or when the Gally-foist is but a-float to Westminster. A trumpeter could not be conceiu'd but then', *Ben Jonson*, ed. C. H. Herford and Percy Simpson (Oxford: Clarendon Press, 1937), vol. 5, 3.2.124–7. Clearly, Jonson was very well aware that a trumpet was unlikely to sound 'peace', and it is not impossible that *The House of Fame* lurks behind the description. Stentor was, after all, the brass-voiced herald of Troy.

13  *The Staple of News* 3.2.113–21, in *Ben Jonson*, ed. Herford and Simpson (vol. VI).

14  Smith discusses how soundscapes create and divide communities: zones of resonance may or may not map on to geographical demography, but local soundscapes can create listening communities through their acoustic profiles, *The Acoustic World*, p. 17, p. 46.

15  Martha Carlin, *Medieval Southwark* (London: Hambledon Press, 1996), calls the suburb of Southwark a chimera. Outside the jurisdiction of the city, it was a parliamentary borough without a charter of incorporation, a group of autonomous manors sharing a communal name and a bad reputation, p. 48.

16 A point made by Sylvia Federico, *New Troy: Fantasies of Empire in the Late Middle Ages* (Minneapolis: University of Minnesota Press, 2003), p. 3.

17 Federico, *New Troy*, provides extensive study of the symbolic appropriation of Troy in the works of Chaucer, Gower, the *Gawain*-poet and the anonymous *St Erkenwald*. See also Christopher Baswell, *Virgil in Medieval England: Figuring the Aeneid from the Twelfth Century to Chaucer* (Cambridge: Cambridge University Press, 1995). Heather James, *Shakespeare's Troy: Drama, Politics and the Translation of Empire* (Cambridge: Cambridge University Press, 1997), provides stringent examination of the mobilisation of Troy legends in the early modern period. *Troilus and Cressida* is discussed pp. 85–115. James includes Chaucer's *House of Fame* amongst those works which subject to scepticism the translation of empire from Virgil's *Aeneid* to London, pp. 1–30.

18 See also James Simpson, 'The Other Book of Troie: Guido delle Colonne's *Historia Destructionis Troiae* in Fourteenth- and Fifteenth-Century England', *Speculum* 73 (1998), 397–423, and C. David Benson, *The History of Troy in Middle English Literature: Guido delle Colonne's Historia destructionis Troiae in Medieval England* (Woodbridge: D. S. Brewer, 1980).

19 There are over five hundred textual differences between the Folio and Quarto versions of the play. The Quartos lack the Prologue.

20 The textual and early performance history of the play is problematic. Registered in February 1603, a Quarto version was published in 1609 with two different title pages and prefatory materials. The epistolary advertisement added to the second state of the Quarto presents the play as a comedy to an 'ever Reader', claiming that the play was never acted. The title pages of the two Quartos call the play either 'The Historie of Troylus and Cresseida' or 'The Famous Historie of Troylus and Cressida'. Inserted late into the 1623 Folio between the Histories and the Tragedies, the first page calls it a 'Tragedie' but it is unclear from the 'Catalogue', or table of contents, to which generic category the play belongs.

21 A summary of the debate is rehearsed in J. W. Ramsey, 'The Provenance of *Troilus and Cressida*', *Shakespeare Quarterly* 21 (1970), 223–40.

22 Robert Crowley's epigram 'Of Bearbaytynge' (1550) excoriates the licentiousness of the entertainments on Bankside, and names Paris Gardens specifically, *The Select Works of Robert Crowley*, ed. J. M. Cowper (EETS ES 15, 1872, 16–17).

23 *Epicoene* 3.3.12–18.

24 The textual indeterminacy of the 'end' of *Troilus and Cressida*, a concluding feature it shares with Chaucer's *House of Fame*, is discussed, along with the possibilities it provides for performance decisions,

in, Roger Apfelbaum, *Shakespeare's Troilus and Cressida: Textual Problems and Performance Solutions* (Newark: University of Delaware Press, 2004), pp. 192–241. The play's multiple and disruptive moments of closure are caused partly by the repetition of Troilus's 'final' words to Pandarus: '[h]ence, brother-lackey! Ignominy and shame / Pursue thy life and live aye with thy name' (5.11.33–4). They appear twice in the Folio version; the earlier placement is the end of 5.3. Both Folio and Quarto print the remainder of the text, Pandarus's final speech, at the end of the play. In performance, however, the exchange between Pandarus and Troilus, as in Boyd's (1998) RSC production, can be moved to its earlier position and Pandarus's 'epilogue' cut. Payne (1936) and Quayle (1948) also ended the play with Troilus's last words (promptbooks). Nunn's (1998) National Theatre production included the 'epilogue' but brought Troilus and Cressida back on stage with Pandarus in an attempt at reconciliation which was scripted from earlier lines of the play. The last person on stage was Sophie Okenedo as Cressida; silent in distressed confusion as the sound of gunshot continued. David Bevington's Arden Shakespeare edition of *Troilus and Cressida* (1998) provides extensive discussion of the textual complications and justification for his decision to print the 'epilogue' as the end of the play, pp. 416–22. Kenneth Muir's Oxford Classics edition (Oxford University Press, 1982), Dawson's Cambridge edition and R. A. Foakes for Penguin all include the epilogue at the end of the play. In *The Oxford Complete Works*, Gary Taylor prints the QF ending as 'Additional Passage B', though fitted on the same page as Troilus's last speech. The Norton text prints Oxford's additional passages in QF position, but indents and italicises them.

25 H. Bonheim, 'Shakespeare's "Goose of Winchester"', *Philological Quarterly* 51 (1972), 940–1. He notes that the park of the Bishop of Winchester was separated from the Globe only by a drainage ditch. Quayle (1948) cut the reference to the galled Winchester goose (promptbook), as did Barton/Kyle (1976), and RSC/Wooster Group production, Le Compte/Ravenhill (2012). Barton (1968) kept it.

26 James argues of these lines that Pandarus 'makes his anachronistic intrusion to complete the movement of the "translation imperii" through time, geography, genre, textual variants and ideology to Elizabethan England and the moment of performance', *Shakespeare's Troy*, p. 96.

27 See especially Marion Turner, *Chaucerian Conflict: Languages of Antagonism in Late Fourteenth-Century London* (Oxford: Clarendon Press, 2007), pp. 31–5, her 'Greater London' in Ardis Butterfield (ed.), *Chaucer and the City* (Cambridge: D. S. Brewer, 2006), pp. 25–40, and, in the same volume, Barbara Nolan, 'Chaucer's "Poetics of Dwelling" in *Troilus and Cressida*', pp. 57–78.

28  The most recent argument for this reading of the end of *Troilus and Criseyde* is by Jamie Fumo, *The Legacy of Apollo: Antiquity, Authority and Chaucerian Poetics* (Toronto: University of Toronto Press, 2010), pp. 125–6, p. 152, and p. 160.

29  Carlin, *Medieval Southwark*, p. 254. The final resting place of the poem is as complex as that of Shakespeare's play. Editors supply the rubric 'unfinished' in modern printed editions. The fragment breaks off in the middle of a sentence which has been taken to suggest that corrupt manuscript dissemination is responsible for the abrupt ending. Caxton supplied twelve lines of his own which Thynne appended in a slightly altered form. More recent criticism regards the end as a deliberate metafictional statement, see *Riverside*, p. 990, and for the textual details, pp. 1142–3.

30  'Fama tenet summaque domum sibi legit in arce, / innumerosque aditus ac mille foramina tectis / addidit et nullis inclusit limina portis; / nocte dieque patet. tota est ex aere sonanti, / tota fremit uocesque refert iteratque quod audit. / nulla quies intus nullaque silentia parte, / nec tamen est clamor, sed paruae murmura uocis, / qualia de pelagi, siquis procul audiat, undis / esse solent, qualemue sonum, cum Iuppiter atras / increpuit nubes, extrema tonitrua reddunt. / atria turba tenet; ueniunt, leue uulgus, euntque / mixtaque cum ueris passim commenta uagantur / milia rumorum confusaque uerba uolu tant' (*Metamorphoses* XII.43–55).

31  Alexandra Gillespie notes that the sounds are those specifically of physical activity: 'chirkynges' are the grinding of two hard surfaces together, and 'gygges', a word nowhere else recorded, the sound made by a bow on a string, *Print Culture and the Medieval Author: Chaucer, Lydgate and Their Books 1473–1557* (Oxford: Oxford University Press, 2006), p. 61. The juxtaposition of these two very different sounds: one industrial, the other from music, is a tiny example in itself of the discordance of this section of *The House of Fame*.

32  Derek Attridge argues that what is often viewed as onomato-poeia is a distinctive and carefully arranged set of phonaesthemes. Onomatopoeia is a convention and requires interpretation as much as any other system of signs, *Peculiar Language* (London: Routledge, 2004), pp. 136–57 (p. 141).

33  Competitive urban noise would not have been confined solely to Southwark, but the presence of crowded tenements in the same location as Marshalsea prison, Paris Gardens, a hospital for the poor sick, and incessant travellers, alongside the sounds of the trades such as lime-burning, tanning and the manufacture of gunpowder would have created a soundscape more likely to have been heard without the city walls than within. Smith notes this with reference to early modern Southwark, *The Acoustic World*, p. 55.

34 It also provided a convenient point of access into the city traversed along the same route in the other direction; a feature of Southwark's unruliness which commentators on the 1381 uprising were not slow to excoriate, see R. B. Dobson, *The Peasants' Revolt of 1381* (London: Macmillan, 1983), 2nd edn, pp. 155–6, 209, 217 and 222–3.

35 David J. Johnson, *Southwark and the City* (Oxford: Oxford University Press, 1969), notes how the presence of travellers of every kind – servants, sailors in port, foreign merchants and craftsmen – fuelled Southwark's reputation as a centre for affrays, broils and criminality, especially with the rich opportunities for consorting at taverns (pp. 61–75). The presence of large numbers of aliens and immigrants (see Carlin, *Medieval Southwark*, pp. 146–9 and p. 167) added both to the suburb's social eclecticism and the diversity of its linguistic registers.

36 Carlin, *Medieval Southwark*, provides extensive discussion of the population of Southwark that ran its service economy: victuallers, innkeepers and hucksters. Tabulated figures for the 1381 Poll Tax return show that they were amongst the most numerous of the residents counted: shipmen (17); brewers (24); hostellers (22); and hucksters (25), pp. 280–4.

37 In his *Mirour de l'Homme*, Gower's figure of Wantonness is a Southwark prostitute who is 'ever available', as common in her wantonness as the roads of the country are common, over which all men, both worthy and miserable, may go at will, John Gower, *Mirour de l'Homme*, ed. William Burton Wilson (East Lansing: Colleagues Press, 1992), p. 127. Federico, *New Troy*, notes how this description resonates with the opening up of the city to the rebels in 1381, p. 155 n. 30.

38 Carlin notes that one of the questions asked in ordinances designed to regulate the stews was whether stewmongers kept their doors open on holidays, *Medieval Southwark*, p. 216. Stewmongers were forbidden to keep boats to prevent their soliciting custom from across the river, thus opening up access to the brothels even more widely, p. 215.

39 Though, strictly speaking, Faustus is addressing a succuba in the shape of Helen of Troy.

40 Far from being an image of harmony, lines 130–5 of Ulysses's speech evoke a 'crowd of unruly aspirants trying to jostle each other off the rungs of an unstable scaffold', Dawson, *Troilus*, p. 45. Compare the end of *The House of Fame* with the scrambling of the emulous 'hepe' of folk stamping on each other's heels, and pushing their noses and faces out of the way (2150–4).

41 Smith discusses the distinctions between bodily hearing and psychological listening, *The Acoustic World*, pp. 6–7.

42 The eagle is right. Sound is nothing more than the movement of air particles: the frequency with which they are moved in air creates

pitch, and the force of that movement amplification. Humans assign taxonomies and significance to the combination of pitch and volume.

43  Martin Irvine, 'Medieval Grammatical Theory and *Chaucer's House of Fame*', *Speculum* 60 (1985), 850–76.

44  'Every' is a keyword of this poem. It appears in the first line and there are seventy more instances. In collocation with speech and sound; indiscriminateness is foregrounded, e.g.: '[o]f every speche, of every soun' (832); 'every speche of every man' (849); 'every word of thys sentence' (877); 'every word that spoken ys' (881); 'wente every tydyng fro mouth to mouth' (2076).

45  The eagle in the *House of Fame* recalls those in Dante's *Divina Comedia, Purgatorio* 9.19–33, and *Paradiso* 1.62–3, neither of whom, in contrast to the reference to the eagle's 'mannes vois' (556), draws attention to their prosopopoeia.

46  Minnis comments wryly, 'perhaps his wife, stereotypically shouting to get him up in the morning? Or perhaps a servant, performing the same duty? Certainly not St Lucy', *The Oxford Guides to Chaucer: The Shorter Poems* (Oxford: Clarendon Press, 1995), p. 202.

47  Words and sound are collapsed into animal noise at other places in the poem: magpies (700–6); mouse (785); bears (1589); apes (1212); rooks' nests (1516), and hives of bees (1521–2).

48  This is not the only instance of collapsing the world of text into sound: a reverse example is the simile that compares the 'crying' folk who flock to the House of Fame with a twenty-foot-thick book (1334–5).

49  Thomas C. Kennedy, 'Rhetoric and Meaning in *The House of Fame*', *Studia Neophilologica* 68 (1996), 9–23, discusses how the reduction of language to sound is illustrated by random patterns of rhyme. He mentions name/fame etc. but does not list the occurrences. They are: Name/fame (305–6; 1145–6; 1153–4; 1275–6; 1311–12; 1405–6; 1411–12; 1489–90; 1555–6; 1609–10; 1619–20; 1695–6; 1715–16; 1735–6; 1761–2; 1871–2; 1899–1900; 2111–12); Fame/game (663–4; 821–2; 1199–1200; 1473–4); Shame/name (557–8; 1815–16); Shame/diffame (1581–2).

50  As it is also in *Troilus* V.1794–6.

51  James, *Shakespeare's Troy*, notes that the displaced scriptedness of Cressida's words is emphasised by the use of the metaphor of printing, pp. 106–12. Any authority, origin or integrity that might have been allotted to the Troy legend or any of its eponymous heroes is dispersed through the deconstruction of sight and words and grammar.

52  Unless otherwise indicated, references to specific production details are based on my own notes from watching and/or hearing recordings of performance.

53  This is discussed by Apfelbaum, *Shakespeare's Troilus and Cressida*, p. 49. Hall realises something of the play between textual instability and acoustic reception that is dramatised in the Prologue that begins

*Satiromastix* acted at the Globe in 1601. Addressed 'Ad Lectorem' the prologue lists a series of printing mistakes that are described as a 'comedy of errors', Thomas Dekker, *Satiromastix* in *The Dramatic Works of Thomas Dekker*, ed. Fredson Bowers (Cambridge: Cambridge University Press, 1953), I.306.

54 Gayle Green, 'Language and Value in *Troilus and Cressida*', *SEL* 21 (1981), 271–85; T. McAlindon, 'Language, Style and Meaning in *Troilus and Cressida*', *PMLA* 84 (1969), 29–43; James Shaw, '*Troilus and Cressida*', in Keith Parsons and Pamela Mason (eds), *Shakespeare in Performance* (London: Salamander, 2000), pp. 220–6, p. 224, and Jane Adamson, *Troilus and Cressida* (Brighton: Harvester, 1987), pp. 11–84.

55 There are 85 examples. Only four other plays have more: *Antony and Cleopatra*, 93; *Hamlet*, 107; *Othello*, 142, and *Romeo and Juliet* 133; statistics taken from searches in Crystal, Shakespeare's Words: http://shakespeareswords.com/Search.aspx. If directors move Pandarus's final speech to 5.3, the play ends with Troilus's sound [o:] in the rhyme of his final couplet: 'go/woe' (5.11.30–1).

56 Smith discusses its communicative range, *The Acoustic World*, pp. 116, 22–9 and p. 130.

57 As Paul Hardwick did in Quayle (1948), Shirley, *Troilus*, p. 30.

58 Shirley, *Troilus*, pp. 110–111.

59 Michael Coveney, *Financial Times*, 27 June (1985).

60 Judge (1996) was a performance of some acoustic force. Loud drunkenness was prominent at the start of 5.2.

61 Poel (1912); Payne (1936), Shirley, *Troilus*, p. 197.

62 As in Providence Trinity Rep's performance in 1971, Shirley, *Troilus*, p. 50. Davies (1985) had flashes and sounds of gunfire; Boyd (1998) guns on stage and shells exploding off it, Shirley, *Troilus*, p. 223. After the bugle calls at the start of Act 1 Scene 1, Davies (1985), Troilus laid down his sword at l. 5 with a 'noise'. Clashing with the military signals at the start of the scene, the first sound of a military weapon struck a domestic object. The instruction to Agamemnon to bang his stick on the table (Davies (1985) promptbook (3.1)) sounds a similar deflation of legendary pomp.

63 E.g. BBC (1981), and Pelican audio recording.

64 Shirley, *Troilus*, p. 43; the Canadian production, noted by Shirley, p. 234, was by David William at the Stratford Festival, Ontario.

65 Yale University production (1916), cited Shirley, *Troilus*, p. 13; Barton (1968), Shirley, *Troilus*, p. 175; Guthrie (1957), Shirley, *Troilus*, p. 33; Barton/Kyle (1976), promptbook. Achilles audibly scrunched Andromache's letter in 5.1.46 (BBC (1981)); in the same production, Troilus's tearing of Cressida's letter (5.3) was accompanied by martial din and much coughing and spluttering from Pandarus.

66 The audience reaction to this moment in Mendes (1990) is very audible on the RSC videotape of the production.

67 Voice casting merges soundworlds lands apart when the Middle Eastern shawms and shofars of the Pelican audio recording usher in a Troilus who declaims in the unmistakable Ambridgean voice of Roy Tucker (Ian Pepperell) in BBC Radio 4's long running serial *The Archers*.

68 Russell Jackson and Robert Smallwood (eds), *Players of Shakespeare* (Cambridge: Cambridge University Press, 1995), p. 163.

69 It is not clear from the promptbook's separate section on music and sound for production whether this treatment of 'theme' was intended to pick up on the musical pun in Troilus's description of Helen as a 'theme of honour and renown' (2.3.204).

70 The sound of the typewriter was a conspicuous element in the sound-scape of Davies (1985), along with Ilona Sekacz's piano score.

71 Of the productions that end the play with the sound of howling wind (BBC (1981)) stands out. Even more so in Judge (1996), where the effect is all the more poignant given the sustained use of brass music throughout. An interview with Juliet Stevenson just before the start of the Davies (1985) run of performances at Stratford captures the dissonance of Troy perfectly: '[b]ugles and other martial noises came from the speakers that relays what's happening on stage to the dressing rooms; you can turn it down, but never off. Next door, the builders' hammers lay a muffled barrage. It sounds like the Trojan war rumbling all through the theatre at Stratford', Hugh Hebert, 'Love on a Battlefield', *The Guardian*, 24 June 1985.

72 It has been noted that *Troilus* sounds the words 'oblivion' and 'fame' more often than any other play. Frank Kermode, '"Opinion" in *Troilus and Cressida*', in Susanne Kappeler and Norman Bryson (eds), *Troilus and Cressida*', *Teaching the Text* (London and Boston: Routledge & Kegan Paul, 1983), pp. 164–79. Fame is heard eight times; opinion ten; scores which are confirmed by searches in Crystal, *Shakespeare's Words*.

73 Literally so in Mendes (1990), when Agamemnon rifled through screwed-up briefing papers and coffee mugs on the general's map table to find his name plate and shook it exasperatedly under Aeneas's nose, Shirley, *Troilus*, p. 119.

74 Hector (99); Achilles (68); Crystal, *Shakespeare's Words*.

75 Cf. 4.5.75–6 when Aeneas asks Achilles, '[i]f not Achilles, sir / What is your name?' The answer: '[i]f not Achilles, nothing' (77).

76 This textual crux is discussed extensively by Apfelbaum, *Shakespeare's Troilus and Cressida*, pp. 171–4. 'Call' is the play's opening word after the Prologue and it is heard a further 40 more times, along with 'tell' (61); 'speak' (46); 'say' (64) 'words' (20); 'praise' (27); 'hear' (19).

77  Apfelbaum, *Shakespeare's Troilus and Cressida*, pp. 77–8, and Barbara
    Hodgdon, 'He Do Cressida in Different Voices', *English Literary
    Review* 20 (1990), 254–86.
78  Judge (1996) had this pronunciation at 2.1.67 and 3.3.245, as does the
    Pelican audio recording.
79  There is even more: '[w]hat Troy means fairly shall be spoke aloud'
    (1.3.260); 'Of every syllable that here was spoke' (5.2.116); 'I can
    tell them that' (1.2.49, 51); 'tell him of Nestor, one that was a man'
    (1.3.292); '[g]o tell him this' (2.3.120); 'who were those went by'
    (1.2.1); 'and so I'll tell her the next time I see her' (1.1.76–7); 'tell
    her I have chastised the amorous Trojan' (5.5.4); 'Ajax was here'
    (2.1.88); 'Cressid was here but now' (5.2.127); 'what were you talking
    of when I came?' (1.2.41); '[t]he noise goes' (1.2.12). And more that
    has not been quoted for reasons of space.
80  Macowan (1938); Guthrie (1956); and Boyd (1998), Shirley, *Troilus*,
    p. 124.
81  Judge (1996) and Dromgoole (1999–2000) had Ulysses mimic
    Achilles's voice, Shirley, *Troilus*, p. 111. Which he does again in the
    scene in which he gulls Ajax into responding to Hector's challenge.
    Not content with speaking rumour and report about both men,
    Ulysses slips into Agamemnon's voice in performing the leader's
    refusal to dance attendance on Achilles, 'And say in thunder "Achilles
    go to him!"' (2.3.183).
82  Amongst the most noteworthy examples of this persistent habit of
    characters speaking in quoted voice is Hector's voicing of a town crier
    in the voice of Fame herself, 'on whose bright crest Fame with her
    loud'st "Oyez"' (4.5.143).
83  Clive Merrison's Pandarus (Mendes (1990)) audibly put on a 'woman's
    voice' for Helen at lines 142ff; but was inconsistent in impersonating
    either her or Paris during his performance of 1.2.143–295. Thersites's
    impersonation of Ajax at 3.3.251–62 occasioned comic voice switch-
    ing in 1990, 1985, 1996 and especially in 2012.
84  This feature of the play was especially stressed in the RSC/Wooster
    (2012) production. The Trojans were wired for sound. Not only did the
    microphones flatten and distort their voices but the overhead speakers
    placed centrally above the playing space made it often unclear who was
    speaking; an effect intensified because their lines were delivered in flat
    monotone. The Greeks were unmiked but Thersites sometimes spoke
    through a hand-held microphone his voice vacillating between bari-
    tone and falsetto. The chanting of lines textually cued for individual
    Greeks by the whole Greek ensemble in 2.3 and 3.3 also contributed to
    the instability between voice and individual origins. While she focuses
    on textual citationality rather than its aural representation, Elizabeth
    Freund demonstrates how Shakespeare's insistent quotation of quota-
    tion of quotation in the play strips '*both* his sources *and* his own text

of their "original" substance with spirited iconoclasm', '"Ariachne's broken woof": The Rhetoric of Citation in *Troilus and Cressida*', in Patricia Parker and Geoffrey Hartman (eds), *Shakespeare and the Question of Theory* (London: Routledge, 1985), pp. 20–35 (p. 34). See also Linda Charnes, *Notorious Identity: Materializing the Subject in Shakespeare* (Cambridge, MA, and London: Harvard University Press, 1993), pp. 70–102.

85  As he has done at 5.7.3–8 when he gathers his Myrmidons around him to school them in butchery.

86  Ralph Berry writes on how the play at this point expresses itself in the flat assertiveness of rhyme, noting especially Achilles's final couplet, with the pun on 'trail'-ing Hector's body attached to his horse's tail (5.8.21–2), *Shakespeare and the Awareness of the Audience* (London: Macmillan, 1985), pp. 115–27 (p. 126).

87  In keeping with the more nuanced tones of his production, Mendes (1990) cut these lines.

88  Payne (promptbook (1936)) cues shouts for 'bruit'.

89  The airy hissing is particularly pronounced in the long-drawn-out final lines in the Pelican audio recording,

90  RSC/Wooster (2012) had Ulysses (Scott Handy) so red in the face and breathless at the end of delivering 1.3.75–138 that he had to use an inhaler. Particular emphasis was given to 'choking' (127).

91  While Berry cites 15, twice the number in any other Shakespeare play, p. 117, when stage directions are included the trumpet count is 22: Crystal, Shakespeare's Words.

92  While their technical limitations were a challenge to playing melody, they could signal recognisable battle instructions, and those series of notes could be modified and polished to sound flourish, sennets and tuckets, Frances A. Shirley, *Shakespeare's Use of Offstage Sounds* (Lincoln: University of Nebraska Press, 1963), pp. 53–7.

93  The quarto prologue to Dekker's *Satiromastix* refers to the 'trumpets sounding thrice', p. 306, and relishing their cessation, the Epilogue describes the trumpet sound as one that 'set men together by the eares' with its 'Tantara-rag', p. 385. While Sternfeld notes that trumpeters were associated with aristocratic guilds, trumpets played by actors were from a profession vilified as the scourge of social distinction by anti-theatre pamphleteers: *Music in Shakespearean Tragedy* (London: Routledge, Kegan and Paul, 1963), p. 196.

94  Even though they were softer in tone than modern trumpets, they were considered too strident to play real music and were used mostly for signalling, Shirley, *Offstage Sounds*, p. 18. She quotes in support the stage direction from the Quarto version of *Dr Faustus* 4.1, 'Trumpets cease and music sounds.' Cornets, a wooden instrument with fingerholes, could stand in for trumpets. Their sound was a coarser and louder version of the oboe.

95   As noted by Smith, *The Acoustic World*, p. 93.
96   H. T. Riley, *Memorials of London* (London: Longmans, Green and Co., 1868), p. 316.
97   My research is not a complete record of early dramatic texts. But a useful profile emerged from the 188 different collocations I found in the LION database. The most was 'sound' (220), which attests to the sheer forcefulness of the acoustic presence of trumpets in early drama. Apart from 'flourish' (12), no other word reached double figures: the closest were 'call' and 'proclaim' (8). There were equal returns for pairs of antonyms such as angels/devils; disgrace/renown, dishonour/honoured, impudent/valiant (2). The results suggested an instrument capable equally of praise or blame.
98   RSC/Wooster (2012) mixed heavy rock, American Indian chant, nursery rhyme and Elizabethan song. The music by Ilona Sekacz in Davies (1985) drew extensive commentary from reviewers who used phrases such as 'twisted echoes' (*The Times*, 27 June), 'distorted' (*Guardian*, 27 June), 'dissonant' (*Sunday Times*, 30 June), 'collectively free-associated' (*New Statesman*, 5 July). The score provided a counterpoint to the work of trumpets in the play with a piano world which moved between Strauss pastiche, 1940s movie soundtracks, off-key Chopin and tortured Weill. As Pandarus exited, the piano was left playing by itself.
99   Smith, *The Acoustic World*, p. 93.
100  Smith, *The Acoustic World*, p. 51. It moves non-human sounds in the direction of speech, and speech in the direction of human sounds.
101  Adamson argues for this contrast, *Troilus and Cressida*, pp. 76–7. Sternfeld argues that the music, though harmonious, does not reform Paris and Helen; rather it appeals to their depravity and confirms it, *Music in Shakespearean Tragedy*, p. 205.
102  Lute (Payne (1938); Quayle (1948)); a flute (Barton/Kyle (1976)); and a piano (Guthrie (1956) and Davies (1985)).
103  Apfelbaum, *Shakespeare's Troilus and Cressida*, devotes pp. 108–34 to a review of music and staging possibilities in performance history of Act 3 Scene 1.
104  Sternfeld notes how the puns on 'broken' music allude to the consort ensemble that included both stringed and wind instruments. It was especially associated with lavish entertainment and banquets, *Music in Shakespearean Tragedy*, pp. 206–7.
105  The insistent repetition of the verbal sounds of 'sweet honey love' (chiefly, but not only by Pandarus), conflates 'sweet queen' with its homophone 'quean' as prostitute. It's a soundplay that has its answering refrain in Pandarus's last speech when he sings/croaks: '[s]weet honey and sweet notes together fail' (5.11.43). David Lindley notes how the available contrast in Act 3 Scene 1 is muted not just by the later treatment of the trumpets but by what he sees

as excessive effeminacy: 'Shakespeare's Provoking Music', in John Caldwell, Edward Olleson and Susan Wollenberg (eds), *The Well Enchanting Skill: Music, Poetry and Drama in the Culture of the Renaissance: Essays in Honour of F. W. Sternfeld* (Oxford: Clarendon, 1990), pp. 79–90 (pp. 81–2).

106 Lindley notes that 'the full force of the ambiguity that attends music [in *Troilus*] is revealed in the use of the martial trumpet', 'Shakespeare's Provoking Music', p. 82.

107 Though the competition for 'top trumps' is tough to call when one remembers the cartwheeling Pentecostal fart at the end of *The Summoner's Tale* (IV.2253–80).

108 First noted by A. P. Rossiter, *Angel with Horns* (London: Longman, 1961), p. 133.

109 In both Quarto and Folio the reading is 'Troyans'.

110 The pun is illustrated with enigmatic clarity in the Barton (1968) promptbook. Ajax is cued to speak '[t]he Trojans' trumpet!' (16) followed by '[t]he Trojan strumpet' written out in the promptbook and attributed to Achilles. The second instruction is then crossed out. The pun was clearly heard in Judge (1996), accompanied by a discordant fanfare. I return to the issue of speech prefixes in performance in the final section of the chapter.

111 There is rich discussion of the excess of trumpets in Berry, *Shakespeare and the Awareness of the Audience*, pp. 119–20, who argues that the trumpet of fame has great resonance in the play but it does not deliver. In addition to Lindley, Shirley and Sternfeld, see also John H. Long, *Shakespeare's Use of Music in the Histories and Tragedies* (Gainsville: University of Florida Press, 1971), pp. 130–44, and R. W. Ingram, 'Music as a Structural Element in Shakespeare', in Clifford Leech and J. M. R. Margeson (eds), *Proceedings of the World Shakespeare Congress Vancouver, 1971* (Toronto: University of Toronto Press, 1972), pp. 174–89 (pp. 182–7).

112 Judge (1996) had brass playing almost continuously throughout the parade scene in Act 1 Scene 2. The promptbook for Payne (1936) cues for sounds of trumpets with great regularity, and especially at entrances and exits.

113 The first of these stage directions (3.3.1), recorded only in the Folio, marks the entry of the Greek politicians to parley with Calchas. The second (4.5.64), again recorded only in the Folio, is for the entry for 'all of Troy' just after '[t]he Troyans trumpet'. Both Greeks and Trojans get a flourish each, but, while the Greek parliament scene in 1.3.1 is prefaced with a sennet in the Folio, no brass is cued for the Trojan council in 2.2. For a 'noble' play, royal flourishes are comparatively scarce, Long, *Shakespeare's Use of Music*, p. 132.

114 Trumpets and drums are sounded in Mendes (1990); Judge (1996), and the Pelican sound recording.

115 Hector's call for a trumpet in Act 5 is before the battle starts (5.3.13) and Andromache immediately pleads with him for no 'notes of sally'.

116 Trojan trumpets F. Troyans trumpet Q. This line is spoken by one of the Myrmidons, the only time one of these anonymous thugs ever utters word in the play. I discuss this in more detail in the final section of the chapter.

117 E.g. in *Othello* 2.1.174, 'The Moor! I know his trumpet', and *The Merchant of Venice* 5.1.122, 'Your husband is at hand, I hear his trumpet'. The Trojans recognise the sound of Hector's trumpet at the end of the scene in which the Greeks have come to take Cressida to the Greek camp (4.4.139).

118 QF call for an 'alarum' before the fight, and at 1. 116 both have the SD 'trumpets cease'.

119 R. A. Foakes discusses this feature of *Troilus* in 'Stage Images in *Troilus and Criseyde*', in Marvin and Ruth Thompson (eds), *Shakespeare and the Sense of Performance* (London and Toronto: Associated University Presses, 1989), pp. 150–61 (p. 157).

120 The use of trumpets to undermine reputation even as characters call for them to enhance it is not solely confined to *Troilus*. It is a conspicuous feature of *Antony and Cleopatra*, the first tetralogy, *Richard II* and *Richard III*. Space prohibits detailed comparison here. Berry, Ingram, Lindley, Shirley, *Offstage Sounds*, and Sternfeld all discuss the role of trumpets in these plays in relation to this issue.

121 There is no SD in the Quarto, but the Folio calls for a Tucket.

122 In RSC/Wooster (2012) Ajax, played throughout as a thuggish wrestler by Aidan Kelly, performed a thrash metal amplified guitar riff, standing on a metal hospital trolley. When no answer came he played it again even more loudly. With still no reply forthcoming, he burst into tears and left the stage, trailing his guitar disconsolately behind him.

123 The appellation is a misnomer (we are told that he only 'semes' to be a person of great authority). In the absence of a Proper Name, critical tradition has christened him with this sobriquet, simply so he can be written about.

124 'Chaucer' is never named in poems where there is a first-person narrator. 'Chaucer' is named solely in the *Introduction to the Man of Lawe's Tale* where the fictional narrator excoriates his 'lewed' rhyming and his mediocrity as a storyteller (II.47). Compare the discussion of 'Geffrey', pp. 73–4 above in Chapter 2.

125 Antenor is named (though does not speak) in *Troilus and Criseyde*. The narrator explicitly comments on the dreadful irony of exchanging him for Criseyde since he subsequently brought Troy to destruction because he was a traitor (IV.203–5).

126 Characters who are named in other Shakespeare plays, present on stage, but mute, include: Matthew Goffe (*Henry VI, Part 2*);

Mortimer, Stafford, Pembroke and Young Richmond (*Henry VI, Part 3*); Thomas Erpingham (*Henry V*) and, as discussed in Chapter 4 above, Philostrate in the Folio version of *A Midsummer Night's Dream*. None of these characters, possibly with the exception of Young Richmond, has the structural and thematic importance of Antenor. Richmond, Stafford and Erpingham appear in five scenes; Stafford and Pembroke in four.

127 The list of 'dramatis personae' added to the play by Rowe and Malone names Antenor, along with Aeneas, as a 'Trojan commander'. Antenor was played by Simon Westwood in Judge (1996). The programme had a section 'Who's Who in the War'. Antenor was mentioned neither here nor in the 'What Became of Them' section a few pages further on.

128 The common root of 'trader' and 'traitor' is Latin 'tradere'. In Pandarus's final speech, he addresses 'traitors and bawds' (5.11.36). Dawson discusses W. J. Craig's conjecture that 'traitors' be emended to 'traders', *Troilus and Cressida*, ed., p. 232.

129 In Mendes (1990), the Trojans gave Antenor an especially warm welcome when he was returned in Act 4.

130 Ben Iden Payne (1936) kept the list of Trojans who filed past intact, but cut all Pandarus's descriptions of them (promptbook). Antenor was thus stripped of Pandarus's accolade. In BBC (1981), when Pandarus spoke of Antenor's wit and judgement, he raised his eyebrows and spoke archly as if those qualities were in doubt.

131 Painted cloths are wall hangings painted with scenes and mottoes. Those who speak with the simplistic clichés they represent are mocked in *As You Like It* (3.2.266). Pander's hall hung with tapestries that speak could be seen as a version of Chaucer's House of Fame.

132 In addition to Pandarus, Antenor's name is spoken by Paris (4.1.39), and by Troilus (4.4.109). And by the traitors to Troy: Aeneas (4.2.62) and Calchas.

133 Davies (1985) deleted the role entirely.

134 T. J. King, *Casting Shakespeare's Plays: London Actors and Their Roles 1590–1642* (Cambridge: Cambridge University Press, 1992), counts 14 men for 15 principal parts (significantly more than the average of 10 for other plays), and 6 men for the 18 minor roles, pp. 89–90. Table 64, pp. 214–15, lists the appearance of roles scene by scene and the number of lines that each speaks.

135 'Within' is a stage direction supplied by Hanmer. Calchas was not seen in BBC 1981. He was just an outline in the tent.

136 Such significance does not always attach. In Barton/Kyle (1976) Leonard Preston who played Antenor is listed as Deiphobus in the cast list in the promptbook, and as Antenor in the public cast lists. In Act 4 Scene 4 Antenor's name is crossed out and that of Deiphobus

inserted. He spoke the line '[l]et us make ready straight'. In Act 4 Scene 1 Antenor's name is kept for those entering and that of Deiphobus is crossed out.

137 Douglas Stender's initials appear at the top left of the V-shaped diagram for the phalanx of Myrmidons, promptbook (1968), p. 57. Leonard Preston is named in the actors present in the scene and his initials appear in the V-shaped diagram for the positions of the Myrmidons on stage, promptbook (1976), p. 60B.

138 Promptbooks and programmes often obscure the other roles the Antenor actor would have played. It is clear from the Hands (1981) promptbook that Peter MacKriel (Antenor) was on stage in the scenes where he is cued, including 5.11. The same applies to Roy Dotrice in Barton (1960). Quayle (1948) moved Pandarus's last speech to 5.3 and ended the play with Troilus's anguished speech back in the Greek camp. Antenor was on stage throughout it (promptbook).

139 Cf. the eagle's use of 'every' discussed above.

140 As we have seen, *The House of Fame* also plays with the last trumpet and judgement, and there is an analogue to Pandarus's lines in the eagle's argument that when it comes to the House of Fame every speech from any person is identical to the person who uttered it on earth. The eagle is playing with notions of the resurrection of the bodies of the redeemed on the Last Day.

141 Cf. discussion of Chaucer's left and right hands, pp. 116–18 above.

# 7
# Da capo

The cover image for this book shows Chaucer doubling up as himself. In reproduction, Ellesmere Chaucer is re-pointed: he rides back from the place where we are accustomed to see him in Harley. The Ellesmere manuscript border that margined him floats in space as a shared speech caption that resembles a theatre notice, or a plaque. Reprising the courteous deferral of the lie and the truth that fly 'compouned' (2108) out of the window in *The House of Fame*, these Chaucers outface teleology and refuse taxonomy. Chaucer was copied from a digitised image of Ellesmere which was then rotated and flipped, but because both figures were painted by hand, even as they appear to be opposites they are non-identical mirror images.

Chaucer has gone through several stages of production. The original artwork was a fully built puppet theatre which was dismantled and reassembled before being turned into a digital image. Shaped and sized into a cover, Chaucer has lost some of his Ellesmere girth, and, in their transport from stage to page, the poles which suspend the horses are without fixed attachment. The Canterbury pilgrimage has become an endlessly recursive carousel – a merry-go-round. Between landscape and portrait, Chaucer points to a made-up version of himself in staged role-play, and, while the final image occupies two dimensions, it was formed from a layered collage of multi-media materials in three. The 'you' in the framed speech was scraped out of fabric coated with acetate. Who is after whom?

# Select bibliography

## Primary

### Manuscripts

London, British Library, MS Harley 4866.
London, British Library, MS Royal 6.E.VI and 6.E.VII.
London, British Library, MS Royal 17.D.VI.
Manchester, John Rylands University Library, MS English 63.
Northumberland, MS 455.
Oxford, Bodleian Library, MS Bodley 686.
Oxford, Bodleian Library, MS Douce 104.
Oxford, Bodleian Library, MS Lansdowne 851.
Oxford, Bodleian Library, Bodleian MS Rawlinson.poet 223.

### Early printed books

*The prologue to His Majesty at the First Play Presented at the Cock-pit in Whitehall; Being part of that Noble entertainment Which Their Majesties received Novemb. 19 from His Grace the Duke of Albemarle.* London, 1660.

Davenant, William. *Macbeth.* London: P. Chetwin, 1674.

Davenant, William and John Dryden. *The Enchanted Isle.* London: Printed by F. M. for *Henry Herringman* at the *Blew Anchor* in the *Lower-walk* of the *New-Exchange*, MDCLXX.

Davenant, William, *The Rivals: A Comedy.* William Cademan, at the Pope's Head in the Lower Walk of the New Exchange, 1668.

### Facsimiles

*The Ellesmere Manuscript of Chaucer's Canterbury Tales: A Working Facsimile,* ed. Ralph Hanna. Cambridge: D. S. Brewer, 1989.

*The Holkham Bible Picture Book: A Facsimile,* ed. Michelle P. Brown. London: British Library, 2007.

*Poetical Works: A Facsimile of Cambridge University Library MS GG.4.27,* ed. M. B. Parkes and Richard Beadle. Cambridge: D. S. Brewer, 1980.

*Theatrical productions, promptbooks, films and musical scores*
*A Midsummer Night's Dream* (Ben Fairfull, The Moment Theatre Company, Courtyard Theatre London (2012).
*A Midsummer Night's Dream* (Michael Hoffman, Fox Searchlight Pictures, 1999).
*A Midsummer Night's Dream* (Adrian Noble, Channel Four Films, 1996).
*Troilus and Cressida* (Elizabeth Le Compte/Mark Ravenhill, RSC/ Wooster Group production, 2012).
*Troilus and Cressida* (Trevor Nunn, 1998, National Theatre production).
*Troilus and Cressida* (Michael Boyd, 1998, RSC production).
*Troilus and Cressida* (Ian Judge, 1996, RSC production).
*Troilus and Cressida* (Sam Mendes, 1990, RSC videotape).
*Troilus and Cressida* (Howard Davies, 1985, RSC production promptbook).
*Troilus and Cressida* (Jonathan Miller, BBC TV, 1981).
*Troilus and Cressida* (Terry Hands, 1981, RSC production promptbook).
*Troilus and Cressida* (John Barton/Barry Kyle, 1976, promptbook).
*Troilus and Cressida* (John Barton, 1968, RSC production promptbook).
*Troilus and Cressida* (Tyrone Guthrie, 1957, RSC production promptbook).
*Troilus and Cressida* (Clive Brill, Archangel Shakespeare, Auburn, CA 95604, 2003).

Editions
Augustine. *De Doctrina Christiana*, ed. and trans. R. P. H. Green. Oxford: Clarendon Press, 1995.
*The Babees Book* in *Education in Early England*, ed. F. J. Furnivall. EETS OS 32 (1867).
Baldwin, William. *Beware the Cat*, ed. William A. Ringler Jr and Michael Flachman. San Marino: Huntington Library, 1988.
*Ben Jonson*, ed. C. H. Herford and Percy Simpson. Oxford: Clarendon Press, 1937.
*Bérinus: Roman en prose du XIVe siècle*, ed. Robert Bossuat. Paris: SATF, 1931.
Boccaccio, Giovanni. *Teseida*, ed. Salvatore Battaglia. Florence: G. C. Sansoni, 1938.
*The Book of Vices and Virtues*, ed. F. W. Nelson. EETS OS 217 (1942).
Bowers, John, ed. *The Canterbury Tales: Fifteenth-Century Continuations and Additions*. Kalamazoo, MI: Medieval Institute Publications, 1992.
Bulwer, John. *Chirologia, or, The naturall language of the hand* (1644), accessed via EEBO.
Chaucer, Geoffrey. *The Riverside Chaucer*, ed. Larry D. Benson et al., 3rd revd edn. Oxford: Oxford University Press, 2008.
Chaucer, Geoffrey. *The Text of the Canterbury Tales*, 8 vols, ed. John M. Manly and Edith Rickert. Chicago: University of Chicago Press, 1940.
Chaucer, Geoffrey. Urry, John, ed. *The Works of Geoffrey Chaucer, Compared with the Former Editions, and Many Valuable MSS. Out of*

*which, Three Tales are Added which were Never Before Printed*. London, 1721.

Chaucer, Geoffrey. Wright, Thomas. *The Canterbury Tales of Geoffrey Chaucer: A New Text with Illustrative Notes in Early English Poetry, Ballads and Popular Literature of the Middle Ages*. London: Percy Society 24 and 26, 1847 and 1857.

Chaucer, Geoffrey. Skeat, Walter W. *Chaucerian and Other Pieces*. Oxford: Clarendon Press, 1897.

Chaucer, Geoffrey. *The Tale of Beryn with a Prologue of the Merry Adventure of the Pardoner with a Tapster at Canterbury*, ed. F. J. Furnivall and W. G. Stone. EETS ES 105 (1909).

Chaucer, Geoffrey. *The Tale of Beryn with a Prologue of the merry Adventure of the Pardoner with a Tapster at Canterbury*, ed. F. J. Furnivall and W. G. Stone. EETS OS 1901.

Crowley, Robert. *The Select Works of Robert Crowley*, ed. J. M. Cowper. EETS ES 15 (1872).

Dekker, Thomas. *The Dramatic Works of Thomas Dekker*, ed. Fredson Bowers. Cambridge: Cambridge University Press, 1953.

*The Digby Poems: A New Edition of the Lyrics*, ed. Helen Barr. Exeter: Exeter University Press, 2009.

Downes, John. *Roscius Anglicanus or an Historical Review of the Stage from 1660–1706* (1708), ed. Judith Milhous and Robert D. Hume. London: The Society for Theatre Research, 1987.

Dryden, John. *The Poems of John Dryden*, 5 vols, V: *1597–1700*, ed. Paul Hammond and David Hopkins. Harlow: Pearson, 2005.

Dryden, John. *The Works of John Dryden: Volume VII, Poems 1697–1700*, ed. Vinton A. Dearing. Berkeley: University of California Press, 2000. 20 vols.

*The Floure and the Leaf*, ed. Derek Pearsall. Kalamazoo, MI: for TEAMS by Medieval Institute Publications, 1990.

Galen. *Galen on the Usefulness of the Parts of the Body*, ed. and trans. Margaret Tallmadge May. Ithaca, NY: Cornell University Press, 1968.

Gower, John. *Confessio Amantis*, in *The English Works of John Gower*, ed. G. C Macaulay. EETS ES 81 (1900).

Gower, John. *Mirour de l'Homme*, ed. and trans.William Burton Wilson. East Lansing: Colleagues Press, 1992.

Gray, Douglas, ed. *A Selection of Religious Lyrics*. Oxford: Clarendon Press, 1975.

*Handlyng Synne*, ed. F. J. Furnivall. EETS OS 123 (1903).

Hoccleve, Thomas. *The Regiment of Princes*, ed. Charles R. Blyth. Kalamazoo, MI: Medieval Institute Publications, 1999.

*Isidore of Seville: The Medical Writings*, ed. and trans. William D. Sharpe, *Transactions of the American Philosphical Society* n.s. 2 (1964), 1, 66–71.

Jonson, Ben. *The Complete Masques*, ed. Stephen Orgel. New Haven and London: Yale University Press, 1969.

Kempe, Margery. *The Book of Margery Kempe*, ed. Hope Emily Allen. EETS OS 212 (1940).

Kempe, Margery. *The Book of Margery Kempe*, ed. Barry Windeatt. Harlow: Longman, 2000.

Langland, William. *Piers Plowman: A Parallel-Text Edition of the A, B, C and Z Versions*, ed. A. V. C. Schmidt. London: Longman, 1995.

Langland, William. *The Vision of Piers Plowman: A Complete Edition of the B-Text*, ed. A. V. C. Schmidt. London: Everyman, 1991.

*Looke About You*, ed. W. W. Greg. London: Malone Society, 1913.

Lydgate, John. *Lydgate's Siege of Thebes*, ed. Axel Erdmann. EETS ES 108 (1911).

Lydgate, John. *Minor Poems of John Lydgate* ed. H. N. MacCracken. EETS OS 192 (1934).

*The Lytylle Childrenes Lytil Boke*, in *Education in Early England*, ed. F. J. Furnivall. EETS OS 32 (1867).

Malory, Thomas. *Complete Works*, ed. Eugène Vinaver, 2nd edn. Oxford: Oxford University Press, 1971.

*Materials for the History of Thomas Becket, Archbishop of Canterbury*, ed. J. C. Robertson and J. B. Shepherd. London, Rolls Series, 1875–85, 7 vols.

*Medieval English Verse and Prose in Modernized Versions*, ed. Roger Sherman Loomis and Rudolph Willard. New York: Appleton-Century-Crofts, 1948.

*The Minor Poems of the Vernon Manuscript Part II*, ed. F. J. Furnivall. EETS OS 117 (1901).

*Myrc's Instructions for Parish Priests* ed. E. Peacock. EETS OS 31 (1868).

Ovid (P. Ovidus Naso). *Metamorphoses*, ed. R. J. Tarrant. Oxford: Oxford University Press, 2004.

*The Philobiblon of Richard de Bury*, trans. Andrew Fleming West. New York: P. C. Duschnes, 1945.

*The Piers Plowman Tradition: A Critical Edition of Pierce the Ploughman's Crede, Richard the Redeless, Mum and the Sothsegger and The Crowned King*, ed. Helen Barr. London: J. M. Dent, 1993.

Quintilian. *The Institutio Oratoria of Quintilian*, ed. H. E. Butler, Loeb Classical Library. Cambridge, MA: Harvard University Press, 1920–22, 4 vols.

Riley, H. T. *Memorials of London*. London: Longmans, Green and Co., 1868

*Le Roman de la Rose*, ed. Daniel Poiron. Paris: Garnier-Flammarion, 1974.

Shakespeare, William. *A Midsummer Night's Dream*, ed. Harold F. Brooks. London: Methuen, 1979.

Shakespeare, William. *A Midsummer Night's Dream*, ed. Peter Holland. Oxford: Clarendon Press, 1994.

Shakespeare, William. *A Midsummer Night's Dream*, ed. Stanley Wells, introduction by Helen Hackett. London: New Penguin, 2005.

Shakespeare, William. *As You Like It*, ed. Juliet Dusinberre. London: Methuen, 2006.

Shakespeare, William. *Measure for Measure: The Text of the Folio of 1623, with that of 'The Law against Lovers' by Sir William D'Avenant, 1662*, ed. B. Frank Carpenter. New York: The Shakespeare Society of New York, 1908.

Shakespeare, William. *The Complete Works*, ed. Gary Taylor and Stanley Wells. Oxford: Oxford University Press, 1988.

Shakespeare, William. *The Tempest*, ed. Stephen Orgel. Oxford: Oxford University Press, 1987.

Shakespeare, William. *The Two Noble Kinsmen*, ed. Lois Potter. London: Methuen, 1997.

Shakespeare, William. *The Two Noble Kinsmen*, ed. Eugene Waith. Oxford: Clarendon Press, 1989.

Shakespeare, William. *The Two Noble Kinsmen by William Shakespeare and John Fletcher*, Royal Shakespeare Company. London: Methuen, 1986.

Shakespeare, William. *Troilus and Cressida*, ed. Jonathan Bate and Eric Rasmussen. Basingstoke: Macmillan, 2010.

Shakespeare, William. *Troilus and Cressida*, ed. David Bevington. London: Methuen, 2006.

Shakespeare, William. *Troilus and Cressida*, ed. Anthony B. Dawson. Cambridge: Cambridge University Press, 2003.

Shakespeare, William. *Troilus and Cressida*, ed. R. A. Foakes, introduction by Colin Burrow. Harmondsworth: Penguin, 1967.

Shakespeare, William. *Troilus and Cressida*, ed. Kenneth Muir. Oxford: Oxford University Press, 1982.

Shakespeare, William. *Troilus and Cressida*, ed. Frances A. Shirley. Cambridge: Cambridge University Press, 2005.

Trevisa, John. *On the Properties of Things: John Trevisa's Translation of Bartholomaeus Anglicus*, ed. M. C. Seymour et al., 2 vols. Oxford: Oxford University Press, 1975.

*The Wakefield Pageants in the Townley Cycle*, ed. A. C. Cawley. Manchester: Manchester University Press, 1958.

*York Mystery Plays*, ed. Richard Beadle and Pamela King. Oxford: Clarendon Press, 1984.

## Secondary

Abbott, E. A. *St Thomas of Canterbury: His Death and Miracles*. London: Adam and Charles Black, 1898.

Abrams, R. '*Two Noble Kinsmen* as Bourgois Drama', in *Shakespeare, Fletcher and the Two Noble Kinsmen*, ed. Charles H. Frey. Columbia: University of Missouri Press, 1989, pp. 145–62.

Adamson, Jane. *Troilus and Cressida*. Brighton: Harvester, 1987.

Allen, Elizabeth. 'The Pardoner in the Dogges Boure: Early Reception of *The Canterbury Tales*', *Chaucer Review* 36 (2001), 91–127.

Allen, Rosamund S. '*The Siege of Thebes*: Lydgate's Canterbury Tale', in *Chaucer and Fifteenth Century Poetry*, ed. Julia Boffey and Janet Cowen. London: King's College London, 1991, pp. 122–42.

Andreas, James R. 'Remythologising *The Knight's Tale*: A *Midsummer Night's Dream* and *Two Noble Kinsmen*', *Shakespeare Yearbook* 2 (1991), 49–68.

Apfelbaum, Roger. *Shakespeare's Troilus and Cressida: Textual Problems and Performance Solutions*. Newark: University of Delaware Press, 2004.

Attridge, Derek. *Peculiar Language*. London: Routledge, 2004.

Bakhtin, M. M. *The Dialogic Imagination*, ed. and trans. M. Holquist. Austin: University of Texas Press, 1981.

Barasch, Moshe. *Giotto and the Language of Gesture*. Cambridge: Cambridge University Press, 1987.

Barney, Stephen A., ed. *Annotation and Its Texts*. Oxford: Oxford University Press, 1991.

Barr, Helen. *Socioliterary Practice in Late Medieval England*. Oxford: Oxford University Press, 2001.

Barr, Helen. 'Religious Practice in Chaucer's *Prioresse's Tale*: Rabbit and/or Duck?', *Studies in the Age of Chaucer* 32 (2010), 39–66.

Barr, Helen. '"Wrinkled deep in time": Emily and Arcite in *A Midsummer Night's Dream*', *Shakespeare Survey* 65 (2012), 12–25.

Bashe, E. J. 'The Prologue of the *Tale of Beryn*', *Philological Quarterly* 12 (1933), 1–16.

Baswell, Christopher. *Virgil in Medieval England: Figuring the Aeneid from the Twelfth Century to Chaucer*. Cambridge: Cambridge University Press, 1995.

Beidler, G. 'The Miller's Tale', in *Sources and Analogues of the Canterbury Tales*, 2 vols, ed. Robert M. Correale and Mary Hamel. Cambridge: D. S. Brewer, 2002–5, vol. 2, pp. 249–76.

Benson, C. David. *The History of Troy in Middle English Literature: Guido delle Colonne's Historia destructionis Troiae in Medieval England*. Woodbridge: D. S. Brewer, 1980.

Benson, C. David. 'Chaucer's Pardoner', *Mediaevalia* 8 (1982), 337–49.

Benson, C. David. 'Their Telling Difference: Chaucer the Pilgrim and His Two Contrasting Tales', *Chaucer Review* 18 (1983), 61–77.

Benson, C. David. *Chaucer's Drama of Style: Poetic Variety and Contrast in The Canterbury Tales*. Chapel Hill: University of North Carolina Press, 1986.

Benson, Larry D. 'The Queynte Puns of Chaucer's Critics', *Studies in the Age of Chaucer* 1 (1984), 23–47.

Benson, R. G. *Medieval Body Language: A Study of the Use of Gesture in Chaucer's Poetry*. Copenhagen: Rosenkilde and Bagger, 1980.

Berry, Ralph. *Shakespeare and the Awareness of the Audience*. London: Macmillan, 1985.

Bertram, Paul. *Shakespeare and Two Noble Kinsmen*. New Brunswick, NJ: Rutgers University Press, 1965.

Bevis, Richard W. *English Drama: Restoration and the Eighteenth Century 1660–1789*. London and New York: Longman, 1988.

Binski, Paul. *Becket's Crown: Art and Imagination in Gothic England 1170–1300*. New Haven and London: Yale University Press, 2004.

Blanch, R. J. and J. N. Wasserman. *From Pearl to Gawain: Forme to Fynisment*. Gainesville: University Press of Florida, 1995.

Blick, Sarah. 'Reconstructing the Shrine of Thomas Becket in Canterbury Cathedral', in *The Art and Architecture of the Late Medieval Pilgrimage in Northern Europe and the British Isles*, ed. Sarah Blick and Rita Tekippe. Leiden: Brill, 2005. pp. 405–41.

Blyth, Charles R. 'Thomas Hoccleve's Other Master', *Medievalia* 16 (1993), 349–59.

Boitani, Piero, 'The Genius to Improve an Invention: Transformations of *The Knight's Tale*', in *Chaucer Traditions: Studies in Honour of Derek Brewer*, ed. Ruth Morse and Barry Windeatt (Cambridge: Cambridge University Press, 2006), pp. 185–98.

Bonheim, H. 'Shakespeare's "Goose of Winchester"', *Philological Quarterly* 51 (1972), 940–1.

Bowers, John M. '*The Tale of Beryn* and *The Siege of Thebes*: Alternative Ideas of *The Canterbury Tales*', *Studies in the Age of Chaucer* 7 (1985), 23–50.

Bowers, John M. 'Controversy and Criticism: Lydgate's *Thebes* and the Prologue to *Beryn*', *Chaucer Yearbook* 5 (1998), 91–115.

Brewer, D. S., ed. *Chaucer and Chaucerians: Critical Studies in Middle English Literature*. London: Nelson, 1970.

Brown, Peter. 'Journey's End: The Prologue to *The Tale of Beryn*', in *Chaucer and Fifteenth Century Poetry*, ed. Julia Boffey and Janet Cowen. Kings College London: Exeter University Press, 1991, pp. 143–74.

Burgwinkle, Bill and Cary Howie. *Sanctity and Pornography in Medieval Culture: On the Verge*. Manchester: Manchester University Press, 2010.

Burgwinkle, William E. *Sodomy, Masculinity and Law in Medieval Literature: France and England 1050–1230*. Cambridge: Cambridge University Press, 2004.

Burrow, John. *Gestures and Looks in Medieval Narrative*. Cambridge: Cambridge University Press, 2002.

Butler, John. *The Quest for Becket's Bones: The Mystery of the Relics of St Thomas Becket of Canterbury*. New Haven and London: Yale University Press, 1995.

Cairns, Anthony G. 'The Bindings of the Ellesmere Manuscript', Special issue 'Reading from the Margins: Textual Studies, Chaucer and

Medieval Literature', ed. Seth Lerer, *Huntington Library Quarterly* 58 (1996), 127–57.

Camille, Michael. *Image on the Edge: the Margins of Medieval Art.* Cambridge, MA: Harvard University Press; Warwick: Reaktion, 1992.

Carlin, Martha. *Medieval Southwark.* London: Hambledon Press, 1996.

Carlson, David R. 'Thomas Hoccleve and the Chaucer Portrait', *Huntington Library Quarterly* 54 (1991), 283–300.

Carruthers, Mary J. *The Book of Memory: A Study of Memory in Medieval Culture*, 2nd edn. Cambridge: Cambridge University Press, 2008.

Caviness, Madeleine Harrison. *The Windows of Christ Church Cathedral Canterbury.* London: Oxford University Press, 1981.

Charnes, Linda. *Notorious Identity: Materializing the Subject in Shakespeare.* Cambridge, MA, and London: Harvard University Press, 1993.

Clanchy, Michael. *From Memory to Written Record: England 1066–1307*, 2nd edn. Oxford: Basil Blackwell, 1995.

Clark, Sandra, ed. *Shakespeare Made Fit.* London: J. M. Dent, 1997.

Cloud, Random. 'The Very Names of the Persons: Editing and the Invention of Dramatick Character', in *Staging the Renaissance: Reinterpretations of Elizabethan and Jacobean Drama*, ed. David Scott Kastan and Peter Stallybrass. London and New York: Routledge, 1991, pp. 88–96.

Coley, David K. '"Withyn a temple ymad of glas": Glazing, Glossing and Patronage in Chaucer's *House of Fame*', *Chaucer Review* 45 (2010), 59–85.

Cooper, Helen. *The Structure of the Canterbury Tales.* London: Duckworth, 1983.

Cooper, Helen. 'Jacobean Chaucer: *Two Noble Kinsmen* and Other Chaucerian Plays', in *Refiguring Chaucer in the Renaissance*, ed. Theresa M. Krier. Gainsville: University Press of Florida, 1998, pp. 189–209.

Cooper, Helen. 'Chaucerian Representation', in *New Readings of Chaucer's Poetry*, ed. Robert G. Benson and Susan J. Ridyard. Cambridge: Brewer, 2003, pp. 7–29.

Cooper, Helen. *Shakespeare and the Medieval World.* London: Methuen, 2010.

Correale, Robert M. and Mary Hamel, eds. *Sources and Analogues of the Canterbury Tales*, 2 vols. Cambridge: D. S. Brewer, 2002–5.

Dame, Joke. 'Unveiled Voices: Sexual Difference and the Castrato', in *Queering the Pitch*, ed. Philip Brett, Gary Thomas and Elizabeth Wood. London: Routledge, 1994, pp. 139–54.

Darjes, Bradley and Thomas Rendall. 'A Fabliau in the *Prologue to the Tale of Beryn*', *Mediaeval Studies* 47 (1985), 416–31.

David, Alfred. 'An Iconography of Noses: Directions in the History of a Physical Stereotype', in *Mapping the Cosmos*, ed. Jane Chance and R. O. Wells, Jr. Houston: University of Rice Press, 1985, pp. 76–97.

Dimmock, Wai Chee. 'A Theory of Resonance', *PMLA* 112 (1997), 1060–71.

Dinshaw, Carolyn. *Chaucer's Sexual Poetics*. Madison: University of Wisconsin Press, 1989.

Dobson, Michael. *The Making of the National Poet: Shakespeare, Adaptation and Authorship, 1660–1769*. Oxford: Clarendon Press, 1992.

Dobson, R. B. *The Peasants' Revolt of 1381*, 2nd edn. London: Macmillan, 1983.

Doyle, A. I. 'The Copyist of the Ellesmere Canterbury Tales', in *The Ellesmere Manuscript: Essays in Interpretation* ed. Martin Stevens and Daniel Woodward. San Marino, CA: Huntington Library and Yushodo Co. Ltd, 1997, pp. 49–68.

Donaldson, E. Talbot. *The Swan at the Well: Shakespeare Reading Chaucer*. New Haven and London: Yale University Press, 1985.

Duggan, Anne J. *Thomas Becket*. London: Arnold, 2004.

Duggan, Anne J. 'A Becket Office at Stavelot: London British Library Additional MS 16964', in *Omnia Disce: Medieval Studies in Memory of Leonard Boyle O.P.*, ed. Anne J. Duggan, Joan Greatrex and Brenda Bolton. Aldershot: Ashgate, 2005, pp. 161–82.

Dutschke, H. C. *Medieval and Renaissance Manuscripts in the Huntington*. San Marino, CA: Huntington Library, 1966.

Edmond, Mary. *Rare Sir William Davenant*. Manchester: Manchester University Press, 1987.

Egan, Rory B. '*Bulles, Coillons*, and Relics in *The Pardoner's Tale*', *ANQ: A Quarterly Journal of Short Articles, Notes and Reviews* 21 (2008), 7–11.

Ellis, Roger. 'Margery Kempe's Scribes and the Miraculous Books', in *Langland, the Mystics and the Medieval Religious Tradition*, ed. H. Phillips. Cambridge: Brewer, 1990, pp. 161–75.

Emmerson, Rick. 'Text and Image in the Ellesmere Portraits of the Tale-Tellers', in *The Ellesmere Manuscript: Essays in Interpretation,* ed. Martin Stevens and Daniel Woodward. San Marino, CA: Huntington Library and Yushodo Co. Ltd, 1997, pp. 143–70.

Federico, Sylvia. *New Troy: Fantasies of Empire in the Late Middle Ages*. Minneapolis: University of Minnesota Press, 2003.

Foakes, R. A. 'Stage Images in *Troilus and Criseyde*', in *Shakespeare and the Sense of Performance*, ed. Marvin and Ruth Thompson. London and Toronto: Associated University Presses, 1989, pp. 150–61.

Forni, Kathleen. *The Chaucerian apocrypha: A Counterfeit Canon*. Gainesville: University Press of Florida, 2001.

Foster, Allyson. 'A Shorte Treatyse of Contemplacyon: The Book of Margery Kempe in Its Early Print Contexts', in *A Companion to The Book of Margery Kempe*, ed. John H. Arnold and Katherine J. Lewis. Woodbridge: D. S. Brewer, 2010, pp. 95–112.

Frederick, Robert E. 'Introduction to the Argument of 1768', in *The Philosophy of Left and Right*, ed. James Van Cleve and Robert E. Frederick. Dordrecht: Kluwer Academic Publishers, 1991, pp. 1–14.

Freeman, Elizabeth. *Time Binds: Queer Temporalities, Queer Histories*. Durham, NC, and London: Duke University Press, 2010.

Freund, Elizabeth. '"Ariachne's broken woof": The Rhetoric of Citation in *Troilus and Cressida*', in *Shakespeare and the Question of Theory*, ed. Patricia Parker and Geoffrey Hartman. London: Routledge, 1985, pp. 20–35.

Frey, Charles H. 'Grinning at the Moon', in *Shakespeare, Fletcher and the Two Noble Kinsmen*, ed. Charles H. Frey. Columbia: University of Missouri Press, 1989, pp. 109–20.

Fumo, Jamie. *The Legacy of Apollo: Antiquity, Authority and Chaucerian Poetics*. Toronto: University of Toronto Press, 2010.

Furnivall, F. J. *A temporary preface to the six-text edition of Chaucer's Canterbury Tales. Part 1, Attempting to show the true order of the tales, and the days and stages of the Pilgrimage, etc., etc.* London: N. Trübner & Co., 1868.

Galloway, Andrew. *The Penn Commentary on Piers Plowman*. Philadelphia: University of Pennsylvania Press, 2006.

Gameson, Richard. 'The Early Imagery of Thomas Becket', in *Pilgrimage: The English Experience from Becket to Bunyan*, ed. Colin Morris and Peter Roberts. Cambridge: Cambridge University Press, 2002.

Gaylord, Alan T., 'Portrait of a Poet', in *The Ellesmere Chaucer: Essays in Interpretation*, ed. by Martin Stevens and Daniel Woodward (San Marino, CA: Huntington Library and Yushodo Co. Ltd, 1997), pp. 121–42.

Gillespie, Alexandra. *Print Culture and the Medieval Author: Chaucer, Lydgate and Their Books 1473–1557*. Oxford: Oxford University Press, 2006.

Gordon, Dillian, Lisa Monnas and Caroline Elam, eds. *The Regal Image of Richard II and the Wilton Diptych*. London: Harvey Miller, 1997.

Green, Gayle. 'Language and Value in *Troilus and Cressida*', *SEL* 21 (1981), 271–85.

Green, Richard Firth. 'The Sexual Normality of Chaucer's Pardoner', *Mediaevalia* 8 (1982), 351–8.

Green, Richard Firth. *A Crisis of Truth: Literature and Law in Ricardian England*. Philadelphia: University of Pennsylvania Press, 1999.

Green, Richard Firth and Ethan Knapp, 'Thomas Hoccleve's Seal', *Medium Ævum* 77 (2008), 319–21.

Green, Susan. 'A mad woman? We are made boys! The Jailer's Daughter in *Two Noble Kinsmen*', in *Shakespeare, Fletcher and the Two Noble Kinsmen*, ed. Charles H. Frey. Columbia: University of Missouri Press, 1989, pp. 121–32.

Grindley, Carl James. 'Reading *Piers Plowman* C Text Annotation: Notes Towards the Classification of Printed and Written Marginalia in Texts from the British Isles 1300–1641', in *The Medieval Professional Reader at Work: Evidence from the Manuscripts of Chaucer, Langland, Kempe and Gower*, ed. Kathryn Kerby-Fulton and Maidie Hilmo, English Literary Studies. Victoria, BC: University of Victoria, 2001, pp. 73–142.

Gust, Geoffrey W. *Constructing Chaucer*. New York: Palgrave Macmillan, 2009.

Hackett, Helen. *William Shakespeare: A Midsummer Night's Dream*. Plymouth: Northcote House in association with the British Council, 1997.

Hackett, Helen. *Shakespeare and Elizabeth: The Meeting of Two Myths*. Princeton: Princeton University Press, 2009.

Hamel, Christopher de. *A History of Illuminated Manuscripts*. London: Phaidon, 1994.

Hanna, Ralph III. 'Annotation as Social Practice', in *Annotation and Its Texts*, ed. Stephen Barney. Oxford: Oxford University Press, 1991, pp. 178–91.

Hansen, Elaine Tuttle. *Chaucer and the Fictions of Gender*. Berkeley and Los Angeles: University of California Press, 1992.

Hardman, Phillipa. 'Presenting the Text: Pictorial Tradition in Fifteenth-Century Manuscripts of the *Canterbury Tales*', in *Chaucer Illustrated: Five Hundred Years of the Canterbury Tales in Pictures*, ed. William K. Finley and Joseph Rosenblum. London: British Library, 2003, pp. 37–72.

Harper, Stephen. '"Pleying with a yerd": Folly and Madness in the Prologue and *Tale of Beryn*', *Studies in Philology* 101 (2004), 299–314.

Harris, Anne. 'Pilgrimage Performance and Stained Glass at Canterbury Cathedral', in *The Art and Architecture of the Late Medieval Pilgrimage in Northern Europe and the British Isles*, ed. Sarah Blick and Rita Tekippe. Leiden: Brill, 2005, pp. 243–81.

Haskell, Ann. '*Sir Thopas*: The Puppet's Puppet', *Chaucer Review* 9 (1975), 253–9.

Hawkes, Terence. *Meaning by Shakespeare*. London: Routledge, 1992.

Higl, Andrew. *Playing the Canterbury Tales: The Continuations and Additions*. Farnham: Ashgate, 2012.

Hilmo, Maidie. 'Framing the Canterbury Pilgrims for the Aristocratic Readers of the Ellesmere Manuscript', in *The Medieval Professional Reader at Work: Evidence from the Manuscripts of Chaucer, Langland, Kempe and Gower*, ed. Kathryn Kerby-Fulton and Maidie Hilmo, English Literary Studies. Victoria, BC: University of Victoria, 2001, pp. 14–72.

Hilmo, Maidie. *Medieval Images, Icons and Illustrated English Literary Texts from the Ruthwell Cross to the Ellesmere Chaucer*. Aldershot: Ashgate, 2004.

Hodgdon, Barbara. 'Gaining a Father: The Role of Egeus in the Quarto and the Folio', *Review of English Studies* 37 (1986), 534–42.

Hodgdon, Barbara. 'He Do Cressida in Different Voices', *English Literary Review* 20 (1990), 254–86.

Hodges, Laura F. *Chaucer and Costume: The Secular Pilgrims in The General Prologue.* Cambridge: D. S. Brewer, 2000.

Hodges, Laura F. *Chaucer and Clothing: Clerical and Academic Costume in the General Prologue to the Canterbury Tales.* Cambridge: D. S. Brewer, 2005.

Holland, Peter. 'Theseus's Shadows in *Dream*', *Shakespeare Survey* 47 (1994), 139–52.

Horobin, Simon. 'The Scribe of the Helmingham and Northumberland Manuscripts of the Canterbury Tales', *Neophilologus* 84 (2000), 457–65.

Ingram, R. W. 'Music as a Structural Element in Shakespeare', in *Proceedings of the World Shakespeare Congress Vancouver, 1971*, ed. Clifford Leech and J. M. R. Margeson. Toronto: University of Toronto Press, 1972, pp. 174–89.

Irvine, Martin. 'Medieval Grammatical Theory and *Chaucer's House of Fame*', *Speculum* 60 (1985), 850–76.

Jackson, Russell and Robert Smallwood, eds. *Players of Shakespeare.* Cambridge: Cambridge University Press, 1995.

James, Heather. *Shakespeare's Troy: Drama, Politics and the Translation of Empire.* Cambridge: Cambridge University Press, 1997.

Jenkins, Jacqueline. 'Reading and the Book of Margery Kempe', in *A Companion to The Book of Margery Kempe*, ed. John H. Arnold and Katherine J. Lewis. Woodbridge: D. S. Brewer, 2004, pp. 113–28.

Johnson, David J. *Southwark and the City.* Oxford: Oxford University Press, 1969.

Jonassen, Frederick B. 'Cathedral, Inn and Pardoner in the *Prologue to the Tale of Beryn*', *Fifteenth Century Studies* 18 (1991), 109–32.

Jost, Jean E. 'From Southwark's Tabard Inn to Canterbury's Cheker of the Hope: The UnChaucerian *Tale of Beryn*', *Fifteenth Century Studies* 21 (1994), 133–48.

Kant, Immanuel. 'On the First Ground of the Distinction of Regions of Space' [1768], in *The Philosophy of Left and Right*, ed. James Van Cleve and Robert E. Frederick. Dordrecht: Kluwer Academic Publishers, 1991, pp. 27–33.

Kendon, Adam. *Gesture: Visible Action as Utterance.* Cambridge: Cambridge University Press, 2004.

Kendrick, Laura. *Chaucerian Play: Comedy and Control in the Canterbury Tales.* California: University of California Press, 1988.

Kennedy, Thomas C. 'Rhetoric and Meaning in *The House of Fame*', *Studia Neophilologica* 68 (1996), 9–23.

Kerby-Fulton, Kathryn and Denise L. Deprès. *Iconography and the Professional Reader: The Politics of Book Production in the Douce Piers*

*Plowman*. Minneapolis and London: University of Minnesota Press, 1999.

Kermode, Frank. '"Opinion" in *Troilus and Cressida*', in *Troilus and Cressida: Teaching the Text*, ed. Susanne Kappeler and Norman Bryson. London and Boston: Routledge & Kegan Paul, 1983, pp. 164–79.

King, T. J. *Casting Shakespeare's Plays: London Actors and Their Roles 1590–1642*. Cambridge: Cambridge University Press, 1992.

Kinsley, James and Helen Kinsley. *John Dryden: The Critical Heritage*. London: Routledge, 1995.

Knapp, Daniel. 'The Relik of a Saint: A Gloss on Chaucer's Pilgrimage', *English Literary History* 39 (1972), 1–26.

Knapp, Ethan. *The Bureaucratic Muse: Thomas Hoccleve and the Literature of Late Medieval England*. University Park, PA: Pennsylvania State University Press, 2001.

Knapp, Peggy. *Chaucer and the Social Contest*. London: Routledge, 1990.

Kohl, Stephan. 'Chaucer's Pilgrims in Fifteenth-Century Literature', *Fifteenth Century Studies* 7 (1983), 221–36.

Koldeweij, Jos. 'Naked and Shameful Images: Obscene Badges as Parodies of Popular Devotion', in *The Art and Architecture of the Late Medieval Pilgrimage in Northern Europe and the British Isles*, ed. Sarah Blick and Rita Tekippe. Leiden: Brill, 2005, pp. 493–510.

Krier, Theresa M., ed. *Refiguring Chaucer in the Renaissance*. Gainesville: University Press of Florida, 1998.

Krochalis, Jeanne E. 'Hoccleve's Chaucer Portrait', *Chaucer Review* 21 (1986), 234–45.

Kuefler, Matthew S. 'Castration and Eunuchism in the Middle Ages', in *A Handbook of Medieval Sexuality*, ed. Vern L. Bullough and James A. Brundage. New York: Garland, 1996, pp. 279–306.

Laskaya, Anne. *Chaucer's Approach to Gender in the Canterbury Tales*. Cambridge: Cambridge University Press, 1995.

Lawton, David. *Chaucer's Narrators*. Cambridge: Brewer, 1985.

Lee, Jennifer M. 'Searching for Signs: Pilgrims' Identity and Experience Made Visible in the *Miracula Sancti Thomae Cantuarensis*', in *The Art and Architecture of the Late Medieval Pilgrimage in Northern Europe and the British Isles*, ed. Sarah Blick and Rita Tekippe. Leiden: Brill, 2005, pp. 473–91.

Lennep, W. Van, ed. *The London Stage, 1660–1800*, Part I: 1660–1700. Carbondale IL, n.p., 1960.

Lerer, Seth. *Chaucer and his Readers: Imagining the Author in Late-Medieval England*. Princeton: Princeton University Press, 1993.

Levinson, Stephen C. 'Space and Place', in Antony Gormley, *Some of the Facts* (Exhibition: Tate St Ives, 2001), pp. 69–109.

Lindley, David. 'Shakespeare's Provoking Music', in *The Well Enchanting Skill: Music, Poetry and Drama in the Culture of the Renaissance: Essays in Honour of F. W. Sternfeld,* ed. John Caldwell, Edward Olleson and Susan Wollenberg. Oxford: Clarendon, 1990, pp. 79–90.

Long, John H. *Shakespeare's Use of Music in the Histories and Tragedies.* Gainsville: University of Florida Press, 1971.

Loomba, Ania. 'The Great Indian Vanishing Trick: Colonialism, Property and the Family in *A Midsummer Night's Dream'*, in *The Feminist Companion to Shakespeare*, ed. Dympna Callaghan. Oxford: Blackwell, 2000. Blackwell Reference Online [accessed 27 July 2010].

Loxton, Howard. *Pilgrimage to Canterbury.* Newton Abbot: Readers Union, 1978.

Maguire, Laurie. *Shakespeare's Names.* Oxford: Oxford University Press, 2007.

Mallette, Richard. 'Same-Sex Erotic Friendship in *Two Noble Kinsmen'*, *Renaissance Drama* 26 (1995), 29–52.

Mann, Jill. *Chaucer and Medieval Estates Satire: The Literature of Social Classes and the General Prologue to the Canterbury Tales.* Cambridge: Cambridge University Press, 1973.

Martin, Priscilla. *Chaucer's Women: Nuns, Wives and Amazons.* Basingstoke: Macmillan, 1996.

Masten, Jeffrey. *Textual Intercourse: Collaboration, Authorship and Sexualities in Renaissance Drama.* Cambridge: Cambridge University Press, 1997.

Mauss, Katharine Eisaman. 'Playhouse Flesh and Blood: Sexual Ideology and the Restoration Actress', *English Literary History* 46 (1979), 595–617.

Mazzio, Carla. 'The Senses Divided: Organs, Objects and Media in Early Modern England', in *Empire of the Senses: The Sensual Culture Reader*, ed. David Howes. Oxford and New York: Berg, 2005, pp. 85–105.

McAlindon, T. 'Language, Style and Meaning in *Troilus and Cressida'*, *PMLA* 84 (1969), 29–43.

McDonald, Nicola. *Medieval Obscenities.* Woodbridge: Boydell, 2006.

McGilchrist, Iain. *The Master and His Emissary: The Divided Brain and the Making of the Western World.* New Haven, CT, and London: Yale University Press, 2012.

McGregor, James H. 'The Iconography of Chaucer in Hoccleve's *De Regimine Principum* and the *Troilus* Frontispiece', *Chaucer Review* 11 (1977), 338–50.

McGuire, Philip C. *Speechless Dialect: Shakespeare's Open Silences.* Berkeley: University of California Press, 1985.

McGuire, Philip C. 'Egeus and the Implications of Silence', in *Shakespeare and the Sense of Performance*, ed. Marvin and Ruth Thompson. London and Toronto: Associated University Presses, 1989, pp. 103–15.

McMullan, Gordon. 'A Rose for Emilia: Collaborative Relations in *Two Noble Kinsmen'*, in *Renaissance Configurations: Voices/Bodies/Spaces, 1580–1690*, ed. Gordon McMullan. London: Palgrave Macmillan, 2001, pp. 129–47.

McMullan, Gordon and David Matthews, eds. *Reading the Medieval in Early Modern England*. Cambridge: Cambridge University Press, 2007.

McNeill, David. *Hand and Mind: What Gestures Reveal about Thought*. Chicago: University of Chicago Press, 1992.

Menzer, Paul. 'The Weavers' Dream: Mnemonic Scripts and Memorial Texts', in *A Midsummer Night's Dream: A Critical Guide*, ed. Regina Buccola. London: Continuum, 2010, pp. 93–111.

Meyer-Lee, Robert J. *Poets and Power from Chaucer to Wyatt*. Cambridge: Cambridge University Press, 2007.

Minnis, A. J. *The Oxford Guides to Chaucer: The Shorter Poems*, Oxford: Clarendon Press, 1995.

Miskimin, Alice S. *The Renaissance Chaucer*. New Haven: Yale University Press, 1975.

Montrose, Louis Adrian. '"Shaping Fantasies": Figurations of Gender and Power in Elizabethan Culture', *Representations* 2 (1983), 61–94.

Mooney, Linne. 'Some New Light on Thomas Hoccleve', *Studies in the Age of Chaucer* 29 (2007), 293–340.

Mooney, Linne R. and Lister M. Matheson. 'The Beryn Scribe and His Texts: Evidence for Multiple-Copy Production of Manuscripts in Fifteenth-Century England', *Library* 4 (2003), 347–70.

Newhauser, Richard. *The Early History of Greed*. Cambridge: Cambridge University Press, 2000.

Newhauser, Richard. 'The Parson's Tale', in *Sources and Analogues of the Canterbury Tales*, 2 vols, I, ed. Robert M. Correale and Mary Hamel. Cambridge: D. S. Brewer, (2002).

Nichols, Stephen G. 'On the Sociology of Medieval Manuscript Annotation', in *Annotation and Its Texts*, ed. Stephen Barney. Oxford: Oxford University Press, 1991, pp. 43–73.

Nichols, Stephen G. 'Philology in Manuscript Culture', *Speculum* 65 (1995), 1–10.

Nilson, Benjamin John. *Cathedral Shrines of Medieval England*. Woodbridge: Boydell, 1998.

Nolan, Barbara. 'Chaucer's "Poetics of Dwelling" in *Troilus and Cressida*', in *Chaucer and the City*, ed. Ardis Butterfield. Cambridge: D. S. Brewer, 2006, pp. 57–78.

Olson, Glending. 'The Misreadings of the *Beryn Prologue*', *Mediaevalia* 17 (1994 for 1991), 201–19.

Olson, Mary C. *Fair and Varied Forms: Visual Textuality in Medieval Illuminated Manuscripts*. London and New York: Routledge, 2003, pp. 154–76.

Olson, Mary C. 'Marginal Portraits and the Fiction of Orality', in *Chaucer Illustrated: Five Hundred Years of the Canterbury Tales in Pictures*, ed. William K. Finley and Joseph Rosenblum. London: British Library, 2003, pp. 1–36.

Osborn, Marijane. 'Word and Image in Chaucer's Enshrined "Coillons" Passage', *Chaucer Review* 37 (2003), 365–84.

Parker, Patricia. *Shakespeare from the Margins: Language, Culture, Context*. Chicago: University of Chicago Press, 1996.

Parkes, Malcolm B. 'The Influence of the Concepts of *Ordinatio and Compilatio* on the Development of the Book', in *Scribes, Scripts and Readers: Studies in the Communication, Presentation and Dissemination of Medieval Texts*. London: Hambledon, 1991.

Parkes, Malcolm. 'The Planning and Construction', in *The Ellesmere Chaucer: Essays in Interpretation*, ed. Martin Stevens and Daniel Woodward. San Marino, CA: Huntington Library and Yushodo Co. Ltd, 1997. pp. 41–7.

Parsons, Ben. '"For My Synne and for My Yong Delite": Chaucer, The *Tale of Beryn*, and the Problem of *Adolescentia*', *Modern Language Review* 103 (2008), 940–51.

Parsons, Kelly. 'The Red Ink Annotator of the Book of Margery Kempe and His Lay Audience', in *The Medieval Professional Reader at Work: Evidence from the Manuscripts of Chaucer, Langland, Kempe and Gower*, ed. Kathryn Kerby-Fulton and Maidie Hilmo, English Literary Studies. Victoria, BC: University of Victoria, 2001, pp. 143–216.

Partridge, E. *Shakespeare's Bawdy*. London: Routledge, 1968.

Patterson, Lee. *Chaucer and the Subject of History*. London: Routledge, 1991.

Pearsall, Derek. 'The Chaucer Portraits', in *The Life of Geoffrey Chaucer: A Critical Biography*. Oxford: Blackwell, 1992, pp. 285–305.

Pearsall, Derek. 'Thomas Hoccleve's *Regement of Princes*: The Poetics of Royal Self-Representation', *Speculum* 69 (1994), 386–410.

Perkins, Nicholas. *Hoccleve's Regiment of Princes: Counsel and Constraint*. Cambridge: Brewer, 2001.

Perkins, Nicholas. 'Haunted Hoccleve?: *The Regiment of Princes*, the Troilean Intertext, and Conversations with the Dead', *Chaucer Review* 43 (2008), 103–39.

Pinti, Daniel J., ed. *Writing after Chaucer: Essential Readings in Chaucer and the Fifteenth Century*. New York and London: Garland, 1998.

Prendergast, Thomas A. *Chaucer's Dead Body: From Corpse to Corpus*. London and New York: Routledge, 2004.

Prendergast, Thomas A. and Barbara Kline, eds. *Rewriting Chaucer: Culture, Authority, and the Idea of the Authentic Text, 1400–1602*. Columbus: Ohio State University Press, 1999.

Raddadi, Mongi. *Davenant's Adaptations of Shakespeare*. Uppsala: Almqvist & Wiksell International, 1979.

Ramsey, J. W. 'The Provenance of *Troilus and Cressida*', *Shakespeare Quarterly* 21 (1970), 223–40.

Reverand, C. D. 'Dryden's "To the Duchess of Ormond": Identifying Her Plantagenet Predecessor', *Notes and Queries* 54:1 (2007), 57–60.

Richmond, Hugh. 'Performance as Criticism: *Two Noble Kinsmen*', in *Shakespeare, Fletcher and the Two Noble Kinsmen*, ed. Charles H. Frey. Columbia: University of Missouri Press, 1989, pp. 163–85.

Roberts, Jane Addison. 'Crises of Male Self-Definition in *The Two Noble Kinsmen*', in *Shakespeare, Fletcher and the Two Noble Kinsmen*, ed. Charles H. Frey. Columbia: University of Missouri Press, 1989, pp. 133–44.

Robertson, D. W. *A Preface to Chaucer*. Princeton: Princeton University Press, 1962.

Rosenblum, Joseph and William Finley. 'Chaucer Gentrified: The Nexus of Art and Politics in the Ellesmere Miniatures', *Chaucer Review* 38 (2003), 140–57.

Rossiter, A. P. *Angel with Horns*. London: Longman, 1961.

Rowe, Katherine. *Dead Hands: Fictions of Agency, Renaissance to Modern*. Stanford: Stanford University Press, 1999.

Sadlek, Gregory M. 'The Image of the Devil's Five Fingers in the *South English Legendary's St Michael* and Chaucer's *Parson's Tale*', in *The South English Legendary: A Critical Assessment*, ed. Klaus P. Jankofsky. Tübingen: Francke, 1992, pp. 49–64.

Sandler, Lucy Freeman. '*Omne Bonum*: Compilation and Ordinatio in an English Illustrated Encyclopedia of the Fourteenth Century', in *Medieval Book Production: Assessing the Evidence*, ed. L. L. Brownrigg. Los Altos Hills: Anderson-Lovelace; London: The Red Gull Press, 1990, pp. 183–200.

Sanger, Paul. 'Silent Reading', *Viator* 13 (1982), 367–414.

Scala, Elizabeth. 'Seeing Red: The Ellesmere Iconography of Chaucer's Nun's Priest', *Word and Image* 26 (2010), 381–92.

Scheil, Katherine West. 'Sir William Davenant's Use of Shakespeare in *The Law Against Lovers* (1662)', *Philological Quarterly* 76 (1997), 369–86.

Schulz, Herbert C. *The Ellesmere Manuscript of the Canterbury Tales*. San Marino, CA: Huntington Library, 1990.

Searle, John R. 'Proper Names', *Mind* 67 (1958), 166–73.

Shannon, Laurie. *Sovereign Amity: Figures of Friendship in Shakespearean Contexts*. Chicago: University of Chicago Press, 2002.

Shaw, James. '*Troilus and Cressida*', in *Shakespeare in Performance*, ed. Keith Parsons and Pamela Mason. London: Salamander, 2000.

Sherman, William H. 'Toward a History of the Manicule', www.livesand letters.ac.uk. Posted online: March 2005.

Sherman, William H. *Used Books: Marking Readers in Renaissance England*. Philadelphia: University of Pennsylvania Press, 2008.

Shirley, Frances A. *Shakespeare's Use of Offstage Sounds*. Lincoln: University of Nebraska Press, 1963.

Simpson, James. '"Dysemol daies and fatal hours": Lydgate's Destruction of Thebes and Chaucer's *Knight's Tale*', in *The Long Fifteenth Century*, ed. Helen Cooper and Sally Mapstone. Oxford: Clarendon Press, 1997, pp. 15–34.

Simpson, James. 'The Other Book of Troie: Guido delle Colonne's *Historia Destructionis Troiae* in Fourteenth- and Fifteenth-Century England', *Speculum* 73 (1998), 397–423.

Simpson, James. 'Chaucer's Presence and Absence, 1400–1550', in *The Cambridge Companion to Chaucer*, ed. Piero Boitani and Jill Mann. Cambridge: Cambridge University Press, 2004. pp. 251–69.

Sinfield, Alan. 'Cultural Materialism and Intertextuality: The Limits of Queer Reading in *A Midsummer Night's Dream* and *Two Noble Kinsmen*', *Shakespeare Survey* 56 (2003), 67–78.

Slocum, Kay Brainerd. *Liturgies in Honour of Thomas Becket*. Toronto: University of Toronto Press, 2004.

Smith, Bruce R. *The Acoustic World of Early Modern England: Attending to the O-Factor*. Chicago: University of Chicago Press, 1999.

Spencer, Christopher. '*Macbeth* and Davenant's *The Rivals*', *Shakespeare Quarterly* 20 (1969), 225–9.

Spencer, Jane. *Literary Relations: Kinship and the Canon 1660–1830*. Oxford: Oxford University Press, 2005.

Spiegel, Gabrielle M. 'Paradox of the Senses', in *Rethinking the Medieval Senses: Heritage, Formations, Frames*, ed. Stephen G. Nichols, Andreas Kablitz and Alison Calhoun. Baltimore: Johns Hopkins University Press, 2008.

Spurgeon, Caroline F. E. *Five Hundred Years of Chaucer Criticism and Allusion, 1357–1900*, 2 vols. New York: Russell & Russell, 1960.

Staley, Lynn. *Margery Kempe's Dissenting Fictions*. University Park, PA: University of Pennsylvania Press, 1994.

Stallybrass, Peter. 'Shakespeare, the Individual and the Text', in *Cultural Studies*, ed. Lawrence Grossberg, Cary Nelson and Paula A. Treichler. New York: Routledge, 1992, pp. 593–610.

Steiner, Emily. *Documentary Culture and the Making of Medieval English Literature*. Cambridge: Cambridge University Press, 2003.

Sternfeld, F. W. *Music in Shakespearean Tragedy*. London: Routledge, Kegan and Paul, 1963.

Stevens, Martin. 'The Ellesmere Miniatures as Illustrations of Chaucer's *Canterbury Tales*', *Studies in Iconography* 7–8 (1981–82), 113–34.

Stevens, Martin. 'The Ellesmere Chaucer: Essays in Interpretation', in *The Ellesmere Chaucer: Essays in Interpretation*, ed. Martin Stevens and Daniel Woodward. San Marino, CA: Huntington Library and Yushodo Co. Ltd, 1997, pp. 15–28.

Stewart, Susan. 'Remembering the Senses', in *Empire of the Senses: The Sensual Culture Reader*, ed. David Howes. Oxford and New York: Berg, 2005, pp. 59–69.

Storm, Melvin. 'The Pardoner's Invitation: Quaestor's Bag or Becket's Shrine?', *PMLA* 97 (1982), 810–18.

Strohm, Paul. *Social Chaucer*. Cambridge, MA, and London: Harvard University Press, 1989.

Strohm, Paul. *Theory and the Premodern Text*. Minneapolis: University of Minnesota Press, 2000.

Sturges, Robert S. *Chaucer's Pardoner and Gender Theory: Bodies of Discourse*. London: Macmillan, 2000.

Sturges, Robert. 'The Pardoner in Canterbury: Class, Gender and Urban Space in *The Prologue to the Tale of Beryn*', *College Literature* 33 (2006), 52–76.

Sumption, Jonathan. *Pilgrimage*. London: Faber and Faber, 1975.

Taylor, Andrew. 'The Curious Eye and the Alternative Endings of *The Canterbury Tales*' in *Part Two: Reflections on the Sequel*, ed. Paul Vincent Budra and Betty A. Schellenberg. Toronto: University of Toronto Press, 1998, pp. 34–52.

Taylor, Gary. *Castration: An Abbreviated History of Western Manhood*. London and New York: Routledge, 2000.

Taylor, Gary, Stanley Wells et al. *William Shakespeare: A Textual Companion*. Oxford: Clarendon Press, 1987.

Taylor, Mark. 'Female Desire in *A Midsummer Night's Dream*', *Shakespeare Yearbook* 2 (1991), 115–31.

Thompson, Ann. *Shakespeare's Chaucer: A Study in Literary Origins*. Liverpool: Liverpool University Press, 1978.

Traub, Valerie. 'The Insignificance of Lesbian Desire in Early Modern England', in *Erotic Politics: Desire on the Renaissance Stage*, ed. Susan Zimmerman. London: Routledge, 1992.

Tredell, Nicolas. *Shakespeare: A Midsummer Night's Dream: A Reader's Guide to Essential Criticism*. Basingstoke: Palgrave Macmillan, 2010.

Trigg, Stephanie. *Congenial Souls: Reading Chaucer from Medieval to Postmodern*. Minneapolis: University of Minnesota Press, 2002.

Turner, Marion. 'Greater London', in *Chaucer and the City*, ed. Ardis Butterfield. Cambridge: D. S. Brewer, 2006, pp. 25–40.

Turner, Marion. *Chaucerian Conflict: Languages of Antagonism in Late Fourteenth-Century London*. Oxford: Clarendon Press, 2007.

Turner, Victor and Edith Turner. *Image and Pilgrimage in Christian Culture: Anthropological Perspectives*. Oxford: Blackwell, 1978.

Underwood, Richard. *Two Noble Kinsmen and Its Beginnings*. Salzburg: Salzburg University Press, 1993.

Vance, Eugene. 'Chaucer's Pardoner: Relics, Discourse, and the Frames of Propriety', *New Literary History* 20 (1988–89), 723–49.

Wagner, Peter. *Reading Iconotexts: From Swift to the French Revolution*. London: Reaktion, 1995.

Wallace, David. '*Cleanness* and the Terms of Terror' in *Text and Matter: New Critical Perspectives on the Pearl-Poet*, ed. R. J. Blanch, M. Youngerman Miller and J. Wasserman. New York: Whitston Publishing Co., 1991, pp. 93–104.

Webb, Diana. *Pilgrimage in Medieval England*. London and New York: Hambledon, 2000.

Weller, Barry. '*Two Noble Kinsmen*, the Friendship Tradition and the Flight from Eros', in *Shakespeare, Fletcher and the Two Noble Kinsmen*, ed. Charles H. Frey. Columbia: University of Missouri Press, 1989, pp. 93–108.

Wenzel, Siegfried. 'Chaucer's Pardoner and His Relics', *Studies in the Age of Chaucer* 11 (1989), 37–41.

Wickham, Glynne. '*Two Noble Kinsmen* or *A Midsummer Night's Dream*, Part II?', in *The Elizabethan Theatre* VII, ed. G. R. Hibbard. Ontario: University of Waterloo, 1980, pp. 167–96.

Williams, Gordon. *Shakespeare's Sexual Language: A Glossary*. London: Continuum, 2006.

Wilson, Richard. 'The Kindly Ones: The Death of the Author in Shakespearean Athens', in *A Midsummer Night's Dream*, ed. Richard Dutton. Basingstoke: Macmillan, 1996, pp. 198–222.

Windeatt, Barry. 'Gesture in Chaucer', *Medievalia et Humanistica* 9 (1979), 141–61.

Winstead, Karen A. 'The *Beryn*-Writer as a Reader of Chaucer', *Chaucer Review* 22 (1988), 225–33.

Woodman, Francis. *The Architectural History of Canterbury Cathedral*. London: Routledge and Kegan and Paul, 1981.

Woolf, Rosemary. *The English Religious Lyric in the Middle Ages*. Oxford: Clarendon Press, 1968.

Zwicker, Steven N. *The Arts of Disguise: Politics and Language in Dryden's Poetry*. Princeton: University of Princeton Press, 1984.

Online resources

All Saints North Street (Online): http://allsaintsnorthstreet.org.uk/stainedglass.html.

Blackwell Reference Online: www.blackwellreference.com.

Canterbury Cathedral (Online): http://canterbury-cathedral.org/assets/files/docs/pdf/home-news/Gormley_Sculpture.pdf.

Centre for Editing Lives and Letters (Online): www.livesandletters.ac.uk/.

Corpus Vitrearum Medii Aevi: www.cvma.ac.uk/publications/digital/norfolk/sites/eastharling/history.html.

Crystal, Shakespeare's Words: http://shakespeareswords.com/Search.aspx.

Daily Mail (Online) www.dailymail.co.uk/.../Antony-Gormley-unveils-new-artwork-Transport-Canterbury-Cathedral.html.

Early English Books Online (Online): http://eebo.chadwyck.com/search/fulltext?.

Flickr Photos: www.flickr.com/photos/stiffleaf/8244695806/.

# Index